U0906968

中国保险学会 中国保险报 编著
Edited by The Insurance Institute of China
& China Insurance News

Bicentenary Chinese Insurance

中国保险业二百年

(1805–2005)

当代世界出版社
The Contemporary World
Publishing House

图书在版编目（CIP）数据

中国保险业二百年：中国保险学会，中国保险报编著.
－北京：当代世界出版社，2005.6

ISBN 7-80115-963-2

I.中… II.①中…②中… III.保险业—经济史
—中国 IV.F842.9

中国版本图书馆CIP数据核字(2005)第040091号

书名：中国保险业二百年
出版：当代世界出版社
地址：北京市复兴路4号(100860)
网址：http://www.worldpress.com.cn
编务电话：(010)83908403
发行电话：(010)83908410（传真）
(010)83908408
(010)83908409
经销：新华书店
印刷：深圳市彩帝印刷实业有限公司
开本：889×1194 1/16
印张：18
版次：2005年6月第1版
印次：2005年6月第1次
书号：ISBN 7-80115-963-2/F·103
定价：228.00元

《中国保险业二百年》编委会

主　　编：周德英

副 主 编：黎宗剑　童伟明

主要编写人员：
张胜利　罗　健　何六艺　李文英　王　泓　房立群
杨　林　张翠珍　徐文晋　卢　霞　荣晓英　赵　雪
张通福　唐国纲　吴晓明　冉海琼　章　铮　承　杨
成继跃　王　健

翻　　译：杨　林　张翠珍

监　　制：金钟宁

设计制作：北京中新鸿视文化发展有限公司

序
Preface

2005年，恰逢中国保险业走过200年历程。从1805年中国第一家保险机构“谏当保安行”(Canton Insurance Society)在广州成立以来，中国保险业历经清朝、民国和新中国三个不同的历史时期，走过漫长而曲折的发展道路。1949年以前，外资保险机构纷至沓来，民族保险企业在夹缝中成长，留下了许多兴衰存亡的故事；新中国成立之后，中国保险业进入新的发展时期，既遭遇过风风雨雨，又创造了辉煌成就。特别是近二十多年来，保险业在改革开放中获得长足的发展。到2004年底，全国保费收入已从1980年4.6亿元增长到4318.1亿元(未含港澳台地区)，年均增长率超过30%，成为整个国民经济中发展最快的行业之一。

相对于中华民族的文明史而言，200年的时间不算太长，但对于具有特定经济基础和社会功能的保险业来说，200年包含着丰富的历史内涵和重要的现实价值，是一段值得认真回顾和总结的历史，是一个值得隆重纪念的日子。在这一历史时刻，中国保险学会和中国保险报共同编辑的大型历史画册《中国保险业二百年》即将出版，这是一件很有意义的事情。

“欲知大道，必先治史。”提高保险行业广大干部员工的理论素养，不仅需要加强业务知识的学习，而且要注重对保险史的研究，通过对历史的学习更好地掌握保险知识，认识保险业的发展规律。记载和反映历史的方式很多，除了史料浩繁的文献档案、史学著作和各种历史教科书外，也可以采用电影、录像、画册等比较直观的方式。《中国保险业二百年》作为一部大型历史画册，大量采集了分散在全国各处的珍贵历史照片、实物图片和典藏文献，以图文并茂的方式，追忆保险业的发展轨迹，展示保险业的辉煌成就，可以看作是一部“直述”中国保险业200年历史的通俗读本。希望它能帮助读者在轻松的阅读中把握中国保险业的来龙去脉，了解中国保险业的发展状况，同时也希望它在宣传和普及保险知识过程中发挥应有的作用。

以史为鉴，继往开来，是时代赋予我们的历史责任。2004年12月11日，我国保险市场进入了全面对外开放的新时期。尽管经过长期的发展特别是改革开放以来，我国保险业取得了举世瞩目的成就，但从总体上说仍然处于发展的初级阶段，摆在我们面前的任务还十分艰巨。在新的形势下，我们一定要进一步整理中国保险业的文化遗产，努力汲取历史营养，与时俱进，开拓创新，不断提高保险业的整体水平，为构建和谐社会和全面建设小康社会作出积极贡献！

中国保险监督管理委员会主席： 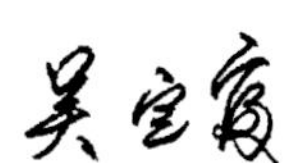

2005年4月28日

目　录
Contents

Bicentenary chinese Insurance
中国保险业二百年(1805—2005)

清代保险业(1805—1911)

Insurance in Late Qing Dynasty (1805-1911)

中国现代保险业从海外泊入。1805 年，英国商人在当时南方对外贸易的惟一口岸——广州设立了“谏当保安行”，这是中国第一个具有现代意义的保险公司。1865 年，上海华商义和公司保险行的创立成为中国第一家民族保险公司，打破了外商独占中国保险市场的局面。

由洋行代理的国外保险机构长期垄断中国保险市场。洋务派首领李鸿章意识到欲求富国自强“须华商自立公司，自建行栈，自筹保险”。1875 年，由唐廷枢、徐润负责筹办的保险招商局成立，开中国人自己经营船舶、货栈、货物运输保险之先河。自办保险获得了民族工商业的支持和欢迎，保险业务迅速拓展。中国民族保险业也由此逐步发展。

在中国民族保险诞生的前后，一批有识之士如魏源、洪仁玕、王韬、郑观应、陈炽等通过其著述向国人介绍西方保险，传播保险思想，对中国民族保险业的兴起产生了积极作用。 鸦片战争之后，中国的门户被迫打开，广州、厦门、福州、宁波、上海，以及汉口、九江、南京、镇江等先后开埠通商，上海以其地理优势成为对外贸易的中心，也成为了清末保险业的中心。

Chinese latter-day insurance was born in from extrinsic influences. Canton Insurance Society, established by British merchandisers at Guangzhou port in 1805, is the first modern-sense insurance company in China, which mainly operated transportation insurance business related with the trade with British merchandisers.

In 1865, 60 years after the emerge of the first Chinese insurer, Chinese initiated to attempt insurance operation, hence the founding of Yihe Co., but in small scale. A decade later, Li Hongzhang, a leader of the westernization movement, deeply felt the pressure from the monopoly by foreign insurance, indicating Chinese merchants should set up their owns to prepare insurance operation and China Merchants Insurance Company was determined to be prepared by China Merchants Navigation Company. In 1875, China Merchants Insurance Company was erected, blazing the earliest trail for vessel, warehouse, and cargo transportation insurance operated by Chinese themselves. Self-operated insurance widely received the support and welcome from the national industry and commerce; insurance business expanded rapidly. To avert risks, China Merchants Insurance Company in the next year founded Renhe Insurance Co. via a public offering, hence the birth of the national insurance of China.

In the period, Chinese insurance market was mainly monopolized by British insurance capital.

一、中国现代保险业的兴起

Rise of Chinese Modern Insurance

1685年，清政府开放海禁。西方商品经济的浪潮开始冲击中国几千年自给自足的自然经济体系。18世纪末19世纪初，以有“世界工厂”之称的英国为代表的西方列强加大了对中国的贸易输出。海上贸易的兴起需要保险的支持。作为中国最早的通商口岸——广州，成为中国保险业的缘起地。

1805年，由东印度公司的达卫森（W S Davidson）发起，在广州开设了广州保险会社(Canton Insurance Society)，又称谏当保安行。

到了1832年，广州保险会社由达卫森拥有的宝顺洋行（Davidson—Dent House）和渣甸（W.Jardine）及麦迪（J.Matheson）创办的怡和洋行（Jardine Matheson&Co.）两家洋行掌管。1835年，宝顺洋行宣布退出后，谏当保安行由怡和洋行独自经营。1836年，怡和对其改组，并易名为谏当保险公司（Canton Insurance Company)，继续在广州开展业务。1857年在上海设立分支机构，并大力吸收华商股份。1881年12月在香港改组，翌年1月1日易名为广东保险公司，重新开业。香港知名的公司在该公司都拥有一定的股份，获利丰厚。

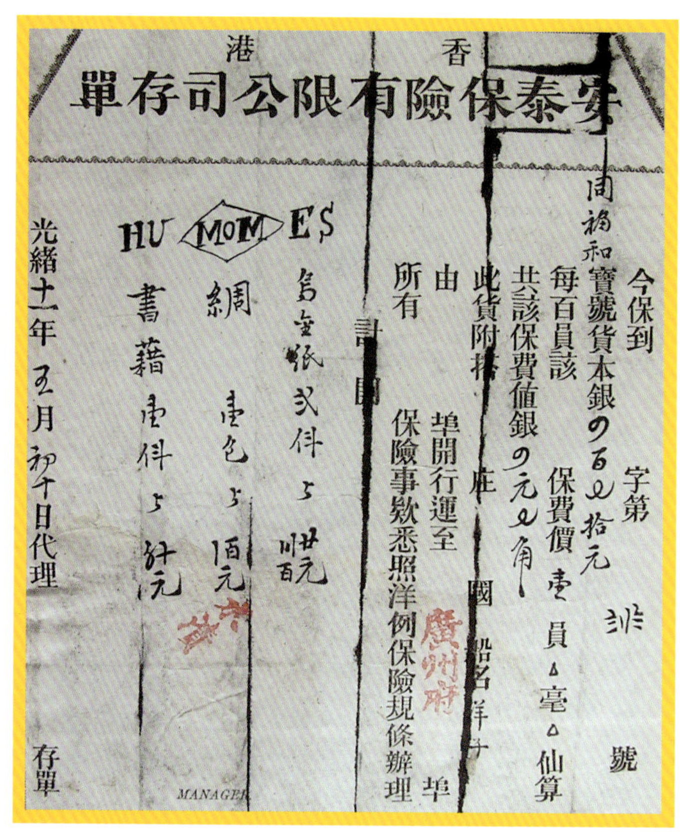

香港

安泰保險有限公司存單

今保到　字第　號

寶號貨本銀

每百員該　保費價　員　毫　仙算

共該保費値銀

此貨附搭　國　船名

由　埠開行運至　埠

所有　保險事欵悉照洋例保險規條辦理

光緒十一年五月初十日代理

存單

MANAGER

1877年安泰保险公司在香港成立。图为光绪11年（1885年）5月10日，香港安泰保险公司签发的水险保单。（资料提供：成继跃）
Marine insurance policy issued by Hongkong Antai Insurance Co. in the reign of Emperor Guangxu of the Qing Dynasty

中国保险业缘起时的广州口岸
Guangzhou Port When Insurance First Appeared in China

19世纪外商“十三行”在广州开设的店铺。“十三行”是清政府指定的专门经营对外贸易的商馆，即小溪馆义和行、荷兰馆集义行、新英国馆保和行、诸州馆丰泰行、旧英国馆隆顺行、瑞典馆瑞行、美国馆广源行、帝国馆孖鹰行、宝顺行、中国街中和行、法国馆高公行、西班牙馆吕宋行、丹麦馆黄旗行。

Shisanhang (thirteen foreign trading houses) in Guangzhou in 19th century

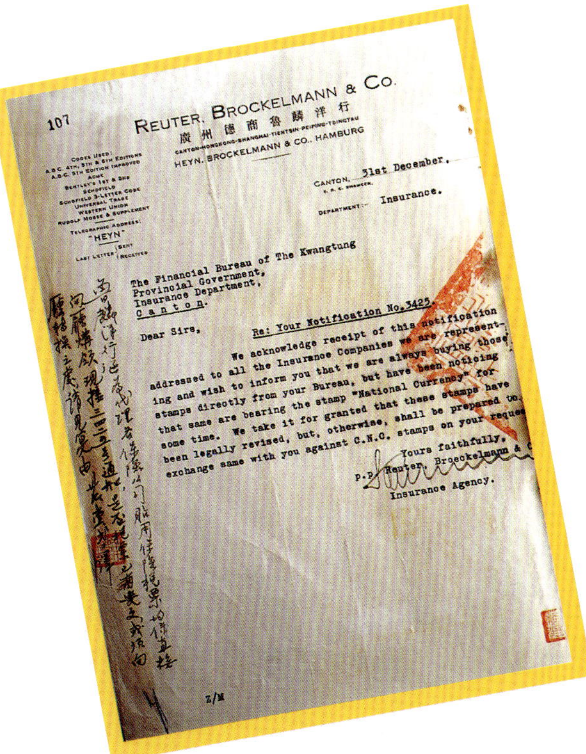

107

REUTER, BROCKELMANN & CO.
廣州德商魯麟洋行
HEYN, BROCKELMANN & CO., HAMBURG

"HEYN"

CANTON, 31st December,

DEPARTMENT:- Insurance.

The Financial Bureau of The Kwangtung
Provincial Government,
Insurance Department,
C a n t o n.

Dear Sirs, Re: Your Notification No.3425.

We acknowledge receipt of this notification addressed to all the Insurance Companies we are representing and wish to inform you that we are always buying those stamps directly from your Bureau, but have been noticing that same are bearing the stamp "National Currency" for some time. We take it for granted that these stamps have been legally revised, but, otherwise, shall be prepared to exchange same with you against C.N.C. stamps on your reque...

Yours faithfully,
p.p. Reuter, Broeckelmann & C...
Insurance Agency.

Z/M

广州德商鲁麟洋行关于代理各保险公司税票的函(资料提供：广州市档案馆)

Letter on insurers' tax receipt deputized by a German Company in Guangzhou

In late 18th century, with the increasing export of Great Britain to China, Insurance first emerged in Guangzhou, the earliest trade port in China.

In 1905, WS Davidson, who worked for the East Indian Company, set up Canton Insurance Society there. It was run by Davidson-Dent House and Jardine Matheson & Co. In 1835; Davidson-Dent House announced to withdraw from the company and Jardine Matheson & Co. became the only owner of the Society. In 1836, Canton Insurance Society was renamed to Canton Insurance Company, while its business continued at Guangzhou. The company set up Shanghai Branch and began to absorb Chinese capital in 1857. In December 1881, the company was reorganized in Hongkong with a new name as Guangdong Insurance Company on January 1, 1881.

香港于仁大厦近景
Union Insurance Co. in HongKong

1887年香港维多利亚区全景
Full scene of Hongkong's Victoria District in 1887

1835年于仁洋面保安行司标
Logo of Union Insurance Society of Canton (1835)

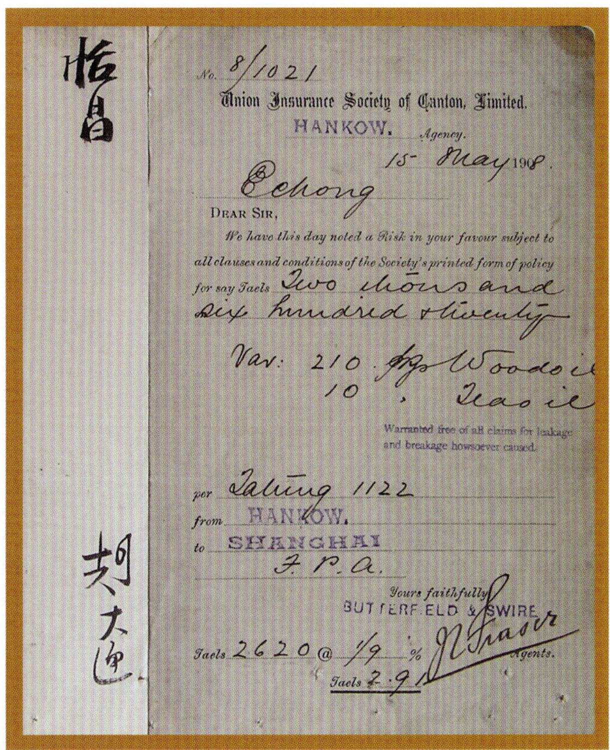

怡昌

No. 8/1021

Union Insurance Society of Canton, Limited.

HANKOW. Agency.

15 May 1908.

Echong

Dear Sir,

We have this day noted a Risk in your favour subject to all clauses and conditions of the Society's printed form of policy for say Taels Two thousand and six hundred & twenty

Warranted free of all claims for leakage and breakage howsoever caused.

per [illegible] 1122

from HANKOW.

to SHANGHAI

F.P.A.

Yours faithfully,
BUTTERFIELD & SWIRE
Agents.

Taels 2620 @ 1/9 %

于仁洋面保安行于1908年5月15日签发的汉口到上海货物运输保险单。(资料提供:成继跃)
Hankou—to—Shanghai cargo transportation insurance policy issued by Union Insurance Society of Canton on May 15, 1908.

1835年，宝顺洋行退出谏当保安行，在广州设立于仁洋面保安行(Union Insurance Society of Canton)，又称友宁保险行。该行在创立之初就允许华商附股。于仁洋面保安行主要承保股东的业务。该行沿续谏当保安行的传统，每三年结算一次。6年后，该行在香港注册，总公司也迁往香港，另在伦敦开设分行，业务也不再限于股东。1868年，在上海设立分支机构，华记、旗昌等洋行加入投资者行列。1882年改名为于仁保险公司(Union Insurance Co.)。

到1838年，广州有洋行约55家，其中15家为外国保险公司(主要是英商公司)代办在华业务。

Founded Davidson-Dent House in Guangzhou in 1835, Union Insurance Society of Canton welcomed Chinese to own the Society's share from the very beginning. The Society's business was limited within its shareholders. Since it's registered in Hongkong, its headquarters was also moved there in the sixth year after its establishment. Later the Society set up its London and Shanghai Branch. It was rename as Union Insurance Co. in 1882.

In the end of 1838, there were 55 foreign companies in Guangzhou, 15 of which operated insurance business.

二、保险思想传播

Spread of Insurance Ideology

第一次鸦片战争打开了中国闭锁了几千年的大门，一批志士仁人开始放眼世界，寻找富国强兵之策，他们在接触西学的过程中感悟到保险在社会经济中的巨大作用，于是将西方保险思想引入中国。第一个将西方保险思想介绍进来的是魏源，他在《海国图志》中对保险有较详尽的描述。其后，产生了一批保险倡导者，如：洪仁玕、王韬、郑观应、张謇等。

The first Opium War broke several—thousand—year closed position; a batch of people with lofty ideals began to take a broad view into the world to seek for the strategy of building prosperous and strong nation. They, in the process of touching western science, comprehend the great function of insurance in society and economy, hence introducing western insurance ideology into China.

中国保险思想传播第一人——魏源(1794—1857)

Wei Yuan: The First Person Introducing Insurance in China

《海国图志》首次向国人介绍了西方的保险，书中将Insurance（保险）译成“担保”，Insurance Company（保险公司）译成“担保会”，Marine Insurance（水险）译成“船担保”，Life Insurance（寿险）译成“命担保”，Fire Insurance（火险）译成“宅担保”。《海国图志》介绍了西方保险公司的三大类型：“一曰船担保。舟航大洋难保沉覆。假如船价二万元载货五万元出海，每月纳会银为会中公费。如或船货有失，视其损失之分类，如仅桅折货湿，会中如数补偿；如或全船沉溺，则会中即偿其半，但必实报实验。众力恤灾，从无推却。英吉利都二十一会，其本银或五六万，或三四万元不等，同休戚，共利害，岁终会计，有利均分，有害分受，要之利多害少。二曰宅担保，城市稠密，回禄堪虞。假如本屋价银二千，每年纳会中银二十元，不幸被灾，则会中亦代偿其半。三曰命担保。假如老妻弱子，身后恐无生计，每年于会中入五十元。死后，如后嗣成立，无需周恤则已；如贫不能自存，则会中赡其家每年一千元。”

Wei Yuan first introduced western insurance to Chinese in details in his great works *Haiguotuzhi*, including three categories: marine, fire, and life insurance.

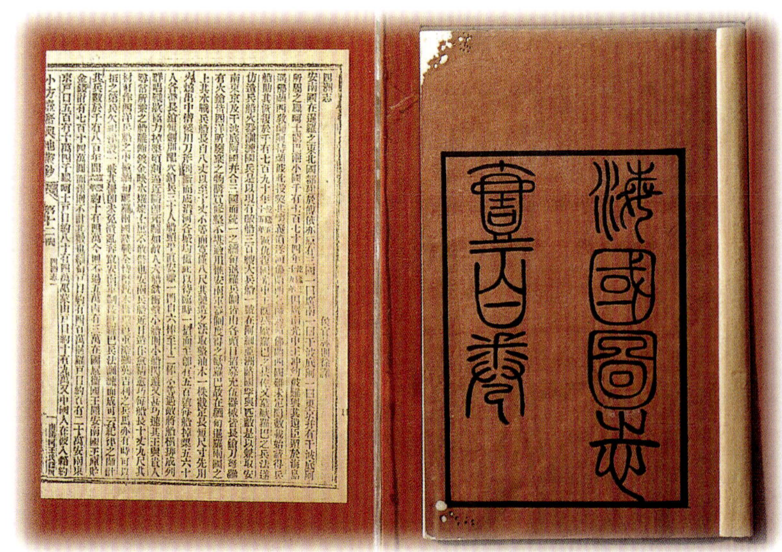

《海国图志》

Haiguotuzhi, by Wei Yuan, the first book introducing western insurance to Chinese.

洪仁玕(1822–1864)，广东花县人。字益谦(又作谦益)，号吉甫，洪秀全的族弟。1859年投奔洪秀全的太平军，后晋为干王，总理朝政。洪仁玕施政后不久，向洪秀全提交实行改革的《资政新篇》。其中在“法法类”中阐述了西方保险的思想：“外国兴保人物之例，凡屋宇、人命、货物、船等有防于火者，失与保人议定，每年纳银若干，有失则保人赔其所值，无失则赢其所奉。若失命，则父母、妻子有赖，失物，则已不致尽亏。”

Hong Rengan(1822-1864) presented western insurance in his well-known *New Guide to Government* written in 1859 shortly after he was appointed as King Gan in Taiping Heavenly Kingdom.

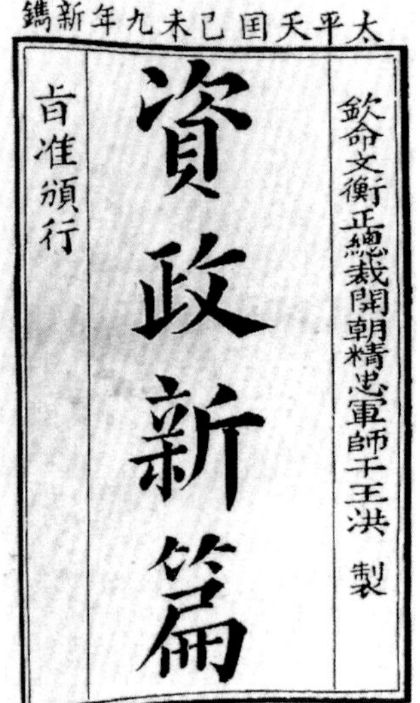

太平天国己未九年新鐫
欽命文衡正總裁開朝精忠軍師干王洪 製
資政新篇
旨准頒行

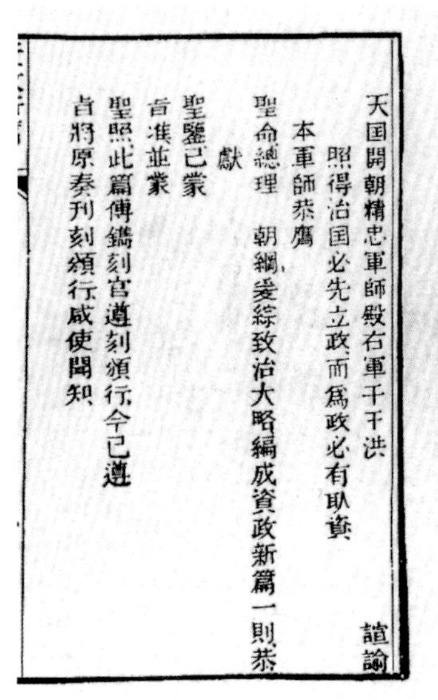

天国開朝精忠軍師殿右軍干王洪 謹諭
照得治国必先立政而爲政必有取資
本軍師恭膺
聖命總理 朝綱爰綜致治大略編成資政新篇一則恭
獻
聖鑒已蒙
旨准並蒙
聖照此篇傳鐫刻官遵刻頒行今已遵
旨將原奏刊刻頒行咸使聞知

《资政新篇》
New Guide to Government by Hong Rengan

王韬
Wang Tao

王韬(1828–1897)，江苏长洲(今吴县)人，清朝最早的改良派思想家之一。王韬在西方各国的游历使他能较全面地阐述保险思想。他认为西方资本主义的发展得利于航海贸易，而航海贸易必然要求保险对其风险给予调剂。他主张轮船招商局与保险应相辅相成。为了保障我国国际贸易的发展，他呼吁在通商口岸以及世界其他各港口，凡我轮船所至之处，设立中国的保险公司或海外代理处。他积极倡导自办保险公司，因为若依赖洋人办保险，中国只有“寄人篱下，权自彼操”，中国保险公司应在二三年间成立，“以中国之人保中国之货，不必假手于外洋，而其利乃尽归于我。”应依靠华侨在国外设立的保险机构，“保险之利开，为商贾之航海者，无所大损，而华人之利仍流于华人中，而不至让西人独据利薮。”王韬的保险思想，对我国自办保险尤其是保险招商局的创立起了直接的推动作用。

Wang Tao (1828-1897) suggested that Chinese insurance company and oversea agencies should be established in order to protect the development of international trade. His thoughts promoted the establishment of China Merchants Insurance Company .

郑观应
Zheng Guanying

郑观应(1841—1920)，广东香山(今中山市)人。字正翔，号陶斋，别号杞忧生等。曾游历过许多国家，先后在英商宝顺、太古等洋行做买办20年。脱离洋行后，以商股代表身份参加洋务派创办的轮船招商局等企业。1894年出版《盛世危言》五卷本，1895年冬刊行增订十四卷本，书中介绍了西方保险史，论述了保险的三大险种："保险有三等(种)：一水险，二火险，三人险。水险保船载货，火险保房屋、货栈，人险保性命、疾病。"指出保险的实质"不过以一人之身之福派及众人"。积极主张自办保险，并亲自参与了1893年进行的招商局船只的换旗与保险一事，在与德商礼和洋行签订的出售与收回合同中，特别列入保险条款。

Zheng Guanying (1841-1920) had been in several foreign companies and took part in the establishment of China Merchants Insurance Company. In his works, he briefed the history of western insurance and introduced marine, fire, and life insurance.

庚申六月

胡不萬年

張謇

张謇为华安合群保寿公司的题词
Zhang Jian's Inscription for China United Assurance Society Ltd.

清末状元、大实业家张謇(1853—1926)1895年创办纱厂。1897年撰述《厂约》，主张仿效西方，从企业盈余中提取保险公积，以防不测。民国后，他就任北洋政府农商总长。在《实业政见宣言书》中主张象西方各国一样，制定农工商法案。他还提出倡办保险的具体政策："各国对于承办保险事业等，每令预交巨款"，"(中国)尚未有此，似可酌量仿行"。

Zhang Jian (1853-1926), who advocated enterprises to draw insurance funds from profits, brought forward detailed polices to promote the development of insurance during his post as chairman of Agriculture Industry and Commerce Bureau.

张謇
Zhang Jian

三、保险中心向上海转移
Insurance Hub to Shanghai

1862年在上海设立的美国扬子保险公司
Yangtze Insurance Co. by American in Shanghai in 1862

1843年11月17日，上海正式开埠。上海优越的地理位置，周边较发达的商品经济环境受到外商的青睐。从此，上海成为外国资本拓展中国市场的桥头堡。中国保险业中心由广州移向上海。

1843年底，怡和洋行423吨的“伊丽莎白·斯图瓦特号”抵达上海。该行在紧靠英国领事馆的地段修建房屋，挂出了“上海怡和洋行”的招牌，成为外商在中国通商口岸建立的第一家最大的商行。

到19世纪60年代，英商保险机构(特别是怡和洋行和宝顺洋行)一直垄断着中国保险业务。其它洋行多通过英商代办保险。

1859年，美国商人在上海成立“上海琼记洋行”(Augustine Heard&Co.)，附设保险代理处，但并没有直接做保险业务，主要依赖怡和及宝顺洋行代办。随着美商在华贸易的增加，琼记洋行与纽约三家保险公司磋商，两年后开始大规模代理美商在华业务，由此揭开了英美争夺中国航运保险市场的序幕。

It was from November 17, 1843 that Shanghai began to be opened to foreign countries. With advantageous geographic location and quite advanced economy, Shanghai became more and more important than Guangzhou for foreign capital to develop in Chinese market. From then on Chinese insurance center moved from Guangzhou to Shanghai.

In late 1843, a ship belonged to Jardine Matheson & Co. arrived in Shanghai and the company became the first largest foreign company established at the open port of China.

Chinese insurance had been in the hands of British insurers till 1860's; in 1859, American merchants set up Augustine Heard & Co. and an insurance agency. Since 1861, the company had started to act as the agent of American insurers; this marked the beginning of the competition in shipping insurance between Britain and America.

上海外滩 Inshore of Shanghai

1862年，美国旗昌洋行(Russell & Co.)筹资100万两，在上海设立第一家外商专业轮船公司——旗昌轮船公司(Shanghai Steam Navigation Co.)。该公司附设扬子保险公司，注资20万两，主要经营货运险，目的在于垄断长江货运险市场。

1872年，英商太古洋行(Butterfield & Swire Co.)在中国创办太古轮船公司。1877年，怡和洋行创办中印轮船公司，他们都兼营保险业务。

19世纪末叶，上海保险市场水险最为发达。经营水险业务的华商保险机构有仁济和、普安等；洋商保险公司有保安、保家、保宁、保宏等；代理行有怡和、旗昌、瑞记等。

American Russell & Co. founded Shanghai Steam Navigation Co. and established Yangtze Insurance Co. in 1862 in order to monopolize the shipping insurance along Yangtze River.

In 1872, British Butterfield & Swire Co. set up Butterfield & Swire Shipping Co. and Jardine Matheson & Co. founded Zhong Yin Shipping Co. in 1877. They both operated insurance business.

In late of 1900's, the most advanced insurance in Shanghai was marine insurance.

19世纪60年代长江航运霸主——旗昌公司金利源码头
Jinliyuan Dock of Shanghai Steam Navigation Co., dominator of shipping in Yangtze River in 1860's

美国旗昌洋行
Russell & Co.

19世纪末上海滩全景
Shanghai's foreshore in late 19th century

1861年在上海紧靠英领馆建造的怡和洋行大楼。该行主要经营进出口贸易、保险、地产、航运、铁路、码头仓储等业务。

Office building of Jardine Matheson & Co. next to British consulate in Shanghai in 1861

1920年重建后的怡和洋行大楼

Office building of Jardine Matheson & Co. after reconstruction in 1920

四、天津保险市场的形成

Tianjin Insurance Market Took Shape

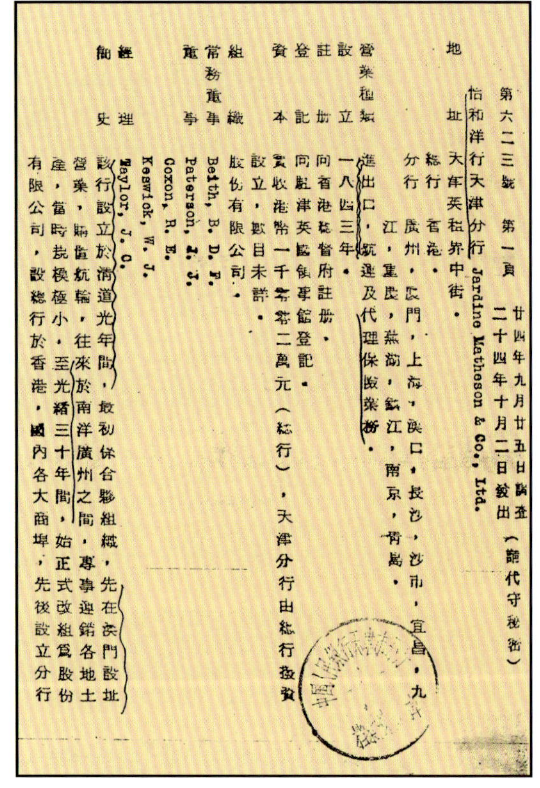

第六二三號　第一頁　廿四年九月廿五日調查　二十四年十月二日發出（請代守秘密）

怡和洋行天津分行 Jardine Matheson & Co., Ltd.

地址　大沽英租界中街。

總行　香港。

分行　廣州，廈門，上海，漢口，長沙，沙市，宜昌，九江，重慶，蕪湖，鎮江，南京，青島。

營業種類　進出口，航運及代理保險業務。

設立　一八四三年。

註冊　向香港總督府註冊。

登記　向駐津英國領事館登記。

資本　實收港幣一千零零二萬元（總行），天津分行由總行發資設立，數目未詳。

組織　股份有限公司。

常務董事　Beith, B. D. F.　Paterson, J. J.

董事　Coxon, R. E.　Keswick, W. J.

經理　Taylor, J. C.

簡史　該行設立於清道光年間，最初係合夥組織，先在廈門設址營業，購置航輪，往來於南洋廣州之間，專事運銷各地土產，當時規模極小，至光緒三十年間，始正式改組為股份有限公司，設總行於香港，國內各大商埠，先後設立分行

怡和洋行天津分行注册登记表

Registration form of Jardine Matheson & Co. Tianjin Branch

第二次鸦片战争后，英商最先登上被列入“五口通商”的天津口岸。伴随英商贸易在天津的发展，现代保险业在天津萌生。

与全国其他各地保险业的历史一样，洋行是保险业最初的载体。1864年怡和洋行在天津设立分行，代理保险业务。仁记洋行(William Forts & Co.)除代理保险业务外，还兼作保险公证。

最早在天津专营保险业务的是英国于仁洋面保安行(又称于仁保险行Union Insurance Society of Canton)。它于1845年在天津设立分支机构。

British merchants became the first to reach Tianjin, one of the five open ports in China after the Second Opium War. Meanwhile, insurance first appeared in Tianjin.

In 1864, Jardine Matheson &Co. set up its branch there and started to be an agent of insurance companies. William Forts & Co. offered insurance notarization .

Union Insurance Society of Canton was the first insurer to specialize in insurance in Tianjin, and its Tianjin Branch was founded in 1845.

天津英租界码头

Port within British Concession in Tianjin

开滦矿务局(1912)旧址。该局曾代理于仁洋面保安行的保险业务。
Site of Kailuan Mining Affairs Bureau (1912), once an agent of Union Insurance Co.

英商仁记洋行(1864)旧址
Site of William Forts & Co. (1864)

汇丰银行旧址。1890年后，于仁洋面保安行曾在此楼二层办公。
Site of HSBC, on the 2nd fl. of which Union Insurance Co. had been after 1890

1921年重建的怡和洋行天津分行营业大楼原景与现景
Original and current look of the business building of Jardine Matheson & Co. after reconstruction in 1921

19世纪60年代怡和洋行在天津海河边的办公大楼及码头
Office building and dock of Jardine Matheson & Co. along Tianjin's Haihe River in 1860's

怡和洋行办公大楼近景
Office building of Jardine Matheson & Co.

到1900年，天津的保险公司已达11家，被代理的保险公司达52家。从事保险代理业务的洋行有：法商立兴洋行(1864年)、中法银公司(1880年后改为中法实业银行)、英商平和洋行(1866年)、太古洋行(Butterfield & Swire Co.，1881年)、德隆洋行(1887年)、德商瑞记洋行(Arnhold Karbery & Co，1880年)、礼和洋行(1880年)、世昌洋行(1888年)、德义洋行(1889年)、日商武斋洋行(1885年)、加藤洋行(1899年)、三井洋行(1899年，Nissen Kissen Kaiza)。

1900年，八国联军攻陷天津，天津租界增至九国，各国商人蜂涌而至。天津人民不仅保险意识日渐提高，而且认识到外商控制中国保险业是“利权外溢”，于是大力发展民族保险业。从1907年起开始组织保险会、防险会和保险公司。上海华商公司也纷纷来天津设立分公司或代理处。

天津保险市场在日益活跃的同时，也出现了“奸商亏累，贪图保险赔偿，放火害人，生出种种纠葛”的现象。为制止不良现象的继续蔓延，刘锡彤等人拟定了对被保险人管理的九条办法。直隶全省巡警道在此基础上又增加了三条对保险人管理的内容，照会天津商会施行。它成为天津最早出现的保险业的法规资料。

在民族保险业兴盛的同时，洋行对保险业务的代理仍占有绝对的优势地位。主要有：博望保险行、普丰洋行、慎昌洋行(Anderzen Mysner & Co.)、德记洋行、开滦矿务局、新泰兴洋行、永兴洋行、瑞丰洋行、光隆洋行、百利洋行、永兴洋行、美最时洋行(Melchers & Co.)等30多家。

The number of insurance companies increased to 11 in 1900. Many foreign companies, such as German Arnhold Karbery & Co., and Japanese Nissen-Kissen Kaiza (NKK) were agents for 52 insurers.

Since 1907, insurance organization appeared in Tianjin and Chinese insurers started to erect their branches there. Meanwhile, the government stipulated regulations to strengthen the control over clients and insurers.

However, Foreign companies still monopolized Tianjin insurance market as they did it in other cities of China. There were about 30 foreign corporations in China then.

日本三井洋行保险公司招贴画
A poster of Nissen Kissen Kaiza

日商三井洋行天津支店(1899)及海河码头。三井洋行曾代理东京海上、东京火灾、明治火灾、日本火灾、共同火灾、大阪海上火灾、太绍火灾、三井海上、三井火灾等保险公司业务。
Haihe River Dock and NNK Tianjin Branch in 1899, once the agent of Tokyo Marine, Tokyo Fire, and many others

五、民族保险业发端

Beginning of Chinese National Insurance

鸦片战争后，以曾国藩和李鸿章等为首的洋务派以“自强”为名，兴办近代军事工业。从19世纪70年代起又以“求富”为名创办民用工业。洋务运动时期一系列工业的兴办，揭开了中国近代工业的序幕，同时也为民族保险业的产生和发展开辟了市场。

1865年5月，中国第一家华商企业——上海华商义和公司保险行成立。但其规模较小，并未开展船舶保险业务，只经营船货保险。真正成为中国民族保险业里程碑的是以李鸿章为首的洋务派创办的保险招商局及其后的仁济和保险公司。

1872年，轮船招商局在上海成立。以招商入股为目的，轮船招商局采取了西方股份制的公司制度。开办后，先后向英国购买伊顿轮、代勃来开轮、其泼利克轮等船只。

After the Opium War, Westernisa-tion Faction leaded by Li Hongzhang and Zeng Guofan initiated modern factories and enterprises mainly dealing business involving in armament production and transportation in order to be self-strengthened. The development of modern industry made it possible for insurance to appear.

In May 1865 Yihe Co., the first Chinese insurer, was founded in so small size that only underwrote vessel and cargo insurance. The real-sense milestone of Chinese national insurance was the founding of China Merchants Insurance Company and Renjihe Insurance Co., which were controlled by the Westernisation Faction.

As a stock company, China Merchants Navigation Company was set up in 1872 in Shanghai; it bought several vessels from Britain.

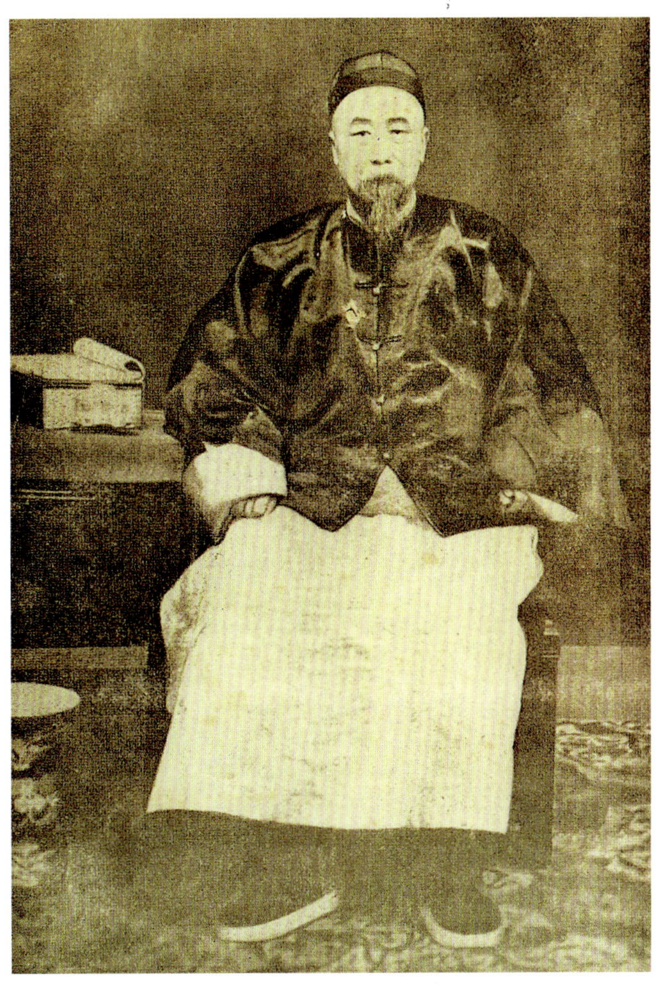

李鸿章(1823-1901)，安徽合肥人，洋务派首领，曾任直隶总督兼北洋大臣，掌管外交、军事、经济重权。1875年委托唐廷枢、徐润筹办中国第一家船舶保险公司——保险招商局。

Li Hongzhang (1823-1901), leader of Westernisation Faction, who, in 1875, entrusted Tang Tingshu and Xu Run to set up the Chinese first shipping insurance company —China Merchants navigation Company.

左图一：轮船招商局总经理徐学禹

Xu Xueyu: General Manager of China Merchants Insurance Company

左图二：轮船招商局副总经理韦焕章

Wei Huanzhang: Vice General Manager of China Merchants Insurance Company

轮船招商局的成立，即刻招致了洋商的排挤。伊顿轮在向上海某洋商保险公司投保时，遭到拒绝，随后转向怡和保安两洋行投保，各保一万五千两，但保险期间只有15天，保费昂贵。洋商保险公司的“冷遇”，使招商局意识到“华商自立公司，自建行栈，自筹保险”的重要性。1875年，李鸿章委托唐廷枢、徐润筹办中国首家船舶保险公司——保险招商局事宜。同年11月1日，《申报》刊登《保险招商局公启》。从4日起，《申报》连续半个月刊登《保险招商局公启》。12月28日，保险招商局正式成立，华商投资踊跃，由于“投股逾额”，将原定股额15万两扩大至20万两，承保能力也有提高。

保险招商局毕竟财力有限，只能承保船值1万两和货值3万两的货船，而当时每艘船的价值大约为10余万两，所以逾额部分还须向外商保险公司投保。但外商公司只限保六成，剩余部分仍需由保险招商局自己承担，所以风险责任依然很大。为此，1876年7月，唐廷枢、徐润等人开始筹资设立仁和保险公司。《申报》曾刊登招股公启，总结了保险招商局的工作，并阐明了设立“仁和”的缘由：“盖保险招商局之设，自乙亥腊月开办，原议集资15万两，嗣以入股者多，复增5万两，共成20万两。业经司有成规，办理颇称起色。凡所保本局及各洋商船货，子母相衡，原有限制，每因投保逾额，至代转保于洋商，傍落利权，能无介意。某等思维再三，允宜循照成章，广集厚资，别分一帜。因与茶商及各帮公议，另立仁和保险公司。”仁和水险公司1876年7月正式成立，资本20万两，保险业务及帐目均由招商局经理。后来，由于投股者众多，股金又增至25万两。公司试办一年后，获利丰富，利润率达30−40%。第二年又添招股本25万两，股本总额共计50万两。

轮船招商局局旗
Flag of China Merchants Navigation Company

Foreign companies refused to insurer Chinese ships or offered strict terms, exp. high premium but short insurance period. Unfair treatment made officers realize the only way is to establish Chinese own insurance company. Therefore Li Hongzhang entrusted Tang Tingshu and Xu Run to prepare China Merchants Insurance Company, which is the first shipping insurer of China.

Due to its limited capital, China Merchants Insurance Company could not insure the overall value of vessels and cargos. So they intended to set up another to mitigate risks and in 1876 established Renhe Insurance Co.

早期轮船招商局各分局长合影
Heads of Branches of China Merchants Navigation Company

早期的外滩轮船招商局大楼
Office building of China Merchants Navigation Company along Shanghai's inshore in early period

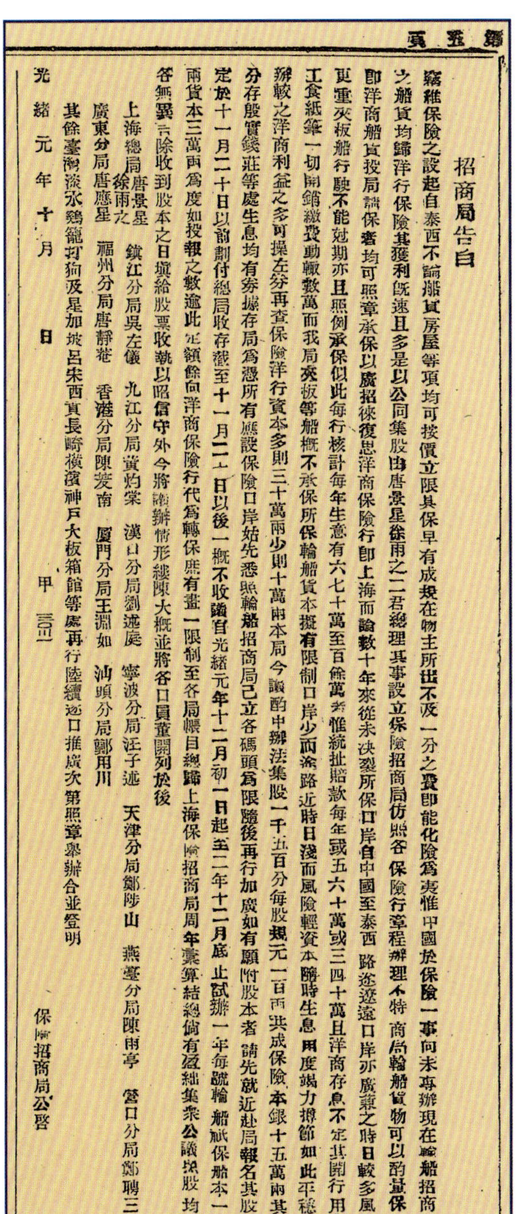

第五頁

招商局告白

竊維保險之設起自泰西不論船貨房屋等項均可按價立限具保早有成規在物主所出不及一分之費即能化險爲夷惟中國於保險一事向未專辦現在輪船招商局之船貨均歸洋行保險其獲利既速且多是以公同集股由唐景星徐雨之二君總理其事設立保險招商局仿照各保險行章程辦理不特商局輪船貨物可以酌量保險即洋商船貨投局請保者均可照章承保以廣招徠復思洋商保險行即上海而論數十年來從未決裂所保口岸自中國至泰西路途遼遠口岸亦廣兼之時日較多風險更重夾板船行駛不能剋期亦且照例承保似此每行核計每年生意有六七十萬至百餘萬者惟統扯賠款每年或五六十萬或三四十萬且洋商存息不定其開行用人工食紙筆一切開銷繳費動輒數萬而我局夾板等船概不承保所保輪船貨本擬有限制口岸少而途路近時日淺而風險輕資本隨時生息用度竭力撙節如此平穩試辦較之洋商利益之多可操左券再查保險洋行資本多則三十萬兩少則十萬兩本局今議酌中辦法集股一千五百分每股規元一百兩共成保險本銀十五萬兩其銀分存殷實錢莊等處生息均有券據存局爲憑所有應設保險口岸姑先悉照輪船招商局已立各碼頭爲限隨後再行加廣如有願附股本者請先就近赴局報名其股本定於十一月二十日以前劃付總局收存截至十一月二十日以後一概不收議自光緒元年十一月初一日起至二年十二月底止試辦一年每號輪船祇保船本一萬兩貨本三萬兩爲度如投報之數逾此定額餘向洋商保險行代爲轉保庶有畫一限制至各局帳目總歸上海保險招商局周年彙算結總倘有盈絀集衆公議照股均派各無異言除收到股本之日填給股票收執以昭信守外今將議辦情形縷陳大概並將各口員董開列於後

上海總局唐景星 徐雨之 鎮江分局吳左儀 九江分局黃灼棠 漢口分局劉述庭 寧波分局汪子述 天津分局鄭陟山 燕臺分局陳雨亭 營口分局鄭聘三

廣東分局唐應星 福州分局唐靜菴 香港分局陳茇南 廈門分局王淵如 汕頭分局鄭用川

其餘臺灣淡水雞籠打狗及呈加坡呂宋西貢長崎橫濱神戶大板箱館等處再行陸續逐口推廣次第照章舉辦合並登明

光緒元年十月 日 保險招商局公啓

甲 三四

中国第一家船舶保险公司——保险招商局在《申报》刊登的告示
Bulletin by China Merchants Insurance Company published in *Shenbao* (Shanghai Newspaper)

重建后的轮船招商局大楼
Rebuilt Office Building of China Merchants Insurance Company

唐廷枢和洋务派首领李鸿章在一起
Tang Tingshu with Li Hongzhang

唐廷枢(1832–1892)，广东中山人。少时肄业香港学堂。1851年，在香港政府巡理厅和大审判院任翻译。1858年，到上海任江海关总翻译，1861年，任英商怡和洋行买办，两年后升为总买办。1867年，唐附股于怡和经营的谏当保险行，为外国保险公司吸收了大量的华商资本。后来，怡和洋行设立香港火烛保险公司，唐同样为之大力招揽保险业务。1873年，唐应李鸿章之邀离开怡和，任轮船招商局总办，从此成为洋务派官僚的得力助手。为改变轮船招商局处处受到外商保险公司排挤的局面，唐廷枢和徐润筹划自设保险公司，定名为保险招商局。经过广募资金，保险招商局于1875年12月28日正式成立，并在多个港口、码头设立分局。由于保险招商局资力有限，遇到大额投保，免不了向洋商保险公司分保。为此，1876年，唐廷枢和徐润等人再次集资组建仁和水险公司，扩大了华商保险公司的自保能力，增强了华人自办保险的信心。1878年，唐廷枢与徐润又将保险招商局扩充资本，并改称济和船栈保险局，大大增强了轮船招商局的生存和竞争能力。

Tang Tingshu (1832-1892), born in Canton, ever worked in Jardine Matheson &Co. and other foreign companies. In 1873 he was invited to prepare for the establishment of China Merchants Insurance Company and from then on he became the loyal and strong assistant of Westernization Faction.

徐润(1838–1911)广东中山人，出生于买办世家，14岁到上海英商宝顺洋行当学徒，1861年升为副买办，大举投资经营茶、丝、麻、烟叶、鸦片买卖。1868年，徐自开宝源祥茶栈。1872年，进入轮船招商局任会办，后与唐廷枢筹办保险招商局及仁和、济和保险公司，实权仅次于唐廷枢。

Xu Run (1838-1911), born in Canton, an apprentice in Davidson-Dent House, with Tang Tingshu together, was entrusted to prepare China Merchants Insurance Company, Renhe, Jihe, and Renjihe Insurance Co.

徐润
Xu Run

随着航运业务的发展，1877年初，利用美国旗昌洋行经营不利的时机，轮船招商局并购了旗昌的轮船和码头栈房。一时间，轮船招商局船只猛增，运量上升。由于仁和水险公司，只保船舶险和运输险，不保码头。栈房和货物的火灾保险，所以每年须向外商投保的数额很大，保费大量外流。于是，唐廷枢、徐润等人在原保险招商局基础上，又招股20万两，专保仁和的逾额部分及轮船招商局的码头仓栈和货物的火险，改称“济和船栈保险局”。《申报》自1878年3月16日起，连续多日刊登招集保险股份公告：“轮船招商局自设仁和保险以来，经历多年，俱臻妥善，第投保者踊跃。每至逾额，历向他处转保，统年计之，为数甚巨。利权外溢，诚可惜也。具有储栈各货屡来局找投保者，而仁和公司以专保船货，并不兼保栈货，因此溢利亦非浅鲜。兹拟召集股银20万两，专保仁和所保逾额，并试办招商局栈储备各货保险，因之曰济和船栈保险局。”1878年4月17日，济和船栈保险局正式开业。此后，唐廷枢一改外国人担任船长的惯例，推举张慎之为“江孚”轮船长，招致外国保险公司不满，并以此为借口拒保。于是，济和船栈保险局再次在原基础上，增资至50万两，扩办为济和水火险公司。

With the development in shipping business, China Merchants Navigation Company had to buy insurance from foreign insurers, for Renhe was operate vessels and transportation insurance. To decrease the outflow of premium, Jihe Insurance Co. was opened on April 17, 1878 to specialize in fire insurance.

20世纪40年代轮船招商局要员合影

Keymen with China Merchants Navigation Company in 1940s

轮船招商局创办仁济和水火保险股份有限公司章程，股东会决议和股东登记暂行条例。
Constitution of Renjihe Marine & Fire Insurance Co.; Decision of Shareholders' Conference; Provisional Rules on Registration of Shareholders

此后的几年内，"仁和"与"济和"的业务不断扩展，并分别在新加坡、菲律宾、旧金山等处设立分支机构，为当地华侨办理保险业务。1881年3月颁布分红帐略，其所属保险公司已付给股东股息25.3万余两。本届由于获利丰厚，另加付余利一分五厘。3月12日的《申报》评论："盖自中国开创以来，其利益之显可见者，胥当以是为嚆矢已。"然而，1884年爆发的中法战争导致了上海金融市场的恐慌，轮船招商局也因此陷入困境，从而仁和、济和的业务也大受影响。为减缓金融恐慌的困扰，振兴民族保险业，仁和、济和两家公司于1886年2月召开董事联席会议，决定将两家公司合并为"仁济和水火保险公司"，股本为规银100万两。合并后的仁济和保险公司名义上是独立的，实际上仍由轮船招商局代办，股款存于轮船招商局。从1888年起轮船招商局进入商办阶段，到20世纪20年代，轮船招商局亏损额高达2000万两。仁济和保险公司大部分资金滞留在轮船招商局，无奈只好缩小业务范围。1927年10月，张静江等人组成的"清查整理招商局委员会"进驻轮船招商局，对仁济和保险公司的整顿意见为："查该公司股本共有80万两，分为8千股。以资本额而论，在国人经营之保险业中，可谓首屈一指。惟其营业状况之腐败，实出乎意料之外。近数年来，该公司除水险红提单外，绝无营业状况可言。最近红提单办法取消，该公司实际上完全停业，所有职员竟终日无所事事。整顿办法，注重营业，添设火险部，同时经营水火险业务。"据《上海市保险业同业公会史略》，仁济和于1934年10月停业。1935年的《中国保险年鉴》记载：仁济和仅存5名职工。1937年的《中国保险年鉴》记载："最近受世界不景气之侵袭，招商局营业感觉极大之威胁。经济逐呈枯竭之象，仁济和保险公司之资本，因滞留于该局而无法收回，致流动资金日趋缺乏，而营业亦无由进展矣。最近该公司经股东会议决定，暂行缩小范围，停保水火险，同时积极向招商局洽商归还方法，以冀早日恢复旧观，继续营业。"1938年后，仁济和保险公司的名字在保险业调查材料名单上已无从查找了。

Since then, Renhe and Jihe Insurance Co.'s business had kept growing and they branched into Singapore, San Francisco, and Philippines to provide insurance for Chinese abroad. They outbreak of Sino-French War in 1884 resulted in the fluctuation and scare in Shanghai finance market and insurance was badly frustrated. The two insurers merged into Renjihe Marine & Fire Insurance Co. in 1886. A team leaded by Zhang JingJiang entered the company and started to clear the company's account in 1927. The company was namely independent, while in fact, it was controlled by China Merchants Navigation Company. It was reportedly known that Renjihe Marine & Fire was closed down in October 1934.

六、火险和寿险的出现
Appearance of Fire and Life Insurance

与世界保险发展史一脉相承，以海上贸易带动的中国最初的保险业务几乎都是水险。直到1866年，怡和洋行才创立了中国第一家火险公司——香港火烛保险公司（HongKong Fire Insurance Company），其生意颇为兴隆，最初几年年均盈利率高达50%，股票飙升400%。

到19世纪末叶，上海火险业中只有保宏一家较为著名，于仁及保家行也兼营火险业务，其他大多是代理行。火险业务仅局限于公共租界内的商店住户，南市区则拒保。保险公司在保户门楣上悬钉一种铜质或铁质火标，既便于警察查视，又提醒救火人员奋勇抢救。一般保户以悬挂保险商标为荣，因为非殷实商店住户，洋商不会贸然承保。

It was not until 1866 that Jardine Matheson &Co. established the first fire insurance company in China: HongKong Fire Insurance Company. By the end of 19th century, New Zealand Insurance Co. was the only well-known in fire insurance in Shanghai. What's more, their business was limited within Public Concession.

上海外滩的扬子保险大厦。当时于仁、保家、保宁、中华等十几家保险公司都租用该楼办公，为当时著名的保险大楼。
Yangtze Insurance Mansion, a well-known insurance building of the time, located in Shanghai's inshore

英商保家水火
保險有限公司

總公司在上海黃浦灘四號

內第　　號保險單
保數五千　両保費

古香齋
寶號
先生　收存

西歷　年四月二十九日起
西歷　年四月二十九日止

英商保家水火保险公司的火险保单
Fire Insurance Policy by North China Insurance Company（资料提供：上海档案馆）

于仁（友宁）保险公司主管兼总经理C.蒙塔古·伊德
Supervisor and General Manager of Union Insurance Company

隔江远眺扬子保险大厦。箭头所指为扬子保险大厦。
Yangtze Insurance Mansion (where the arrow points to)

寿险在中国的起步，比水险大约晚了三四十年。1846年，英国永福（Standard）和大东方（Oriental）在中国南方城市初办寿险业务，但被保险人几乎都是外国人，业务规模很小。随后英商永明人寿和永年人寿也相继拓展寿险市场。

1853年，永福人寿保险公司（Standard Life Assurance Co.）授予托马斯·蒙克里夫（Thomas Moncreiff）为驻上海保险代办处首席代理人。1889年，永福制定了“1846-1900年中国人死亡经验表”。

1897年，英商永年人寿保险公司（The China Mutual Life Insurance Co. Ltd）在上海成立。资本50万银两，发5000 股，每股100两。1924年，该公司与加拿大永明人寿合并。

Life insurance appeared thirty to forty years later than marine insurance. Standard and Oriental Insurance Co. started their business in Southern cities in China in 1846, but most of clients were foreigners .

In 1853, Thomas Moncrief was entrusted as Chief Agent in Shanghai by Standard Life Assurance Co. which then made the Experienced Mortality Table of Chinese People (1846-1900).

The China Mutual Life Insurance Co. Ltd was established in 1897 in Shanghai. Later it merged with Canada Sun Life Assurance Co.

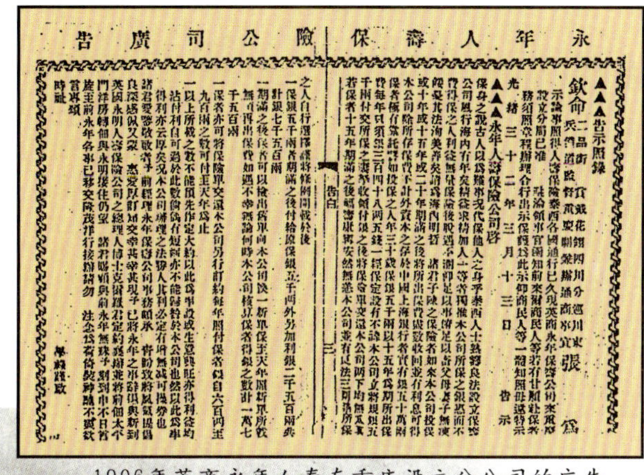

永年人壽保險公司廣告

▲▲▲告示照錄

▲▲▲永年人壽保險公司啓

光緒三十二年三月十三日 告示

1906年英商永年人寿在重庆设立分公司的广告
Ad by Sun Life Insurance Co. for founding of its Chongqing Branch

永年人寿保险公司大楼
Office building of China Mutual Life Insurance Co.

朱葆三，浙江黄岩人，上海商界著名人士。20世纪初在上海工商界中广为流传的一句话："上海道一颗印，不及朱葆三一封信"，足见当时朱葆三在上海商界的重要地位。1905年5月，朱葆三、曾少卿在上海发起成立华兴保险公司。朱葆三出任三总董之一。1906年10月，朱葆三投资参股的华安水火保险公司开业，朱葆三出任董事。同年11月，朱葆三等发起的华成经保火险公司在上海成立，后改为华成保险公司，朱为董事。1907年，身为华兴、华成、华安三家公司总董的朱葆三在上海发起成立华商火险公会，会员公司华兴、华安、华通、华成经保、源安、华侨合众、万丰、福安等家公司。朱葆三为首任会长。华商火险公会为中国第一家保险社团组织，也是1931年改组成立的上海保险同业公会的前身。1909年，朱葆三又投资宁绍商轮公司(其保险部经营有关保险业务)、华安合群保寿公司等。

Zhu Baosan, born in Zhejiang Province, was a very important person in Shanghai business circles. Taking part in the establishment of Huaxing, Huacheng and Hua'an Insurance Co., he took the chair of the three companies. Also he did preparation to found Chinese Fire Insurance Association, the predecessor of Shanghai Insurance Association.

1912年华商火险公会由会长制改为会长与会董并行制。华成经保总董王一亭被推举为会董，左图为改制后的华商火险公会会长、华安水火保险公司总经理沈仲礼。

Shen Zhongli, general manager of Hua'an Fire & Marine Insurance Co and chairman of Chinese Fire Insurance Association

to the credit of General Reserve.
Messrs Booth, Mackenzie and Mountain were appointed a Committee to confer with the auditors on this point.
Secretary's remuneration — It was resolved that the Secretary's remuneration be paid free of Income Tax.
China — Mr E. M. Mountain reported he proposed to appoint a manager to develop the company's business in China, the remuneration to be £400 per annum, which proposal was approved.
It was resolved that the Annual Meeting be held on Wednesday 15th April 1908, at 2.30 o'clock p.m., in the Rooms of the Institute of Directors, 4 Corbet Court E.C.

At a Meeting of the Directors of the British
Holland Persia Trading Co. — was considered and approved and it was resolved that the seal of the Company be affixed and that the same be signed and executed by Harry Simbs Gullick and John William Rogerson, two directors and by John Gardiner the Secretary of the Company. The seal was affixed accordingly in the presence of Mr Walker, a notary, who attended for purposes of legalisation.
China — Mr E. M. Mountain reported he had appointed Sydney Fulcher Esq; to act as manager for the company in China, the remuneration being £450 p.a; which appointment was approved.
Secretary's remuneration — It was resolved that the Secretary's remuneration be increased to £250 p.a, such increase dating from 1 January 1908.

J. B. Rogerson
9.4.08

1908年英国鹰星保险公司董事会会议记录，该记录记载了鹰星公司在华业务的开始，并任命了在中国的第一位经理。

Minutes of board meeting of Eagle Star Insurance Co.; it records business initiation with the first appointed manager in China

七、清末保险市场的格局

Insurance Market in Late Qing Dynasty

清末民族保险业处在初创阶段，从1865年中国最早的民族保险公司——义和保险公司成立至辛亥革命前夜，约有35家民族保险公司创立，其中水火险公司27家，寿险公司8家。

从公司数目上看，民族保险公司已有一定规模，但这些公司在市场上都立足不稳，业务规模不大，其市场份额不足10%。

清末外商对华贸易不断扩展，外商垄断着以水险为主的中国保险市场，其市场份额超过90%。

当时，外商在华创设的保险公司并不多，外商的保险业务主要通过洋行代理。1900年，有52家洋行代理148家保险公司的业务。英商在中国保险市场上占有绝对主导地位，其业务做法、管理模式、费率水平、保单条款等均为其他国家的保险人所仿效。

清末，以英国保险商为核心在上海成立了中国最早的保险行业自律组织——上海洋商保险公会，该会的成立更加强了外商对中国保险市场的垄断，他们共进共退，在佣金、折让、费率、险种、拒保、分保等方面协调一致，共同遵守。这一时期，外商保险公司以上海为核心，向中国沿海、沿江地区扩展业务，设立分公司，其业务范围已扩展到广州、黄浦、澳门、汕头、厦门、台湾、福州、宁波、镇江、九江、汉口、烟台、天津、宜昌、北京等地。

From the establishment of the first Chinese national insurance company to the eve of the Revolution of 1911, thirty-five insurers were founded , twenty-seven of which were fire and marine insurers and eight were life insurance companies. However, their total business only occupied less than 10 percent of the market .

During this period ,Chinese insurance was in the hands of foreign companies which shared more than 90 percent of the market. In reality, there were much more agents than insurance companies. There were totally 52 foreign agents of 148 insurers. British insurers were the super leader of Chinese market. The foundation of Shanghai Foreign Insurance Association at the end of Qing Dynasty strengthened the monopoly. Meanwhile, they established branches along seas and rivers in China.

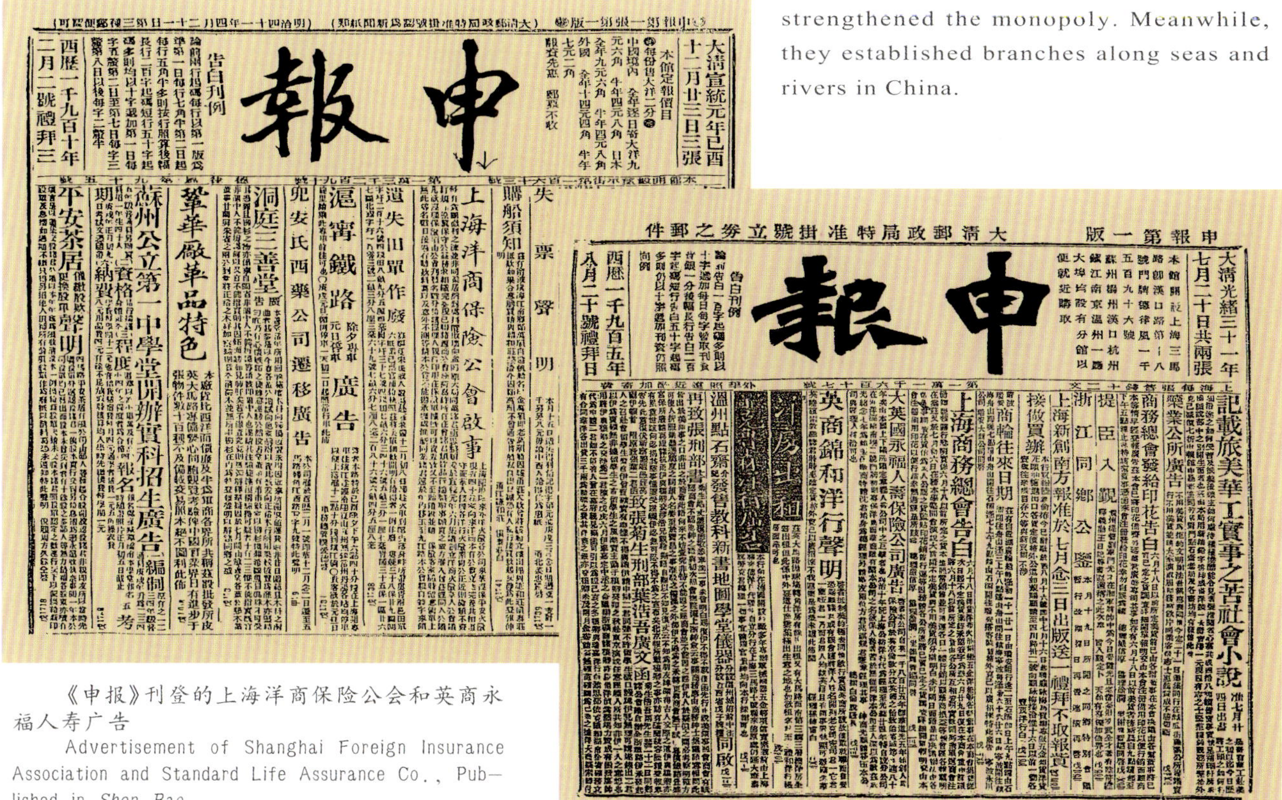

申報
大清宣統元年己酉十二月廿三日三張
西歷一千九百十年二月二號禮拜三
上海洋商保險公會啟事
遺失田單作廢
滬寧鐵路廣告
兜安氏西藥公司遷移廣告
洞庭三善堂
蘇州公立第一中學堂開辦實科招生廣告
平安茶居
購船須知
失票聲明

申報
大清光緒三十一年七月二十日共兩張
西歷一千九百五年八月二十號禮拜日
記載旅美華工實事之苦社會小說
商務總會發給印花告白
提臣入覲
浙江同鄉公鑒
上海新創南方報准於七月念二日出版
接做買辦
上海商務總會告白
大英國永福人壽保險公司廣告
英商錦和洋行聲明
溫州點石齋發售教科新書地圖學堂儀器
再致張刑部書

《申报》刊登的上海洋商保险公会和英商永福人寿广告

Advertisement of Shanghai Foreign Insurance Association and Standard Life Assurance Co., Published in *Shen Bao*

清末时期主要外商保险公司一览表

Major Foreign Insurers in China in Late Qing Dynasty

创办时间 Time Founded	公司名称 Company	注册地点 Register Place
外商水火保险公司 Foreign Fire and Marine Insurers		
1805年	广州保险会社(又称谏当保安行 Canton Insurance Society)	广州 Guangzhou
1835年	於仁洋面保安行(又称友宁保险行Union Insurance Society of Canton)	澳门 Macao
1862年	美国扬子保险公司(Yangtze Insurance Association)	上海 Shanghai
1863年	保家行(North China Insurance Company)	上海 Shanghai
1865年	保宁保险公司(又称中外保众保险公司China Traders Insurance Co.)	香港 HongKong
1866年	香港火烛保险公司(Hong Kong Fire Insurance Co.)中国第一家火险公司	香港 Hong Kong
1868年	英商公裕太阳保险公司(Sun Fire Office,1891年易名Sun Insurance Office)	上海,分支机构 Shanghai, Branch
1868年	巴勒保险公司(North British Mercantile Insurance Co.for Eastern Branch)	上海,分支机构 Shanghai, Branch
1870年	中日水险公司(China and Japan Marine Insurance Co.)	上海 Shanghai
1870年	香港维多利亚保险行(Victoria Fire Insurance Co.)	香港 HongKong
1871年	华商保安公司(华商保险公司Chinese Insurance Co.)	香港 HongKong
1884年	保宏保险公司(New Zealand Insurance Co.)	上海,分支机构 Shanghai, Branch
1893年	利川保险公司(英商立德)	重庆 Chongqing
1899年	日本明治火灾保险株式会社	台湾,分公司 Taiwan, Branch
1902年	沙俄莫斯科火灾保险公司	哈尔滨,分公司 Haerbing,Branch
1903年	日本家畜保险株式会社	台湾 Taiwan
1903年	英商保家水险公司(North China Marine Insurance Co.)	重庆 Chongqing
1906年	英京火险公司	重庆,分公司 Chongqing, Branch
1910年	荷兰望赉(Jana Sea and Fire)公司	上海 Shanghai
外商人寿保险公司 Foreign Life Insurers		
1884年	美商公平人寿保险公司(Equitable Life Insurance Co.)	上海,分公司 Shanghai, Branch
1898年	英商永福人寿保险公司(Standard Life Assurance Co.)	上海,分公司 Shanghai, Branch
1898年	英商永年人寿保险公司(China Mutual Life Insurance Co.)	上海 Shanghai
1899年	美国纽约人寿保险公司(New York Life Insurance Co.)	上海,分公司 Shanghai, Branch
1899年	加拿大宏利人寿保险公司(Manufactrure Life Insurance Co.)	上海,分公司 Shanghai, Branch
1899年	加拿大永明人寿保险公司(Sun Life Assurance Co.)	上海,分公司 Shanghai, Branch
1904年	日本帝国生命保险株式会社	台湾,分公司(寿) Taiwan, Branch
1905年	英商华洋人寿保险公司(Shanghai Life Insurance Co.)	上海 Shanghai
1909年	新加坡大东方人寿保险公司(Great Eastern Life Assurance Co.of Singapore)	上海,分公司 Shanghai, Branch

清末时期主要华商保险公司一览表

Major Chinese Insurance Companies in Late Qing Dynasty

华商水火保险公司		
创办时间 Time Founded	公司名称 Company	注册地点 Register Place
1865年	上海义和保险公司(中国第一家民族保险机构)	上海
1875年	保险招商局(华商自办的第一家船舶保险公司)	上海
1877年	安泰保险公司	海口
1880年	常安保险公司	香港
1882年	上海火烛保险公司	上海
1882年	万安保险公司	香港
1886年	仁济和保险公司	上海
1899年	宜安水火保险公司	香港
1900年	福安保险公司	香港
1901年	协安保险公司	香港
1901年	香港源安洋面火烛保险公司	香港
1905年	华兴火险公司	上海
1905年	华通保险公司	上海
1905年	中国合众水火保险公司	上海
1905年	同益火险公司	上海
1905年	万丰火险公司	上海
1906年	华安水火保险公司	香港
1906年	华成经保保险公司	香港
1906年	源盛保险公司	上海
1907年	四海通银行保险公司	上海
1907年	重庆探矿保险公司	重庆
1908年	中国信益保险公司	上海
1908年	满洲股份公司(经营杂货、兼营保险)	哈尔滨
1908年	冠球联保火险公司	广州
1909年	恒安保险公司	上海
1909年	普华保险公司	上海
1909年	小吕宋益同人保险公司	上海
1909年	恒盛保险公司	上海
1909年	汇通保险公司	上海
1909年	同安保险公司	上海
华商人寿保险公司		
1894年	福安水火人寿保险公司	香港
1905年	华洋永庆人寿保险公司	上海
1907年	华安人寿保险公司	上海
1909年	上海允康人寿保险公司	上海
1909年	上海延年人寿保险公司	上海
1909年	上海永宁人寿保险公司	香港，中外合资

Bicentenary chinese Insurance
中国保险业二百年(1805-2005)

民国保险业(1912-1949)

Insurance in the Republic of China (1912-1949)

辛亥革命推翻了清代统治，南京临时政府采取了一些必要措施保护和奖励工商业。1927年后，国民党在南京成立了国民政府，建立了以“四行”、“两局”、“一库”为代表的官僚资本金融机构，这些机构和民营银行相继投资于保险业，使民族保险事业获得自创立以来的第一个发展高潮。

1937年，抗日战争爆发，大批工商企业内迁，促使大后方的经济有了发展的契机，内地保险业也得以相应发展，陪都重庆一度成为大后方保险业的中心。民族保险业出现了第二次繁荣。

抗战结束后，集中在上海的大量游资，再度竞相投资于保险业，至解放前夕，上海保险机构已达到241家，其中民族保险机构178家，形成了中国民族保险业发展的第三次高潮。

发展并非一帆风顺的民国保险业，总的来说呈现出了前所未有的繁荣景象。民国时期的保险公司数量成倍增加，其分支机构和代理网点星罗棋布，遍及全国各地乃至国外。由于金融业以其雄厚的资金投入保险业，增强了资本实力，改善了公司的经营管理。民国保险业注重专业培养，发展经纪人，广泛开展保险业务，并拓展险种，除一般财产保险、人寿保险、责任保险、信用保险之外，还有战时的兵险和一些专业性质的保险业务。保险同业公会、中国保险学会等团体应运而生，对规范保险市场、繁荣保险学术、培养保险人才作出了贡献。为了加强对保险业的监管，国民政府于1929年颁布了《保险法》。1939年，同时颁布了修订后的《保险法》、《保险业法》和《保险业法实施法》。

As the time required, China United Assurance Society Ltd, which was founded at the same time of the founding of the government of the Republic of China, has a far-reaching significance – a symbol of the rise in the national life insurance.

During the period 3 climaxes surged in the national insurance:

In 1927, Kuomintang established its national government, followed with some financial institutions of bureaucrat capital like “four banks”, “two bureaus”, and “ one treasury”, which cornered the whole country’s economic lifeline. In the period bureaucrat, banking, and commercial capital were invested in the insurance in succession, thus the historically first peak in the national insurance.

After the outbreak of the War of Resistance Against Japan (1937-1945), inland insurance institutions grew fast in quantity under the background of the boom in the insurance business in the vast home front, along with the inward move of the national government and great batches of industry and commerce, therefore came the second prosperity in the conventional underwriting.

After the War, the title of insurance hub re-crowned to Shanghai, where a great amount of idle funds rushed for investment in insurance again, hitting a record of the number of insurance institutions. On the eve of the liberation, there had been 241 insurance organs in Shanghai, of which, 178 from national insurance institutions, which is regarded as the third highlight of the national insurance.

一、民族保险业的涌起

Surge of Chinese National Insurance

民国初期，中国民族保险业获得了快速发展的机遇：一是民国初建需要刺激工商业的发展以稳定政权；二是第一次世界大战的爆发，欧美列强卷入战争，无瑕东顾，大大减缓了洋商对中国保险市场的控制；三是“五四”运动的爆发，反帝斗争的兴起，赢得了整个民族对民族工商业的支持和对洋商的抵制。

1912—1925年，陆续创办的民族保险公司有：上海康年保寿、华安合群保寿、均安水火(香港)、羊城置业(广州)、金星人寿、香安(香港注册、广州)、永康联保人寿、联泰(香港)、华侨合众(前身为中国合众，1917年改组为中华保险公司)、上海联保水火、先施置业(总公司在香港)、广恒(香港)、永宁水火、永安水火(总公司在香港)、爱众联保寿险、众益联保寿险、两利联保寿险、博爱人寿联保、永益联保寿险、永隆人寿、宁绍水火、华年人寿水火(汉口)、中和人寿(天津)、江苏中华商立寿险、福田保寿(福建莆田)、大中华水火人寿(杭州)、中华人寿保险公益会(广东番禺)、船商水运保险(四川富顺)、合记公司(安东)、利运保险公司(浙江兰溪)、仁济保寿(广东番禺)、保众保险(江苏江浦)、公安保险(广东南海)等。

Chinese national insurance got good opportunities to develop in the early period of the Republic : first, the government needed to promote the development of insurance in order to guarantee the development of industry and commerce; secondly, foreign companies were forced to loosen the control over China's insurance market during the interval while the World War I broke out; thirdly , with the outbreak of May Fourth Movement and the deepening of anti-imperalism struggle, people all over the country took action to support the national industry and resist the foreign companies.

A large number of insurance corporations such as China National Life Insurance Co. Ltd (Shanghai), the Venus Life Insurance Co. Ltd and the China United Assurance Society Ltd, were established from 1912 to 1925.

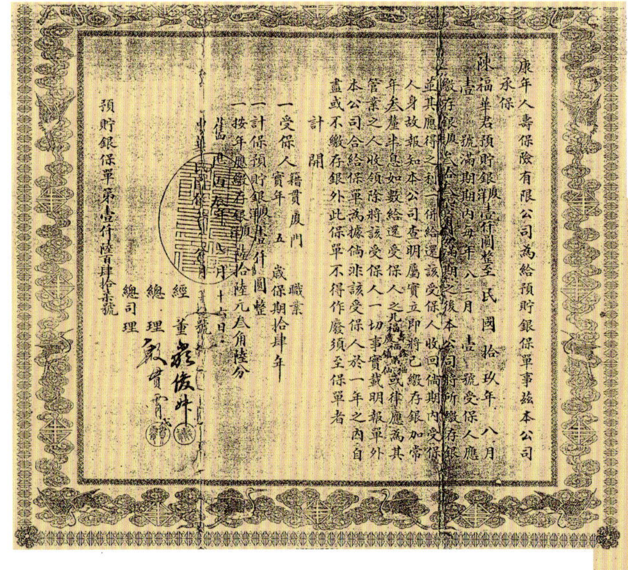

1912年3月上海康年保寿公司成立，资本额为银元100万两。图为上海康年保寿公司保单。

Policy Signed by China National Life Insurance Co. Ltd

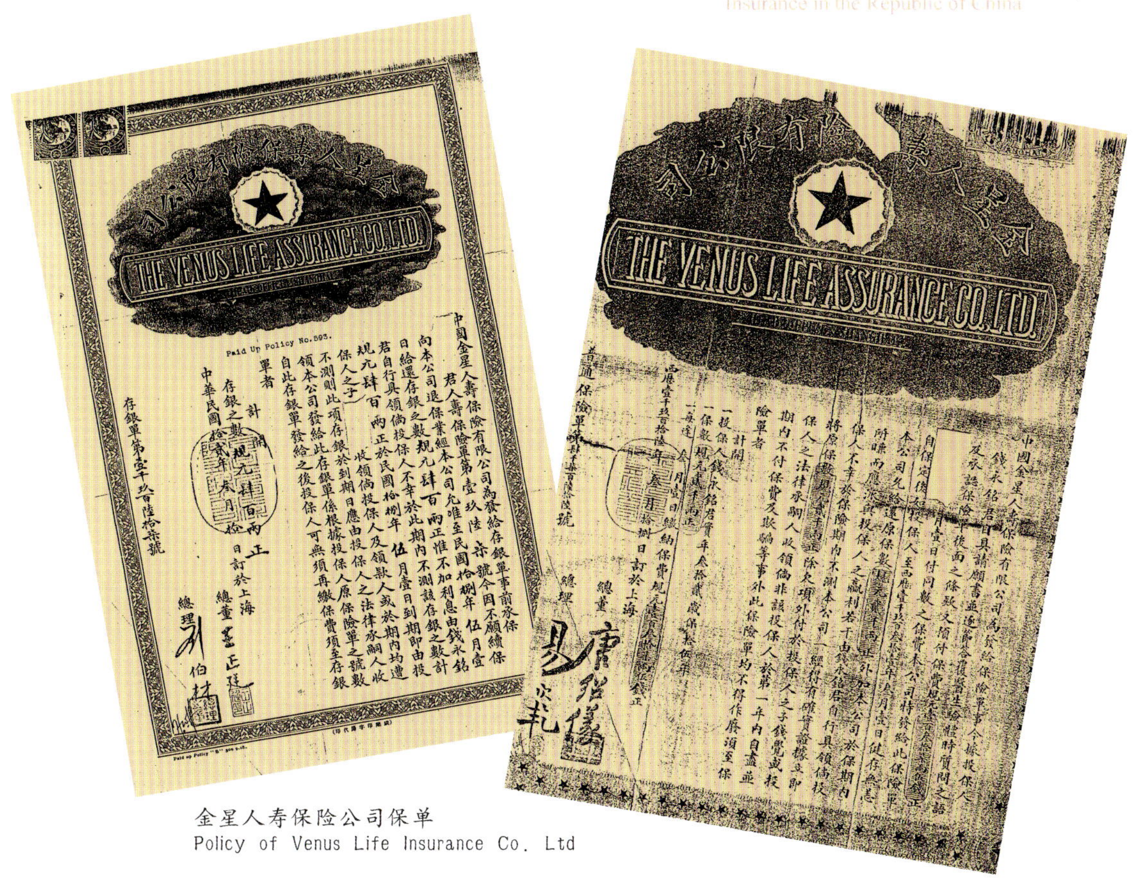

金星人寿保险公司保单
Policy of Venus Life Insurance Co. Ltd

卢作孚(1893—1952)，实业家。四川合川人。1925年创办民生公司，曾任总经理，国民党政府川江航务管理局局长、四川省建设厅厅长和交通部次长。1950年任全国政协委员。

Lu Zuofu, born in Sichuang Province, established Mingsheng Co.in 1925 and ever was the senior official in Guomingdang Government and Member of China People's Political Consulting Conference.

中国民族保险业的成长全赖民族工商界与银行界资本的注入。中国第一代实业家张謇领风气之先，其大生纱厂集团投资创立了自己的保险公司。1926年起，卢作孚的民生实业公司投资于民安、太平洋、中国航运意外、合众、中国人寿、大吉、兴华、航联等保险公司。

与此同时，刘氏集团老板刘鸿生目睹自己的企业每年要花费大量保费，于是想自设保险公司，经与潘学安(时任友邦人寿副总经理)和陈光甫(上海银行总经理)谋划，筹资12万元，于1927年1月19日在上海成立大华保险公司，经营水火险业务。大华经营稳健，并向外商分保，每年均有盈余。1936年资本增至20万元。

The national industry and commerce and banking capital promoted the development of insurance. Zhang Jian, one of the first entrepreneurs in China, founded an insurance company. Since 1926, Minsheng Industrial Company invested in and set up Ming'an, the Pacific, China Navigation Casual, China Life, Daji and Xinghua insurance companies.

At the same time,chairman of Lius' Group founded their own insurance corporation in order to decrease the large amount of premium payment. With the help of Pan Xue'an and Chen Guangpu , Dahua Insurance Company was established in Shanghai on January 1st, 1927, which specialized in marine and fire insurance .

刘鸿生(1888—1956)，实业家。浙江定海人。毕业于上海圣约翰大学。1909年入英商平矿务公司。1920年起创办中华码头公司、中华煤气公司、上海章华毛麻纺织公司、大中华火柴公司、上海水泥公司等企业。1927年投资保险，创办大华保险公司，并任董事。解放后任全国政协委员。

Liu Hongsheng, born in Zhejiang Province, started to work in a British mining co. After graduation from Saint Johnson University, a series of companies were set up by him since 1920. In 1927 he established Dahua Insurance Co. and held the position of the director. He was a member of China People's Political Consulting Conference.

大华保险公司董事长——陈光甫
Chen Guangpu, board chairman of Dahua Insurance Co.

大华保险公司总经理——潘学安，上海人。1931年留学美洲，攻读经济及保险学，回国后，任东南大学经济及保险学教授。1920年，任美亚保险公司创始人史带秘书。1922年与其创办友邦保险公司，后提升为副总经理。1927年与刘鸿生、陈光甫创办大华保险公司，随后又创办中国第一信用保险公司，堪称中国信用保险第一人。潘学安先生在友邦创立初期，即竭力提倡终身保险，大华保险公司创立后，他在管理上采用科学管理办法，并首先与国外公司订立分保合同。除任大华保险公司，中国第一信用保险公司总经理外，还任泰山保险公司常任董事、保险公会执委委员、保管委员会统一华洋保价委员会委员等职。

Pan Xuean, general manager of Dahua Insurance Co., went to America to learn economics and insurance in 1931. He became secretary of CV Starr, the founder of American Asiatic Underwriters in 1920; participated in the foundation of the Asia Insurance Company; later became vice general manager of the company. Pan established China's first credit Insurance Company named China First Credit Insurance Co.

工商实业界投资保险的进程中，别具影响的是当时中国两家顶尖的大型百货公司永安与先施公司对保险业的投入。

郭乐、郭泉兄弟经营的永安资本集团(以百货为基础)于1915年，投资75万元，创办永安水火保险公司(总公司在香港，后在上海、广州、汉口、天津、汕头等地设分公司)。1925年，又投资创办永安人寿保险公司(总公司在香港)。之后，又投资于上海联保水火保险公司。

During this period two large-sized department stores invested in insurance successively. In 1915, Yong'an Group which belonged to the Guos' established Yong'an Marine & Fire Insurance Co.. And in 1925 Yong'an Life Insurance Co. was founded.

郭氏兄弟1918年创建的上海永安公司大楼
Building of Yong'an Co. founded by Guo Le and Guo Quan

上海永安水火保险公司
Office Building of Yong'an Marine & Fire Insurance Co.

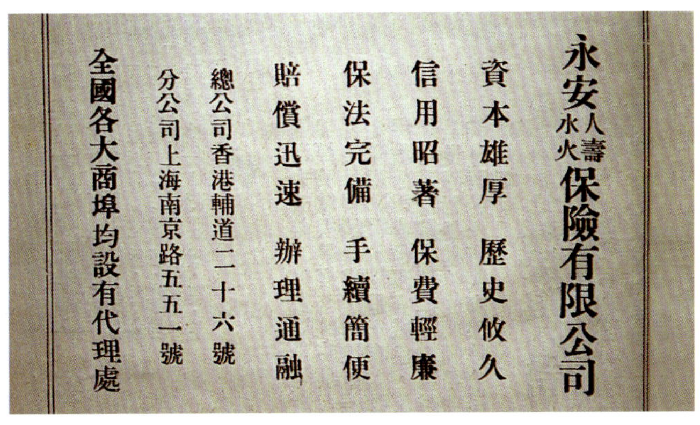

30年代永安保险广告
Ad by Yong'an Marine & Fire Insurance Co. in 1930's

上海永安水火保险公司同仁照
Staff of Yong'an Marine & Fire Insurance Co.

上海永安人寿保险公司同仁照
Staff of Yong'an Life Insurance Co.

1915年先施集团公司董事会同意马应彪关于设立保险公司的提议，决定由香港、广州、上海三处先施公司各出资港币40万元创办先施保险置业公司(总部设在香港，在广州、上海设分公司)。该公司经营状况良好，1935年保费收入为规元15.3万余元，各险结余11.9万余元。

The other large department store Xianshi Group established Xianshi Insurance Co. in 1915 at the request of Ma Yingbiao.

建议先施公司设立保险公司的澳洲华侨马应彪

Ma Yingbiao: advocate for Xianshi Insurance Co.

(照片提供：上海档案馆)

黄泽生，广东人，早年在香港皇仁书院求学。1900年就职于上海礼和洋行。民国初年，香港先施保险置业公司来沪设立分公司，黄泽生参与筹备。分公司成立时任副司理，未及数载，升任司理，主持工作。在先施工作近40年。先施保险业务发展，实赖其主持之功。

Huang Zesheng, born in Canton, manager of Xianshi Insurance Co., greatly promoted the development of Xianshi's insurance business during his nearly 40-year incumbency.

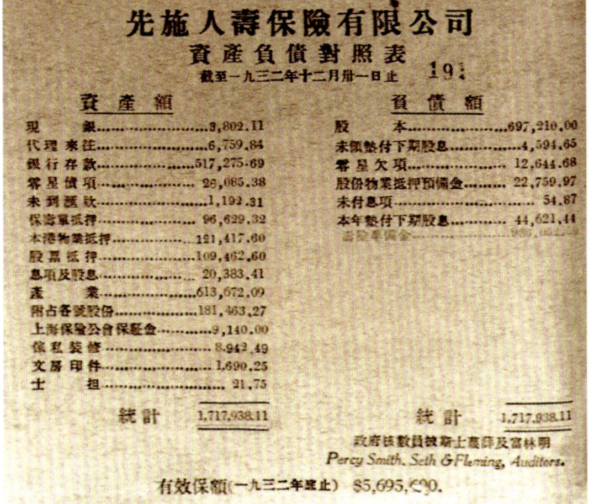

先施人壽保險有限公司

資產負債對照表

截至一九三二年十二月卅一日止

資產額		負債額	
現銀	3,802.11	股本	697,210.00
代理來往	6,759.84	未領墊付下期股息	4,594.65
銀行存款	517,275.69	零星欠項	12,644.68
零星債項	26,085.38	股份物業抵押預備金	22,759.97
未到匯欵	1,192.31	未付息項	54.87
保險單抵押	96,629.32	本年墊付下期股息	44,621.44
本港物業抵押	121,417.60	[illegible]	[illegible]
股票抵押	109,462.60		
息項及股息	20,383.41		
產業	613,672.09		
附占各號股份	181,463.27		
上海保險公會保証金	9,140.00		
傢私裝修	8,942.49		
文房印件	1,690.25		
士担	21.75		
統計	1,717,938.11	統計	1,717,938.11

Percy Smith, Seth & Fleming, Auditors.

有效保額(一九三二年底止) $5,695,€90.

1932年先施人寿资产负债表

Balance sheet of Xianshi Life in 1932

先施保险置业公司总部大楼

Headquarters building of Xianshi Insurance Co.

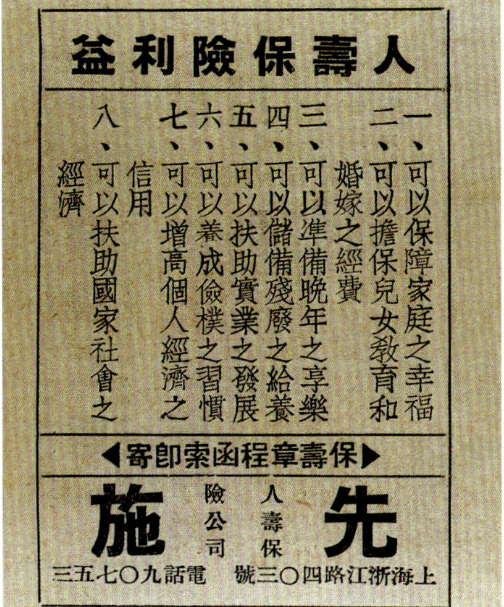

人壽保險利益

一、可以保障家庭之幸福
二、可以擔保兒女教育和婚嫁之經費
三、可以準備晚年之享樂
四、可以儲備殘廢之給養
五、可以扶助實業之發展
六、可以養成儉樸之習慣
七、可以增高個人經濟之信用
八、可以扶助國家社會之經濟

▶保壽章程函索即寄◀

先施人壽保險公司

上海浙江路四〇三號 電話九〇七五三

30年代先施人寿广告

Ad of Xianshi Life in 1930's

二、民族寿险业兴起的标志

Mark of the Surge of National Life Insurance

20世纪初，华资寿险市场曾一度兴起，但由于经营和管理不善，停业者居多。1912年7月1日，开业的华安合群保寿公司在总结以前寿险公司经验教训的基础上，由吕岳泉发起创办，公司征得当时政界要人、工商巨绅的赞同和投资，纯粹华股，并以维护民族权益为宗旨。公司于同年12月向北洋政府工商部注册。黎元洪出任名誉董事长、冯国璋任董事、吕岳泉任总经理，并聘请英国人郁赐为总司理。经营富资保寿、安家保寿、额定经利保寿、终身保寿等寿险业务。

1926年5月，位于上海静安寺的华安大厦落成，成为当时华商保险公司惟一的保险大楼。华安合群还相继在国内外重要商埠设立机构，经营之红火，足以与外商寿险公司抗衡，公司一直经营到解放前夕。

To maintain the national benefit, China United Assurance Society Ltd. (CUASL) was opened on July 1, 1912, with general manager Lu Yuequan and shareholders of some well-known politicians, exp., Li Yuanhong (honorary board chairman); Feng Guozhang (director), etc. Well operated, CUASL branched into all over the country and even overseas as well.

1912年华安合群在外滩开张

Office building of CUASL in 1912

华安合群保寿公司创办人吕岳泉
Lu Yuequan: founder of China United Assurance Society Ltd

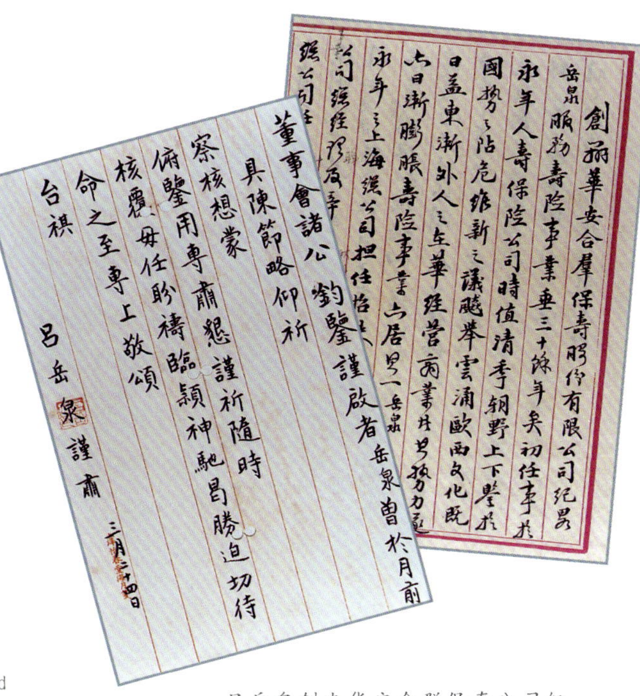

董事會諸公鈞鑒謹啟者岳泉曾於月前
具陳節略仰祈
察核想蒙
俯鑒用專肅懇謹祈隨時
核覆毋任盼禱臨穎神馳昌勝迫切待
命之至專上敬頌
台祺
吕岳泉謹肅
三月二十四日

吕岳泉创办华安合群保寿公司纪略和吕岳泉给董事会的手迹(照片提供:上海档案馆)
Brief record of the establishment of CUASL, and Mr. Lu's autograph letter to the board of directors

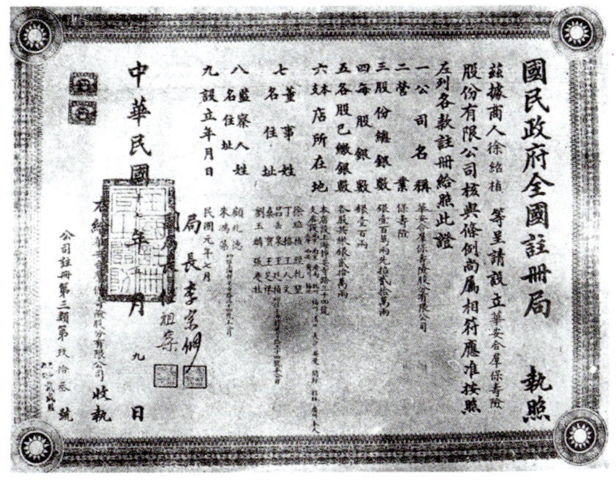

國民政府全國註冊局 執照
茲據商人徐紹楨 等呈請設立華安合羣保壽股份有限公司核與條例尚屬相符應准核照左列各款註冊給照此證
中華民國 年 月 日
局長

1912年民国政府工商部颁发的华安合群保寿公司的工商执照
Business license issued by the Industrial & Commercial Ministry of the Republic of China to CUASL in 1912

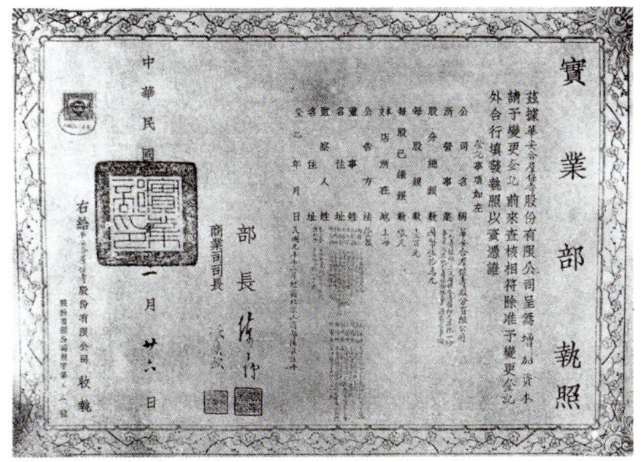

實業部 執照
中華民國 年 一月 廿六日
部長

1930年华安合群保寿公司实行增资扩股,图为民国政府实业部向该公司颁发的执照。
Capital—adding license issued by the government of the Republic of China to CUASL in 1930

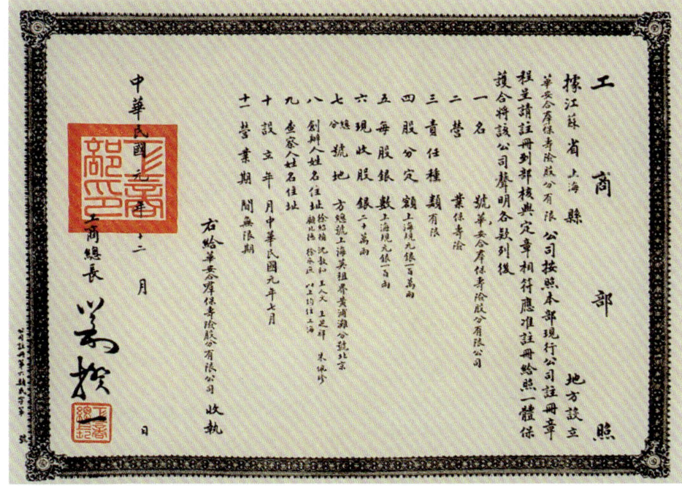

工商部 執照
中華民國 年 二月 日
工商總長

民国政府1928年颁发给华安合群保寿公司的全国注册执照
Registered license issued by the government of the republic of China to CUASL in 1928

公司董事王人文
Wang Wenren: Director of China United Assurance Society Ltd

公司董事桑实
Sang Shi: the Director of China United Assurance Society Ltd

公司董事丁斐章
Ding Feizhang: Director of China United Assurance Society Ltd

公司董事张庆桂
Zhang Qinggui: Director of China United Assurance Society Ltd

华安合群保寿公司创办人之一盛宣怀
Sheng Xuanhuai: One of the Founders of China United Assurance Society Ltd

公司董事颜棣三
Yan Disan: Director of China United Assurance Society Ltd

公司董事徐绍桢
Xu Shaozhen: Director of China United Assurance Society Ltd

公司董事王芝祥
Wang Zhixiang: Director of China United Assurance Society Ltd

华安合群聘请的总司理英国人郁赐
British chief consultant employed by China United Assurance Society Ltd

华安合群保寿公司董事黎元洪
Li Yuanhong: Director of CUASL

言之信者
在乎區蓋
之百
黎元洪

華安合群保壽公司
承保受命
黎元洪

黎元洪为华安合群保寿公司题词
Li Yuanhong's Inscription for CUASL

賦畀於形人生非偶疵癘
夭札天司其任今也不然
責由人負華安可豈馳
譽九有與喜為市自童而
耆類言長年積金山阜欲
盡從心春成著手保我大羣
同躋仁壽
馮國璋

同躋仁壽
馮國璋

冯国璋为华安合群保寿公司题词
Feng Guozhang's Inscription for CUASL

华安合群保寿公司董事冯国璋
Feng Guozhang: Director of CUASL

1930年华安合群保寿公司全体同仁合影
Staff of CUASL in 1930

华安合群公司安家保寿险保单
Life insurance policy issued by CUASL

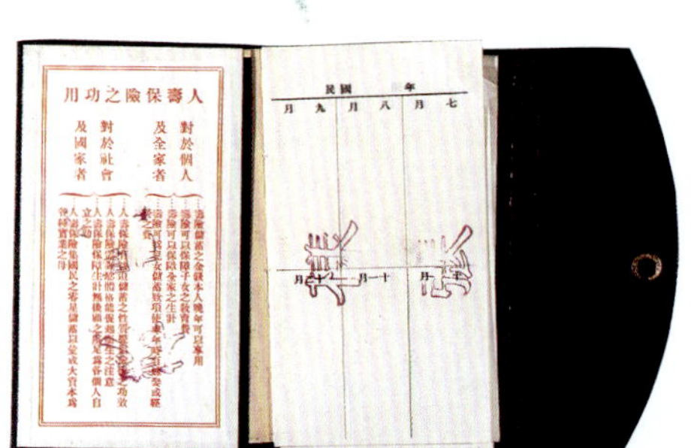

华安合群公司保险证
Insurance Certificate issued by CUASL

华安合群办公场景
Office of China United Assurance Society Ltd.

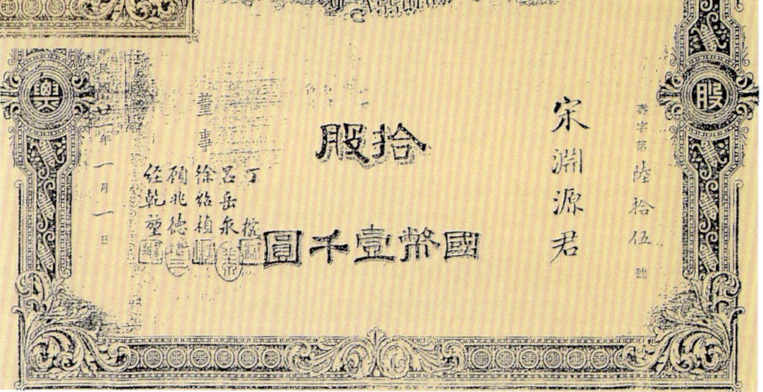

华安合群保寿公司发行的增资股票

Capital-adding stock issued by CUASL

1919年9月9日，华安合群保寿公司设在印尼泗水的分公司开业。

CAUSL's Indonesia Branch opened in 1919

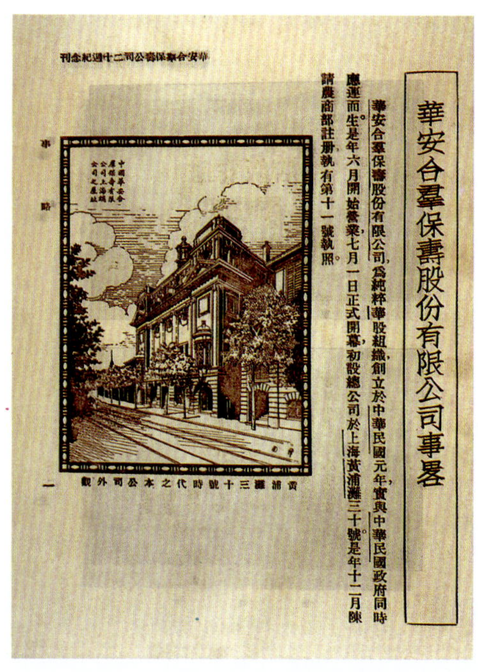

華安合羣保壽公司二十週紀念刊

華安合羣保壽股份有限公司事畧

華安合羣保壽股份有限公司，爲純粹華股組織，創立於中華民國元年，實與中華民國政府同時應運而生。是年六月開始營業，七月一日正式開幕，初設總公司於上海黃浦灘三十號。是年十二月陳請農商部註冊，執有第十一號執照。

黃浦灘三十號時代之本公司外觀

事略 一

华安合群保寿公司20周年纪念刊，刊中画图为华安合群早期办公楼。

Album for the 20th anniversary of the founding of CAUSL

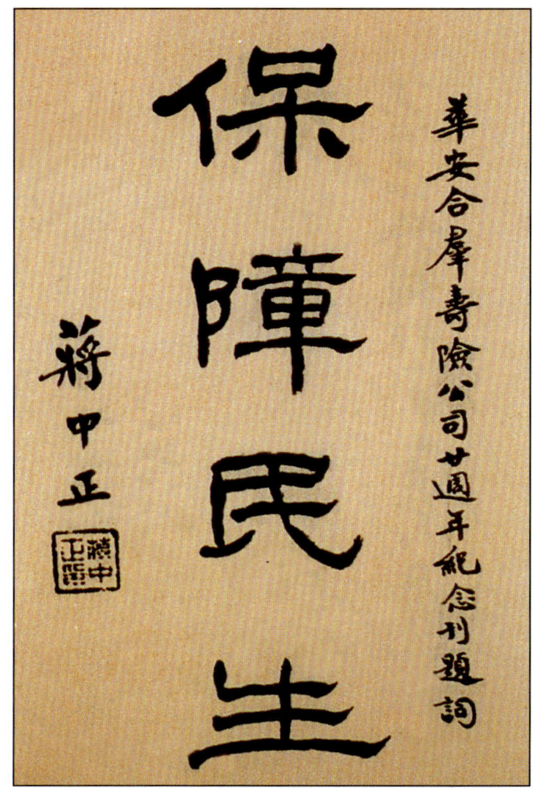

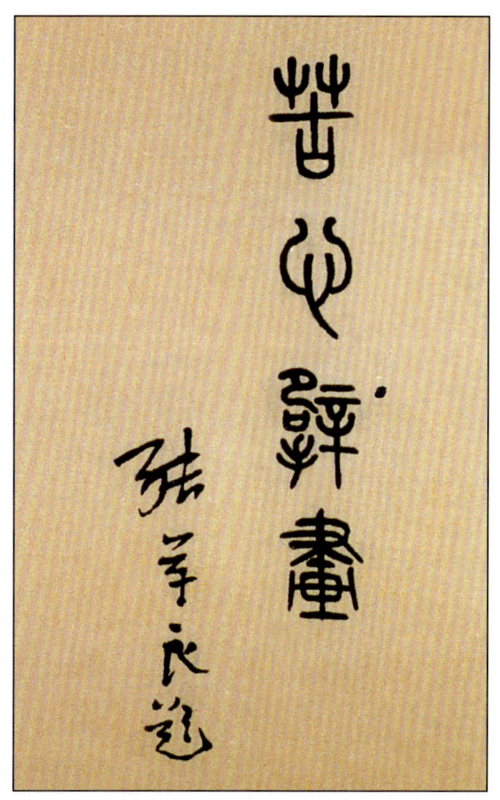

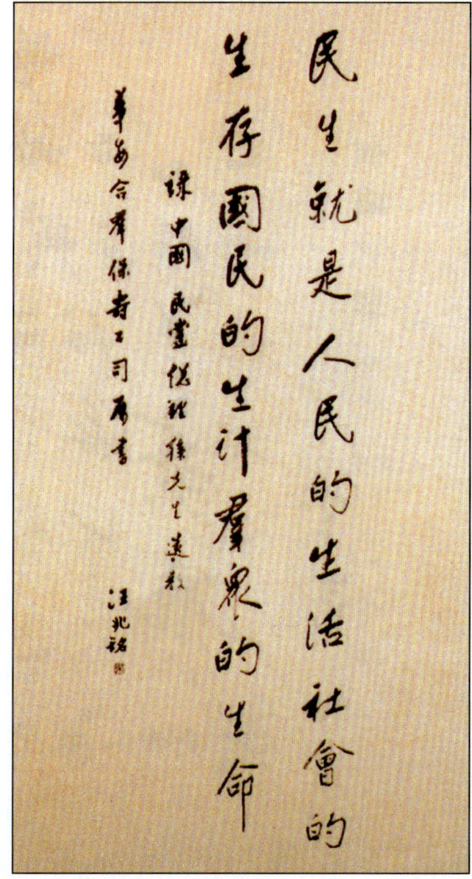

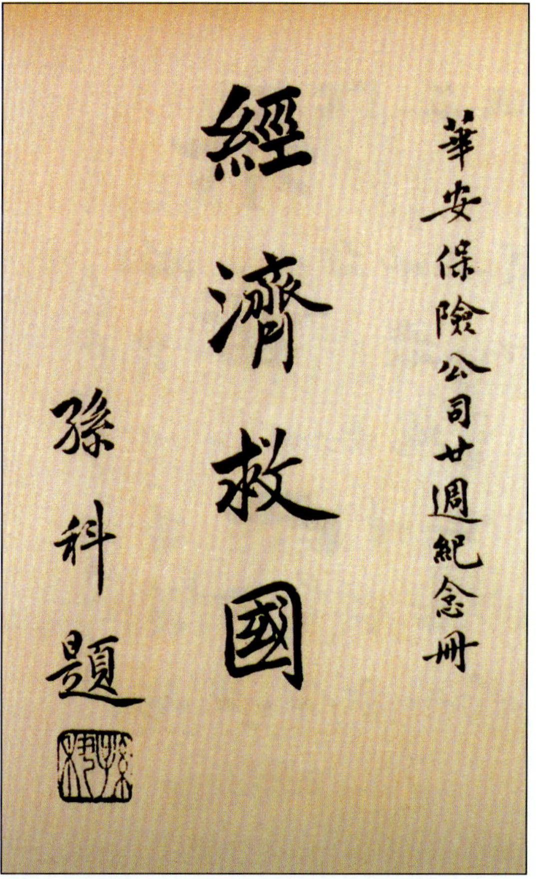

蒋介石、张学良、汪精卫、孙科为华安合群公司20周年题词

Jiang Jieshi's, Zhang Xueliang's, Wang Jingwei's and Sun Ke's Inscriptions for the 20th Anniversary of China United Assurance Society Ltd

三、“壬子兵变”引发中国最早的大赔案

Earliest Huge Claim in China by 1912 Mutiny

当时《大公报》刊登的1912年3月2日晚兵变士兵在天津街头纵火行抢的插图

Illustration of fire-setting and robbery by soldiers on the night of March 2, 1912 published in *Dagongbao*

民国元年(1912)孙中山为和平统一南北，将中华民国大总统让位袁世凯，并派蔡元培、宋教仁到京请袁就职。袁心存疑虑，为拖延离京，策划了震惊中外的兵变，这一年为壬子年，故史称“壬子兵变。”

兵变起自北京，随后波及天津、保定、石家庄、济南、烟台、奉天等北方大部分城市。兵变士兵到处烧杀掳掠。仅天津被焚掠商铺就达2200多家，损失白银12120万两；保定损失白银700余万两；沧州损失白银50余万两……

“壬子兵变”引发了中国时间最早、金额最大、范围最广的保险赔案。仅天津一地就有300多家受损失商铺向保险公司索赔，索赔金额高达白银143万两，这些商铺组成了“索偿保险会”，依靠天津商会向保险人集体索赔，涉及的保险人与保险代理人有：礼和行、德义行、立兴行、禅臣行、兴隆行、福安行、世昌行、立达行、德隆行、华通行、信益行、瑞丰行、隆茂行、瑞记行、太古行、新泰兴行、恒安行、普华行、平和行、北洋行、源安行、仁记行、华安行、三井行等24家。

To peacefully integrate the whole country, Sun Zhongshan demised the Crown to Yuan Shikai in 1912. Nevertheless, Yuan felt doubt about this and designed the 1912 Mutiny, in which, most large cities in north China were involved in and a tremendous loss had been caused, hence the one-year-plus claim.

兵变后北京戏园旅馆被掠的悲凉景象

Beijing's theatre and inn after plunder

四、金融资本投入保险业

Financial Capital Invested in Insurance

周学熙
Zhou Xuexi

1915年8月，曾两任北洋政府财政总长的周学熙在其创办的中国实业银行下创设永宁保险行(1932年6月改组为永宁水火保险公司)，办理水火保险，成为中国银行业兼办保险的先驱。此后，银行业相继投资保险业，成为中国民族保险的一个新形势。早期有东莱银行投资100万元开办的安平保险公司，1929年11月金城银行开办的太平水火保险公司，上海商业储蓄银行分别于1927年和1930年开办的大华保险公司和中国第一信用保险公司。1931年后，金融资本投入保险业的越来越多：1931年上海银行创设宝丰保险公司，中国银行拨资200万创办中国保险公司；1932年浙江兴业银行、中国通商银行、浙江实业银行、中孚银行等四家华商银行，与美亚保险公司联合创立泰山保险公司；1933年四明银行开办的四明保险公司；1934年中国民生银行投资500万元开设中国天一保险公司；1935年中央银行拨资500万成立中央信托局保险部。由于金融业以其雄厚的资金投入保险业，民族保险业有了飞速发展，到1936年，保险公司与1914年相比公司数量增加了两倍多，资本金增加了5倍多，呈现出欣欣向荣的景象。

In August 1915, with the capital of Industrial Bank of China, Zhou Xuexi established Yongning Insurance Co, which specialized in marine and fire insurance and was reorganized into Yongning Marine & Fire Insurance Co. in June 1932. Industry Bank of China was the first to invest in insurance; afterward, many insurance firms like Dahua Insurance Co. were founded by banks.

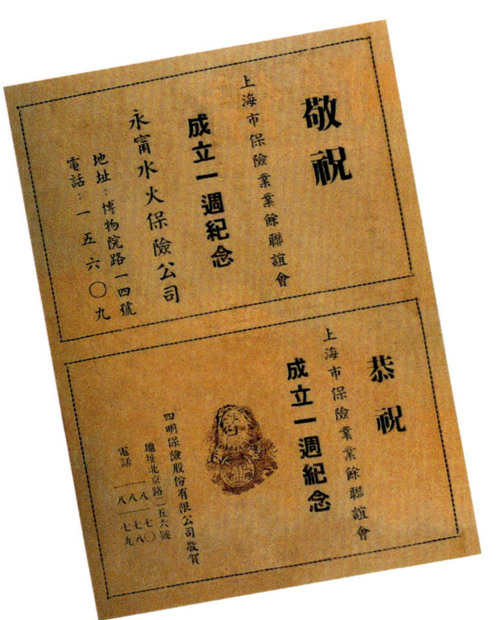

永宁、四明保险公司广告
Ads by Yongning and Siming Insurance Co.

1933年四明银行开设的四明保险公司
Siming Insurance Co. founded by Siming Bank in 1933

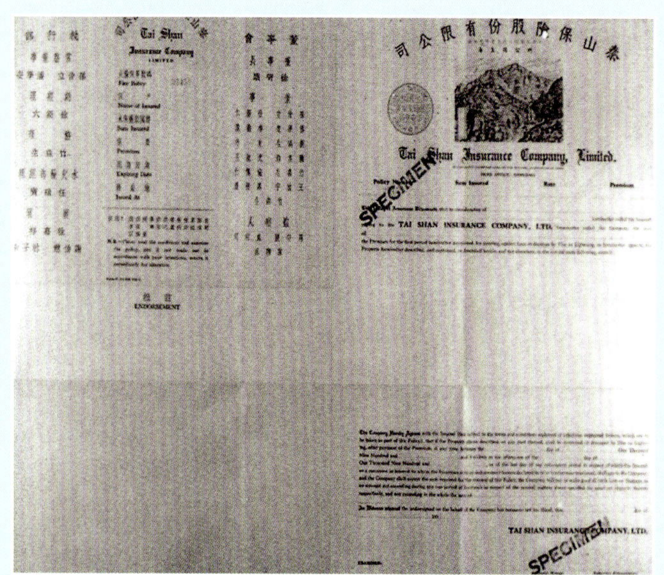

泰山保险公司早期保险单
Policy Signed by Taishan Insurance Co. Early

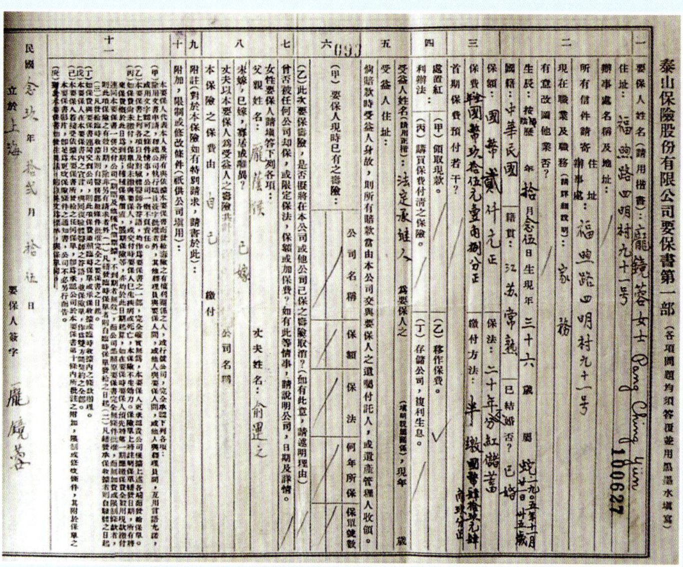

泰山保險股份有限公司要保書第一部

泰山保险公司投保书
Application Form of Taishan Insurance Co.

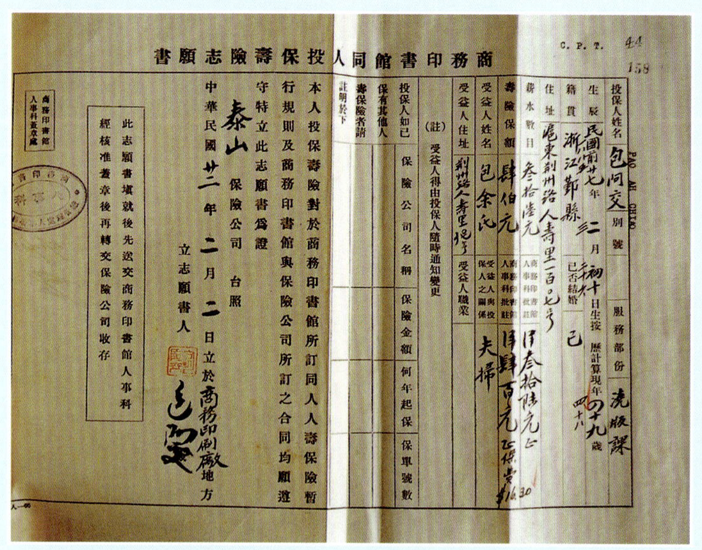

商務印書館同人投保壽險志願書

上海商务印书馆同仁向泰山保险公司投保志愿书
Application of Shanghai Commercial Press to Taishan Insurance Co.

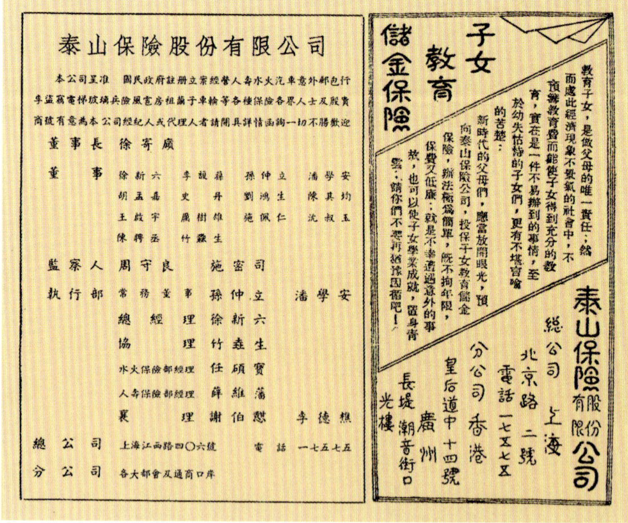

泰山保險股份有限公司

本公司呈准 國民政府註冊立案經營人壽水火汽車意外郵包行李盜竊電梯玻璃兵險風雹房租蘭子車輪等各種保險各界人士及殷實商號有意為本公司經紀人或代理人者請開具詳情函詢一切不勝歡迎

董事長 徐寄廎

董事 徐新六 李馥蓀 孫仲立 潘學安 胡孟嘉 史丹 劉鴻生 陳其均 王啟宇 嚴樹雄 施佩仁 沈叔玉 陳輝丞 竹森生

監察人 周守良 施密司

執行部 常務董事 孫仲立 潘學安
總經理 徐新六
協理 竹森生
水火保險部經理 任碩寶
人壽保險部經理 薛維藩
襄理 謝伯慰 李德樵

總公司 上海江西路四〇六號 電話 一七五七五
分公司 各大都會及通商口岸

泰山保险公司的启事和广告
Notice and Ad released by Taishan Insurance Co.

东莱银行是较早投资保险业的金融企业之一图为天津东莱银行旧址
Site of Donglai Bank in Tianjin (one early financial institutional investor in insurance)

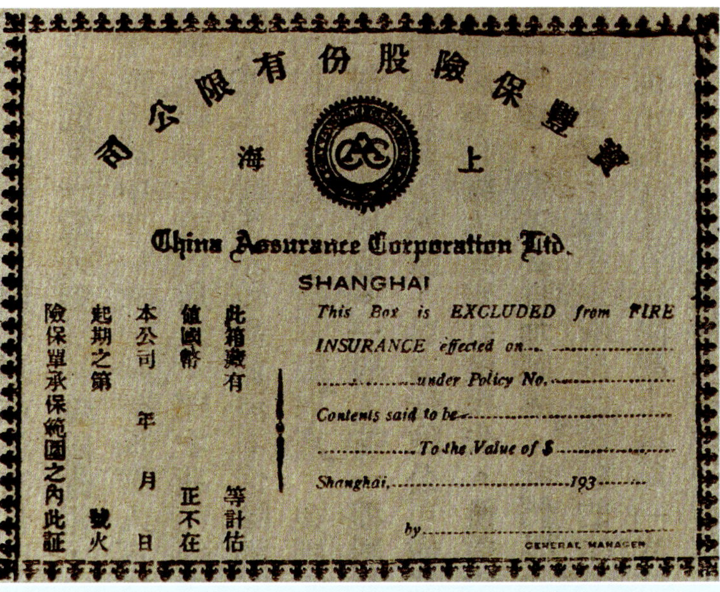
寶豐保險股份有限公司
上海
China Assurance Corporation Ltd.
SHANGHAI
此箱藏有……等計估值國幣……正不在本公司……年……月……日起期之第……號火險保單承保範圍之內此證
This Box is EXCLUDED from FIRE INSURANCE effected on......
......under Policy No......
Contents said to be......
......To the Value of $......
Shanghai,......193......
by......
GENERAL MANAGER

上海银行与太古洋行开设的宝丰保险公司出具的“非保险品箱条”
Note of non-insurance product issued by Baofeng Insurance Co.

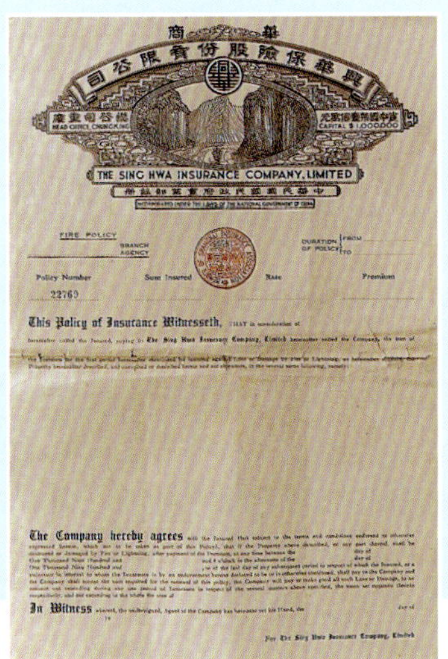
興華保險股份有限公司
THE SING HWA INSURANCE COMPANY, LIMITED
FIRE POLICY
This Policy of Insurance Witnesseth
The Company hereby agrees
In Witness

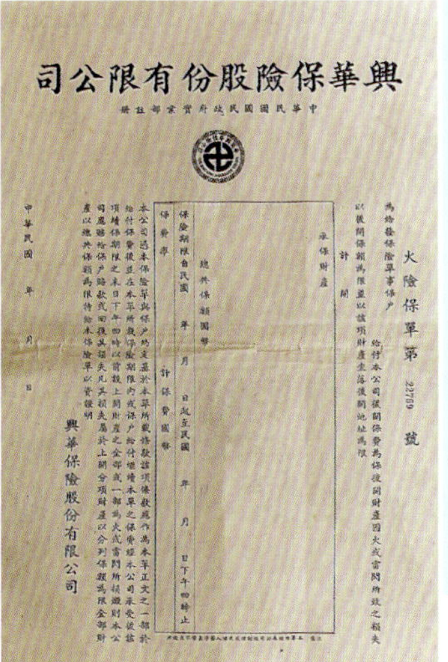
興華保險股份有限公司
火險保單第 22769 號
興華保險股份有限公司

重庆聚兴银行开办的兴华保险公司保险单
Policy Signed by Xinghua Insurance Co. set up by Juxing Bank

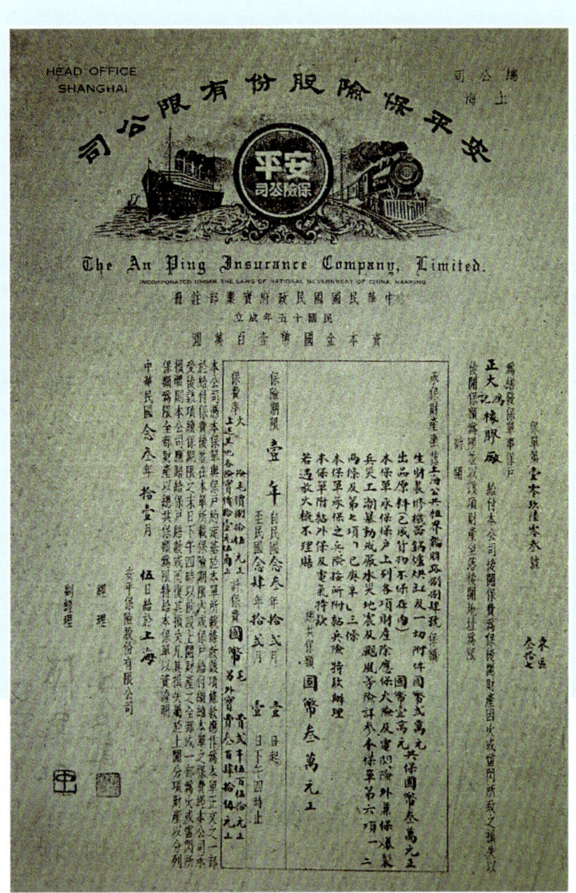
HEAD OFFICE SHANGHAI
安平保險股份有限公司
總公司 上海
平安 保險公司
The An Ping Insurance Company, Limited.

东莱银行投资的安平保险公司火险保单
Fire Policy by Anping Insurance Co. Set Up By Donglai Bank

中国天一保险公司经理——王仁全
Wang Renquan: manager of Tianyi Insurance Co.

王仁全自1914年毕业后，就开始在一家英商保险公司工作。在这家历史悠久、实力雄厚的公司工作8年多的经历，使他积累了丰富的保险理论和实践经验。1923年，他结识了美国美亚保险公司总经理史带先生，深受史带赏识，很快受命全权组织友邦水火保险公司。1924年友邦水火保险公司成立，王任经理。

1921年，史带招英国人投资，组织了英商四海保险公司和法商四海保险公司，王仁全被聘为筹备专员。四海保险公司开业时，王调任该公司经理。1932年史带联合中国金融界和实业界巨子成立华商泰山保险公司，王兼任特种保险部经理。1933年，王仁全曾赴华北等地考察保险业务，回沪后就任美亚保险公司总理帮办。这20年中，王仁全把差不多全部精力和时间，都用来替外国人效力。他深感中国民族保险事业，虽有了今天的进步，但不能与外商保险公司相抗衡，他希望自己的理论和经验，用在民族事业的发展上。于是，1935年春，王仁全应中国天一保险公司董事长聘请就任协理，1936年天一保险公司董事会改组，王就任经理。

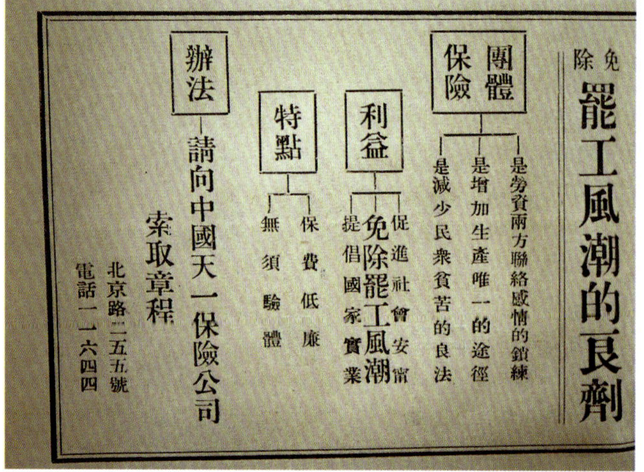

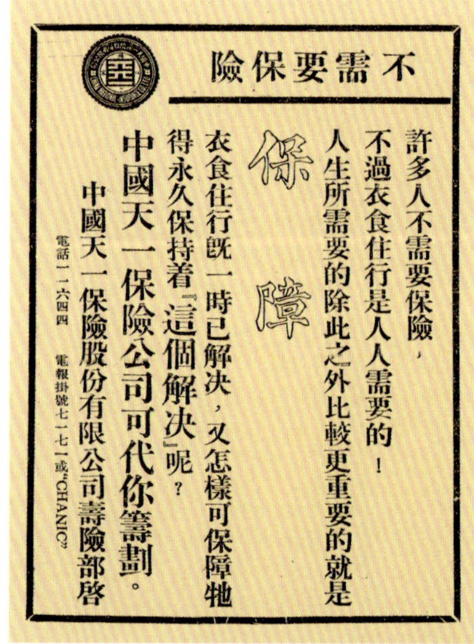

中国天一保险公司广告
Ad of Tianyi Insurance Co.

1937年中国天一保险公司同仁合影
Staff of Tianyi Insurance in 1937

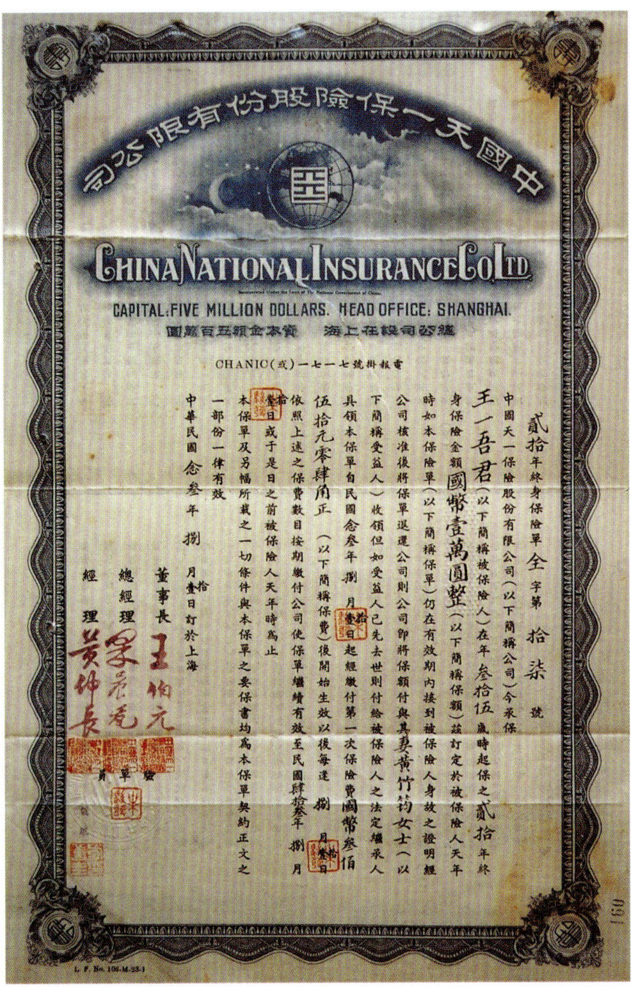
中國天一保險股份有限公司
CHINA NATIONAL INSURANCE CO. LTD.
CAPITAL: FIVE MILLION DOLLARS. HEAD OFFICE: SHANGHAI.
資本金額五百萬圓 總公司設在上海
電報掛號七一七一(或)CHANIC

貳拾年終身保險單全字第拾柒號
中國天一保險股份有限公司(以下簡稱公司)今承保
王一吾君(以下簡稱被保險人)在年叁拾伍歲時起保之貳拾年終
身保險金額國幣壹萬圓整(以下簡稱保額)茲訂定於被保險人天年
時如本保險單(以下簡稱保單)仍在有效期內接到被保險人身故之證明經
公司核准後將保單退還公司則公司即將保額付與其妻黃竹筠女士(以
下簡稱受益人)收領但如受益人已先去世則付給被保險人之法定繼承人
具領本保單自民國念叁年捌月拾壹日起經繳付第一次保險費國幣叁佰
伍拾元零肆角正(以下簡稱保費)後開始生效以後每逢捌月拾壹日
依照上述之保費數目按期繳付公司使保單繼續有效至民國肆拾叁年捌月
拾壹日或于是日之前被保險人天年時為止
本保單及另幅所載之一切條件與本保單之要保書均為本保單契約正文之
一部份一律有效
中華民國念叁年捌月拾壹日訂於上海
董事長 王伯元
總經理
經理

中国天一保险公司保险单
Policy Signed by Tianyi Insurance Co.

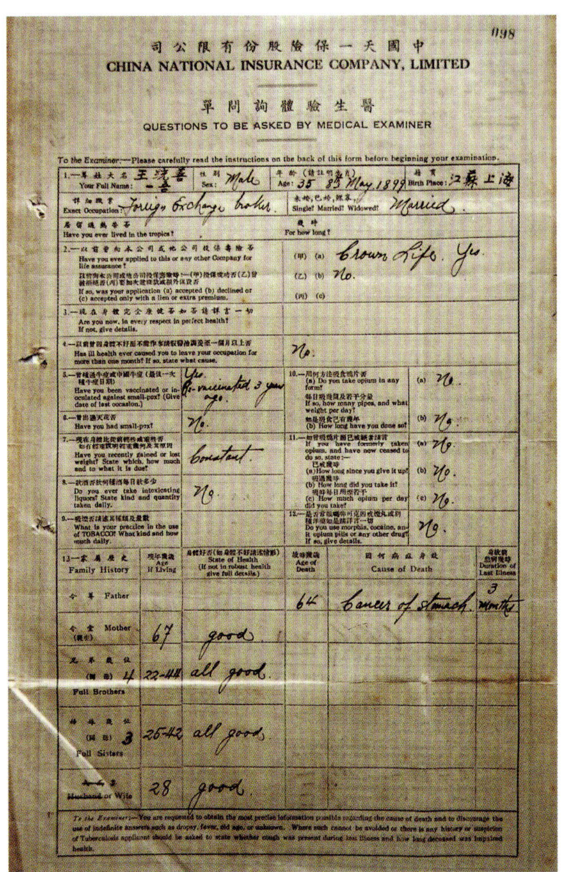
中國天一保險股份有限公司
CHINA NATIONAL INSURANCE COMPANY, LIMITED
醫生驗體詢問單
QUESTIONS TO BE ASKED BY MEDICAL EXAMINER

中国天一保险公司医生验体询问单
Health Questionnaire of Tianyi Insurance Co.

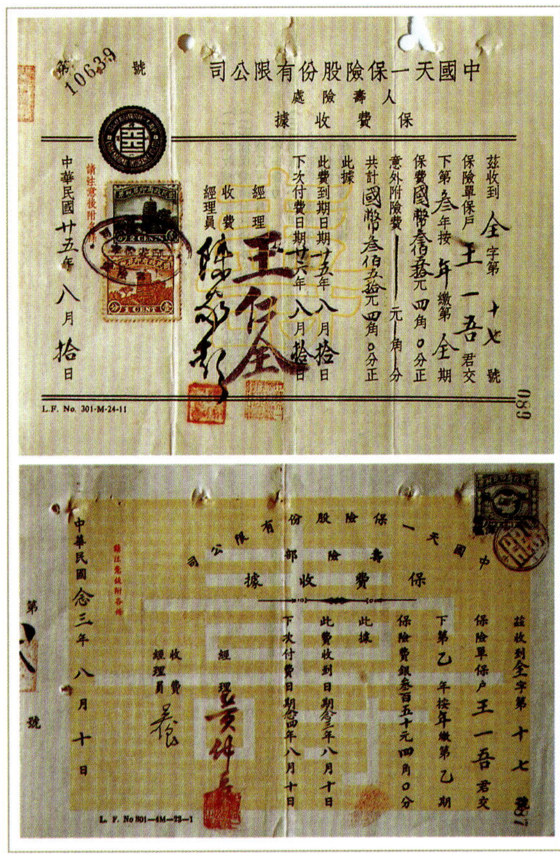
中國天一保險股份有限公司
人壽險處
保費收據
第10639號
茲收到全字第十七號
保險單保戶王一吾君交
下第叁年按年繳第全期
保費國幣叁佰伍拾元四角〇分正
意外附險費—元—角—分
共計國幣叁佰伍拾元四角〇分正
此據
此費到期日期廿五年八月拾日
下次付費日期廿六年八月拾日
經理
收費
經理員
中華民國廿五年八月拾日
L.F. No. 301-M-24-11

中國天一保險股份有限公司
壽險部
保費收據
茲收到全字第十七號
保險單保戶王一吾君交
下第乙年按年繳第乙期
保險費銀叁百五十元四角〇分
此據
此費收到日期念三年八月十日
下次付費日期念四年八月十日
經理
收費經理員
中華民國念三年八月十日
L.F. No 301-4M-23-1

中国天一保险公司保费收据
Premium Receipt of Tianyi Insurance Co.

Wang Renquan started to work for a British insurance company after his graduation in 1914. He knew CV Starr in 1923 and was highly appreciated by Starr. Later he was employed as the senior administrator of Asia Insurance Co. and American Asiatic Underwriters. Meanwhile he felt that he should do something for Chinese national insurance. He held the post of manager in Tianyi Insurance Co. from 1936.

五、史带与美亚保险
Starr & AAU

1916年，一位曾做过保险经纪人的美国年轻人来到中国，在上海他看到了新兴的保险市场的潜力，于1919年12月在上海创设美亚保险公司(American Asiatic Underwirters，简称AAU)，他就是后来有“远东保险王”之称的史带(C.V.Starr)。美亚在百慕大注册，总公司设在上海。

C.V. Starr, ever an insurance broker, recognized the large potential in insurance when he reached China when he was young. He established American Asiatic Underwriters in December 1919. For his great achievement in insurance, he is reputed as the King of Insurance in Far East.

美亚保险创办人史带先生
CV Starr

美亚办公大楼入口近景
Entrance of the Office Building of AAU

史带在中国古庙向客户介绍保险业务(1922)
Mr.Starr introducing Insurance to Chinese in 1922

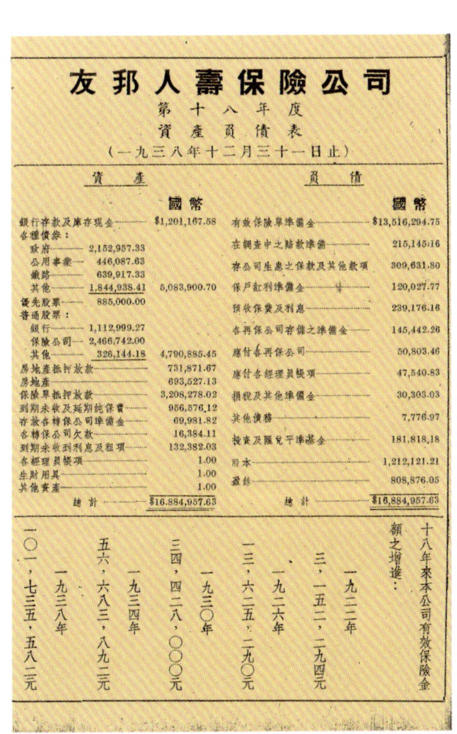

友邦人壽保險公司

第十八年度

資產負債表

（一九三八年十二月三十一日止）

資產		國幣
銀行存款及庫存現金		$1,201,167.58
各種債券：		
政府	2,152,957.33	
公用事業	446,087.63	
鐵路	639,917.33	
其他	1,844,938.41	5,083,900.70
優先股票	885,000.00	
普通股票：		
銀行	1,112,999.27	
保險公司	2,466,742.00	
其他	326,144.18	4,790,885.45
房地產抵押放款		731,871.67
房地產		693,527.13
保險單抵押放款		3,208,278.02
到期未收及延期純保費		956,576.12
存放各轉保公司準備金		69,981.82
各轉保公司欠款		16,384.11
到期未收到利息及租項		132,382.03
各經理員欠項		1.00
生財用具		1.00
其他資產		1.00
總計		$16,884,957.63

負債	國幣
有效保險單準備金	$13,516,294.75
在調查中之賠款準備	215,145.16
存公司生息之保款及其他款項	309,631.80
保戶紅利準備金	120,027.77
預收保費及利息	239,176.16
各再保公司存儲之準備金	145,442.26
應付各再保公司	50,803.46
應付各經理員欠項	47,540.83
捐稅及其他準備金	30,303.03
其他債務	7,776.97
投資及匯兌平準基金	181,818.18
股本	1,212,121.21
盈餘	808,876.05
總計	$16,884,957.63

十八年來本公司有效保險金額之增進：

一九二二年 三，一五二，二九四元

一九二六年 一三，六二五，二九〇元

一九三〇年 三四，四二八，〇〇〇元

一九三四年 五六，六八三，八九二元

一九三八年 一〇一，七三五，五八二元

1938年友邦人寿保险公司资产负债表
Balance sheet of Asia Life Insurance Co. in 1938

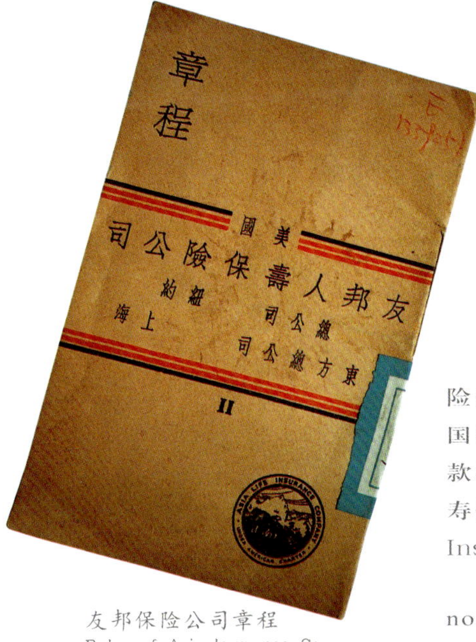

友邦保险公司章程
Rules of Asia Insurance Co.

美亚保险专营中国的非寿险业务。1921年史带又看好中国的寿险市场，利用美亚的赔款准备金，在上海注册友邦人寿保险公司(The Asia Life Insurance Company)。

The AAU specialized in non-life insurance. Mr. Starr used the loss reserve to found the Asia Life Insurance Company in 1921.

美亚保险公司办公场景
Working employees of AAU

1927年，美亚迁入在上海外滩17号的办公大楼。
Office building of AAU in Shanghai (moved in 1927)

美亚同仁合影
Employees of AAU

史带在保险经营上的成功，除了其发奋努力和经营与组织才能之外，还在于他能在中国选贤任能。美亚造就了一批华人保险精英，这些人为美亚的发展立下了汗马功劳。

Starr succeeded in management especially in human resource, hence many elites worked for him, which was a key factor to his achievements.

招徠人壽保險，歐美諸邦，早已認爲專門職業，不特高尚優越，更有服務社會造福人羣之意旨。人壽保險事業，不因時局變幻，或商業凋零而受影響，實爲最穩妥之事業。凡爲經理員者，有下列優異之點：

(一)職業安定

(二)無工作瑣屑之煩惱

(三)收入豐富逐年增加

(四)無減薪之憂慮

人壽保險之於中國，現正蒸蒸日上，前途發展無可限量，實爲有志青年促成經濟獨立之良機。

本公司辦理壽險有年，造就人才頗多，良以訓練得力，誘掖有方諸君有意，請駕臨本公司營業部面洽。

友邦人壽保險公司啓

上海外灘十七號

友邦人寿保险公司招聘广告(1936)
Recruiting ad of Asia Insurance Co.

陆仲义，江苏吴县人。上海沪江大学毕业，中西文学根底深厚。曾任当时华北惟一英文刊物《华北明星报》编辑。1922年与史带相识，史带慕其才华，聘为友邦上海及外埠营业部经理。陆仲义广罗优秀人才，训练有方，故业务发展迅速。旋任续保部主任，对保户的疑问解释详尽，服务周到，因而失效保单大为减少。后又任友邦监理兼业务委员、赔款部主任。

Lu Zhongyi, who got to known Starr in 1922, was the department manger of Asia Insurance Co.

朱孔嘉，美亚初创时期就参加工作，为人谨慎，处事干练，深为史带器重。太平洋战争爆发后，上海沦陷。留沪美籍职员都到了集中营里，美亚的组织全靠朱孔嘉支撑。抗战胜利后，外商保险公司都持观望态度，不敢立刻复业。朱孔嘉不顾美亚美籍职员的异议，毅然放手大干，业务突飞猛进，财源滚滚，创造了美亚的空前繁荣。

Zhu Kongjia took part in the whole process of the establishment of AAU.

美亚创办后，业务蒸蒸日上，随着资本的日益雄厚，史带于1931年又创办英商四海保险公司。在这时期，史带先后在中国筹创了8家保险公司。30年代，庞大的美亚集团在中国保险市场控制了三分之一的业务。

Along with the increasingly boom in AAU's insurance operation, AAU set up Sihai Insurance Co. in 1931. During the period, AAU established 8 insurers in China; it controlled one third of the business in Chinese insurance market in 1930's.

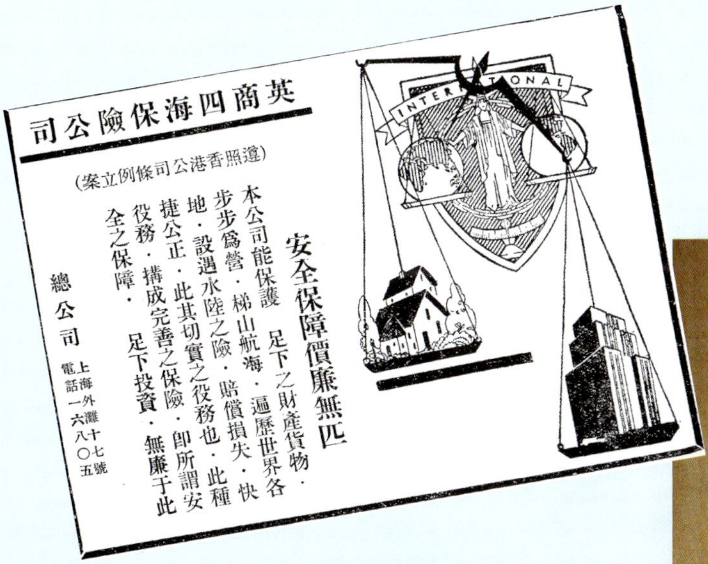

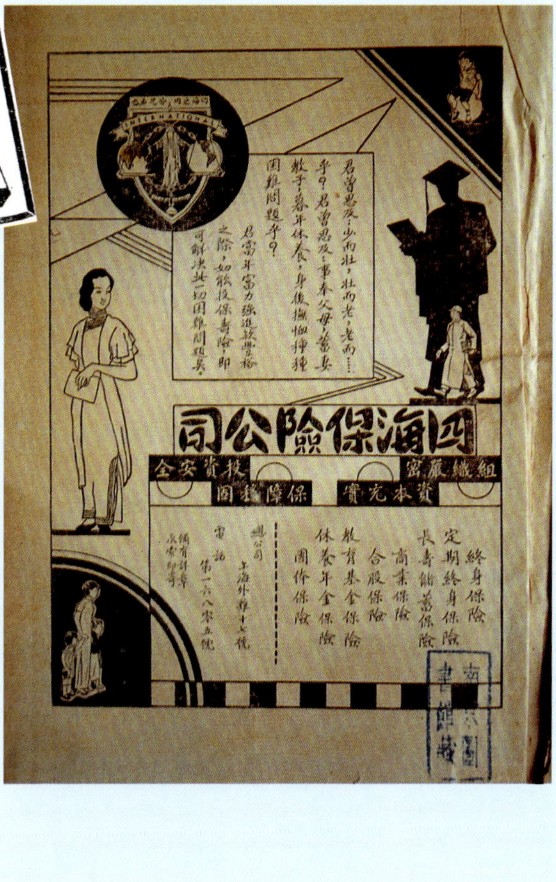

英商四海保險公司
(遵照香港公司條例立案)
安全保障價廉無匹
本公司能保護 足下之財產貨物．步步為營．梯山航海．遍歷世界各地．設遇水陸之險．賠償損失．快捷公正．此其切實之役務也．此種役務．構成完善之保險．即所謂安全之保障． 足下投資．無廉于此
總公司 上海外灘十七號 電話一八〇七五

四海保險公司
終身保險
定期終身保險
長壽儲蓄保險
商業保險
合股保險
教育基金保險
休養年金保險
團体保險

30年代四海保险公司广告
Ad of Sihai Insurance Co. in 1930's

六、北方保险重镇：天津
Tianjin: Insurance Centre of North China

民国初年，天津逐步成为北方金融中心。1927年，天津有外商银行13家，华商银行17家。到了1934年，天津已有外商银行17家，华商银行29家，银号269家，典当行88家。当时的许多银行都代理保险业务。金融业的发展为保险业的扩展奠定了基础。天津迅速成为北方保险市场的中心。

1916—1923年，比较有影响并代理保险业务的外商银行主要有：美商花旗银行、日商朝鲜银行、中法工商银行、美丰银行等。

1919年起，美国的火险公司大规模进入天津。首屈一指的是美国火险公会，它代理大陆、北美洲等19家保险公司的业务。

1924年，美亚保险在天津设立分公司，代理汉诺威、四海、美联等17家保险公司业务。

同年，北美洲保险公司在天津设立分公司，并代理其它保险公司业务。

In early Republic of China, Tianjin, where there were 13 foreign banks and 17 Chinese banks in 1927, gradually grew to be the finance centre of North China. From 1916-1923, the well-known insurance agencies included CitiBank, Koran Bank (Japan), Sino-French Industry and Commerce Bank, and Meifeng Bank, etc. acted as agencies of insurance business.

In 1919, a great number of fire insurers from the USA rushed in Tianjin, while the largest one was American Fire Insurance Union acting as the agent of several insurers.

北美洲保险公司天津分公司同仁合影(1930年)（照片提供：信诺保险公司）
Staff of North America Insurance Co. Tianjin Branch

1917年金城银行在天津创办，1935年总行迁往上海。图为天津金城银行办公大楼全景。1929年金城银行独资创办了太平保险公司。

Office Building of the Kingchen Banking Corporation, Tianjin.

金城银行董事任振采
Ren Zhengcai: Director of the Kingchen Banking Corporation

金城银行董事吴达全
Wu Daquan: Director of the Kingchen Banking Corporation

金城银行董事宁彩轩
Ning Caixuan: Director of the Kingchen Banking Corporation

金城银行董事倪幼丹
Ni Yiudan: Director of the Kingchen Banking Corporation

金城银行监察人胡笔江
Hu Bijiang: Supervisor of the Kingchen Banking Corporation

金城银行监察人范旭东
Fan Xudong: Supervisor of the Kingchen Banking Corporation

七、周作民与太平保险
Zhou Zuomin & Taiping Insurance Co.

创立于1917年5月的金城银行是当时中国重要的私营银行，与盐业、中南、大陆银行合称“北四行”。周作民自金城银行创立到1934年，一直担任总经理，1935年兼任董事长。1929年金城银行独资创办太平水火保险公司，资本金为100万元。办理水、火、船壳、汽车等保险。周作民任总经理，丁雪农任第一协理，王伯衡任第二协理。太平保险公司以“太平保险、保险太平”为口号，团结合作，经过三年的经营，取得了获利20万元（占投资总额40%）的佳绩，为同行侧目。

Kingchen Bank, founded in May 1917, was an importantly private bank then. Zhou Zuomin, from the Kingchen's foundation to 1934, had always been general manager and board chairman of the company. In 1929, the bank established Taiping Marine & Fire Insurance Co. to set foot in marine, fire, and automobile insurance, while Zhou also took up the post of general manger of the insurer, for zhou's achievements more outstanding than his peers.

周作民(1884—1955)江苏淮安县人，近代中国银行家，金城银行总经理。1929年创办太平保险公司兼任总经理，后收购安平、丰盛等保险公司，任总经理处总经理。1955年任全国人大特邀代表。

Zhou Zuomin, born in Jiangsu Province, was a famous banker. He was the Special Deputy to the National People's Congress in 1955.

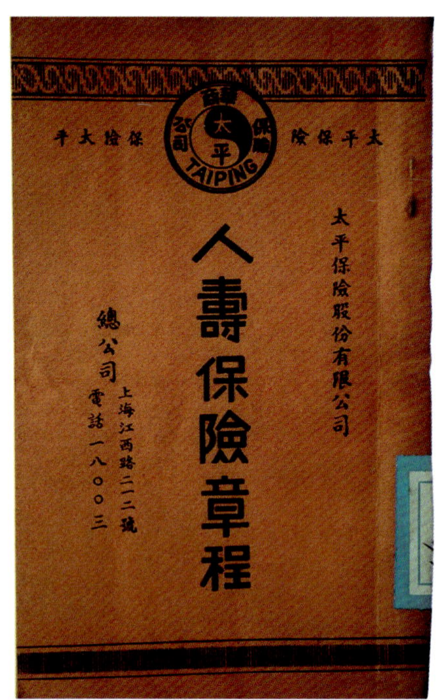

太平保险公司人寿保险章程

Rules on Life Insurance of Taiping Insurance Co.

蔡元培等为太平保险公司寿险部开业题词

Inscriptions by Cai Yuanpei, etc. for the opening of life department of Taiping

太平保险公司董事长黄奕住
Huang Yizhu: board chairmanr of Taiping Insurance Co.

1934年，中南、大陆、交通、国华四家银行入股太平水火保险，使其规模扩大，遂改组为太平保险公司。

1934年4月，太平扩充资本为500万元，实物300万元，由黄奕住任董事长，周作民任总经理，并开设人寿保险部。尔后，东莱银行、四行储蓄会也先后入股。太平保险公司与所有股东银行及各地分支行签订了保险代理协议。太平还在国内外大中城市及西贡、雅加达、新加坡等地开设分支机构及代理处，一时声名鹊起。

In 1934, Taiping Marine & Fire Insurance Co. was transformed into Taiping Insurance Co., by the investment from China & South Sea Bank, Continent, Communication, and China State Bank. Taiping Insurance Co. set up one life insurance department in April 1935 and some branches over the country and abroad as well.

太平保险公司常务董事、大陆银行总经理许汉卿
Xu Hanqing: standing director of Taiping and general manager of Conti—nent Bank

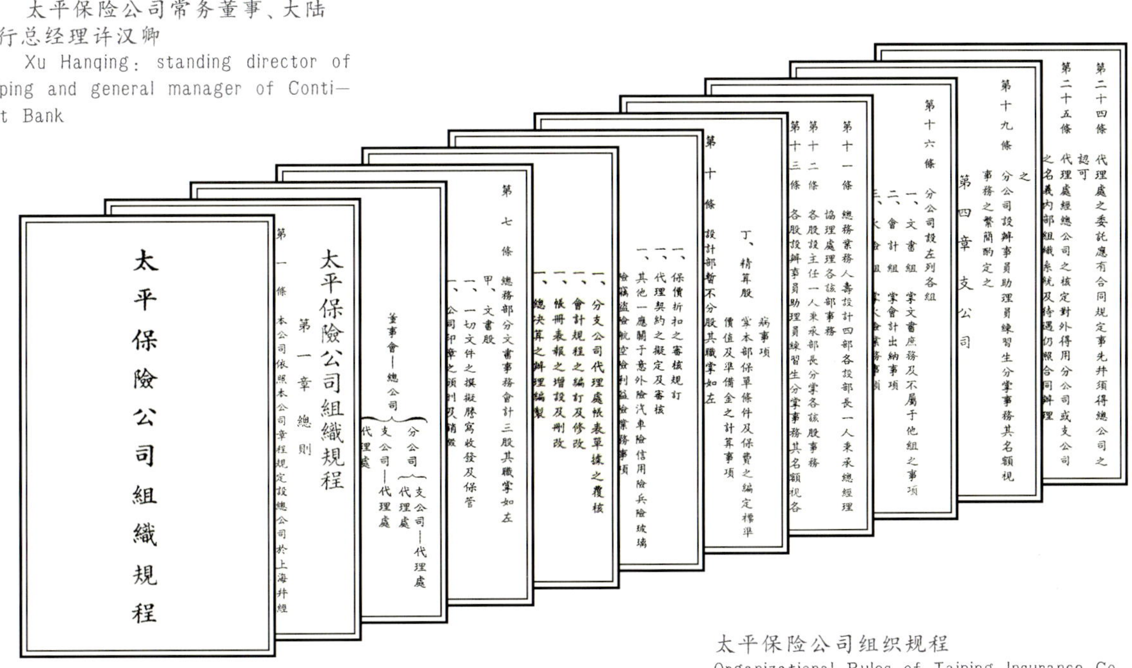

太平保險公司組織規程

太平保險公司組織規程
第一章 總則
第一條 本公司依照本公司章程規定設總公司於上海并經

太平保险公司组织规程
Organizational Rules of Taiping Insurance Co.

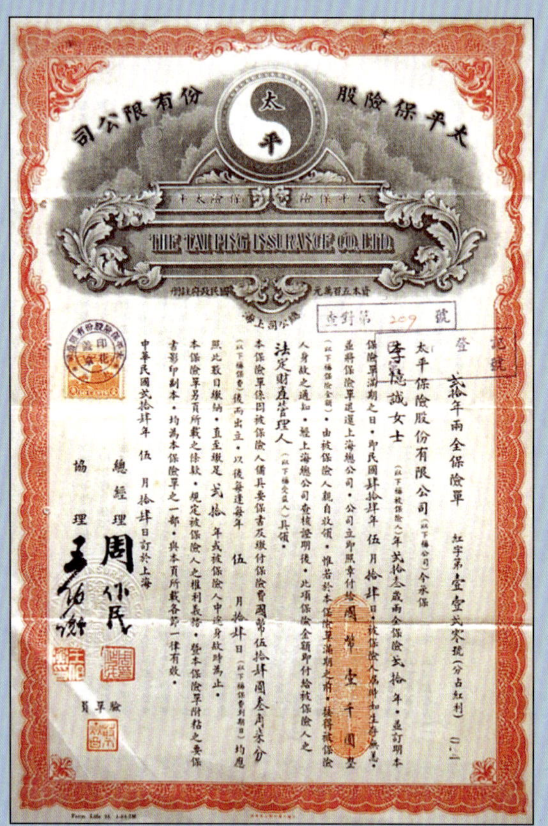

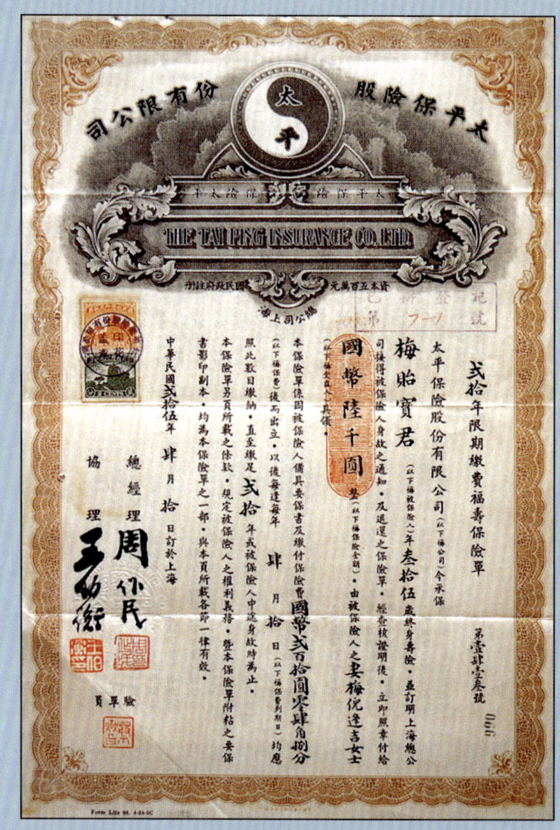

太平保险公司保险单
Insurance Policies Issued by Taiping Insurance Co.

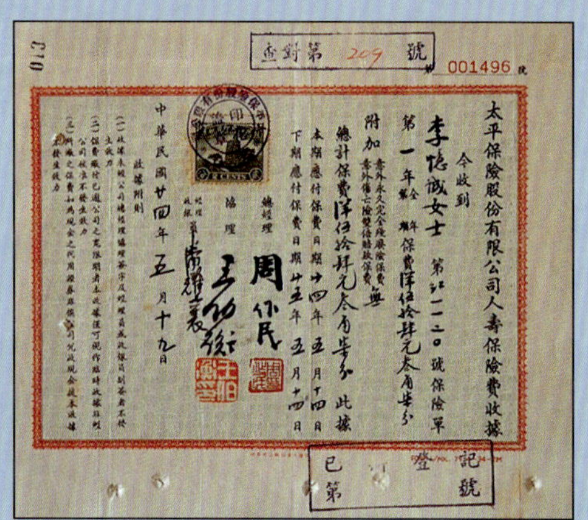

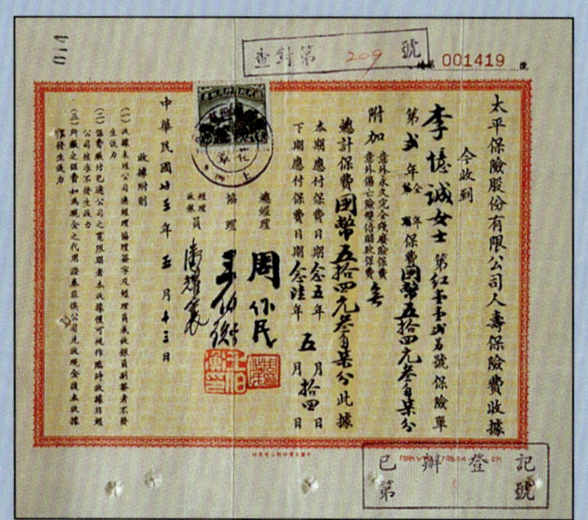

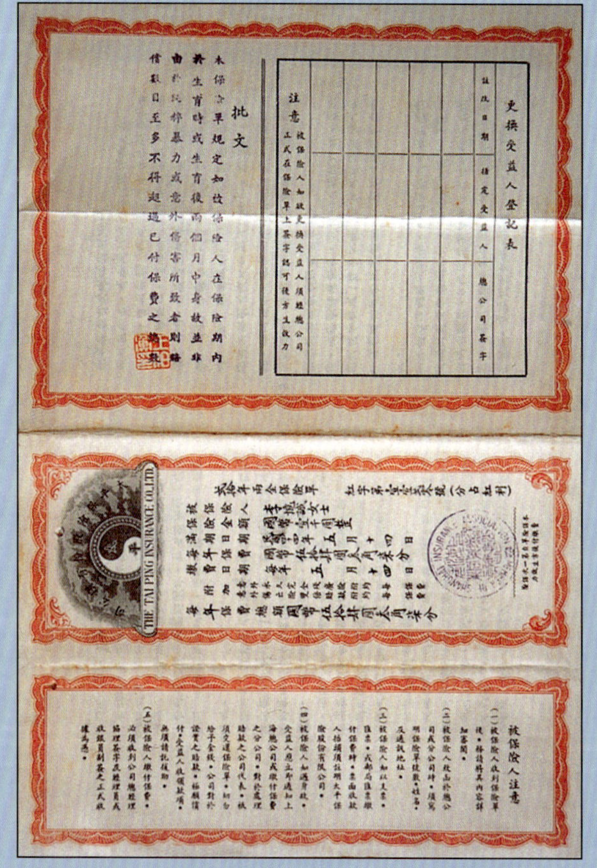

太平保险公司保费收据
Premium receipts of Taiping Insurance Co.

太平保险公司在扩大其自身投资的同时，也开始兼并和接办其他保险公司。1935年5月，太平保险公司联合安平、丰盛保险公司组成“太安丰总经理处”，统一管理三家保险公司。1936年5月收购中国天一保险公司。

While increasing its own investment, Taiping Insurance Co. also began to merger with and undertook other insurers. In 1935, Taiping, with Anping, Fengsheng Insurance Co. formed "Tai An Feng Head Office" to unitedly mange the three insurers. In 1936, Taiping purchased Tanyi Insurance Co.

太平保险公司承保的陆顺记企业麻袋被烧毁，公司赔付该企业一万多元。
Indemnity by Taiping for burned-up Sacks to 10,000 yuan

太平保险公司承保的陆顺记企业遭火灾照片
Burned factory underwritten by Taiping Insurance Co.

太平保险公司承保的卡车倾覆伤鱼贩20多人，死亡一人的现场照片。
the Overturned Truck Insured by Taiping Insurance Co.

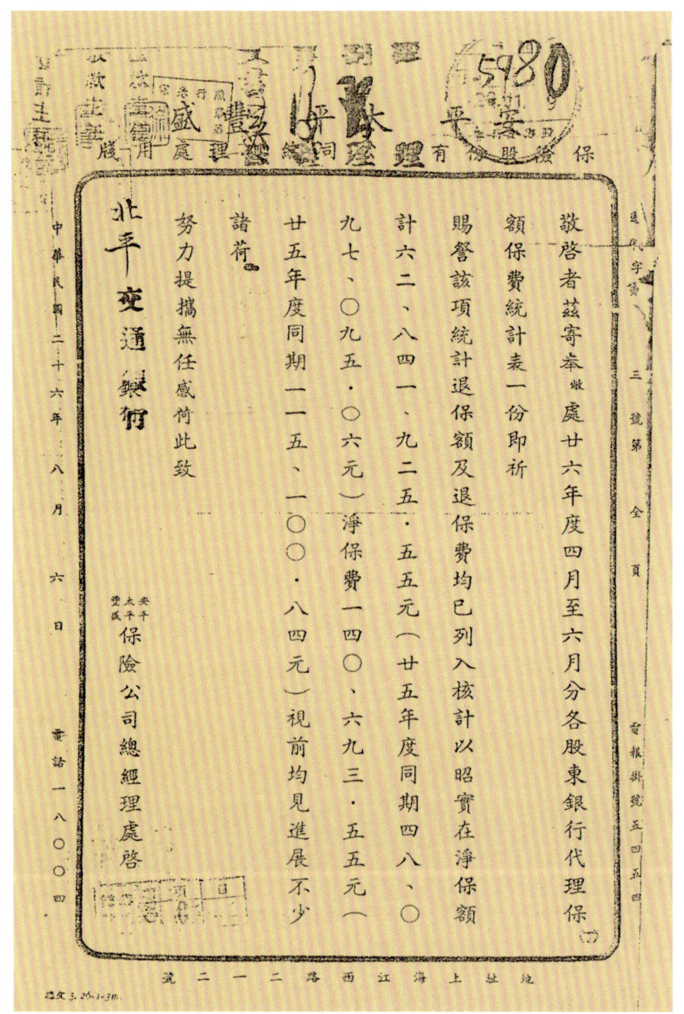

保險股份有限公司總經理處

敬啓者茲寄奉敝處廿六年度四月至六月分各股東銀行代理保額保費統計表一份即祈
賜詧該項統計退保額及退保費均已列入核計以昭實在淨保額計六二、八四一、九二五·五五元（廿五年度同期四八、〇九七、〇九五·〇六元）淨保費一四〇、六九三·五五元（廿五年度同期一一五、一〇〇·八四元）視前均見進展不少
諸荷
努力提攜無任感荷此致
北平交通銀行

安平
太平 保險公司總經理處啓
豐盛

中華民國二十六年八月六日

電話一八〇〇四

地址上海江西路二一二號

太安丰保险公司总经理处致北平交通银行的函

Tai An Feng Head Office's Letter for Communications Bank of Peiping

THE

187

AN PING FIRE & MARINE INSURANCE COMPANY, LIMITED.

ANNUAL ACCOUNTS

FOR

The Year Ended 31st December 1933.

安平保险公司1933报告册

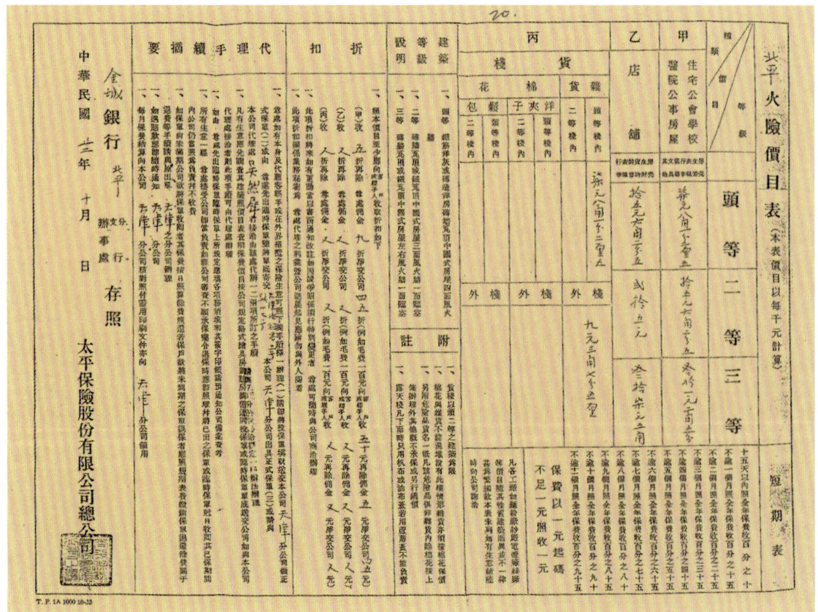

北平火險價目表（本表價目以每千元計算）

等級 / 價目 / 種類：甲 住宅公會學校醫院公事房屋；乙 店舖；丙 貨棧（雜貨、棉花）

頭等　二等　三等

短期表

十五天以內照全年保費收百分之十
不逾一個月照全年保費收百分之十五
不逾二個月照全年保費收百分之二十五
不逾三個月照全年保費收百分之三十五
不逾四個月照全年保費收百分之四十五
不逾五個月照全年保費收百分之五十五
不逾六個月照全年保費收百分之六十五
不逾七個月照全年保費收百分之七十五
不逾八個月照全年保費收百分之八十
不逾九個月照全年保費收百分之八十五
不逾十個月照全年保費收百分之九十
不逾十一個月照全年保費收百分之九十五

保費以一元起碼 不足一元照收一元

建築　附註　折扣　代理手續摘要

金城銀行北平支行存照

中華民國廿年十月　日

太平保險股份有限公司總公司

北平金城银行代理太平保险公司业务火险费率表

The premium rate table of fire insurance of Taiping Insurance Co.

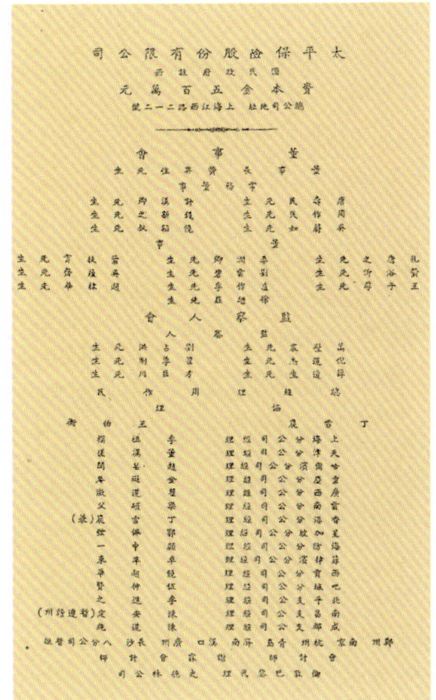

太平保险公司注册情况
Register of Taiping Insurance Co.

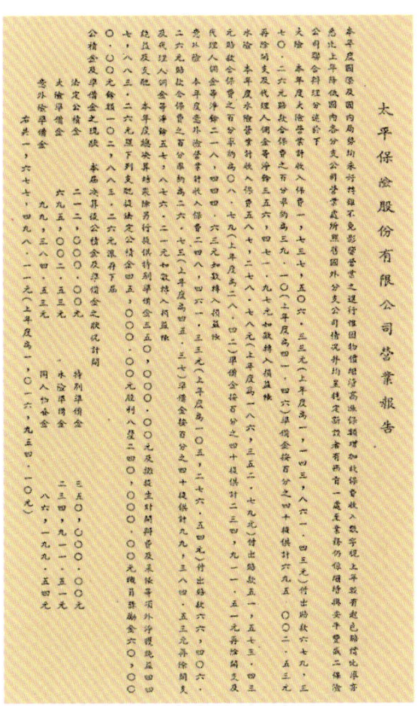

太平保险公司1940年营业报告
The annual Business Report of Taiping Insurance Co. in 1940

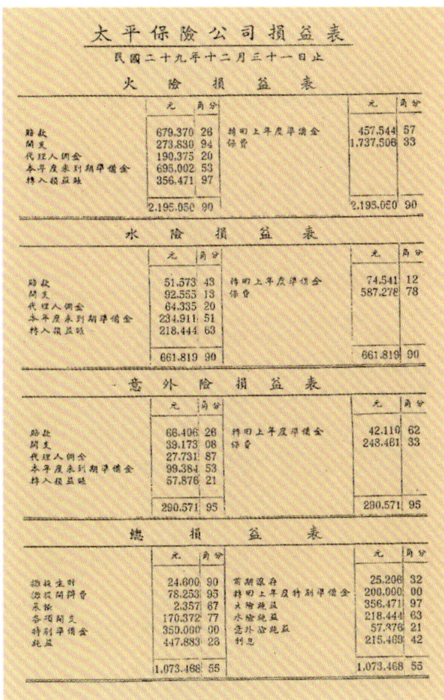

太平保險公司損益表

民國二十九年十二月三十一日止

火險損益表

	元	角分		元	角分
賠款	679,370	26	轉回上年度準備金	457,544	57
開支	273,830	94	保費	1,737,506	33
代理人佣金	190,375	20			
本年度未到期準備金	695,002	53			
轉入損益賬	356,471	97			
	2,195,050	90		2,195,050	90

水險損益表

	元	角分		元	角分
賠款	51,573	43	轉回上年度準備金	74,541	12
開支	92,555	13	保費	587,278	78
代理人佣金	64,335	20			
本年度未到期準備金	234,911	51			
轉入損益賬	218,444	63			
	661,819	90		661,819	90

意外險損益表

	元	角分		元	角分
賠款	68,406	26	轉回上年度準備金	42,110	62
開支	39,173	08	保費	248,461	33
代理人佣金	27,731	87			
本年度未到期準備金	99,384	53			
轉入損益賬	57,876	21			
	290,571	95		290,571	95

總損益表

	元	角分		元	角分
攤提生財	24,600	90	前期滾存	25,206	32
攤提開辦費	78,253	95	轉回上年度特別準備金	200,000	00
呆賬	2,357	67	火險純益	356,471	97
各項開支	170,372	77	水險純益	218,444	63
特別準備金	350,000	00	意外險純益	57,876	21
純益	447,883	26	利息	215,469	42
	1,073,468	55		1,073,468	55

太平保险公司1940年损益表
The annual Profit and Loss Sheet of Taiping Insurance Co. in 1940

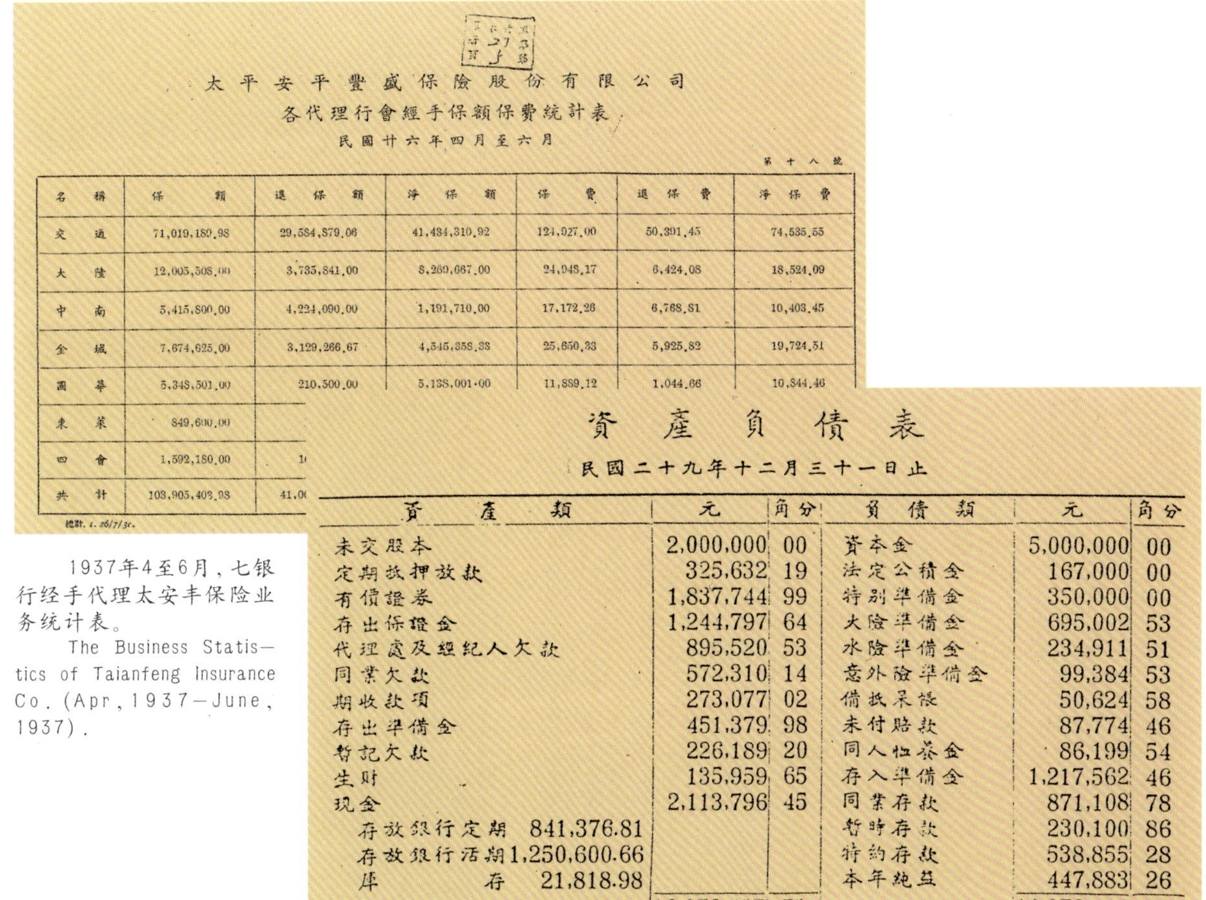

太平安平豐盛保險股份有限公司
各代理行會經手保額保費統計表
民國廿六年四月至六月

第十八號

名稱	保額	退保額	淨保額	保費	退保費	淨保費
交通	71,019,180.98	29,584,879.06	41,434,310.92	124,927.00	50,391.45	74,535.55
大陸	12,005,508.00	3,735,841.00	8,269,667.00	24,948.17	6,424.08	18,524.09
中南	5,415,800.00	4,224,090.00	1,191,710.00	17,172.26	6,768.81	10,403.45
金城	7,674,625.00	3,129,266.67	4,545,358.38	25,650.33	5,925.82	19,724.51
國華	5,348,501.00	210,500.00	5,138,001.00	11,889.12	1,044.66	10,844.46
東萊	849,600.00	[illegible]	[illegible]	[illegible]	[illegible]	[illegible]
四會	1,592,180.00	1[illegible]	[illegible]	[illegible]	[illegible]	[illegible]
共計	103,905,403.98	41,0[illegible]	[illegible]	[illegible]	[illegible]	[illegible]

1937年4至6月，七银行经手代理太安丰保险业务统计表。
The Business Statistics of Taianfeng Insurance Co. (Apr, 1937—June, 1937).

資產負債表

民國二十九年十二月三十一日止

資產類	元	角分	負債類	元	角分
未交股本	2,000,000	00	資本金	5,000,000	00
定期抵押放款	325,632	19	法定公積金	167,000	00
有價證券	1,837,744	99	特別準備金	350,000	00
存出保證金	1,244,797	64	火險準備金	695,002	53
代理處及經紀人欠款	895,520	53	水險準備金	234,911	51
同業欠款	572,310	14	意外險準備金	99,384	53
期收款項	273,077	02	備抵呆賬	50,624	58
存出準備金	451,379	98	未付賠款	87,774	46
暫記欠款	226,189	20	同人恤養金	86,199	54
生財	135,959	65	存入準備金	1,217,562	46
現金	2,113,796	45	同業存款	871,108	78
存放銀行定期 841,376.81			暫時存款	230,100	86
存放銀行活期 1,250,600.66			特約存款	538,855	28
庫存 21,818.98			本年純益	447,883	26
	10,076,407	79		10,076,407	79

太平保险公司1940年资产负债表
The 1940's Balance Sheet of Taiping Insurance Co.

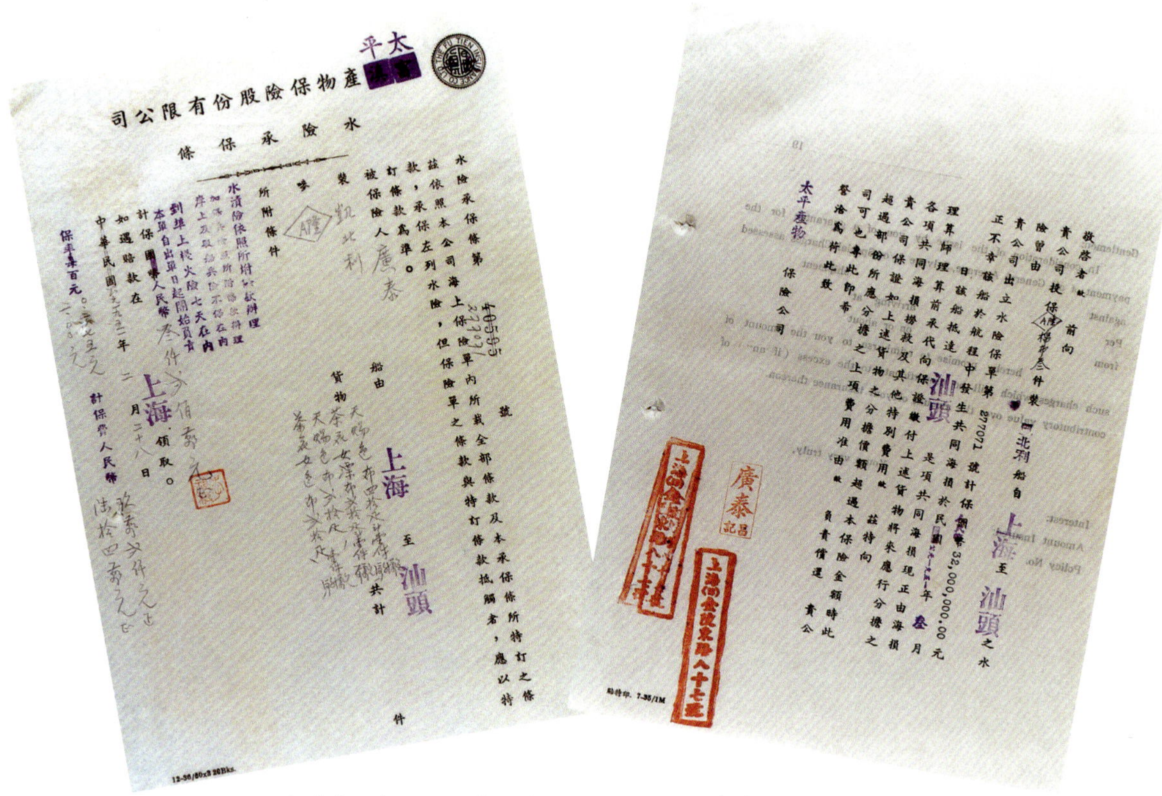

太平产物保险公司使用的保险通知书和要求其承担共同海损的索赔函
The Insurance Notice and the Claim Request Used by Taiping Property Insurance Co.

金城银行代理太平保险公司保险业务合同
Agency contract between Kingchen Banking Corporation and Taiping

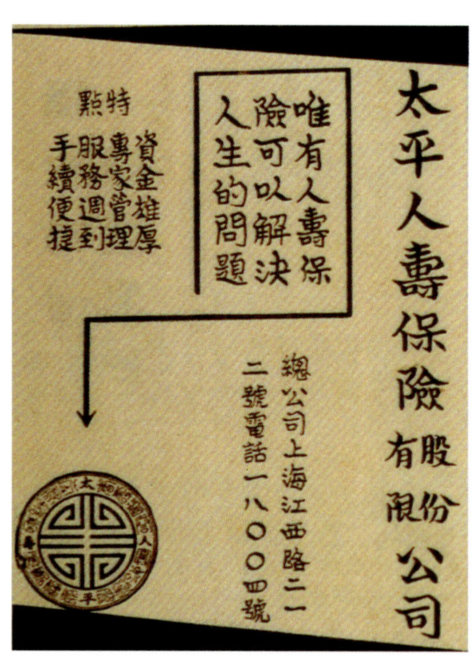

太平保险公司广告
Ad of Taiping Insurance Co.

1937年太平、安平、丰盛保险公司合并后，公司主要领导人赴黄山合影并签名留念。

Heads of the company in Huangshan Mountain (after the integration of Taiping、Anping、and Fengsheng in 1937)；their signatures as a memento (below).

安平丰盛保险公司济南分公司办公楼
Office building of Anping Fengsheng Insurance Co. Ji'nan Branch

太平、安平、丰盛第一届联合业务会议。太平第二协理王伯衡(前左八)、太平总经理周作民(前左九)、太平第一协理丁雪农(前左十)、安平经理董汉槎(前左十一)。
Attendees of the First united conference of Taiping, Anping, and Fengsheng

1935年太平、安平、丰盛保险公司全体同仁在上海合影。
Staff of Taiping, Anping, and Fengsheng Insurance Co. in Shanghai in 1935

八、中国银行与中国保险公司
Bank of China & China Insurance Co.

1928年，南京政府建立中央银行，中国银行成为经营国外汇兑的专业银行。1931年中国银行投资200万元设立中国保险公司，并于11月正式开业，宋汉章兼任董事长。中国保险公司初期主要经营火灾保险。兼营茧子险、银钞险。以后业务范围又扩展到汽车险和邮包险。1933年秋，增办人寿保险业务，主要险种有终身人寿保险、限期缴费终身保险、储蓄保险、人身意外保险、劳工保险和雇主责任保险等。

1937年，“八·一三”事变后，中国保险公司一方面积极向海外发展业务，成立中国保险公司驻港办公处；另一方面向内地延伸，在重庆设立经理处，先后在重庆、桂林、昆明、贵阳、成都开展业务。太平洋战争爆发后，海外机构停业，宋汉章在重庆组建了中国保险公司总管理处。

1946年，宋汉章由重庆返回上海，中国保险公司也迁沪办公，宋汉章仍兼董事长。解放后，中国保险公司作为官僚资本被人民政府接管。

1931年中国保险公司办公大楼
Office building of the China Insurance Co. in 1931

The Central Bank was set up by the Nanjing government in 1928 to specialized in foreign exchange. In 1931, the Bank of China invested 200 million yuan to found the China Insurance Co., while Song Hanzhang was concurrent board chairman. Early its business was limited within fire insurance; later it's broadened to automobile and parcel post insurance. It started to operate life insurance in the autumn 1933. Since the outbreak of August Thirteenth Incident in 1937, the China Insurance Co. began to develop in overseas market. Song Hanzhang organized the head office in Chongqing after the outbreak of the Pacific War. It was in 1946 that Song returned to Shanghai and the China Insurance Co. was also moved back. The China Insurance Co., as a bureaucrat-capital, was taken over by the government after China's liberation.

宋汉章(1872—1968)，浙江余姚人。早年随父到上海，就读于中西书院，毕业后进上海电报局工作。1891年，中国第一家自办银行中国通商银行成立，宋进入该行工作。此后曾任北京储蓄银行经理、上海大清银行经理。1911年辛亥革命后，大清银行改组为中国银行，宋被任命为中国银行上海分行经理。1931年，中国银行董事会投资建立中国保险公司，宋任董事长，全权办理。中国保险公司初期以经营火灾保险为主，以后中国保险公司的业务又扩充运输险及汽车险、邮电险等。又把水上运输险，分为平安险、水渍险。对海洋运输险另加费用，还可加保兵险及破碎险。1933年，又增办人寿保险业务。1937年，"八·一三"事变后，中国保险公司一方面积极向海外发展业务，在香港开办保险业务，成立中国保险公司驻港办公处；另一方面又向内地发展，在重庆设立经理处，先后在重庆、桂林、昆明、贵阳、成都开展保险业务。太平洋战争后，中国保险公司在海外的营业机构后停业，人员撤退。宋汉章在重庆组成中国保险公司总管理处。

1946年，宋汉章从重庆返回上海，中国保险公司总部亦复员回沪，领导各地分公司及经理处，宋汉章仍兼董事长。上海解放后，中国保险公司与英国伦敦承担分保业务的各公司关系中断。宋汉章赴香港后，接通、恢复关系。后宋汉章辞职，1968年12月去世。

Song Hanzhang (1872—1967) was employed by China Trading Bank in 1891; later he took up the post of manager of Shanghai Great Qing Bank. He was appointed as manager of the Bank of China Shanghai Branch after the Shanghai Great Qing Bank was reorganized to the Bank of China for the outbreak of 1911 Revolution. Song, as board chairman, was responsible for the establishment of the China Insurance Co. He had been chairman of Insurance Company since it's foundation.

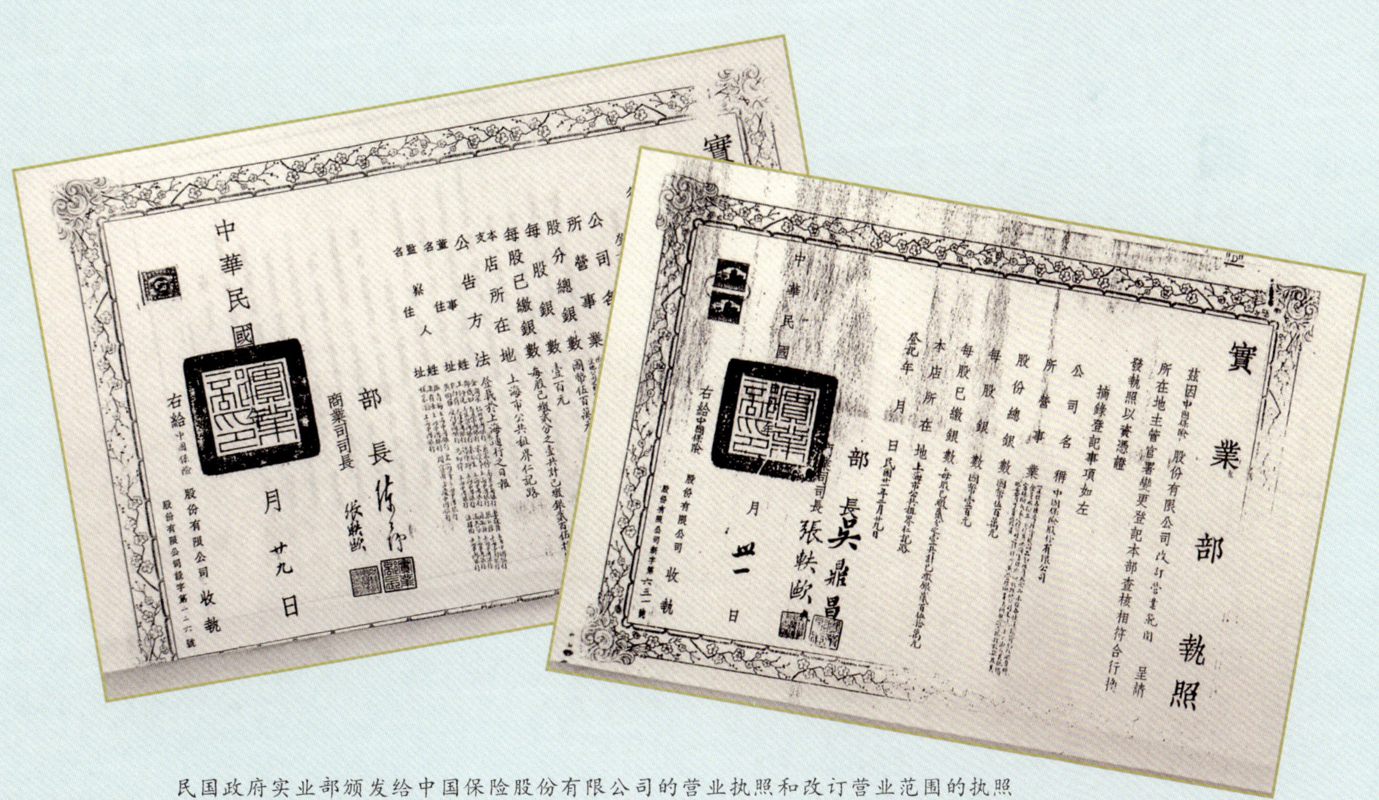

實業部執照

公司名稱
所營事業
股份總銀數 國幣伍百萬元
每股銀數 壹百元
每股已繳銀數 每股已繳貳分之壹共計已繳銀貳百伍拾萬元
本店所在地 上海市公共租界仁記路
公告方法 登載於上海通行之日報
董事姓名住址
監察人姓名住址

部長
商業司司長 張軼歐

右給中國保險股份有限公司收執
股份有限公司設字第一二六號
中華民國 年 月 廿九 日

實業部執照

茲因中國保險股份有限公司改訂營業範圍 呈請
所在地主管官署變更登記本部查核相符合行換
發執照以資憑證
摘錄登記事項如左
公司名稱 中國保險股份有限公司
所營事業
股份總銀數 國幣伍百萬元
每股銀數 國幣壹百元
每股已繳銀數
本店所在地 上海市公共租界仁記路
登記年月日 民國廿一年二月廿九日

部長 吳鼎昌
司長 張軼歐

右給中國保險股份有限公司收執
股份有限公司新字第六三一號
中華民國 年 月 廿一 日

民国政府实业部颁发给中国保险股份有限公司的营业执照和改订营业范围的执照
Business license and license on business scope changing issued by the Industrial Department of the Republic of China to the China Insurance Co.

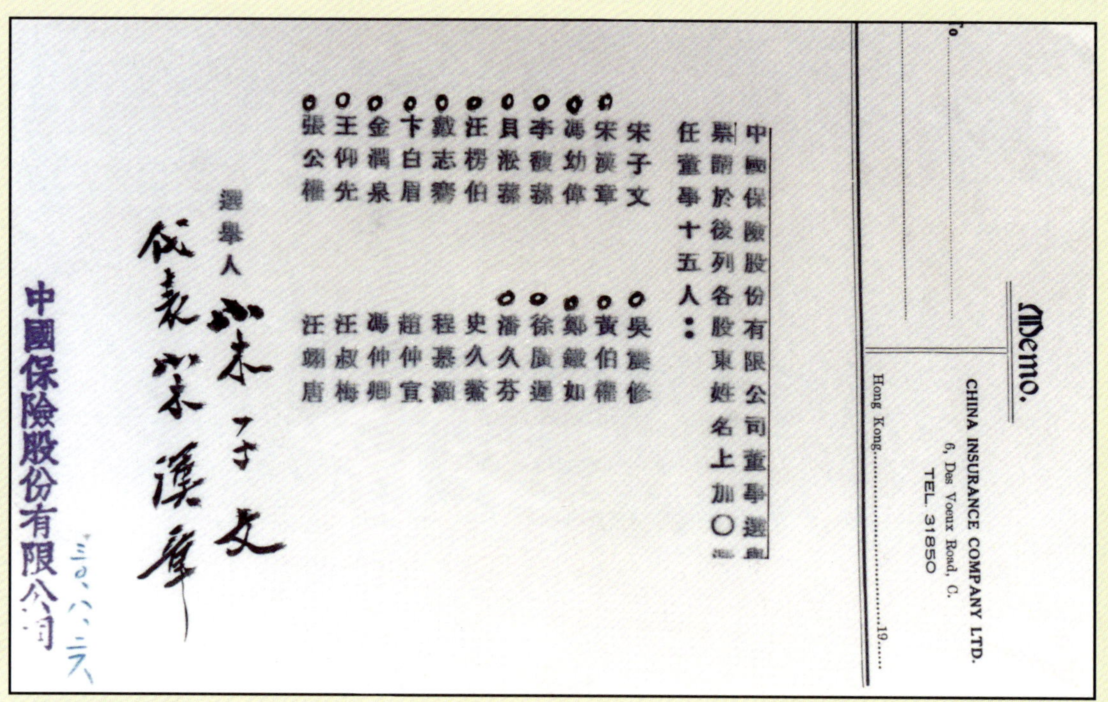

Memo.
CHINA INSURANCE COMPANY LTD.
6, Des Voeux Road, C.
TEL. 31850
To
Hong Kong..................19....

中國保險股份有限公司董事選舉票
謹於後列各股東姓名上加〇為
選任董事十五人：

〇宋子文 〇宋漢章 〇馮幼偉 〇李馥蓀 〇貝淞蓀 〇汪楞伯 〇戴志騫 〇卞白眉 〇金潤泉 〇王仰先 〇張公權

〇吳震修 〇黃伯權 〇鄭鐵如 〇徐廣遲 〇潘久芬 史久鰲 程慕灝 趙仲宣 馮仲卿 汪叔梅 汪翊唐

選舉人 宋子文
代表 宋漢章

中國保險股份有限公司
三〇、八、二八

中国保险股份有限公司董事选举票，图为公司董事长宋汉章代表宋子文填写的选票。（资料提供：中国第二历史档案馆）

Vote for directors filled in by Shong Hanzhang (board chairman of the China Insurance Co.) delegated for Shong Ziwen

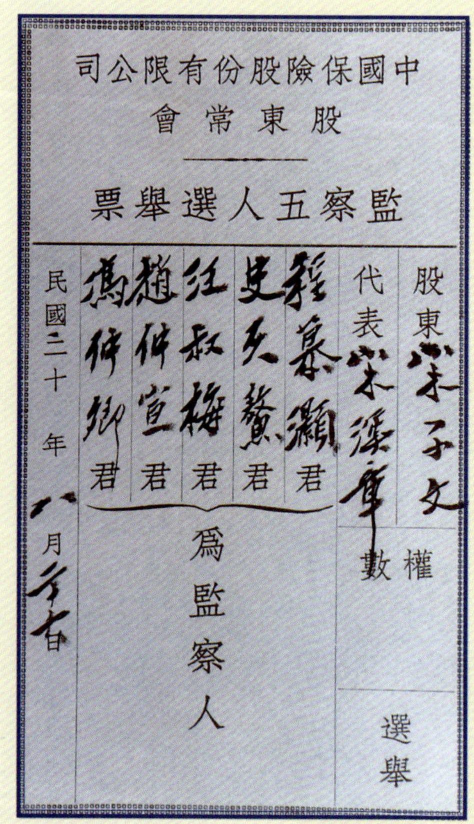

中國保險股份有限公司
股東常會
監察人五人選舉票

股東 宋子文
代表 宋漢章

程慕灝君
史久鰲君
汪叔梅君
趙仲宣君
馮仲卿君
為監察人

權數
選舉

民國三十年八月廿八

宋汉章代表宋子文填写的中国保险股份有限公司监事会选票（资料提供：中国第二历史档案馆）

Vote for directorate filled in by Shong Hanzhang delegated for Shong Ziwen

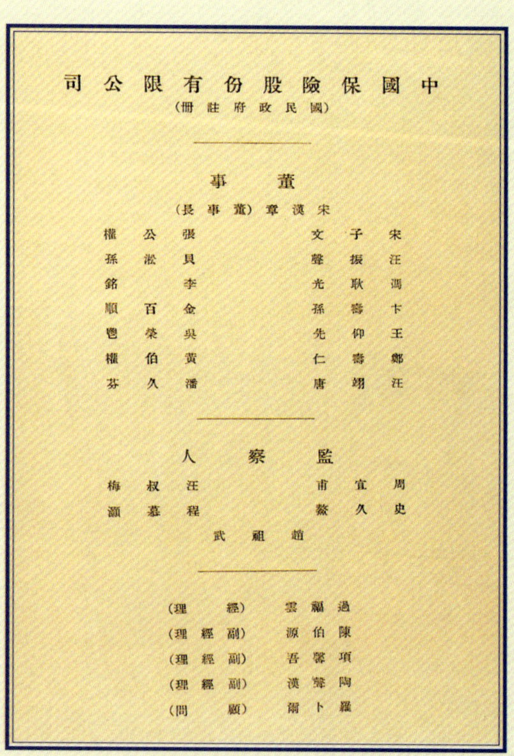

中國保險股份有限公司
（國民政府註冊）

董事
宋漢章（董事長）
宋子文 張公權
汪振聲 貝淞孫
馮耿光 李銘
卞壽孫 金百順
王仰先 吳榮鬯
鄭壽仁 黃伯權
汪翊唐 潘久芬

監察人
周宜甫 汪叔梅
史久鰲 程慕灝
趙祖武

過福雲（經理）
陳伯源（副經理）
項馨吾（副經理）
陶聲漢（副經理）
羅卜爾（顧問）

中国保险公司董事和监察人名单

List of directors and supervisors of the China Insurance Co.

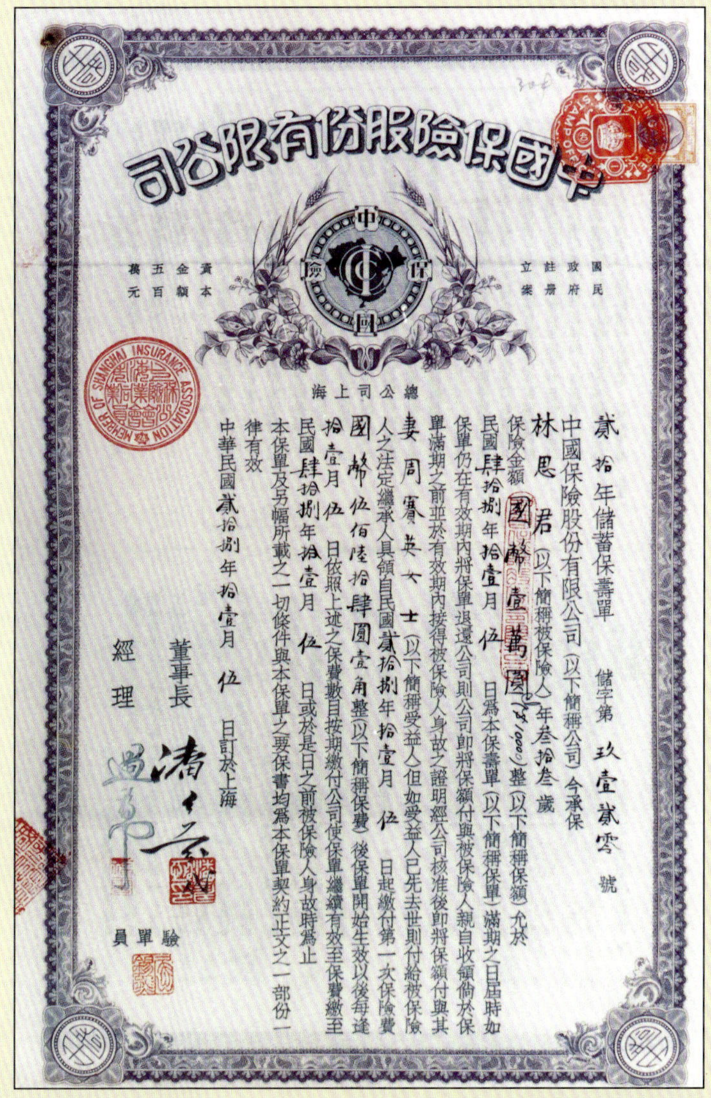
中國保險股份有限公司

國民政府註冊立案

資本金額五百萬元

總公司上海

貳拾年儲蓄保壽單　儲字第玖壹貳零號

中國保險股份有限公司（以下簡稱公司）今承保
林思君（以下簡稱被保險人）年叁拾叁歲
保險金額國幣壹萬圓（$10000）整（以下簡稱保額）允於
民國肆拾捌年拾壹月伍日為本保壽單（以下簡稱保單）滿期之日屆時如
保單仍在有效期內將保單退還公司則公司即將保額付與被保險人親自收領倘於保
單滿期之前並於有效期內接得被保險人身故之證明經公司核准後即將保額付與其
妻周賽英女士（以下簡稱受益人）但如受益人已先去世則付給被保險
人之法定繼承人具領自民國貳拾捌年拾壹月伍日起繳付第一次保險費
國幣伍佰陸拾肆圓壹角整（以下簡稱保費）後保單開始生效以後每逢
拾壹月伍日依照上述之保費數目按期繳付公司使保單繼續有效至保費繳至
民國肆拾捌年拾壹月伍日或於是日之前被保險人身故時為止
本保單及另幅所載之一切條件與本保單之要保書均為本保單契約正文之一部份一
律有效

中華民國貳拾捌年拾壹月伍日訂於上海

董事長

經理

驗單員

中国保险有限公司储蓄寿险保险单
Policy of deposit life insurance issued by China Insurance Co.

中國保險股份有限公司

資產負債表

中華民國二十四年十二月三十一日

資產	人壽險部	水火及雜險部	總額
投資			
抵押放款	$ 500,000.00	$ 2,176,686.55	$ 2,676,686.55
內國公債		397,006.00	397,006.00
經理處往來	3,140.27	167,410.45	170,550.72
經紀人往來	15,237.75	136,856.37	152,094.12
未收同業各款		72,344.11	72,344.11
存出同業保險準備金		36,621.64	36,621.64
未收保費	20,354.26	7,447.76	27,802.02
未收利息	12,029.17	47,322.59	59,351.76
各戶欠	2,742.54	237,321.20	240,063.74
營業用器具		1.00	1.00
存放銀行	165,512.25	489,510.49	655,022.74
銀行往來及法幣	15,524.08	340,403.85	355,927.93
	$ 734,540.32	$ 4,108,932.01	$ 4,843,472.33

負債		人壽險部	水火及雜險部	總額
已收股本				
股本總額	$ 5,000,000.00			
未收股本	2,500,000.00	$ 500,000.00	$ 2,000,000.00	$ 2,500,000.00
公積金			67,550.57	67,550.57
特別公積金			607,955.19	607,955.19
投資準備金			130,000.00	130,000.00
房地產基金			20,000.00	20,000.00
火險準備金			380,523.04	380,523.04
水險及雜險準備金			89,110.82	89,110.82
人壽險準備金		196,794.72		196,794.72
本年純益			267,323.17	267,323.17
		$ 696,794.72	$ 3,562,462.79	$ 4,259,257.51
未付火險賠款			63,245.28	63,245.28
未付水險及雜險賠款			5,489.15	5,489.15
未付同業各款		7,892.81	144,675.54	152,568.35
各戶存		29,852.79	315,082.80	344,935.59
備抵呆帳			17,976.45	17,976.45
		$ 734,540.32	$ 4,108,932.01	$ 4,843,472.33

損益計算表

中華民國二十四年度

損失	金額
營業用器具折舊	$ 7,408.99
買賣公債佣金	1,062.20
投資準備金	80,000.00
房地產基金	20,000.00
呆帳	12,627.94
純益	267,323.17
	$ 388,422.30

利益		金額
利息		
存放款項	$ 235,085.58	
有價證券	104,693.30	$ 339,778.88
兌換損益		2,083.69
火險部餘額		25,938.72
水險及雜險部餘額		16,355.00
人壽險部餘額		4,266.01
		$ 388,422.30

1934年，中国保险股份有限公司资产负债表。
The 1934's Balance Sheet of the China Insurance Co.

中国银行总裁宋子文
Song Ziwen: president of the Bank of China

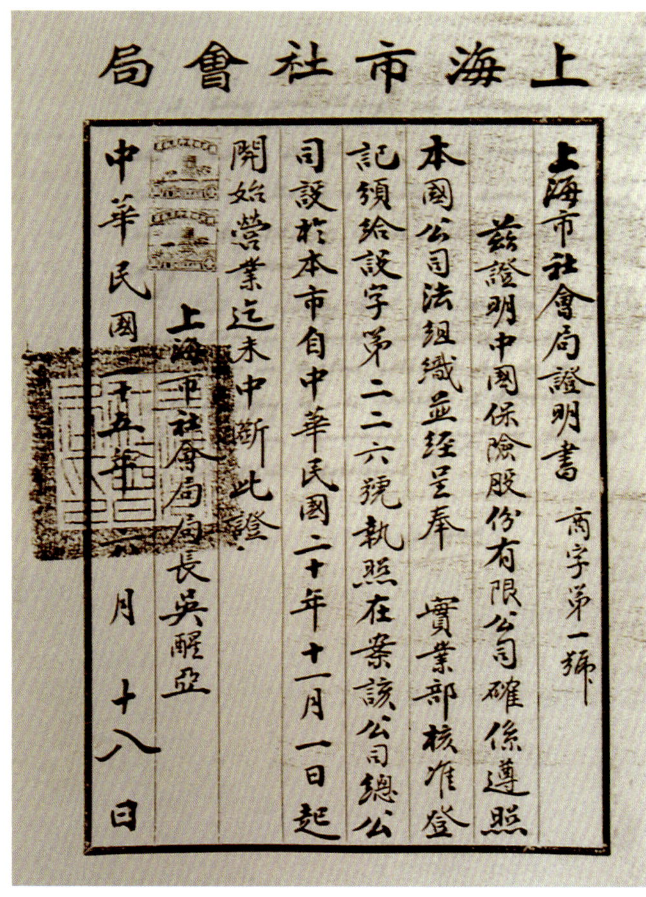

上海市社會局

上海市社會局證明書　商字第一號

茲證明中國保險股份有限公司確係遵照本國公司法組織並經呈奉實業部核准登記領給設字第二二六號執照在案該公司總公司設於本市自中華民國二十年十一月一日起開始營業迄未中斷此證

上海市社會局局長吳醒亞

中華民國二十五年　月　十八日

1936年上海市社会局为中国保险股份有限公司开具的证明
Certificate issued by Shanghai Social Bureau for China Insurance Co. in 1936

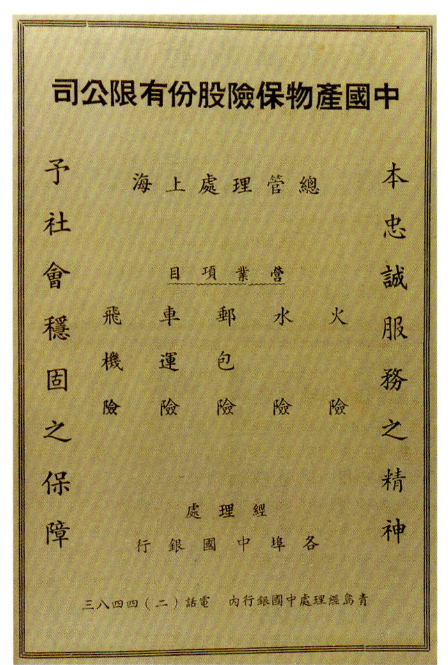

中国产物保险股份有限公司广告
Ad of China Property Insurance Co.

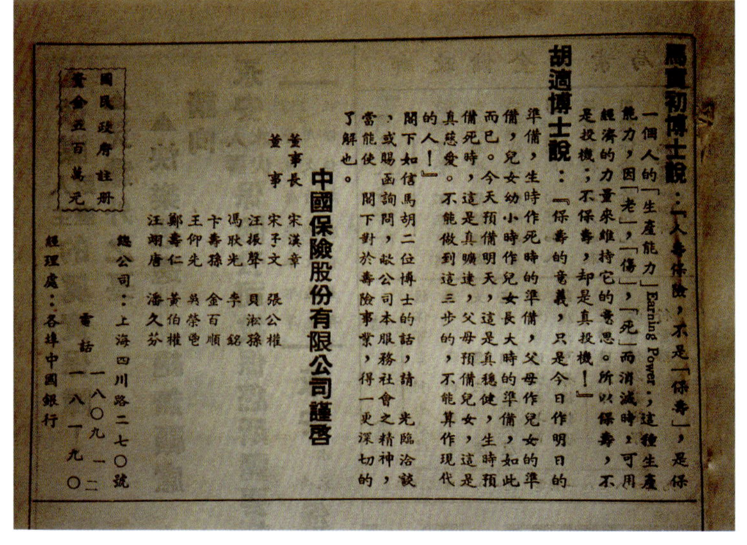

馬寅初博士說：『人壽保險，不是「保壽」，是保一個人的「生產能力」Earning Power；這種生產能力，因「老」，「傷」，「死」而消滅時，可用經濟的力量來維持它的意思。所以保壽，不是投機；不保壽，卻是真投機！』

胡適博士說：『保壽的意義，只是今日作明日的準備，生時作死時的準備，父母作兒女的準備，兒女幼小時作兒女長大時的準備，如此而已。今天預備明天，這是真穩健，生時預備死時，這是真曠達，父母預備兒女，這是真慈愛。不能做到這三步的，不能算作現代的人！』

閣下如信馬胡二位博士的話，請光臨洽談，或賜函詢問，敝公司本服務社會之精神，當能使閣下對於壽險事業，得一更深切的了解也。

中國保險股份有限公司謹啓

董事長 宋漢章
董事 宋子文 汪振聲 馮耿光 卞壽孫 王仰先 鄭壽仁 汪湖唐 張公權 貝淞孫 李銘 金百順 吳榮鬯 黃伯權 潘久芬

總公司：上海四川路二七〇號 電話 一八〇九一 一八一九〇
經理處：各埠中國銀行

國民政府註冊 資金五百萬元

登有马寅初、胡适名言的中国保险公司启事，这两句名言至今仍广为传用。
China Insurance Co.'s notice with Ma Yanchu's and Hushi's wisdom

中国保险元老——过福云

过福云，江苏武进县人。1884年进入怡和洋行保险部，1894年被该公司聘为顾问。鉴于当时南洋一带商市发达，过于1909年赴新加坡创立华通保险分公司，任总经理，后任中国保险公司总经理，直至1955年退休。

过福云从事保险事业六十余年，实现了他为民族保险事业奋斗终身的愿望。以其从事保险事业的时间和对民族保险业的贡献，堪称中国保险元老。

Guo Fuyun, born in Jiangsu Province, entered into the Insurance Department of the Jardine-Madison House in 1884 and was employed as its consultant in 1894. He went to Singapore to establish the Huatong Insurance Co. Singapore Branch in 1909 and later he held the position of general manager of the China Insurance Co. till he retired in 1955.

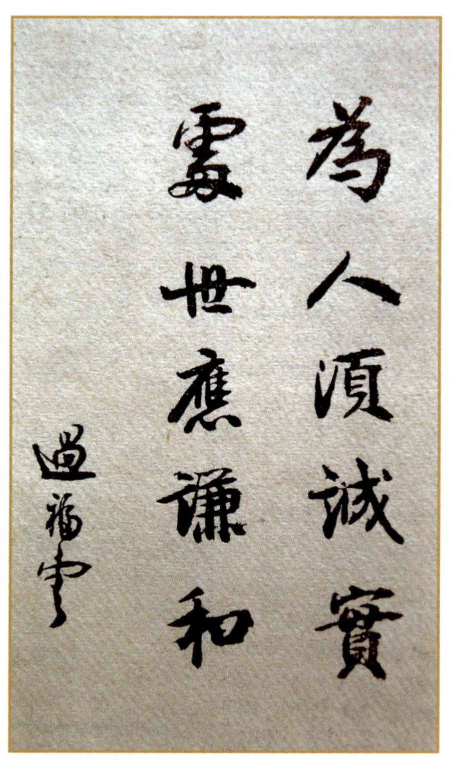

过福云的手迹反映了他的处世原则

Guo Fuyun's script reflecting his principle of self-conducting

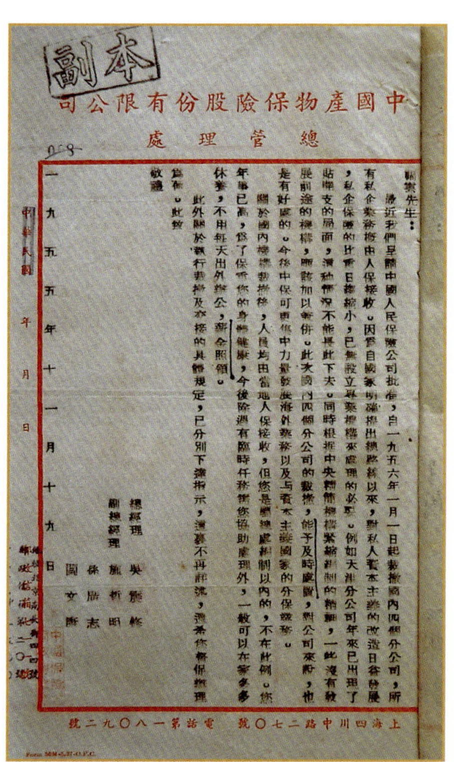
副本

中國產物保險股份有限公司
總管理處

驥雲先生：

最近我們呈請中國人民保險公司批准，自一九五六年一月一日起撤銷國內四個分公司，所有私企業務均由人保接收。因為自國家明確提出總路線以來，對私人資本主義的改造日益發展，私企保業的比重日益縮小，已無設立專業機構來處理的必要。例如天津分公司年來已出現了貼保支的局面，這種情況不能長此下去。同時根據中央對簡化機構緊縮編制的精神，一些沒有發展前途的機構，應該加以合併。此次國內四個分公司的撤撤，能予及時處置，對公司來說，也是有好處的。今後中保可更集中力量發展海外業務以及与資本主義國家的分保業務。

關於國內機構撤銷後，人員均由當地人保接收，但您是屬總處編制以內的，不在此例。您年事已高，為了保重您的身體健康，今後除遇有臨時任務需您協助處理外，一般可以在家多多休養，不用每天出外辦公，薪金照領。

此外關於執行業務及交接的具體規定，已分別下達指示，這裏不再詳述，還希你查照辦理為荷。此致

敬禮

總經理 吳震修
副總經理 施哲明 徐品志 周文斯

一九五五年十一月十九日

上海四川中路二七〇號 電話第一八〇一九二號

1955年，过福云退休前，中国人民保险公司上海分公司代表总公司致过福云的函的附件。

Official letter to Guo Fuyun from Shanghai Branch on behalf of China Property Insurance Co. in 1955 before his retirement

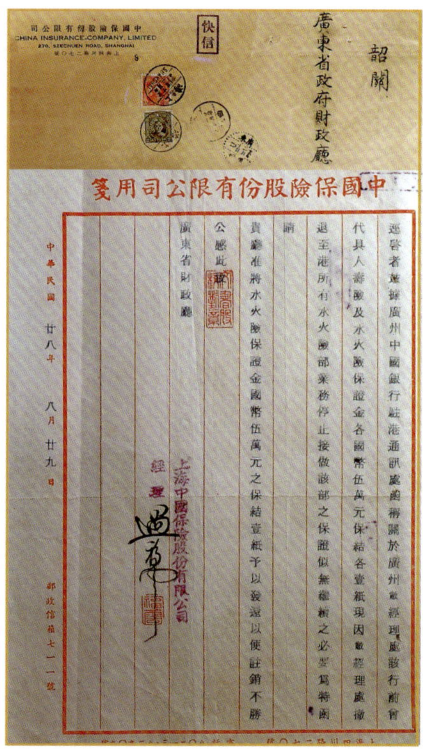
中國保險股份有限公司
CHINA INSURANCE COMPANY, LIMITED

快信

廣東省政府財政廳

韶關

中國保險股份有限公司用箋

逕啓者兹據廣州中國銀行駐港通訊處函稱關於廣州敝經理處該行前曾代具人壽險及水火險保證金各國幣伍萬元保結各壹紙現因敝經理處撤退至港所有水火險部業務停止接做該部之保證似無繼續之必要爲特函請

貴廳准將水火險保證金國幣伍萬元之保結壹紙予以發還以便註銷不勝

公感此致

廣東省財政廳

上海中國保險股份有限公司
經理 過福雲

中華民國廿八年八月廿九日

郵政信箱七一一號

过福云签名的中国保险股份有限公司公函

The China Insurance Co.'s official letter signed by Guo Fuyun

九、胡咏骐与宁绍保险公司

Hu Yongqi & Ningshao Insurance Co.

胡咏骐，浙江鄞县人。1926年，留学美国哥伦比亚大学，学习人寿保险和商业管理。1929年回国后，任宁绍商轮公司保险部经理，后任宁绍水火保险公司总经理。1931年，创办宁绍人寿保险公司并出任总经理。

1935年中国保险学会成立，胡咏骐为常务理事。1935年以后，胡咏骐出任上海保险业同业公会主席，其间，主持翻译了保险单上长期沿用的英文条款，结束了我国民族资本保险公司在保险单上没有中文条款的历史。1938年，上海市保险业余联谊会成立，胡咏骐被聘为顾问。1939年，中国共产党中央委员会特别批准胡咏骐加入中国共产党。1940年11月5日，胡咏骐因病在上海逝世。

宁绍水火保险公司和宁绍人寿保险公司总经理胡咏骐
Hu Yongqi: General Manager of Ningshao Marine and Fire Insurance Co. and Ningshao Life Insurance Co.

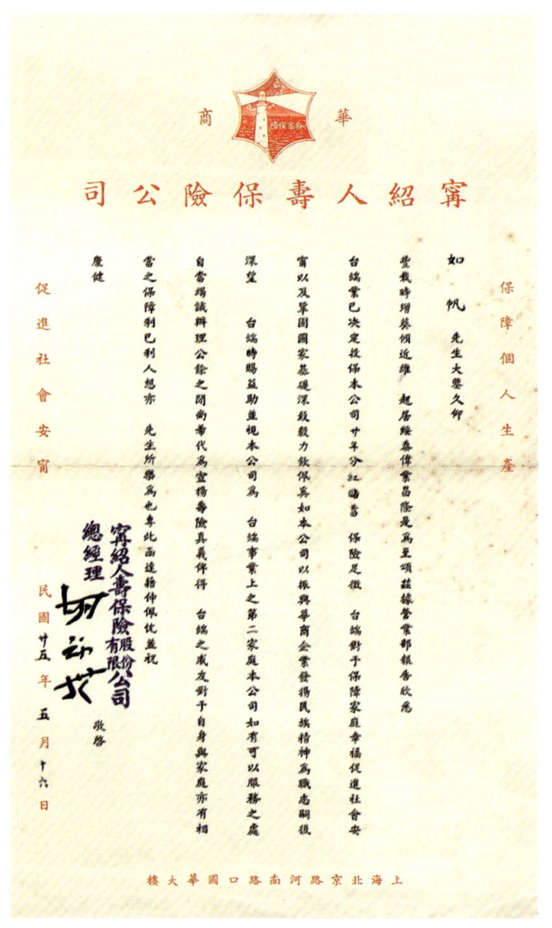

華商

寗紹人壽保險公司

保障個人生產

如帆先生大鑒久仰
豐裁時增景仰近維起居綏泰偉業昌隆是爲至頌茲據營業部報告欣悉
台端業已決定投保本公司廿年分紅儲蓄保險足徵台端對于保障家庭幸福促進社會安
寗以及鞏固國家基礎深致毅力欽佩奚如本公司以振興華商企業發揚民族精神爲職志嗣後
深望台端時賜益助並視本公司爲台端事業上之第二家庭本公司如有可以服務之處
自當竭誠辦理公餘之閒尚希代爲宣揚壽險真義俾得台端之戚友對于自身與家庭亦有相
當之保障利己利人想亦先生所樂爲也專此函達藉伸保忱並祝
康健

寗紹人壽保險股份有限公司
總經理　敬啓

民國廿五年五月十六日

促進社會安寗

上海北京路河南路口國華大樓

胡咏骐致宁绍人寿保险公司保户信
Hu Yongqi's letter to policyholders of Ningshao Life Insurance Co.

After his study on life insurance and business administration at Columbia University in America, Hu Yongqi return to China and was employed as manager of the Insurance Department of Ningshao Commercial Shipping Co. and later general manager of Ningshao Marine & Fire Insurance Co. In 1935, Hu established Ningshao Life Insurance Co.; he took up the post of general manger of the company.

Hu devoted all his life to Chinese insurance. He had been the standing member of China Insurance Society founded in 1935, chairman of Shanghai Insurance Association, consultant of China Insurance Employees Federation founded in 1938. He directed the translation of insurance clauses from English into Chinese, giving the end to the history that Chinese national insurers had no Chinese insurance clauses. In 1939, the Central Party Committee of the Communist Party of China specially approved Hu to join the Party. He died of cancer in Shanghai on November 5, 1940.

胡咏骐在宁波斐迪中学毕业,居中者为胡咏骐。
Hu Yongqi (middle) with his middle-school classmates

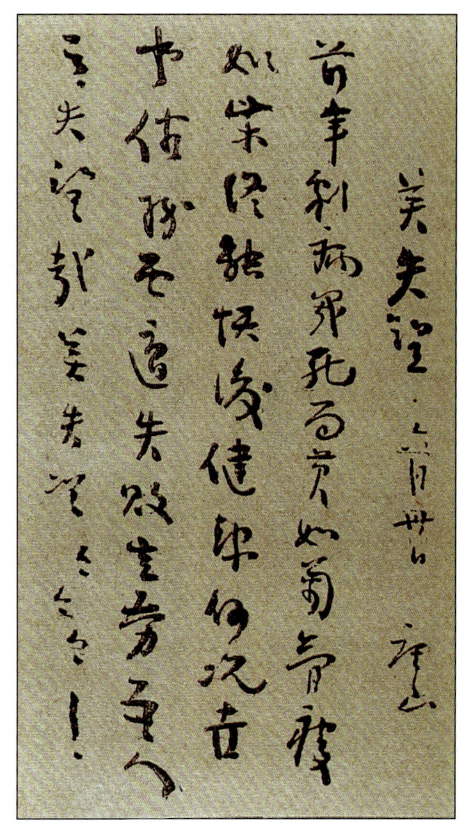

胡咏骐墨迹,1937年6月30日,胡咏骐书于庐山。全文为:前年剧病几死,面黄如菊,骨瘦如柴,终能恢复健康。何况世事俗务,虽遭失败,岂劳我人之失望哉?莫失望!莫失望!勉人努力事业,勿以失败而堕志。胡咏骐坚忍奋斗百折不挠之精神,于此可窥一斑。
Calligraphy by Hu Yongqi at Lushan Mountain in June 30, 1937.

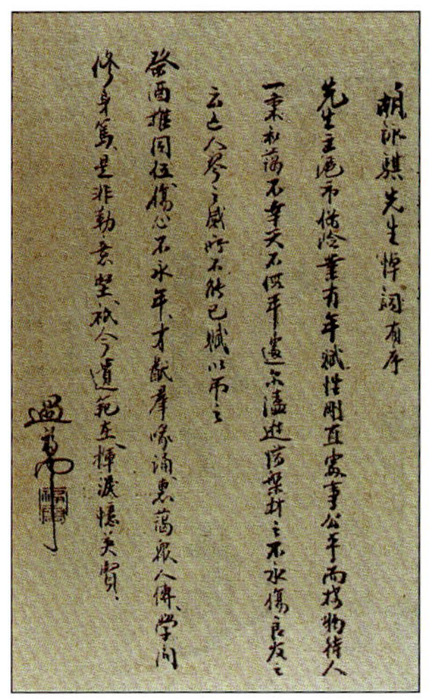

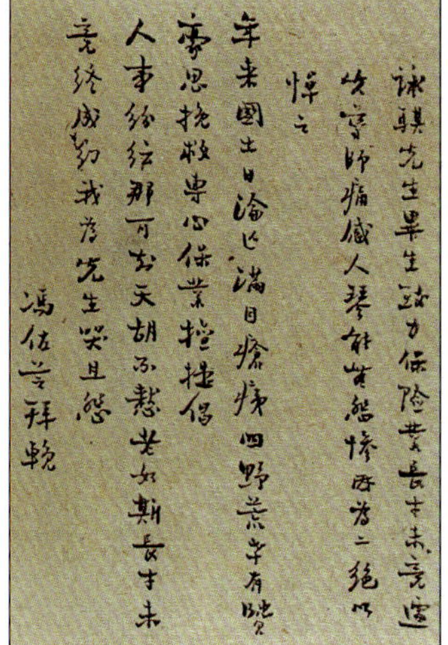

追懷胡詠騏先生
畢生事業付東流
慨嘆長才未竟酬
碩畫良規留景式
頻揮老淚念同儔
呂岳泉

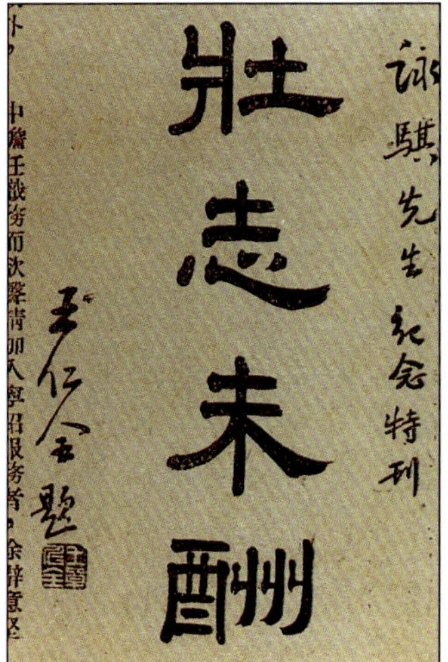

詠騏先生紀念特刊
壯志未酬
王仁全題

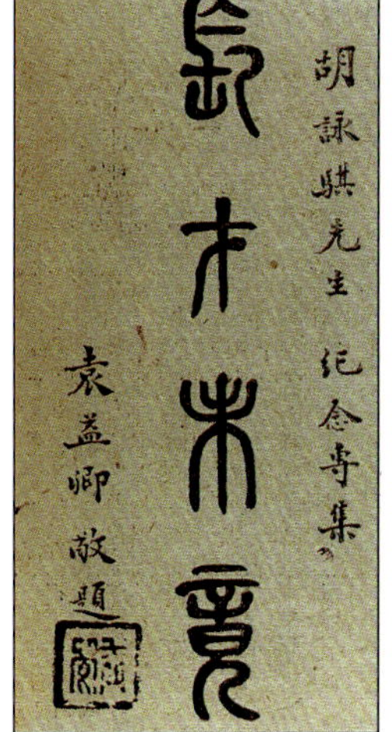

胡詠騏先生紀念專集
長才未竟
袁益卿敬題

我国民族保险业的精英吕岳泉、过福云、陈干青、王仁全、冯仁芸等为悼念胡咏骐逝世题写悼词。
Laments by some elites of Chinese national insurance for Hu Yongqi's passing away

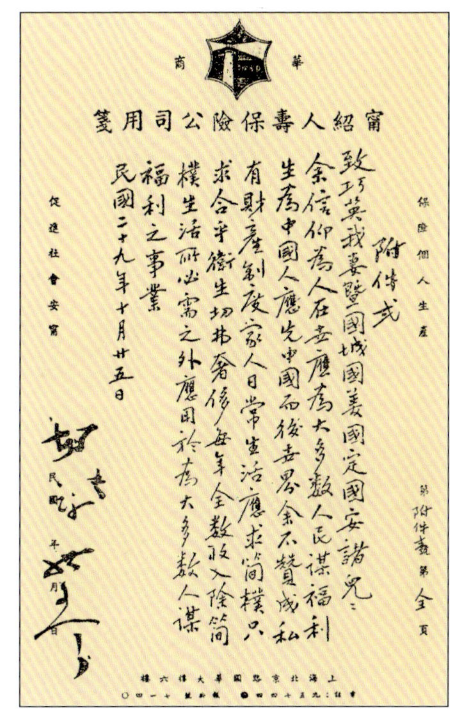

華 商
甯紹人壽保險公司用箋

附件式

致巧英我妻暨國城國義國定國安諸兒:
余信仰為人在世應為大多數人民謀福利
生為中國人應先中國而後吾界余不贊成私
有財產制度家人日常生活應求簡樸只
求合乎衛生切戒奢侈每年全數收入除簡
樸生活所必需之外應用於為大多數人謀
福利之事業
民國二十九年十月廿五日

胡詠騏

1940年11月5日,胡咏骐因患癌症逝世,终年42岁。图为胡咏骐的遗嘱。
Hu Yongqi's Testament

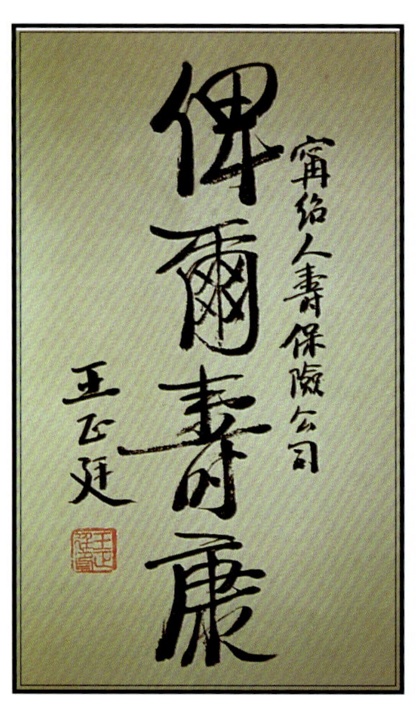

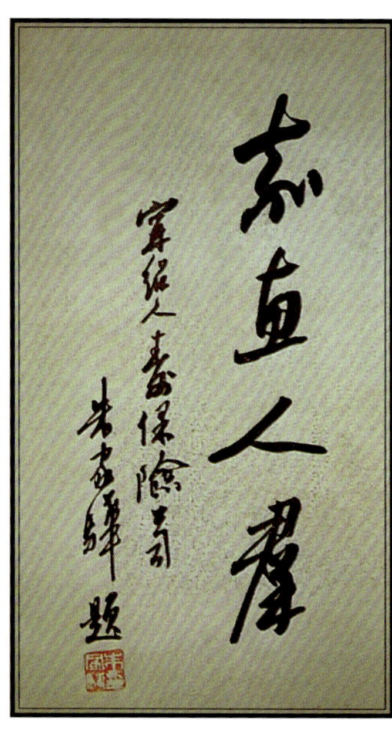

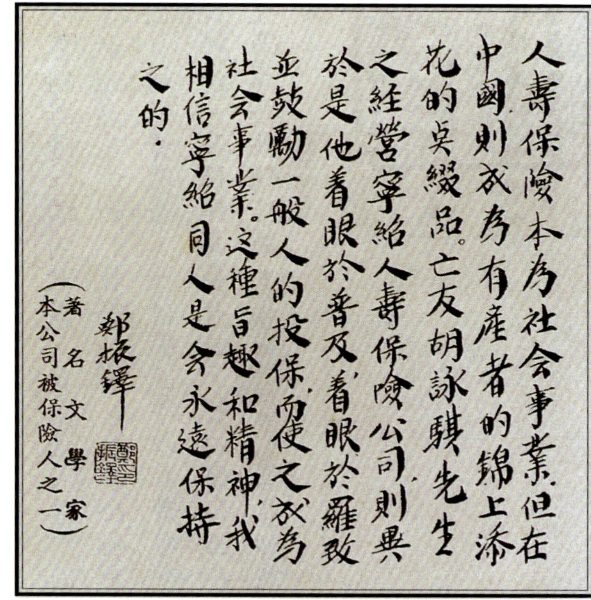

國人經營之甯紹人壽保險公司開業十年，認真服務，有利社會，裨益人群，各界稱許。值十週紀念，承先啓後，時見信譽日隆，爰弁數語，藉誌欽佩。

樊正康謹題

（滬江大學校長 本公司被保險人之一）

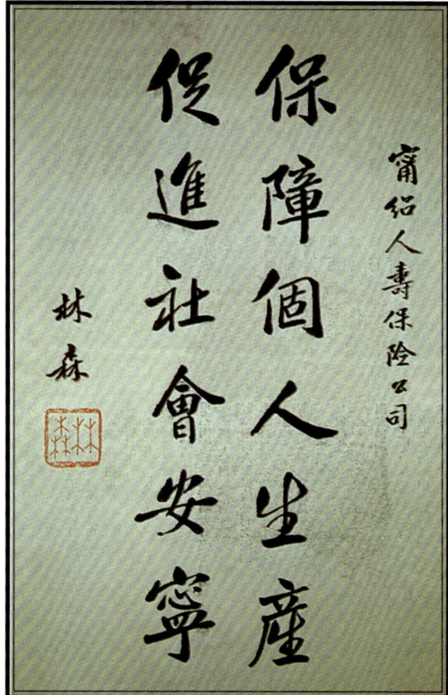

甯紹人壽保險公司十周紀念

十年基礎 如日方升 規模宏遠 造福人羣

何炳松敬題

（暨南大學校長 本公司被保險人之一）

社会名人为宁绍人寿保险公司题词

Inscriptions by notables for Ningshao Life Insurance Co.

宁绍商轮公司保险部全体同仁合影
Staff of the Insurance Department of Ningshao Commercial Shipping Co.

1933年宁绍水火保险公司同仁合影
Staff of Ningshao Marine & Fire Insurance Co. in 1933

上海商界巨头虞洽卿，他与朱葆三、严筱舫等人创办了宁绍轮船公司，该公司保险部为宁绍水火保险公司和宁绍人寿保险公司的前身。

Yu Qiaqing: a magnate in Shanghai commercial circle

宁绍人寿保险公司董事邵长春

Shao Changchun: Director of Ningshao Life Insurance Co.

宁绍人寿保险公司办公楼

Office Building of Ningshao Life Insurance Co.

宁绍人寿保险公司襄理兼发展部主任杨培之，公司襄理周永德，精算兼会计部主任李宁坤。
Ningshao Life's assistant manager/Development Department director Yang Peizhi, assistant manager Zhou Yongde, director of Actuary and Accounting Department.

宁绍人寿保险公司推荐杨培之赴美留学，公司同仁欢送留影。图中左五为胡咏骐，右五为杨培之。
Ningshao Life's staff to send off Yang Peizhi to study in America; Hu Yongqi (L5); Yang Peizhi (R5).

宁绍人寿保险公司开展业务培训
Business training in Ningshao Life Insurance Co.

宁绍人寿保险公司开展服务月恢复失效保单活动
Ningshao Life's Service Month to validate ineffective polices

宁绍人寿保险公司医务人员询问保户身体情况和为保户办理投保手续时情景
Ningshao Life's medical clerk inquiring a policyholder's health condition to transact cover-insurance procedure

寗紹水火保險公司

寧紹水火保險公司 (一)

公 司 名： 寧紹水火保險股份有限公司
英 文 名： Ning Shao Fire & Marine Insurance Company, Limited.
創立年月： 民國十四年十一月寧紹商輪公司兼營保險業務二十四年改組爲保險公司
組織性質： 股份有限公司
資本總額： 國幣五十萬元
實收資本： 國幣二十五萬元
股份數目： 二千五百股
每股金額： 國幣二百元

營業種類：
1.水險 3.汽車險
2.船壳險 4.火險

董事長： 方椒伯
董 事： 袁履登 孫梅堂 樂振葆 金廷蓀 何楳軒 謝蘅牕 傅品圭 張繼光
監察人： 張永祥 王雲甫 洪賢鈁
總經理： 胡詠騏

總公司所在地：
上 海

代理處所在地：
寧 波 漢 口 九 江
蕪 湖 長 沙 蘇 洲
常 州 南 京 湖 洲
杭 洲 無 錫 温 洲
南 潯 嘉 興 烟 台
營 口 海 門 北 平
青 島 天 津

公司所在地及職員

所在地	職務	姓名	詳細地址及電報電話
上海	總經理	胡詠騏	北京路356號
	協理	龔渭源	電話95744 電報7140
	經理	王其培	
	副經理	包鏡第	
	水險部主任	趙嘉晉	
	火險部主任	羅振英	
	汽車部主伍	趙嘉晉	

——130——

宁绍水火保险公司概况
General situation of Ningshao Marine & Fire Insurance Co.

全國保險公司總覽

甯紹人壽保險公司 (一)

公 司 名： 甯紹人壽保險股份有限公司
英 文 名： Ning Shao Life Insurance Co., Ltd.
創立年月： 民國二十年十一月一日
註册年月： 民國二十一年五月十七日
註册年限： 五十年滿期後經股東會决議得呈准續展之
組織性質： 股份有限公司
資本總額： 國幣二十五萬元
實收資本： 國幣二十五萬元
股份數目： 二千五百股
每股金額： 國幣一百元

營業種類：
1.終身保險
2.限期繳費終身保險
3.儲蓄保險
4.薪資儲蓄養老金保險
5.子女教育金保險
6.子女婚嫁金保險
7.團體保險
8.意外保險

董事長： 樂振葆
總經理： 胡詠騏

總公司所在地：
上 海

分公司所在地：
廣 州 青 島
漢 口 北 平

代理處所在地：
九 江 重 慶 蘇 州
南 京 杭 州 烟 台
濟 南 開 封 汕 頭
甯 波 長 沙 威海衞
鎮 江 無 錫 南 昌
濰 縣 廈 門

— 127 —

宁绍人寿保险公司概况
Bird's-eye view of Ningshao Life Insurance Co.

十、民族保险市场的扩展

Expansion of Chinese National Insurance Market

随着银行业及企业投资相继介入保险业，大大促进了保险业的发展，保险分支机构和代理网点遍及全国。

随着民族保险业的迅速发展，中外保险公司的竞争日趋激烈，一些规模较大的保险公司，逐渐向海外开拓保险市场，扩展国外保险业务。

1909年12月，华通保险公司在新加坡设立分公司，总经理为过福云，该公司是中国最早的驻外保险分支机构。

从1925年起，华安合群保寿公司陆续在荷属东印度群岛12座城市设立分支机构。另外广州羊城保险公司在香港、新加坡等地设有分公司，在吉隆坡设有代理分公司。其他在海外设有分支机构的保险公司还有上海联保、羊城置业、四海通、先施置业、永安水火、永安人寿、陆海通人寿、泰山、宝丰、中国、爱群人寿、香安以及先施人寿保险公司等。

With the successive investment from banking and enterprises, Chinese national insurance had been greatly promoted to a further development; insurance branches and outlets of agencies covered the whole country. Meanwhile, the competition between Chinese and foreign insurers had been increasingly fierce; some large-scale insurers gradually expanded business toward overseas market.

In December 1909, Huatong Insurance Co set up branch in Singapore, which is the earliest Chinese insurance branch set up abroad, while Guo Fuyun took up the post of general manger.

Since 1925, China United Assurance Society Ltd. had successively established branches in 12 cities in indies under abroad the governance of Holland, followed with a series of branches abroad set up by some other insurers.

1937年各地保险公司统计

Statistics of Number of Insurers in China (1937)

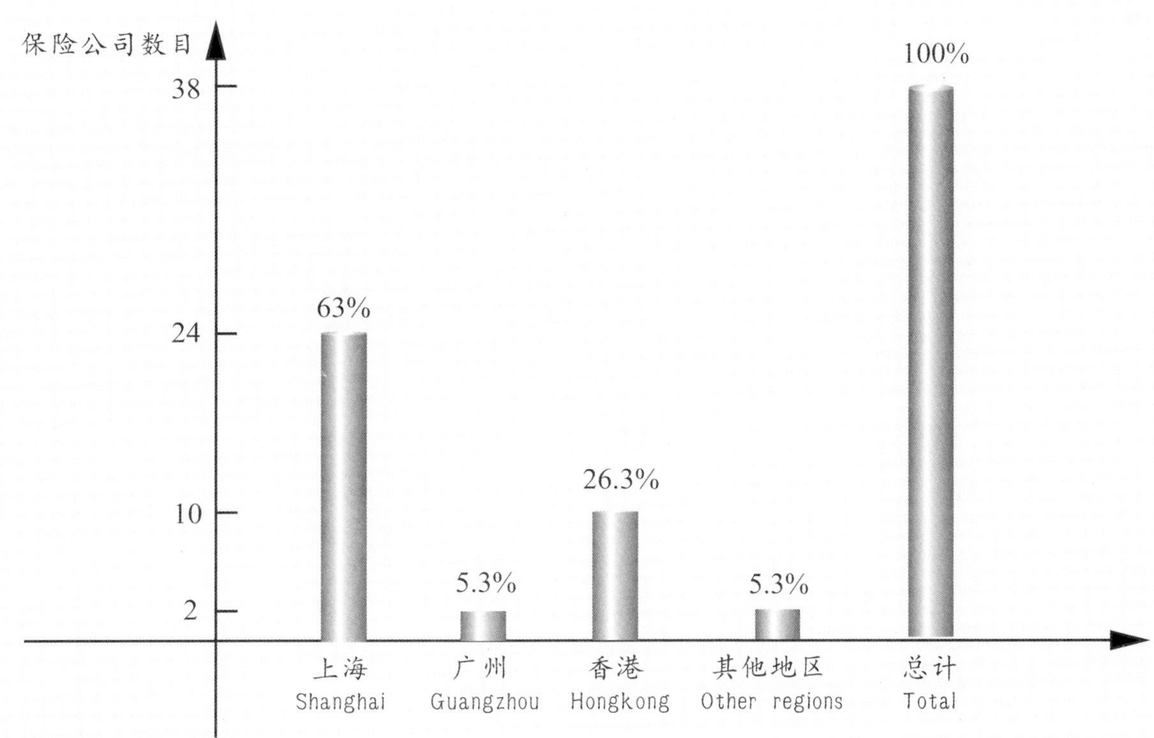

1937年各地保险公司分支机构数目统计表

Statistic of Number of Insurance Branches in Cities of China (1937)

地区	天津	北平	济南	青岛	南京	汉口	重庆	广州	其他中心城市	总计
分支机构数	10	4	5	6	10	4	7	20	60	126

1937年各地保险公司代理处数目统计表

Statistics of Number of Insurance Agencies in China (1937)

地区	江苏	浙江	湖北		福建		广东	四川	辽宁		安徽	河南	天津	其他	总计
保险代理处数	161	109	52	其中汉口 12	27	其中福州 11	44	33	47	其中营口 8	35	40	10	1130	1688

1937年主要保险公司分支机构和代理处一览表

Main Insurers' Branches and Agencies in 1937

	分支（家）	代理处（个）
中央信托局保险部	26	19
中国保险公司		82
太平洋保险公司	15	240
安平保险公司	14	224
宝丰保险公司	11	46
丰盛保险公司	12	170
华安合群保寿公司	17	14

十一、邮政储汇局与简易人寿保险

Postal Savings & Remittance Co. and Postal Life Insurance

1935年5月10日，国民政府公布《简易人寿保险法》，采取国办主义，由邮政储汇局兼办。该法规定：简易人寿保险为国营事业，属交通部主管，其他保险业者不得经营；第二三条规定：邮政储汇局对被保险人负给付保险金额之责。简易人寿保险分终身保险和定期保险两种。终身保险，其被保险人死亡时，给付保险金额。保险金额以国币50元至500元为限。被保险人必须在契约满期时或未满期而被保险人死亡时，方可领受全部保险金额。未满二年发生死亡时，则视时间之长短，而规定其权利。如未满一年死亡时，领受所纳之全部保险费；逾期一年而未满二年死亡时，领受保险金额之半数。并规定了保户遇有需要时，可凭保险单作抵押向保险公司借款。

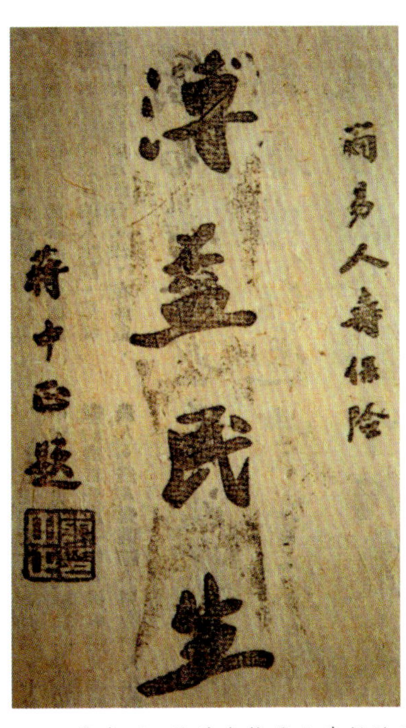

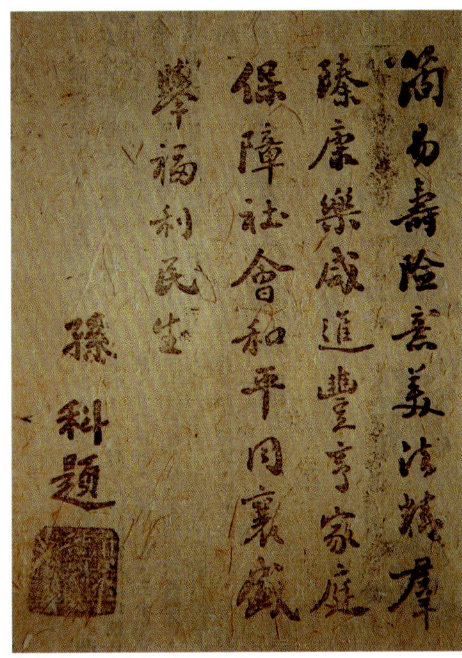

蒋介石、孙科为简易人寿保险的题词
Inscriptions of Jiang Kaishi and Sun Ke for postal life insurance

简易人寿保险法

1935年5月10日国民政府公布的《简易人身保险法》
Postal Life Insurance Law Promulgated by the Republic of China in 1935

1935年5月，简易人寿保险公布后，邮政储汇局于同年12月1日正式开业并在局中设置保险处，专门从事简易人寿保险业务。初期在上海储汇总局汉口分局试办，很快推广到了江苏、浙江、安徽、福建、广东、湖南、湖北等省。各省邮政局及邮局304处。至1936年末，签订简易人寿保险契约17900余种，月收保费2000多元，保险金额386万元。1937年抗战爆发，这项业务受到影响。

1939年，邮政储汇局由上海迁至昆明，次年其保险处迁到重庆，积极督导各地业务。到1942年底，签订简易人寿保险契约6万余件，月收保费6万余元，保额达970万元。

此后十余年，简易人寿保险业务又得到了迅速发展，到简易人寿保险开办10周年之时（即1945年8月），签订保险契约达35.3万件，月收保费860多万元，保险金额超过12亿元。

On May 10, 1935, the Republic of China promulgated *the Postal Life Insurance Law* that stipulated the postal life insurance should be run by the Post Savings & Remittance Co. (PSRC).

An insurance department specialized in postal life insurance was set up in 1935 by the PSRC. During the decade after 1939 in which year the Company moved to Kunming, postal life insurance had made a rapid progress.

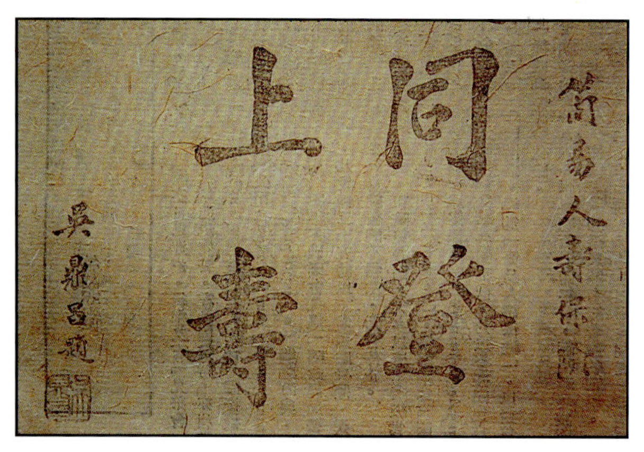

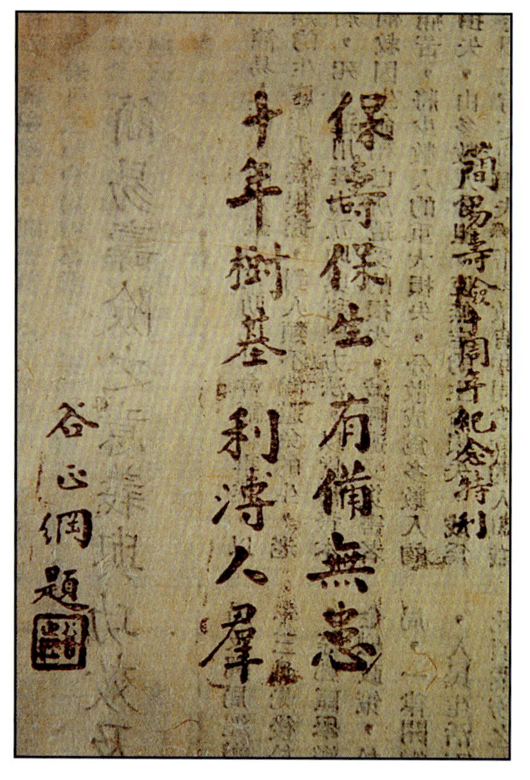

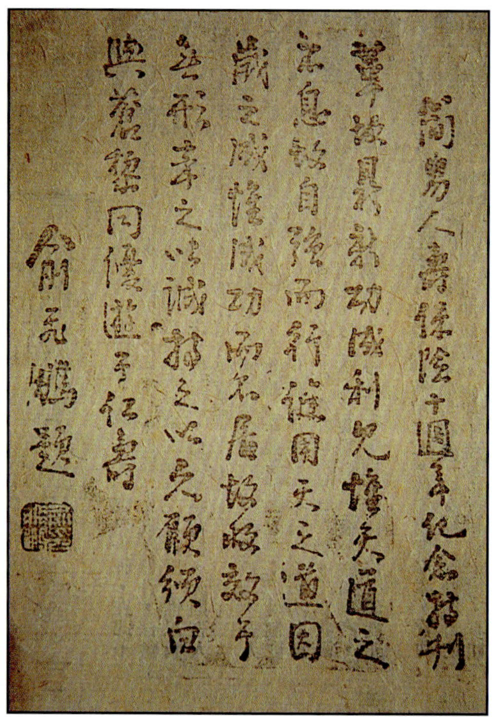

民国要人为简易人寿保险题词
Inscriptions by VIPs of the Republic of China for postal life insurance

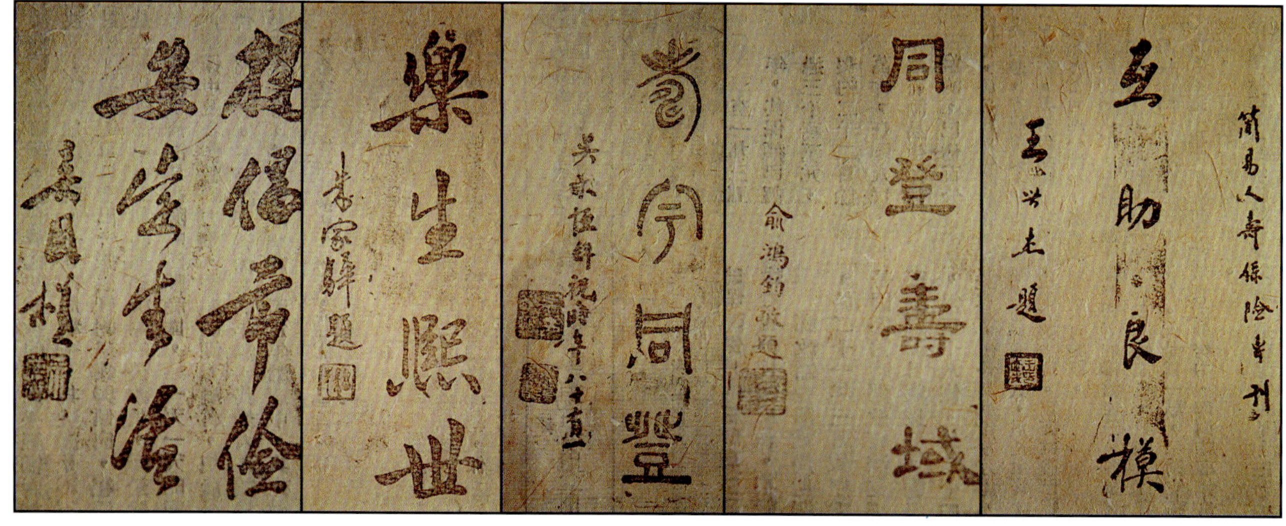

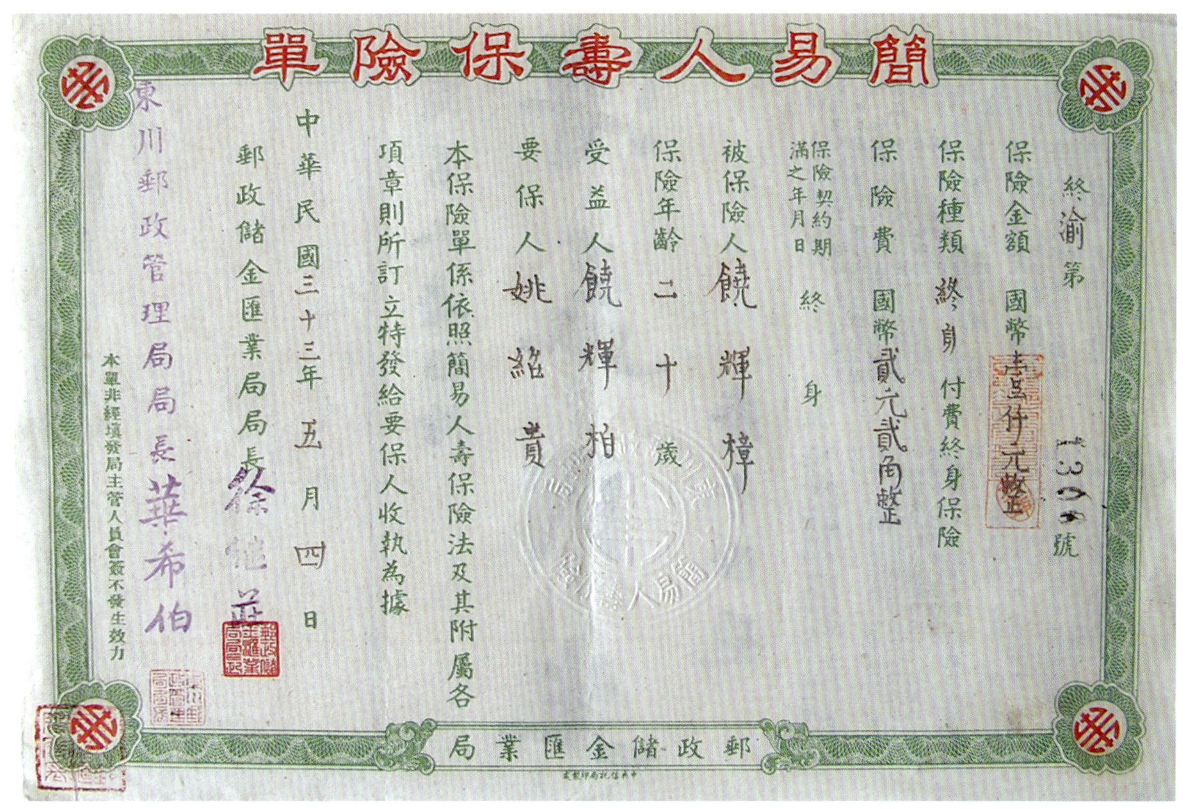

簡易人壽保險單

終渝第1306號

保險金額 國幣壹仟元整
保險種類 終身付費終身保險
保險費 國幣貳元貳角整
保險契約期滿之年月日 終身
被保險人 饒輝樟
保險年齡 二十歲
受益人 饒輝柏
要保人 姚紹貴

本保險單係依照簡易人壽保險法及其附屬各項章則所訂立特發給要保人收執為據

中華民國三十三年五月四日

郵政儲金匯業局局長 徐[illegible]

東川郵政管理局局長 華希伯

本單非經填發局主管人員會簽不發生效力

郵政儲金匯業局

1944年5月4日，东川邮政局签发的简易人寿保险单。（资料提供：成继跃）
Postal life insurance policy issued by Dongchuan Post Office in 1944

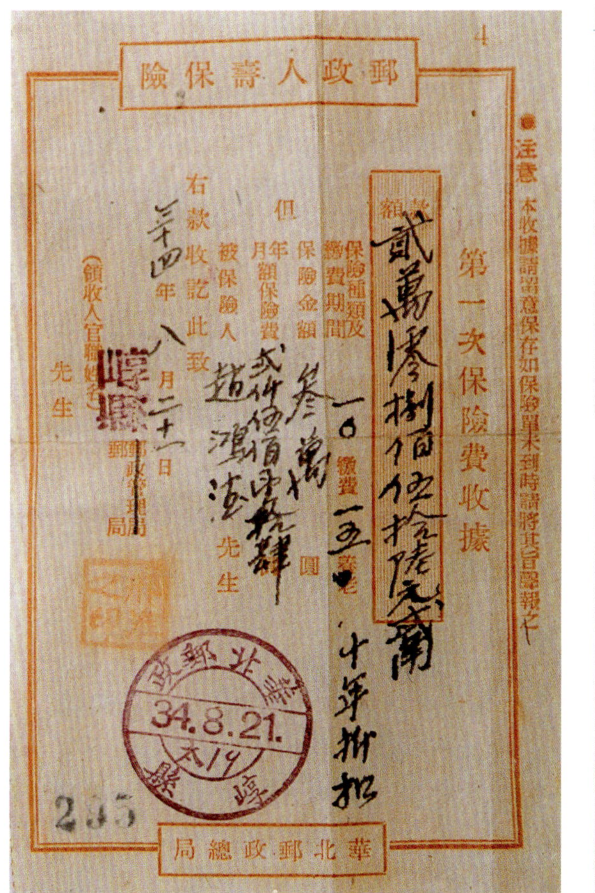

郵政人壽保險

第一次保險費收據

保險種類及繳費期間
保險金額
月額保險費
被保險人 先生
右款收訖此致
年 月 日
（領收人官銜姓名）
郵政局

注意 本收據請留意保存如保險單未到時請將其[illegible]

34.8.21.

華北郵政總局

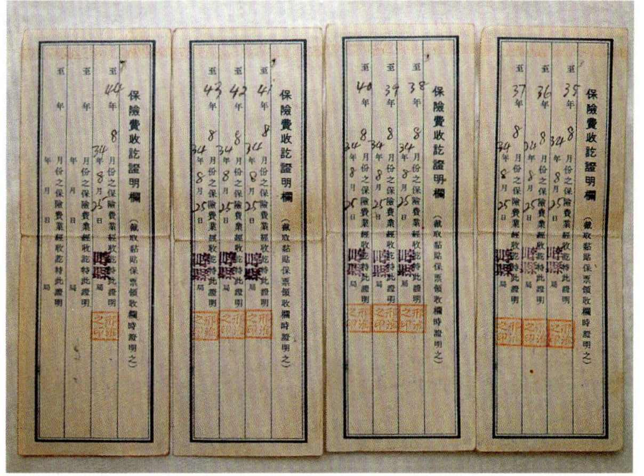

华北邮政总局签发的简易人寿保险保费收据
Premium receipt of postal life insurance issued by North China Post General Office

十二、保险同业公会

Insurance Association

随着民族保险市场的发展，保险同业为联络感情，讨论随时发生的保险事项，保险同业公会组织开始成立。最早成立的类似的组织，是朱葆三于1907年发起成立的华商火险会(上海市保险同业会前身)。1917年改名为华商水火公会。1928年11月改为上海保险同业公会。1931年10月根据国民政府公布的《工商同业会法》，改名为上海市保险业同业公会。由于上海是当时中国保险业的中心，大多数保险公司的总部都设在上海，因此上海市保险业同业公会实际上成为具有全国地位的中国民族保险的同业公会组织。

Some insurance self-discipline organizations came up with the development of Chinese national insurance. The first insurance association is the Chinese Fire Insurance Association initiated by Zhu Baosan, which, in 1931, was reorganized into the Chinese Marine & Fire Insurance Association with its new name as Shanghai Insurance Association in 1928 according to the local law. As a matter of fact, the association was equivalent to a nationwide one, because Shanghai, where it's located in, was the insurance centre of China at that time.

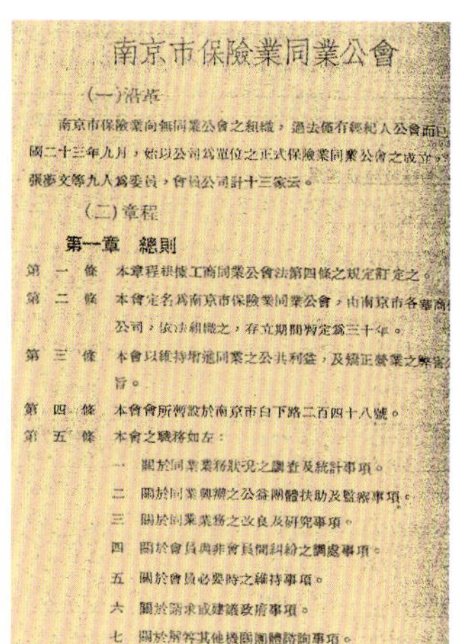

南京市保險業同業公會

(一)沿革

南京市保險業向無同業公會之組織，過去僅有經紀人公會而已……國二十三年九月，始以公司為單位之正式保險業同業公會之成立，……張夢文等九人為委員，會員公司計十三家云。

(二)章程

第一章 總則

第一條 本章程根據工商同業公會法第四條之規定訂定之。

第二條 本會定名為南京市保險業同業公會，由南京市各華商……公司，依法組織之，存立期間暫定為三十年。

第三條 本會以維持增進同業之公共利益，及矯正營業之弊害……旨。

第四條 本會會所暫設於南京市白下路二百四十八號。

第五條 本會之職務如左：

一 關於同業業務狀況之調查及統計事項。

二 關於同業興辦之公益團體扶助及監察事項。

三 關於同業業務之改良及研究事項。

四 關於會員與非會員間糾紛之調處事項。

五 關於會員必要時之維持事項。

六 關於請求或建議政府事項。

七 關於解答其他機關團體諮詢事項。

南京市保险业同业公会章程
Rules of Nanjing Insurance Association

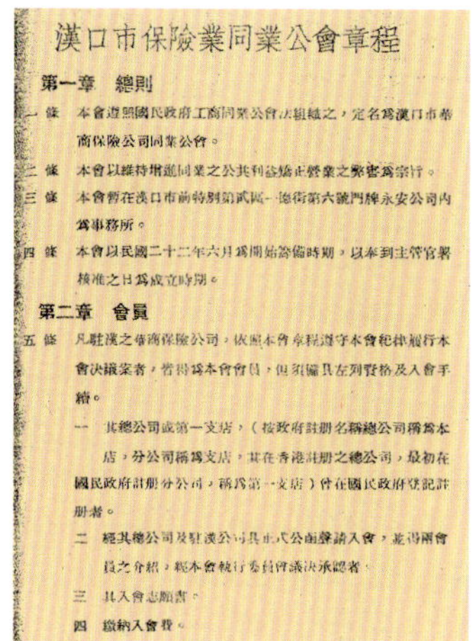

漢口市保險業同業公會章程

第一章 總則

一條 本會遵照國民政府工商同業公會法組織之，定名為漢口市華商保險公司同業公會。

二條 本會以維持增進同業之公共利益矯正營業之弊害為宗旨。

三條 本會暫在漢口市前特別第貳區一德街第六號門牌永安公司內為事務所。

四條 本會以民國二十二年六月為開始籌備時期，以奉到主管官署核准之日為成立時期。

第二章 會員

五條 凡駐漢之華商保險公司，依照本會章程遵守本會紀律履行本會決議案者，皆得為本會會員，但須備具左列資格及入會手續。

一 其總公司或第一支店，（按政府註冊名稱總公司稱為本店，分公司稱為支店，其在香港註冊之總公司，最初在國民政府註冊分公司，稱為第一支店）曾在國民政府登記註冊者。

二 經其總公司及駐漢公司具正式公函聲請入會，並得兩會員之介紹，經本會執行委員會議決承認者。

三 具入會志願書。

四 繳納入會費。

汉口市保险业同业公会章程
Rules on Hankou Insurance Association

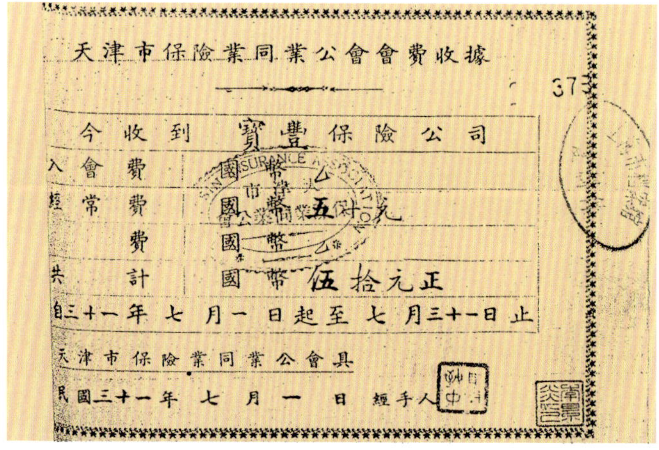

天津市保險業同業公會會費收據

37

今收到	寶豐保險公司
入會費	國幣
經常費	國幣五拾元
費	國幣
共計	國幣伍拾元正

自三十一年七月一日起至七月三十一日止

天津市保險業同業公會具

民國三十一年七月一日 經手人

天津市保险业同业公会会费收据
Receipt of membership fee of Tianjin Insurance Association

1931年10月1日，上海市保险业同业公会成立，图为会议代表合影。
Members Attending the Foundation Conference of the Shanghai Insurance Association

十三、张似旭和中华人寿保险协进社
Zhang Sixu & China Life Insurance Promotion Society

为了传播寿险常识，使更多的国人了解寿险，参加寿险。1932年9月，美国友邦人寿保险公司营业总监，保华保险公司董事张似旭发起组织中华人寿保险协进社。参加的保险公司及代表有，泰山保险公司沈景星、华安合群保寿保险公司薛维藩、四海保险公司杨士珍、宁绍人寿保险公司张素民，先施人寿保险公司霍永区、中国保险公司樊兆鼎。推举张似旭为社长，总编辑郭佩弦、陈克勤、欧阳婉、沈雷春。

Zhang Sixu, supervisor of the Business Department of the Asia Insurance Co. and director of Baohua Insurance Co. initiated to found China Life Insurance Promotion Society (CLIPS) in September 1932 with members as: Shen Jingxing (Taishan Insurance Co.), Xue Weifan (China United Assurance Society), Yang Shizhen (Sihai Insurance Co.), Zhang Sumin (Ningshao Life), Huo Yongqu (Xianshi Life), and Fan Zhaoding (China Insurance Co.); Zhang Sixu was recommended as president; Guo Peixian, Chen Keqin, Ouyang Wan, and Shen Leichun as chief editors.

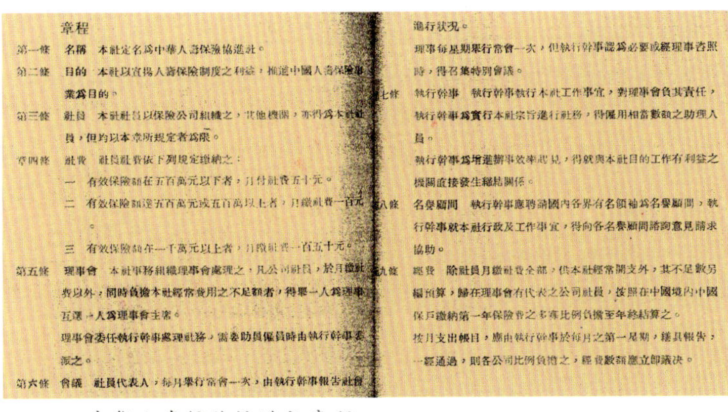

章程

第一條　名稱　本社定名爲中華人壽保險協進社。

第二條　目的　本社以宣揚人壽保險制度之利益，推進中國人壽保險事業爲目的。

第三條　社員　本社社員以保險公司組織之，其他機關，亦得爲本社社員，但均以本章所規定者爲限。

第四條　社費　社員社費依下列規定繳納之：

一　有效保險額在五百萬元以下者，月付社費五十元。

二　有效保險額達五百萬元或五百萬以上者，月繳社費一百元。

三　有效保險額在一千萬元以上者，月繳社費一百五十元。

第五條　理事會　本社事務組織理事會處理之，凡公司社員，於月繳社費以外，同時負擔本社經常費用之不足額者，得舉一人爲理事，互選一人爲理事會主席。

理事會委任執行幹事處理社務，需要助員僱員時由執行幹事委派之。

第六條　會議　社員代表人，每月舉行常會一次，由執行幹事報告社務進行狀況。

理事每星期舉行常會一次，但執行幹事認爲必要或經理事咨照時，得召集特別會議。

第七條　執行幹事　執行幹事執行本社工作事宜，對理事會負其責任，執行幹事爲實行本社宗旨進行社務，得僱用相當數額之助理人員。

執行幹事爲增進辦事效率起見，得就與本社目的工作有利益之機關直接發生締結關係。

第八條　名譽顧問　執行幹事應聘請國內各界有名領袖爲名譽顧問，執行幹事就本社行政及工作事宜，得向各名譽顧問諮詢意見請求協助。

第九條　經費　除社員月繳社費全部，供本社經常開支外，其不足數另編預算，歸在理事會有代表之公司社員，按照在中國境內中國保戶繳納第一年保險費之多寡比例負擔至年終結算之。

按月支出帳目，應由執行幹事於每月之第一星期，繕具報告，一經通過，則各公司比例負擔之，經費數額應立即議決。

中华人寿保险协进社章程
Rules of China Life Insurance Promotion Society

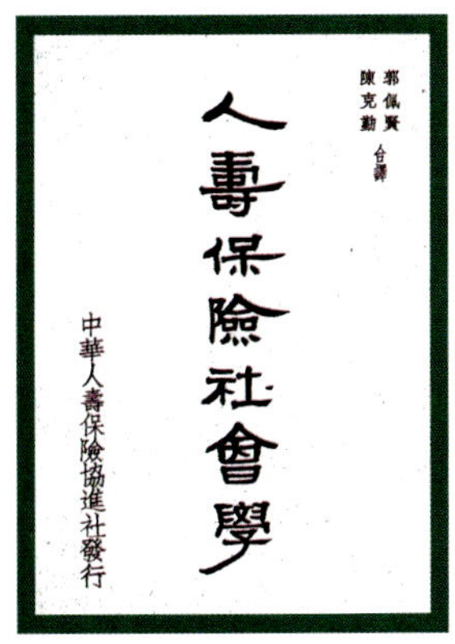

中华人寿保险协进社出版发行的《人寿保险社会学》
Sociology of Life Insurance published by the CLIPS

中华人寿保险协进社社长张似旭
Zhang Sixu: president of the CLIPS

张似旭，美国哈佛大学学士，曾在哥伦比亚大学攻读新闻学。历任华北明星报编辑、苏州东吴大学教授、上海交署秘书、上海国民新闻社编辑、上海大陆报总编辑、国民政府外交部情报司司长、美商友邦人寿保险公司董事、营业总监、保华保险公司总监。1932年9月，发起创办中华人寿保险协进社，被推举为社长。1940年，身为“保卫大中国同盟”上海分会成员的张似旭，因积极参加抗日运动，开展捐献资助新四军活动，于7月19日被日本特务暗杀。

Zhang Sixu worked as a news editor, a college professor, and a government official after his graduation from Havard University and Columbia University. Later he worked for several insurance companies. In 1940, he was assassinated by Japanese spy.

友邦人壽保險公司營業總監

張似旭先生遇害

本月十九日下午四時卅分，靜安寺路七十二號起士林咖啡館中，突發生一恐怖血案，遇害者爲在中外社會負盛譽之張似旭氏。卽友邦人壽保險公司營業總監，暨發行中英文大美晚報及大美報之大美印刷公司董事。兼保華保險公司董事。前中華人壽保險協進社社長。罹難之時身中五鎗，慷慨以殉，消息傳出，全滬震驚，茲分誌各情如下，

最近上海情勢特殊張氏親友及大美印刷公司同事，曾一再敎勸張氏離滬，但張氏，轉惓惓以同人之安危爲念，而不欲「獨善其身」，唯其間會僱有工部局警務處保鏢一名，以資防衛，但旋卽於上星期辭去，該日午後三時許，張氏在大美公畢，卽驅車出外，四時許，氏曾派車夫至其寓取球衣及網拍，四時半，當張氏獨坐起士林咖啡館二樓小憩時，突有暴徒二人，匆匆登樓，不發一言，卽以徒手之張氏爲敵，手出槍遽加轟擊，當時槍聲如珠，張氏不及閃避，隨卽受傷踣地，血流涓涓，默然殞命。

張氏遺體，於下午五時三十分先送宏恩醫院，嗣轉送海格路紅十字會醫院，衣淡灰色小方格華絲紗長衫，週身爲殷紅血跡所浸染，胸前袒露，右頸右臂及背部均有槍痕，張氏遺體，已於翌晚移送萬國殯儀館，當由大美印刷公司組織治喪委員會，其夫人爲美國鹽湖市之華僑，有家屬多人在彼，其夫人之母家中人，與美國議員金格，均係好友，遺有一女，年十二歲，能操三國語言，噩耗所佈，聞耗痛悼者，不獨我保險界人士而已！中外人士，莫不同聲哀悼，其遺氏慷慨殉難後，我國僑彥，業於二十三日晨七時，由萬國殯儀館移至貝當路美國敎堂，於九時舉行莊嚴肅穆之大殮儀式，然後送虹橋公墓下葬，萬方同弔，舉國震悼，張氏身後哀榮，當可隨其貞勇精神，含笑九泉矣。

当时报刊对张似旭死讯的报道
News report on Zhang Sixu's death from murder

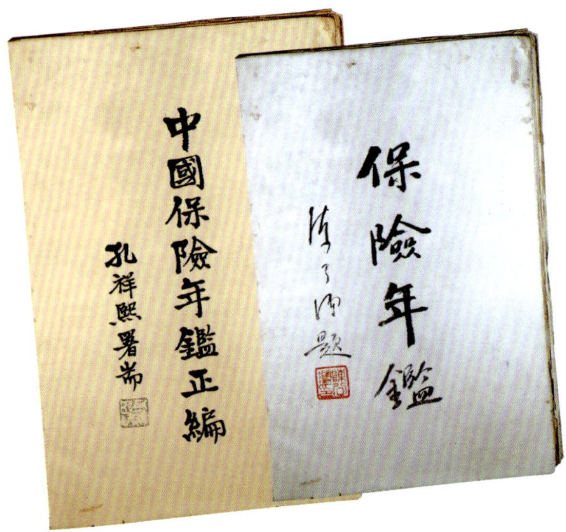

1935、1936年《中国保险年鉴》
China Insurance Yearbooks (1935,1936)

中华人寿保险协进社成立后，积极开展各项活动。主要是演讲会，创办函授学校，在大学中增设保险科，并组织编印出版物。如太平保险公司主办的《保险界》，宁绍人寿保险公司主办《人寿季刊》，还在当时各大报刊上创办专栏。1935年，开始出版了《中国保险年鉴》。这时期，中华人寿保险协进社在保险学术和保险实务研究及宣传工作上作出了重要贡献。

After its foundation, China Life Insurance Promotion Society organized various activities mainly including lecture meetings, originating correspondence schools, adding insurance subject to universities, and organizing complication and publication of journals and yearbooks, etc.

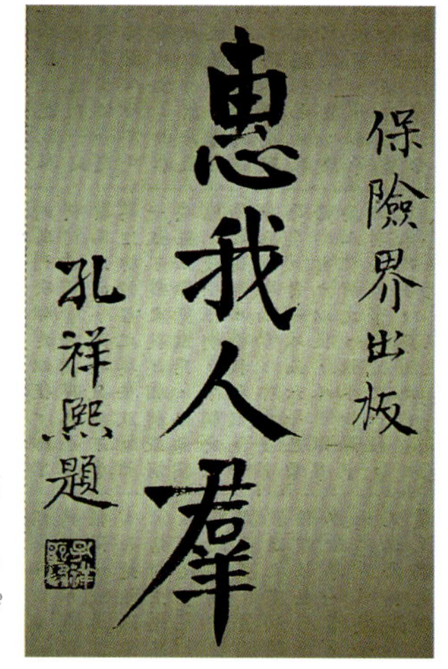

孔祥熙为《保险界》刊物出版题词

Kong Xiangxi's inscription for publication "*Insurance Sector*"

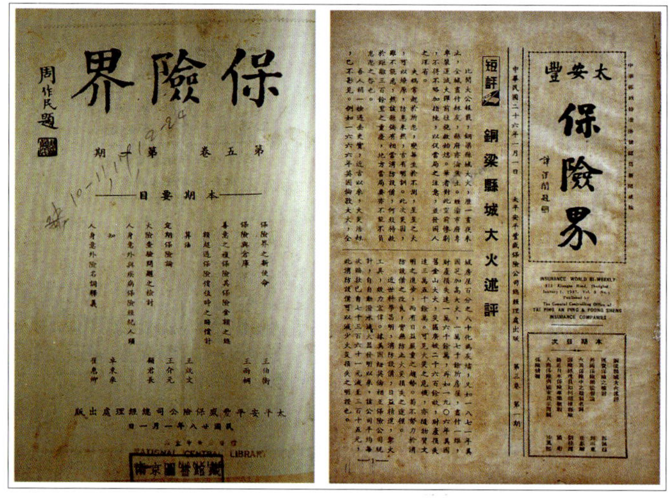

太平(后合并为太安丰)保险公司主办的《保险界》刊物

Publication "*Insurance Sector*" directed by Taiping Insurance Co.

当年出版物上的火险宣传画

A fire insurance poster of the time

宁绍人寿保险出版的《人寿》季刊，马寅初、张公权等分别题写刊名。

Quarterly *Life Insurance* published by Ningshao Life

十四、中国第一个保险学术团体：中国保险学会

China Insurance Society: First Academic Body of Chinese Insurance

1935年8月3日，中国第一个保险学术团体——中国保险学会在上海静安寺路（现南京西路）华安大厦（现华侨饭店）二楼正式举行成立大会。出席大会的代表30余人，公推宋汉章为大会主席。会上选出宋汉章、张素民、罗北辰、丁雪农、胡咏骐、张明昕、刘聪强、王效文、朱如堂、项馨吾、吕岳泉、徐可升、经乾坤、顾庆毅、董汉槎15人为第一届理事，互选宋汉章、胡咏骐、张明昕、丁雪农、刘聪强5人为常务理事，公推宋汉章为理事长，王效文为名誉秘书，项馨吾为名誉会计。8月21日，举行会员临时大会，通过了理事会修订的《中国保险学会章程》，共7章23条。在总纲第二条开宗明义地提出，中国保险学会以研究保险学理，促进保险事业为宗旨。章程第5条规定了保险学会的任务为：(1)研究保险学理；(2)调查保险实务；(3)编制保险统计；(4)拟订保险条款；(5)训练保险人才；(6)举办保险演讲；(7)发行保险书刊；(8)创设保险图书馆；(9)组织各种保险研究会。

China Insurance Society, China's first academic body of insurance, was founded on August 3, 1935 in Shanghai; over 30 delegates attended the inauguration of the society; Song Hanzhang was elected as chairman of the society. Thereafter, the society has played an important role in promoting the development of insurance.

1935年8月5日，中国保险学会成立大会合影。
A group photo to memorialise the founding of the Society in 1935

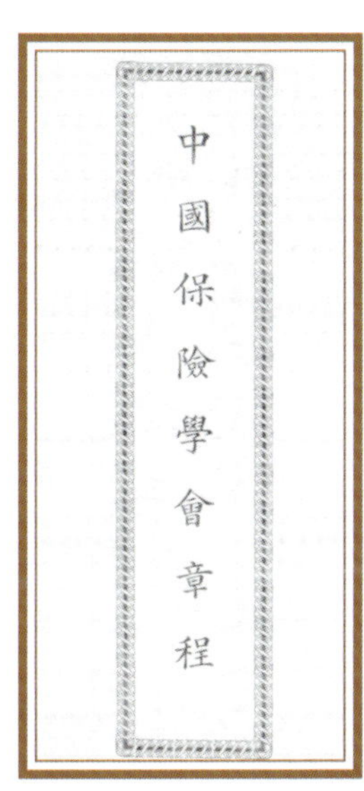

Rules of China Insurance Society

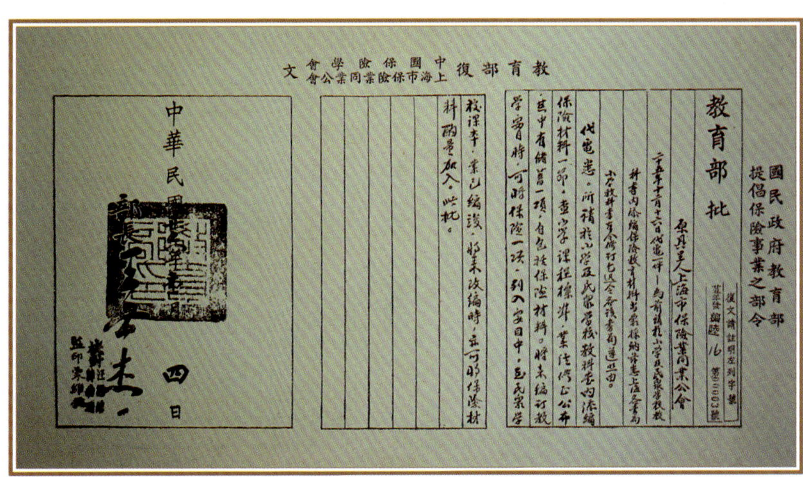
教育部復中國保險學會 上海市保險業同業公會文

國民政府教育部提倡保險事業之部令

教育部批

中華民國 四 日

国民政府教育部与中国保险学会、上海市保险业同业公会发布的提倡保险事业的部令。
Directive to develop life insurance, Issued by the Education Ministry, China Insurance Society and Shanghai Insurance Association

中国保险学会第一届年会合影
Members Attending the First Annual Conference of China Insurance Society

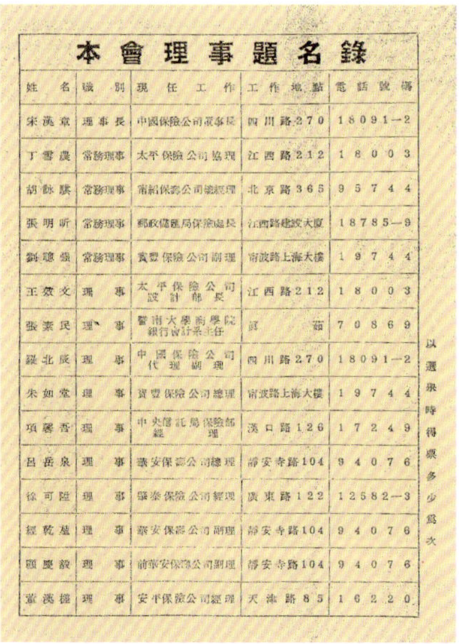

本會理事題名錄

姓名	職別	現任工作	工作地點	電話號碼
宋漢章	理事長	中國保險公司董事長	四川路270	18091—2
丁雪農	常務理事	太平保險公司協理	江西路212	18003
胡詠騏	常務理事	寧紹保險公司總經理	北京路365	95744
張明昕	常務理事	郵政儲匯局保險處長	江西路建設大厦	18785—9
劉聰強	常務理事	寶豐保險公司副理	寧波路上海大樓	19744
王效文	理事	太平保險公司設計部長	江西路212	18003
張素民	理事	暨南大學商學院銀行會計系主任	真茹	70869
羅北辰	理事	中國保險公司代理副理	四川路270	18091—2
朱如堂	理事	寶豐保險公司總理	寧波路上海大樓	19744
項馨吾	理事	中央信託局保險部經理	漢口路126	17249
呂岳泉	理事	泰安保險公司總理	靜安寺路104	94076
徐可陞	理事	肇泰保險公司經理	廣東路122	12582—3
經乾堃	理事	華安保險公司副理	靜安寺路104	94076
顧慶毅	理事	前華安保險公司副理	靜安寺路104	94076
董漢槎	理事	安平保險公司經理	天津路85	16220

以選舉時得票多少爲次

中国保险学会理事名录
Director list of China Insurance Society

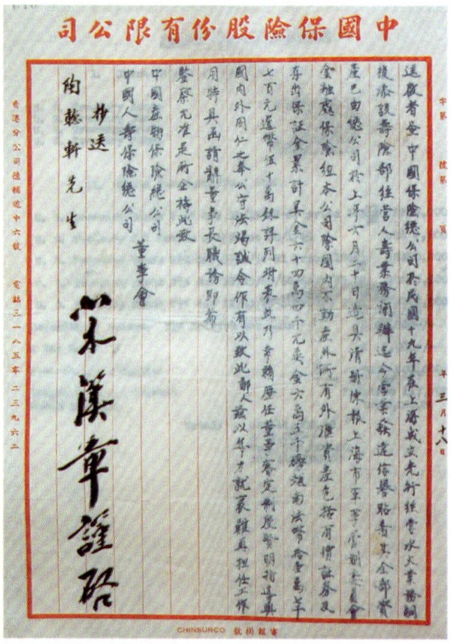

解放后宋汉章写给中国保险公司的辞职函
Song Hanzhang's resignation letter to China Insurance Co.

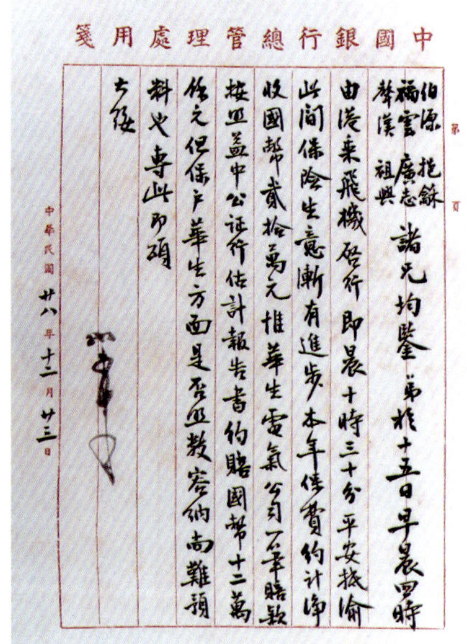
中國銀行總管理處用箋

伯源 福雲 華漢 艳鉌 廣志 祖興 諸兄均鑒：弟於十五日早晨四時由港乘飛機啓行，即晨十時三十分平安抵渝。此間保險生意漸有進步，本年保費約計净收國幣貳拾萬元，惟華生電氣公司不幸賠款，按照益中公證行估計報告書約賠國幣十二萬餘元，但保戶華生方面是否照數容納，尚難預料也。專此，即頌大綏。

中華民國廿八年十二月廿三日

1939年，宋汉章致过福云等人的信函。
Song Hanzhang's letter to Guo Fuyun, etc. in 1939.

創刊詞

宋漢章

嘗聞欲覘一國國民經濟興替消長之跡象，但觀國內保險事業發展之榮枯，斯言也，不佞始疑而終信之。良以保險事業，實操整個社會經濟基礎安定與否之重要關鍵，安定則趨繁榮，反是則殆，表裏相因，事理至明。

不佞學殖荒疏，對於保險知識，初屬門外，卒因感於我國保險事業之落後，及與國計民生關係之重要，雖年逾耳順，而忘其衰庸，毅然從事，精衛塡海，志切補裨。客歲復承中國保險學會諸君子之謬愛，推長理事，一載以還，建樹毫無，尸位之咎，衾影滋慚。

此次本會有刊行保險季刊之舉，環顧國內保險定期刊物，寥若晨星，本刊之產生，自有其重大之意義與必要。不惟業斯者藉可溝通聲氣，灌輸新知，以達事實與學理互相印證，共作進一步之切磋。即各界人士對於保險事業，亦可因此而獲正確之認識，加強其信仰，以收

宋汉章为《保险季刊》撰写的创刊词
Prologue by Song Hanzhang for the *Insurance Quarterly*

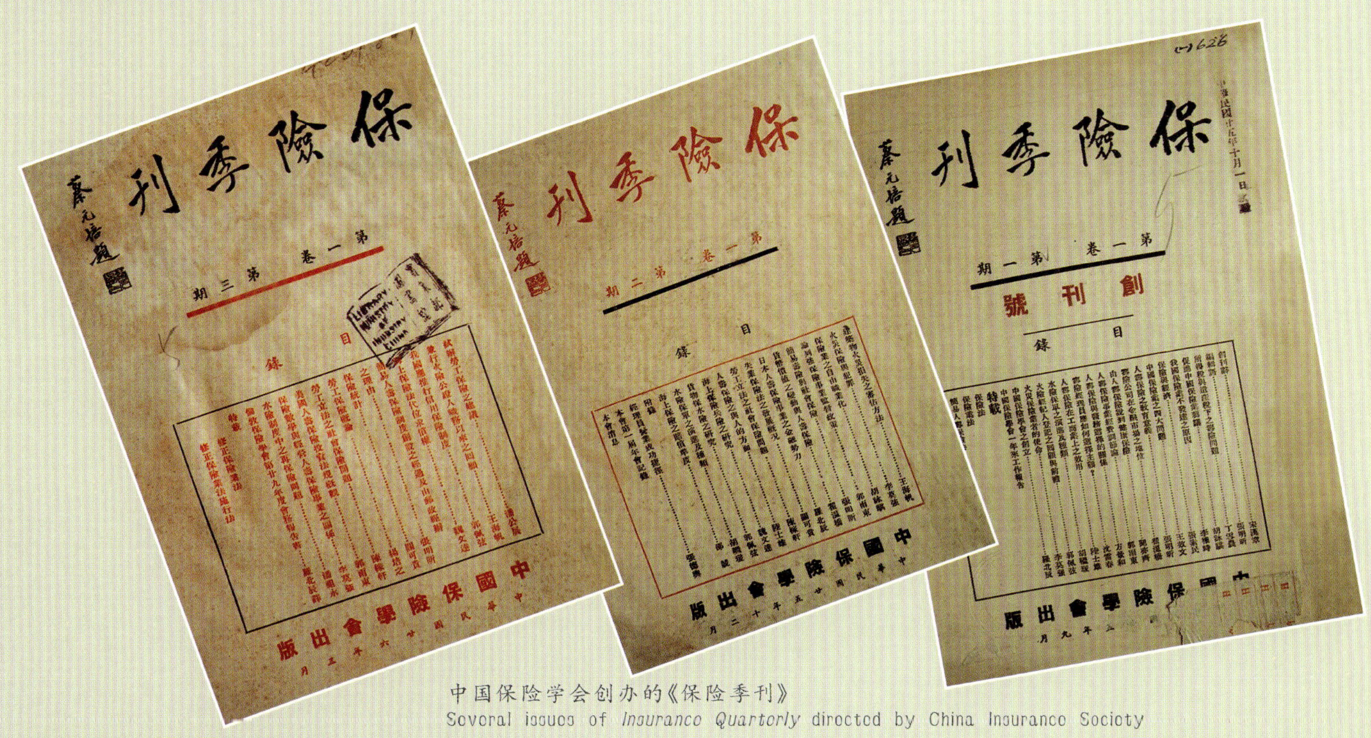

中国保险学会创办的《保险季刊》
Several issues of *Insurance Quarterly* directed by China Insurance Society

十五、中央信托局的保险业务
Insurance Business by the Central Trust Co.

1935年10月1日，中央信托局在上海正式成立，经营各种信托业务，理事长由孔祥熙兼任。成立时由中央银行拨给资本1000万元，开始只经营信托、储蓄、易货、运输等业务。1935年11月，为扩大资金来源，追求丰厚的保险盈利及保障自身资金的安全，由中央银行一次拨款500万元增设保险部，办理火险、水险、兵盗险、汽车险、寿险、一切产物及人身意外险，并经营分保业务。

中央信托局保险部开业后，业务飞速增长。1935年承保金额仅3702.3万元(其中火险为为487.2万元；水险为3215.1万元)，保费收入7.5万元。到1937年，承保金额（不包括兵险）猛增为100696.4万元（其中火险为23509.9万元，水险为77186.5万元），共收入保费207万元。1937年抗战开始后，业务重心转向西南、西北诸省。1937年10月18日，为配合战时需要，中央信托局保险部正式承保运输兵险（1940年改为战时运输兵险）。1939年12月8日，又承保战时陆地兵险，其承保对象大都是工厂与仓库，以及部分指定的商店和轮渡设施。承办战时运输兵险和战时陆地兵险，对保障农工矿产品的运输安全，充实战时资源，安定后方生产起了积极作用。1941年3月，中央信托局将保险部寿险办事处扩充改组为人寿保险处，投资国币1000万元，主要办理免检的国民寿险、储蓄寿险、终身寿险、公务人员团体寿险、厂矿职工团体保险、养老年金以及人寿再保险等业务。原保险部则更名为产物保险处，主要办理再保险和战时兵险业务。

抗战胜利后，中央信托局人寿保险处和产物保险处随中央信托局总局迁回上海。返沪后每月仅保费收入就在2亿元左右，主要为各政府机关投保的运输险。1949年底中央信托局被人民政府接管，其保险业务宣告结束。

Operating diversified trust businesses, the Central Trust Co. was established on October 1, 1935, while Kong Xiangxi took concurrent board chairman. In November 1935, the Insurance Department of the Central Trust Co. was established with the capital of the Central Bank to run businesses including property, life insurance, and reinsurance. During the War of Resistance Against Japan, it underwrote transportation war insurance, which made it pay a large amount of indemnity for the insured. The Central Trust Co. was taken over by the government of the People's Republic of China after the liberation.

中央信托局理事长——孔祥熙
Kong Xiangxi: director-general of the Central Trust Co.

项馨吾(1899—1982)，江苏嘉定人，毕业于上海澄衷学堂，1915年进入中国银行实习并拜总经理张嘉嫩为师。1929年，被派至伦敦中国银行办事处任秘书。1931年，中国银行开设保险部，并指命项馨吾在伦敦改学保险。研究保险学说，同时进入伦敦经济学院就读，1932年，他入伦敦太阳保险公司实习。1933年返国，出任中国保险公司副经理。

1935年，中央信托局成立保险处，项出任经理。保险处后分为产物保险处及人寿保险处，项又改任产物保险处经理直至1948年。抗战胜利后，项应国营招商局邀请筹办中国航联意外责任保险及中国航联产物保险两大保险公司。公司开业前，于1948年初又奉中央信托局委派前往美国纽约设立中央信托局纽约分局，经营财产保险业务，为中国第一家在保险发达国家开设的保险公司，后于1957年停办。1958年应美亚保险公司创办人Starr的邀请参加该公司，任职于火险部及再保险部。1974年退休，时年75岁。1982年病逝于美国新泽西州。

Xiang Xinwu (1899—1982), born in Jiangsu, was employed as the manager of the Insurance Department of the Central Trust Co. in 1935 and manager of the Property Insurance Department when the Insurance Department was separated into property and life insurance department. In the spring of 1948, Xiang was sent to the USA to prepare the foundation of the Central Trust Co. New York Branch (closed down in 1957) to specialize in property insurance. In 1958, Mr. Starr invited him to work for the Fire Insurance and Reinsurance Department of the American Asiatic Underwriters. He retired in 1974 and passed away in 1982 in America.

中央信託局保險部業務規則

民國二十四年十一月印行

1935年中央信托局保险部业务规则

Regulations on Insurance Business of the Central Trust Co. (1935)

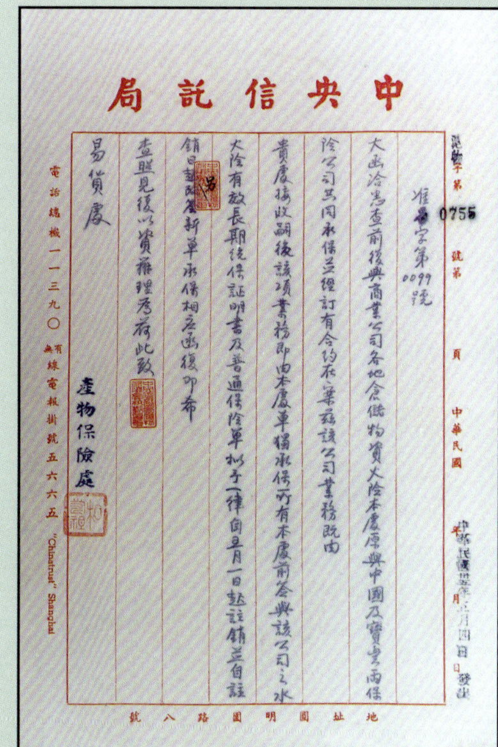

中央信託局

准產字第0099號

大函洽悉查前後與商業公司各地倉儲物資火險本處原與中國及寶豐兩保險公司共同承保並經訂有合約在案茲該公司業務既由貴處接收嗣後該項業務即由本處單獨承保所有本處前簽與該公司之水火險有效長期統保證明書及普通保險單擬予一律自五月一日起註銷並自註銷日起改簽新單承保相應函復即希查照見復以資辦理為荷此致

易貨處

產物保險處

中華民國廿五年五月四日發出

電話總機一一一三九〇 有無線電報掛號五六六五 "Chinatrust" Shanghai

地址 圓明園路八號

1936年5月，中央信托局产物保险处业务函。

Business Letter of the Property Insurance Department of the Central Trust Co.

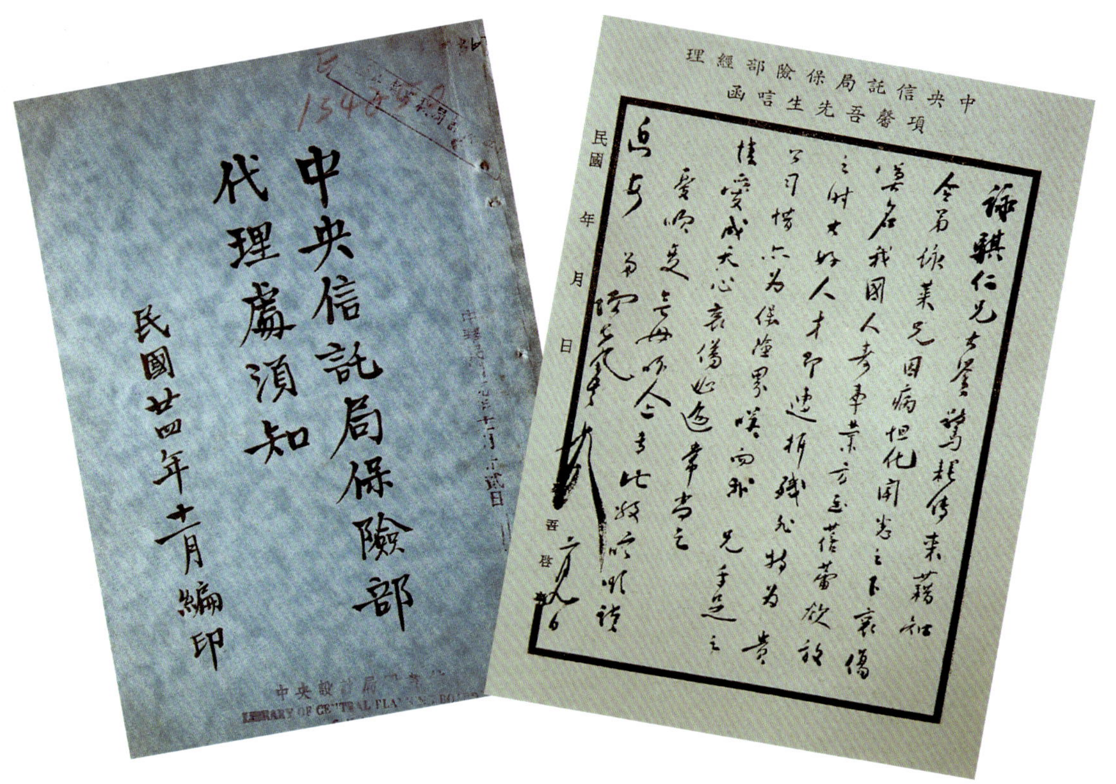

1935年，中央信托局保险部代理处须知。
Guide of the Agency Department of the Central Trust Co. (1935)

中央信托局保险部经理项馨吾致胡咏骐的手写函
Xiang Xinwu's original letter to Hu yongqi

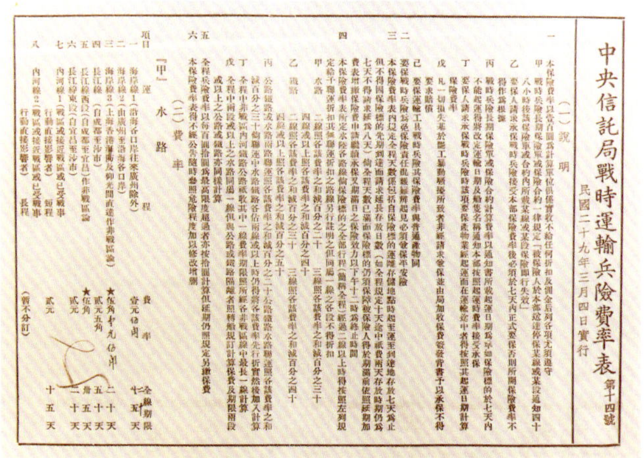
中央信託局戰時運輸兵險費率表 第十四號
民國二十九年三月四日實行

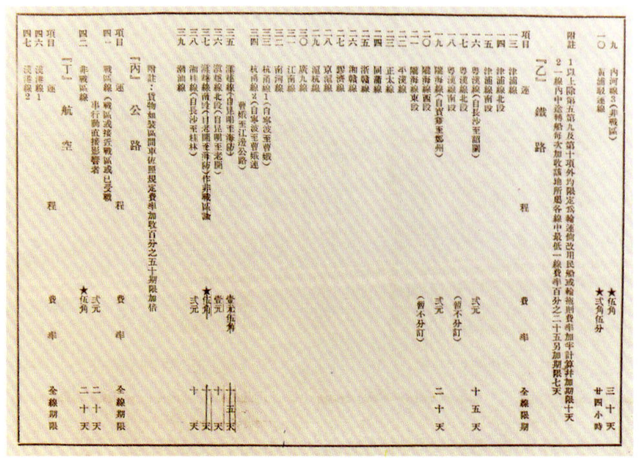

中央信託局
保險部
國民政府特准設立
資本國幣伍百萬圓
業務種類
火險 一般船舶險 水陸聯運險 郵包險 汽車險 電梯意外險 壽險 意外傷害險 航空意外險
局址上海漢口路一二六號
電話 一七二四九 一四〇八六
電報掛號 五六六五號
各埠均有代理處

中央信托局保险部广告
Ad of the Insurance Department of the Central Trust Co.

1940年3月，中央信托局实行的战时运输兵险费率表。
The Central Trust Co.'s rate scale for wartime transportation war insurance in March 1940

1939年7月，中央信托局保险部为开办战时陆地兵险业务，从上海选聘13位保险界优秀人物南下昆明联系业务。后被保险界誉为“十三太保”，他们是：张仲良（美亚保险公司）、林震峰（中国保险公司）、程恩树（宁绍保险公司）、包玉刚（英商保裕保险公司）、唐雄俊（中国保险公司）、沈雍康（四明保险公司）、茅子嘉（华商联合保险公司）、徐曾渭（中国保险公司）、周志斌（英商上海保险行）、胡肇忠（四海保险公司）、沈尔元（中国保险公司）、童肇麟（四明保险公司）、赵镇圭（美商慎昌保险公司）。

上列13人在“一切为了祖国”的口号下，组成了一个坚强的团体，在当时内地大片领土被日军占领的情况下，绕道香港、越南海防，辗转来到昆明，顺利完成陆地兵险的组织与筹备工作。

中央信托局上海办事处旧址
Site of the Central Trust Co. Shanghai Branch

In July 1939, to launch land war insurance, the Central Trust Co. selected and engaged 13 excellent persons in Shanghai to go southward to Kunming to prepare the land war insruance; they are later reputed as “thirteen go-getters” by the sector.

In the situation that a majority of the inland was occupied by Japanese troops, the 13 persons floundered to Kunming via the detour to Hongkong and Vietnamese coast defence, and smoothly completed their commission to prepare the insurance.

1939年中央信托局选聘的13名业务骨干(誉称“十三太保”)合影于榆园西楼(照片提供：林震峰)
The selected 13 business elites at the Xilou of Yuyuan (1939)

抗战时期，在日机轰炸下的重庆中央信托局保险部。

Insurance Department of the Central Trust Co. after Japanese bombing

包玉刚，浙江宁波人。1931年，离家到汉口父亲包兆龙的平和鞋庄学做生意，不久包玉刚对制鞋业失去兴趣。他向父亲提出，要到英商安利洋行保险部工作。包兆龙同意了他的要求。此后，包玉刚又就职于中央信托局保险部。

Bao Yugang: first worked at a British Company; later a employee of the Insurance Department of the Central Trust Co.

50年代中期，相寿祖（右一，中央信托局产物保险处）、陈萱（右二，中国航联保险公司）、朱孔嘉（右三）、史带（右四，美亚保险公司）、陈长桐（右五，中国保险公司）、丁雪农（太平保险公司）在台北合影。（照片提供：康继超）

Xiang Shouzu (R1, Insurance Dept. of Central Trust Co.), Chen Xuan (R2, China Aviation Federation Insurance Co.), Zhu Kongjia (R3), Shi Dai (L3, AAU), Chen Changtong (L2, China Insurance Co.), and Ding Xuenong (L1, Taiping Insurance Co.) in Taipei in mid-1950's.

十六、保险印花税与保险印纸
Insurance Stamp Tax & Insurance Yinzhi (Tax Receipt)

中国保险印花税和征收起始于清朝末年，正式实施于民国初期，延续至新中国解放初期。1911年，北洋政府决定将清末酝酿已久的印花税付诸实施。1912年10月21日，北洋政府由临时大总统令公布施行《印花税法》。在这部税法中，北洋政府对三类35种凭证征收印花税。保险单被列为第二类凭证。1934年12月8日，国民政府公布了24条、3类35个税目的《印花税法》，并制定了执行细则，定于1935年9月1日起在全国施行。保险单被列为第一类商事产权凭证，适用税率为“按保额每千元贴花2分，超过之数不及1000元的按1000元计贴。每件保额不满1000元的免贴。”

保险印纸属于印花税票的一种，目前发现的有“中国图”保险税票、“长城图”保险印纸和“华北人寿”保险票。这些保险税票产生于抗日战争开始前后，大量使用于抗日战争时期，因受日本经济文化的影响，保险印花税票被称为印纸，为了区分印花税票，人们习惯上把保险税票统称为保险印纸。

Chinese insurance stamp tax and its being levied is started from the late Qing Dynasty and officially carried out in the early Republic of China till the early period of the liberation of China.

As a kind of stamp tax receipts, insurance Yinzhi has been currently found in the ways of insurance tax receipt with “Chinese Map”, insurance tax receipt with “Great Wall Picture”, and insurance receipt with “North China Life Insurance”, which came into being in the period of the War of Resistance Against Japan. Influenced by Japanese economy and culture, insurance stamp tax receipt is called Yinzhi and, in order to distinguish it from stamp tax receipt, it's customarily called by a joint name as insurance Yinzhi.

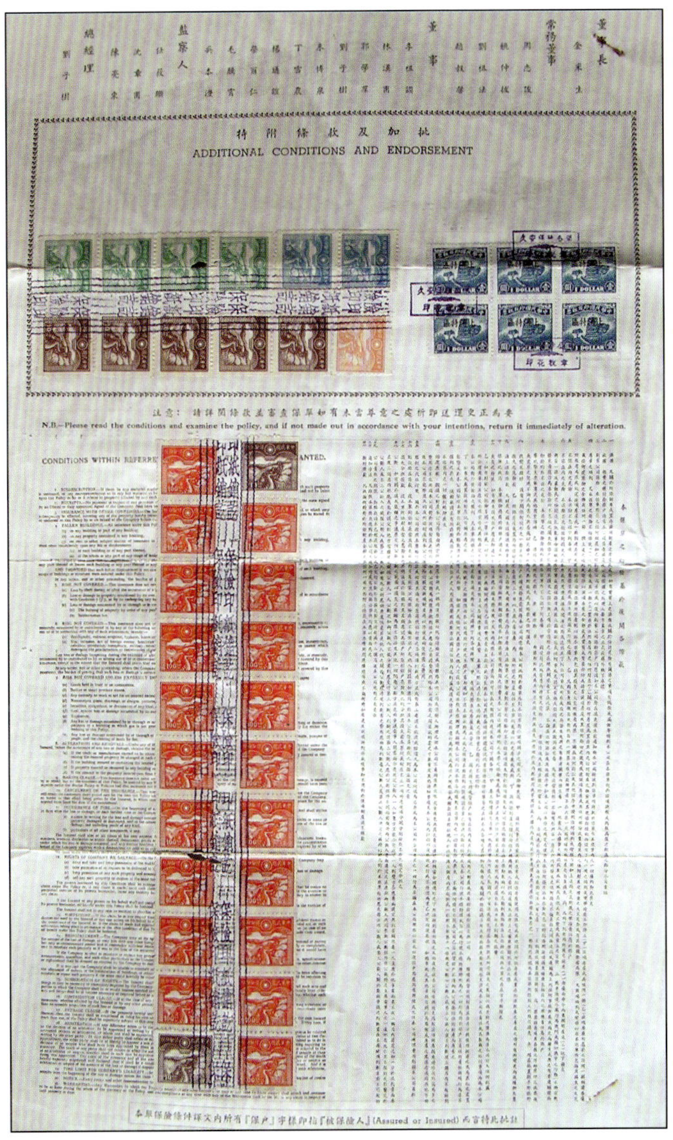

1943年5月12日，上海久安保险公司签发的火险保险单，保单背面贴“长城图”保险印纸（印花税票）40张。（资料提供：成继跃）

Fire insurance policy with 40 “Great-Wall-Picture” stamp tax receipts on its back issued by Shanghai Jiuan Insurance Co. in 1943

民国政府发行的面值壹角的"长城图"保险印纸(资料提供:成继跃)

"Great-Wall-Picture" insurance Yinzhi with par value of 1 Jiao (0.1 yuan) issued by the Republic of China

抗日战争时期,伪华北政府对人寿保险业征收印花税,图为伪华北邮政局设计的人寿保险税票样票。(资料提供:成继跃)

Specimen of life insurance tax receipt designed by Post office under the Japanese North-China government during the War of Resistance Against Japan

十七、早期保险学术著作
Early Insurance Compositions

由于中国民族保险业是一项新兴的事业，比之外商保险公司，它的历史短，实力差，专业人才缺乏，处于劣势地位。华商保险公司的一切章程、契约、保险单证等，都是照搬外国保险公司的成规，对于保险原理、业务技术等方面，很少注意研究改进，至于有关保险书籍更属凤毛麟角。鉴于上述情况，保险业有识之士大力提倡研究保险学术理论，宣传普及保险知识，振兴民族保险事业。

王效文所著的《保险学》，出版于1925年，马寅初在序言中称："吾国向无所谓保险学，有之，自本书始。"

In 1925, *Insurance* by Wang Xiaowen was published in Shanghai, which, as the first insurance monograph in China, was highly appreciated by Ma Yanchu in its prologue. Thereafter lots of books of this kind were published.

王效文著的《保险学》是我国第一部保险学术专著
Insurance by Wang Xiaowen

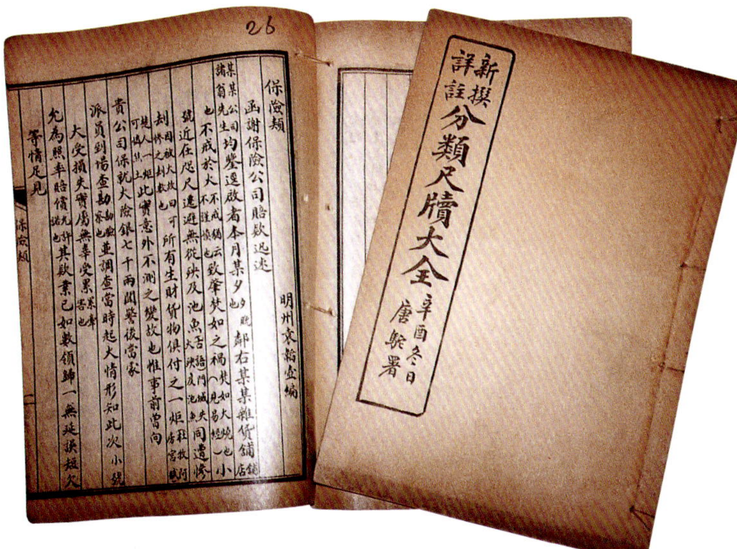

1921年出版的新撰译注《分类尺牍大全》，全书共31类，保险类编排在第30类，介绍了关于保险公文信函的写作。
Collection of Classified Correspondences published in 1921, introducing the composition of insurance archives

商务印书馆发行的早期保险著作
Books on insurance theory

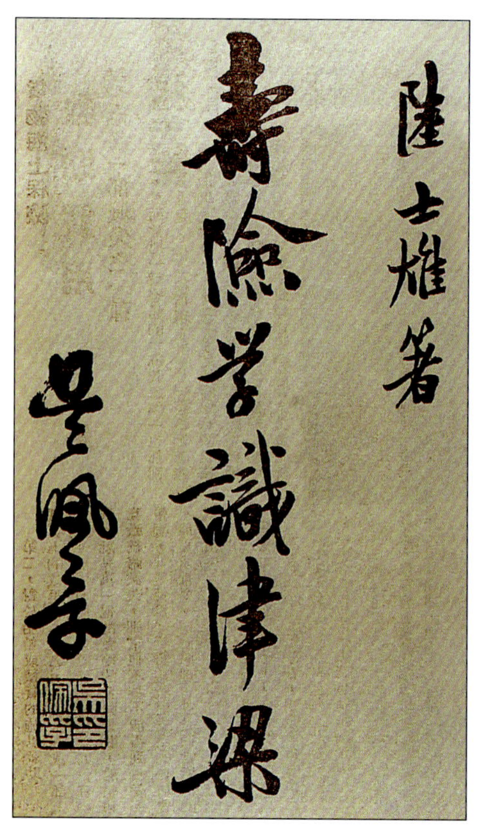

吴佩孚为陆士雄著书题字
Life Insurance Guide by Lu Shixiong

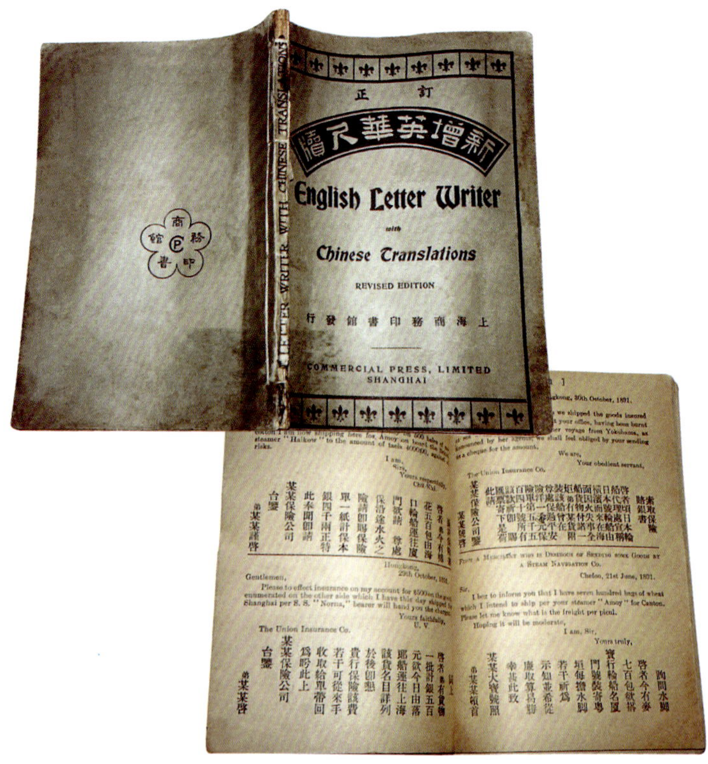

1922年上海商务印书馆出版的《新增英华尺牍》，介绍了保险公文的写作方法。
New Added Sino—British Correspondences published by Shanghai Commercial Press in 1922, introducing the composition of insurance archives

十八、保险中介的发展

Development of Insurance Intermediary

上海聯保水火險公司

上海聯保水火險公司(三)

代理處所在地及代理人

代理處所在地	代理人姓名	詳細地址及電報電[話]
天津	龍孝治	日租界明石街20
鎮江	吳季衡	江邊馬路
九江	李廣記	
杭州	何劍夏	蠡頭巷34
烟台	馬翼君	劉公祠街
烟台	關瑞芬	朝陽街
青島	仇光齋	北平路82東泰號
威海衛	公盛利	
龍口	熾昌厚	
遼甯	聯保公司	大淸宮前
營口	孫辛堂	
長春	趙繩武	
吉林	翟雅泉	
大黑河	東安祥	
大黑河	王昇恆	
黑龍江	廣信號	
富錦	義泰	
富錦	東記茶莊	
珠河	大合泰	
海拉爾	興亞商店	
滿洲里	源茂號	
阿什河	復興永號	
一面坡	復昌盛號	
泰安鎮	合順昌號	
三岔河	福玉恆絲房	
公主嶺	張磐九	
郭家店	永豐泰號	一道街
范家屯	張磐九	
安東	聚祥泰號	
普蘭店	永慶棧	
卅里堡	玉成和	
富爾基	裕順厚	
金州	程香閣	
星加坡	亞洲公司	

30年代上海联保水火保险公司代理人一览表

Agency list of Shanghai United marine & Fire Insurance Co. in 1930's

中国保险的中介始于洋行和银行的保险代理，继而有了保险经纪人和保险公估行。

1861年，琼记洋行与三家纽约保险公司签订代理合同，开始了大规模的保险业务，成为第一家在中国充当美国大保险公司代理人的美国洋行，直到1912年才有华商保险代理处出现。1912年1月，天津老顺记五金商号代理华兴保险公司经营火险，是华商最早出现的保险代理处之一。

到了30年代，各大保险公司在全国都设有几十个代理处或代理人。

The intermediary of Chinese insurance started from the insurance agencies by foreign firms and banks, and then, they developed into insurance brokers and insurance survey & loss rating companies.

It's not until in 1912, Tianjin Laoshunji Metals Co. began to act as the agency of fire insurance business of Huaxing Insurance Co., marked a first Chinese insurance agency appeared in China.

上海保险业经纪人公会第一届执监委员合影

Executive and Supervisory Members (First Session) of Shanghai Insurance Brokers Association

1924年9月，外商保险公会与保险公司买办及保险经纪人签订一项新协议，成立保险买办及经纪人组织公会，买办须交纳500两保证金，经纪人为100两，公会发给经纪人由外商保险公司董事会签发的护照。买办薪金一般由外商保险公会审定，大约在100—300两之间，一般提取其招揽保险额的一成为佣金。

宿晋初是英商怡和保险公司的经纪人。1925年5月宿晋初在《新无锡》报上刊登招揽本年度蚕茧险公启，费率为20%，此时该公司所定费率为15%。

1932年5月，上海保险公会推选丁雪农等5位代表与外商保险公司讨论火险实价问题，在其后所作的汇报中指出："……将定率登中西各报，一一公布，使保户明了价额，无论其向公司亲自投保，或委托经纪人代为投保，均应照定率实付。至经纪人所招揽之生意，由公司在所交保费内提出百分之十五为佣金，保户但照费实付，无须过问。"

1936年4月，华商组织的上海保险业同业公会和洋商组织的上海火险公会联合设置的华洋联合委员会，制定并由双方公会通过《火险经纪人登记与管理规章》，规定：(1)禁止经纪人非法发还回扣与被保险人；(2)限定经纪人之营业资格；(3)限定经纪人佣金，为实收保费的20%；(4)举办经纪人登记。同年12月6日，上海保险业经纪人公会成立，第一届常务会员为朱晋椒、郭佩弦、王梅卿、李百祥、潘垂统。朱晋椒为主席。

In September 1924, foreign insurance associations and brokers came to an agreement to jointly found an insurance brokers association.

In April 1936, *Regulations on Registration & Management of Fire Insurance Brokers* was promulgated by Shanghai Fire Insurance Association. In the same year, Shanghai Fire Insurance Brokers Association was founded; Zhu Jinjiao was selected as Chairman of the association.

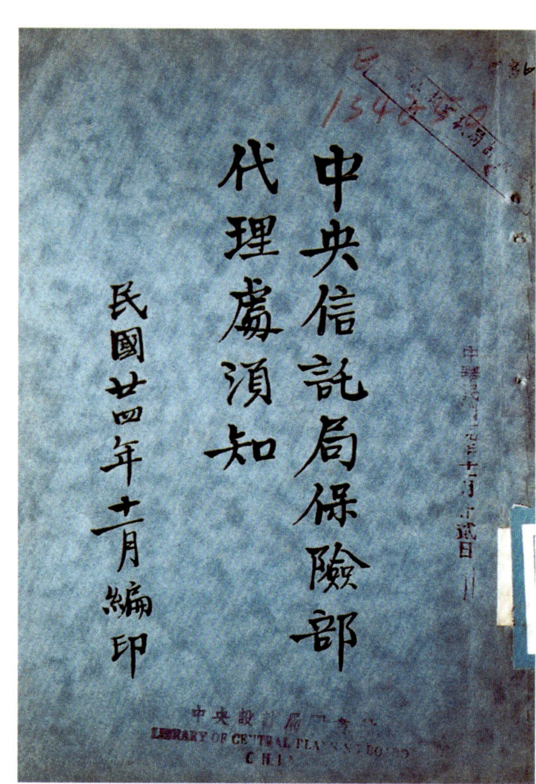

中央信托保险部为加强代理处管理编印的手册
Handbook to Strengthen the Management of Agency, edited by Insurance Department of Central Trust Co.

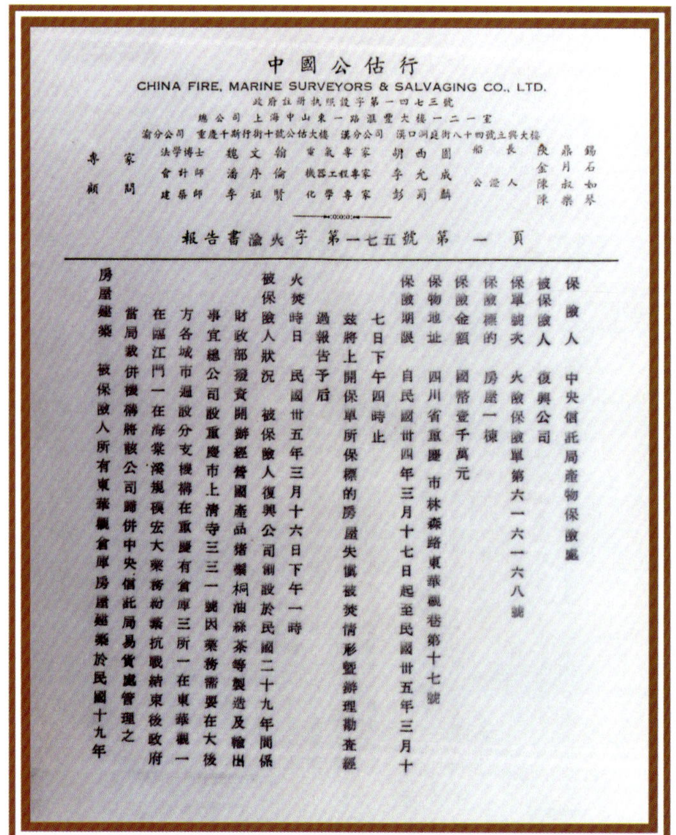

中國公估行
CHINA FIRE, MARINE SURVEYORS & SALVAGING CO., LTD.
政府註冊執照設字第一四七三號
總公司 上海中山東一路滙豐大樓一二一室
渝分公司 重慶千廝行街十號公估大樓 漢分公司 漢口洞庭街八十四號立興大樓

專家顧問 法學博士 魏文翰 電氣專家 胡西園 船長 [illegible]鼎錫
會計師 潘序倫 機器工程專家 李允成 公證人 金月石 陳叔如 陳樂琴
建築師 李祖賢 化學專家 彭司勳

報告書渝火字第一七五號 第一頁

保險人 中央信託局產物保險處
被保險人 復興公司
保單號次 火險保險單第六一六一六八號
保險標的 房屋一棟
保險金額 國幣壹千萬元
保物地址 四川省重慶市林森路東華觀巷第十七號
保險期限 自民國卅四年三月十七日起至民國卅五年三月十七日下午四時止
茲將上開保單所保標的房屋失慎被焚情形暨辦理勘查經過報告予后
火焚時日 民國卅五年三月十六日下午一時
被保險人狀況 被保險人復興公司創設於民國二十九年間係財政部發資開辦經營國產品猪鬃桐油絲茶等製造及輸出事宜總公司設重慶市上清寺三三一號因業務需要在大後方各城市遍設分支機構在重慶有倉庫三所一在東華觀一在區江門一在海棠溪規模宏大業務紛繁抗戰結束後政府當局裁併機構將該公司歸併中央信託局易貨處管理之
房屋建築 被保險人所有東華觀倉庫房屋建築於民國十九年

1946年中国公估行出具的火险报告书
Fire Insurance Checking Report by China Evaluator Co. in 1946

英商普来公证行保险公证案卷
Insurance notarising files by a British surveyor

朱晋椒——浙江鄞县人，上海保险业经纪人公会第一任主席。早年供职于原籍钱庄业，后出任上海汇通洋行保险部经理，在职4年间，业绩显著。1923年，禅臣洋行聘其为保险部中国总经理，由于管辖业务突飞猛进，使其名声大振。但他目睹中国资金滚滚外流，心中总有隐痛。1934年，中国保险公司董事长宋汉章聘其为业务部经理，这是他服务民族保险业的开始。1936年，上海华洋保险联合委员会改订火险经纪人规章，朱看到那时上海的保险经纪人多数以个人业务为前提，缺乏团体组织能力，于是着手组织保险经纪人公会，被推选为主席。就任后，他倾力于会务工作，重视同业的福利和会员的学术修养。同年，天一保险公司聘其为协理，仍兼中国保险公司业务经理。

Zhu Jinjiao, the initiator and first chairman of Shanghai Insurance Brokers Association, acted as the manager of several foreign companies. In 1934, Zhu was employed as manager of the Business Department of China Insurance Co., which marked the beginning for him to work for Chinese national insurance.

华商盖安公证行的保险公证案卷
Insurance notarising files by Chinese Gaian Surveyor Co.

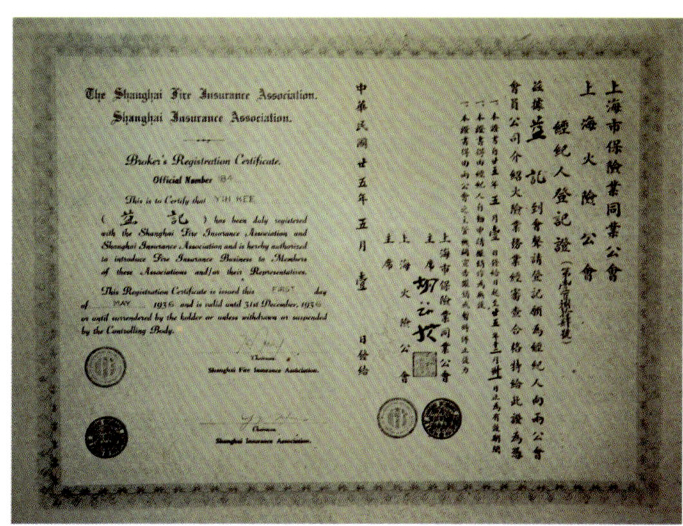

上海市保險業同業公會
上海火險公會
經紀人登記證

茲據 益記 到會聲請登記願為經紀人向兩公會會員公司介紹火險業務業經審查合格特給此證為憑

上海市保險業同業公會 主席
上海火險公會 主席

中華民國廿五年五月壹日發給

The Shanghai Fire Insurance Association.
Shanghai Insurance Association.

Broker's Registration Certificate.

Official Number 184

This is to Certify that YIH KEE (益記) has been duly registered with the Shanghai Fire Insurance Association and Shanghai Insurance Association and is hereby authorized to introduce Fire Insurance Business to Members of these Associations and/or their Representatives.

This Registration Certificate is issued this FIRST day of MAY 1936 and is valid until 31st December, 1936 or until surrendered by the holder or unless withdrawn or suspended by the Controlling Body.

Chairman
Shanghai Fire Insurance Association.

Chairman
Shanghai Insurance Association.

1936年上海保险业同业公会、上海火险公会颁发的经纪人登记证
Certificate of registration for insurance brokers issued by Shanghai Insurance Association and Shanghai Fire Insurance Association in 1936

Agreement of Acceptance

Agreement of Acceptance

THE EQUITABLE ADJUSTERS

THE EQUITABLE ADJUSTERS

THE EQUITABLE ADJUSTERS

华商永平公证行的保险公证案卷
Insurance—notarising files by Yongping Co.

保险公证原由洋行把持，1935年，上海联合保险公证事务所成立，同年上海益中公证行在汉口开设分行，打破了外商垄断的局面。

1937年共有6家公证行，华商有益中公证行及华商联合保险公证事务所两家，有时洋商也委托益中勘灾估损，洋商有麦礼洋行、鲁意斯摩洋行、普来公证行、三义洋行、保险审估公司、博禄公证行、瑞和及远东公证行等。

1937年2月国民政府上海市警察局颁发“上海市火险公估行火场通行证”，规定持证才能进入火场。当时上海有火险公估行10余家。1941年上海益中公证行在重庆设立分支机构，不久改为中华保险公证事务所。1942年重庆成立公估行，卢作孚任董事长。1943年中国公估行制定《中国公估行各项委案费率及付费章程》。1947年中国公证事务所制订《各项委案收费规章》，委案包括货物丈量、货物重量、散油测量、木船检验、代行标卖等12种项目。1948年上海中国公证事务所设立。

Insurance notarisation was originally controlled by foreign companies; until in 1935 Shanghai United Insurance Notarisation Office was founded and in the same year, Shanghai Yizhong Notarisation Co. set up a branch in Hankou, breaking the situation of monopoly by foreign companies.

英商麦礼洋行保险公证案卷
Insurance—notarising files by a British Co.

REPORT

华商益中公证行的保险公证案卷
Insurance—notarising files by Yizhong Notarisation Co.

十九、早期再保险业
Early Reinsurance

旧中国的民族再保险起步很晚。保险前辈杨经才曾慨叹："中国的再保险，一直操在洋商保险公司手里，中国的保险公司，充其量不过是洋商公司的经纪而已。"

直到1928年，中国才出现了第一个同业分保集团"上海四行联合总经理处"。上海联保，联泰、肇泰、羊城四家保险公司加入。

中国第一个专营再保险的公司——华商联合保险公司于1933年6月成立，发起人为邓东明，肇泰、华安、永宁、永安、先施、中国海上、通易、宁绍等保险公司积极响应，邓东明被聘为经理。

Chinese national reinsurance was rather late in its development, just as Yang Jingcai, an insurance veteran, had sighed with regret "since Chinese reinsurance has always been in the hands of foreign insurers, Chinese insurers, at most, merely act as the brokers of foreign insurers".

Till 1928, first Chinese reinsurance group, Shanghai Four-Insurer United Head Office, was established, while the four insurers were Shanghai United, Liantai, Zhaotai, and Guangzhou Insurance Co.

In 1933, Chinese United Insurance Co., the first insurers specialized in reinsurance, was set up in Shanghai with Deng Dongming as the manager.

开中国专业再保险先河的邓东明
Dengdong Ming: Pioneer of Chinese specialized reinsurance

中国再保险公司总经理张昌祈
Zhang Changqi: General Manager of China Reinsurance Co.

中国第一个同业分保集团——上海四行联合总经理处经理徐可升
Xu Kesheng: Manager of the General Manager Department of Shanghai Four-Insurer United Head Office

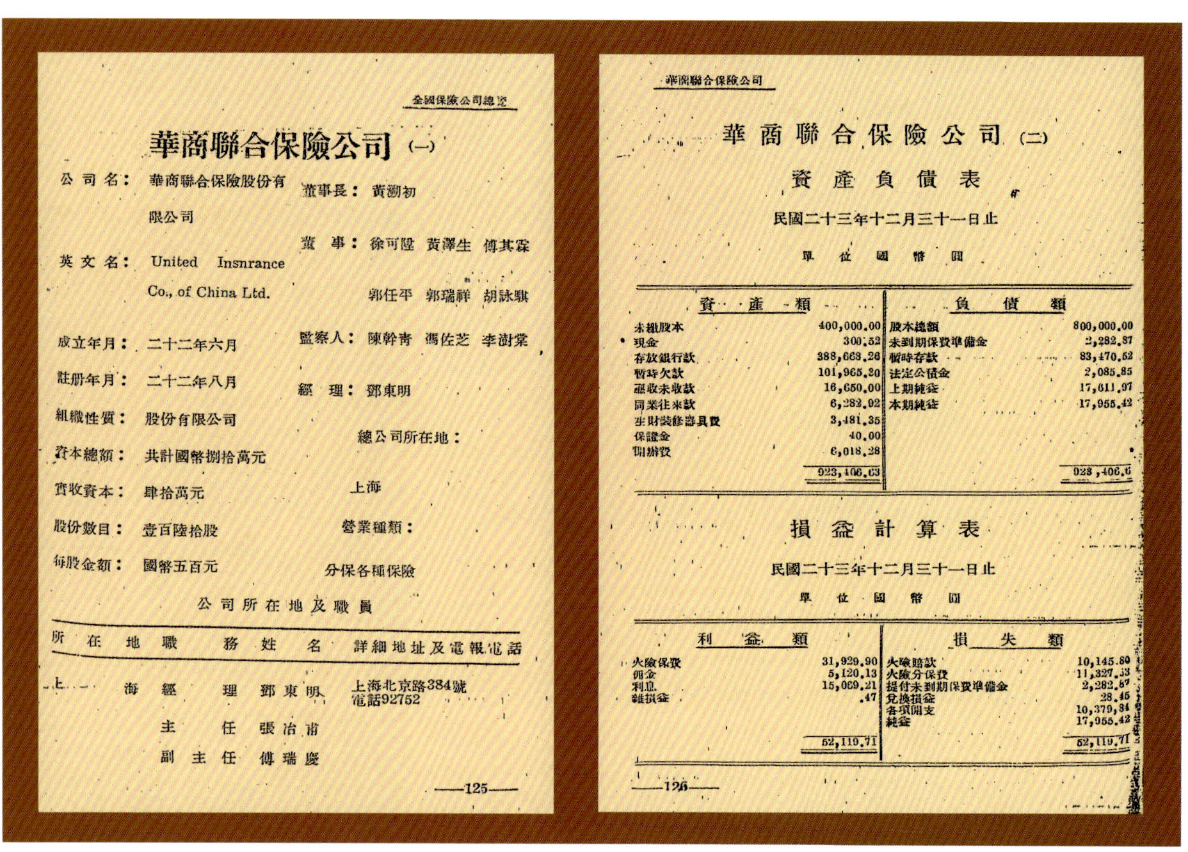

全國保險公司總覽

華商聯合保險公司 (一)

公司名：華商聯合保險股份有限公司

英文名：United Insnrance Co., of China Ltd.

成立年月：二十二年六月

註册年月：二十二年八月

組織性質：股份有限公司

資本總額：共計國幣捌拾萬元

實收資本：肆拾萬元

股份數目：壹百陸拾股

每股金額：國幣五百元

董事長：黃溯初

董　事：徐可陞　黃澤生　傅其霖　郭任平　郭瑞祥　胡詠騏

監察人：陳幹青　馮佐芝　李澍棠

經　理：鄧東明

總公司所在地：上海

營業種類：分保各種保險

公司所在地及職員

所在地	職務	姓名	詳細地址及電報電話
上海	經理	鄧東明	上海北京路384號 電話92752
	主任	張治甫	
	副主任	傅瑞慶	

—125—

華商聯合保險公司

華商聯合保險公司 (二)

資產負債表

民國二十三年十二月三十一日止

單位國幣圓

資產類		負債類	
未繳股本	400,000.00	股本總額	800,000.00
現金	300.52	未到期保費準備金	2,282.87
存放銀行款	388,663.26	暫時存款	83,470.52
暫時欠款	101,965.20	法定公積金	2,085.85
應收未收款	16,650.00	上期純益	17,611.97
同業往來款	6,282.92	本期純益	17,955.42
生財裝修器具費	3,481.35		
保證金	40.00		
開辦費	6,018.28		
	923,406.63		923,406.6

損益計算表

民國二十三年十二月三十一日止

單位國幣圓

利益類		損失類	
火險保費	31,929.90	火險賠款	10,145.80
佣金	5,120.13	火險分保費	11,327.33
利息	15,069.21	提付未到期保費準備金	2,282.87
雜損益	.47	兌換損益	28.45
		各項開支	10,379.84
		純益	17,955.42
	52,119.71		52,119.71

—126—

1936年《中国保险年鉴》刊登的华商联合保险公司资料

Materials about China United Insurance Co. published on 1936's *China Insurance Yearbook*

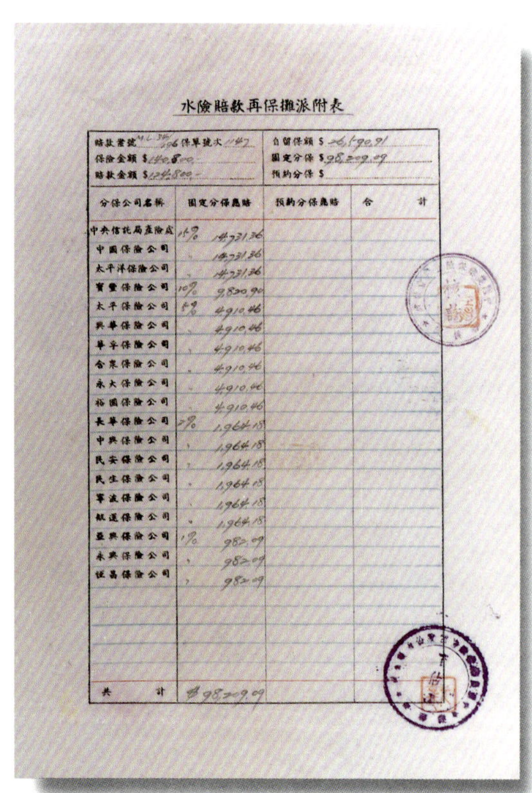

水險賠款再保攤派附表

賠款案號 ML-341/196　保單號次 1147　自留保額 $26,590.91

保險金額 $140,800　固定分保 $98,209.09

賠款金額 $124,800.-　預約分保 $

分保公司名稱	固定分保應賠	預約分保應賠	合計
中央信託局產險處	15% 14,731.36		
中國保險公司	14,731.36		
太平洋保險公司	14,731.36		
寶豐保險公司	10% 9,820.90		
太平保險公司	5% 4,910.46		
興華保險公司	4,910.46		
華孚保險公司	4,910.46		
合衆保險公司	4,910.46		
永大保險公司	4,910.46		
裕國保險公司	4,910.46		
長華保險公司	2% 1,964.18		
中興保險公司	1,964.18		
民安保險公司	1,964.18		
民生保險公司	1,964.18		
寧波保險公司	1,964.18		
航運保險公司	1,964.18		
亞興保險公司	1% 982.09		
永興保險公司	982.09		
恆昌保險公司	982.09		
共計	$98,209.09		

中国农业保险公司制作的水险赔款再保分摊附表

China Agriculture Insurance Co.'s attached list of reinsurance apportionment of indemnity for marine insurance

40年代中期，中国再保险市场成三足鼎立之势：一是以国家财政为后盾的官僚资本再保险机构，这类机构以中央信托局产物保险处为代表，它们被赋予集中办理再保险特权。1946年由中央信托局参股控制的中国再保险公司在上海成立。张昌祈任总经理，其全部业务为合约分保和临时分保。二是上海华商分保集团，主要有太平、久联、华商联合、大沪、中国5家。其中由中国保险公司组建的中国分保集团有成员公司三四十家，多为民营公司；三是外商保险公司经营的再保险，以美亚保险为最。这三方势力主宰中国再保险市场。

A three-dominator situation had shaped in the mid-1940's: the first was bureaucrat-capital-funded insurance institutions backed by the national finance, with its model as the Insurance Department born from the Central Trust Co.; the second was Shanghai Chinese Reinsurance Group, mainly composed of Taiping, Jiulian, China United, Dahu, China Insurance Co.; the third that monopolized Chinese reinsurance market was reinsurance operated by foreign insurers, among which, AAU kept the leading position.

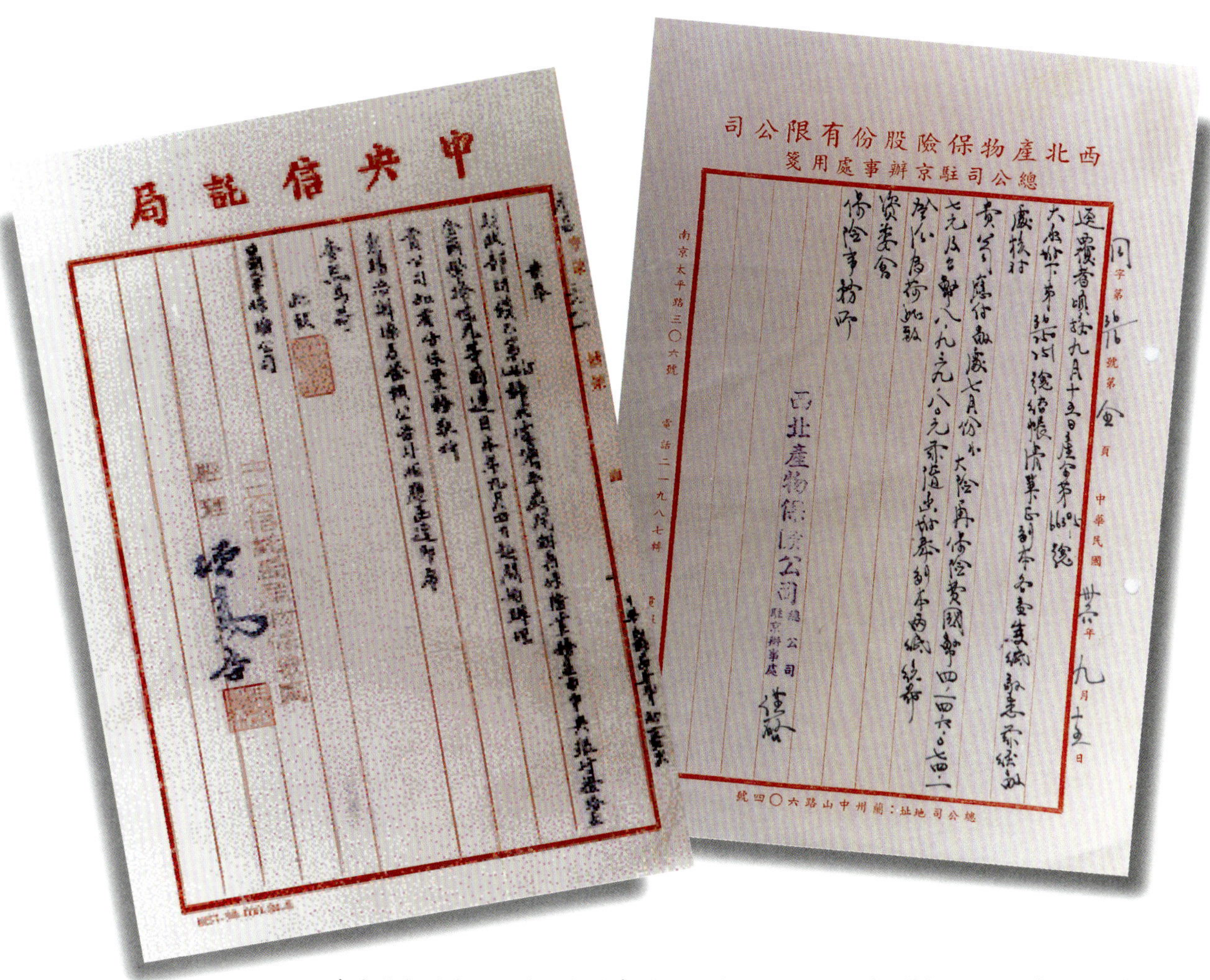
中央信託局

西北產物保險股份有限公司
總公司駐京辦事處用箋
南京太平路三〇六號
電話二一九八七號
總公司地址：蘭州中山路六〇四號

中央信托局和西北产物保险有限公司关于再保险的函(资料提供：广州市档案馆)
Letters on Reinsurance by the Central Trust Co. and Northwest Property Insurance Co.

二十、上海保险职工运动

Insurance Employees Movement in Shanghai

上海保险业业余职工联谊会(简称“保联”)是中国共产党领导下的广泛团结保险业职工和中上层人士的群众性团体，成立于1938年7月。

“保联”根据党在抗日战争和解放时期的总任务、总要求，结合不同时期形势的发展变化以及保险业的特点，采取灵活多样的、政治经济相结合的、改善生活福利与寓教于乐的斗争形式和组织形式，开展了丰富多采的群众性联谊活动。

Founded in July 1938, Shanghai Insurance Part-Time Employees' Fraternity (briefed as the Fraternity), under lead of the Communist Party of China, was a mass organization widely united insurance employees and persons of middle and high layers.

“保联”会址爱多亚路(现上海延安东路)160号
Site of the Fraternity (160, Yan'an East Road)

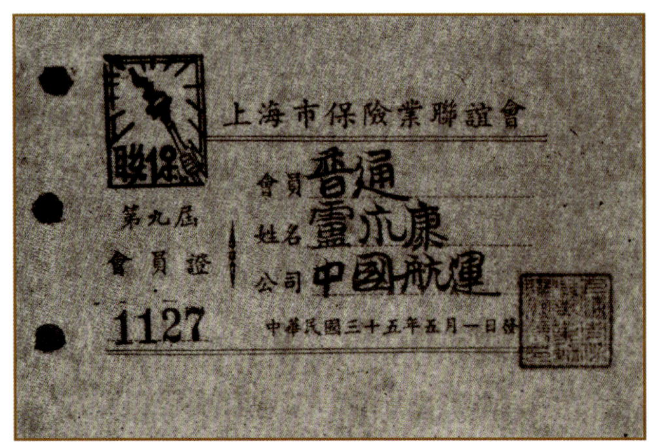

“保联”会员证
Membership card of the Fraternity

1940年"保联"第三届理事会成员合影
Directors attending the 3rd Council of the Fraternity in 1940

1938年7月1日，"保联"召开成立大会，参加大会的有华商和洋商保险公司的职员400余人。大会选举胡咏骐、谢寿天、董国清、程恩树、林震峰、关可贵(保险业同业公会秘书长)、王中振(保险业同业公会秘书)、朱懋仁、郭雨东等组成第一届理事会，推选郭雨东为理事会主席。理事会下设了秘书处、会员部、总务部、娱乐部、体育部、学术部、妇女部、出版委员会、图书委员会及福利委员会等工作部门。各部、会根据工作需要再分设若干组，广泛吸收各公司会员参加各项会务活动，并向当时的公共租界当局工部局政治部办理团体登记，于1938年10月4日，领到"华人总会"第5号执照，取得了合法的社会团体的地位。

"保联"成立后展开了各种形式的职工活动，吸引了广大保险职工参加。1940年1月"保联"会员达1402人，约占整个上海保险职工总数的70%。

On July 1, 1938, the foundation conference of the Fraternity was held; more than 400 employees from Chinese and foreign insurance companies attended the conference.

After its foundation, the Insurance Fraternity launched multiform activities, absorbing widely spread insurance employees to take part in it; by January 1940, the number of members of the Fraternity had come to 1,402, approximately accounting for 70 per cent of the entire insurance staff.

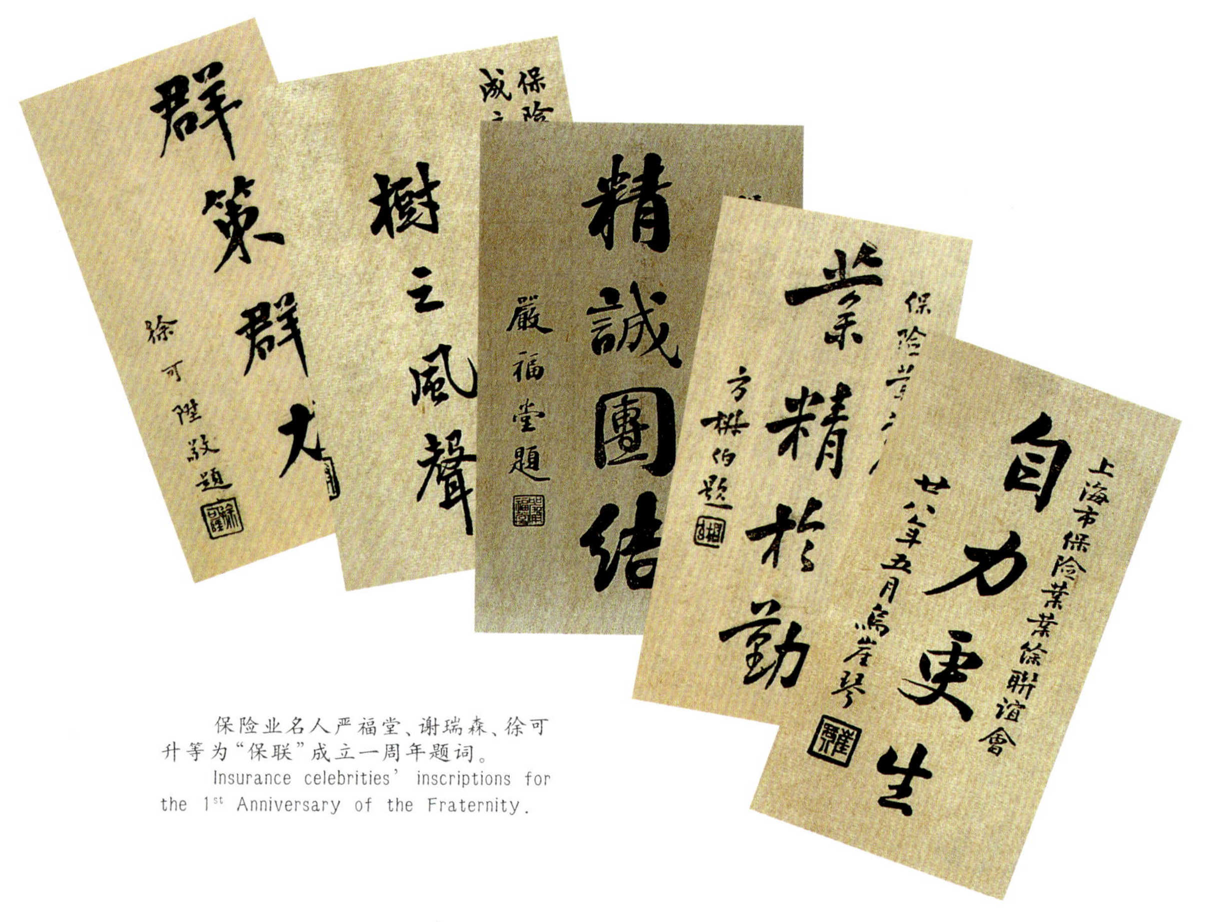

保险业名人严福堂、谢瑞森、徐可升等为"保联"成立一周年题词。

Insurance celebrities' inscriptions for the 1st Anniversary of the Fraternity.

"保联"学术部主办保险学术研究讲座全体师生合影

Teachers & Students attending the lecture on insurance academic studies sponsored by the Fraternity

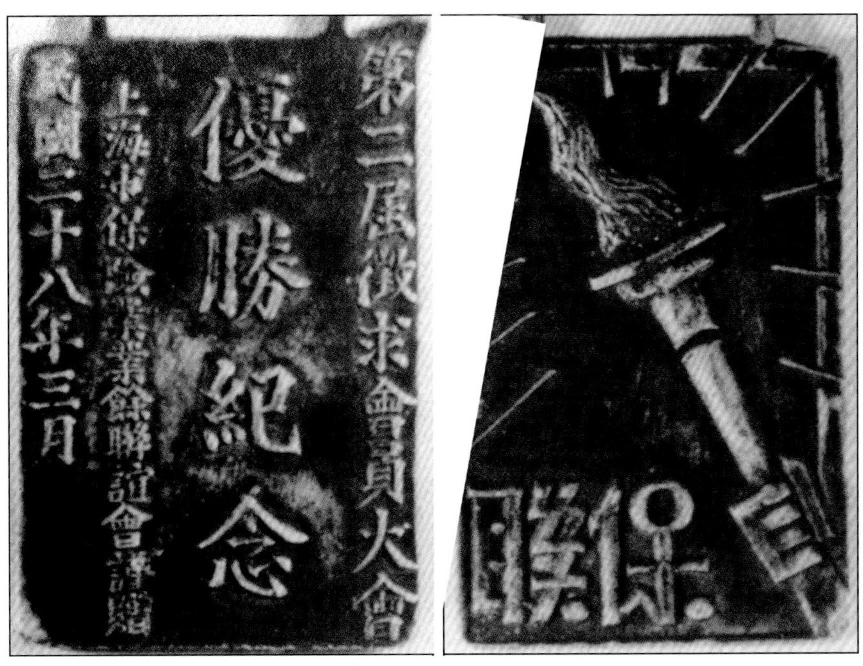

1939年3月"保联"第三届征求会员大会优胜纪念章，右图为"保联"会徽。
Badge for the winner in an activity by the Fraternity; emblem of the Fraternity (R)

1940年保联杯、1941年咏骐杯两届冠军得主保裕足球队全体合影。
Baoyu Football Team winning two football matches in 1940, 1941.

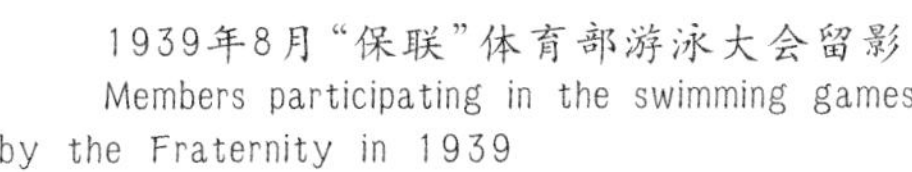

1939年8月"保联"体育部游泳大会留影
Members participating in the swimming games by the Fraternity in 1939

上海市保險界同仁進修會

保險學術講習班

結業證書

學員趙京生係鎮江縣人現年二三歲於本班修業期滿成績及格准予結業此證

理事長 羅北辰

班主任 唐雄俊

中華民國三十六年九月二十五日

改名保险进修会的会员证
Member card of Insurance Retraining Society renamed from the Fraternity

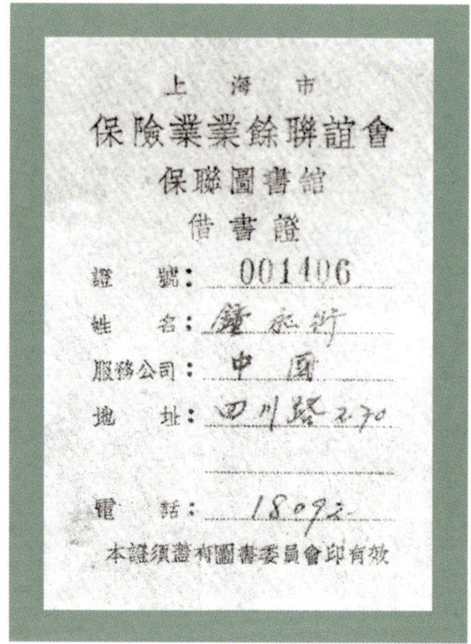

上海市

保險業業餘聯誼會

保聯圖書館

借書證

證號：001406

姓名：鐘永衍

服務公司：中國

地址：四川路270

電話：18092

本證須蓋有圖書委員會印有效

“保联”图书馆借书证
Library card of the Library of the Fraternity

1937年“保联”组织的话剧演出《日出之前》剧照
Drama *Before Sunrise* organized by the Fraternity in 1937

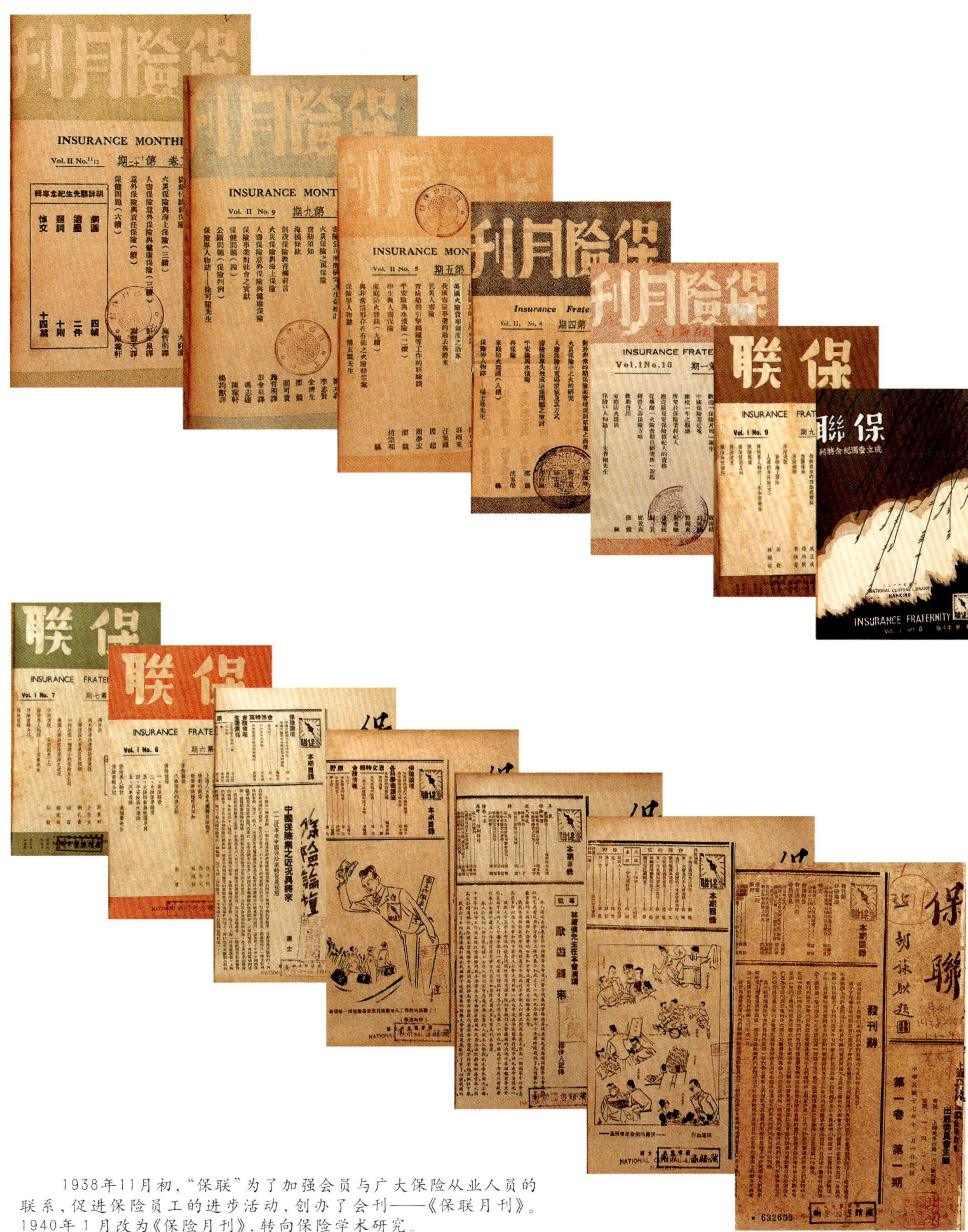

1938年11月初,"保联"为了加强会员与广大保险从业人员的联系,促进保险员工的进步活动,创办了会刊——《保联月刊》。1940年1月改为《保险月刊》,转向保险学术研究。

Issues of *Insurance Monthly* and *Insurance Fraternity* (changed to the former in 1940)

二十一、早期保险立法
Early Insurance Legislations

随着中国保险业的发展，对保险经营逐步有了法律规范。1903年，清政府设立商部。1904年，设立法律修订馆。1907年，徐锐拟订了《保险业章程草案》。1910年，日本人志田钾太郎参与起草的《大清商律草案》颁布，第七章为损害保险营业(共49条)，第八章为生命保险营业(共10条)。

1913年，当时任北洋政府农商总长的张謇在《实业政见宣言书》中倡言：应尽快制定公司法、破产法、运输保险等法规。北洋政府修订法律馆聘请法国人爱斯嘉拉为顾问，拟订《保险契约法草案》，共四章109条。由于1928年北洋政府瓦解，此法未获公布。

1918年，《银行周报》刊登北洋政府农商部拟订，1917年法制局修订的《保险业法案》，共42条，规定外国人经营保险业，应呈报农商部。

With the development of Chinese insurance, some laws began to be worked out to regulate insurance operations. In 1907, Xu Rui drew out the *Draft of Insurance Rules*. In 1908, the *Banking Weekly* published the news that the Agriculture & Commercial Ministry of the Northern Government drew out the *Act of Insurance* revised by the Legislation Bureau in 1917, which, with 42 articles, stipulates foreigner should submit a report to the Ministry to operate insurance.

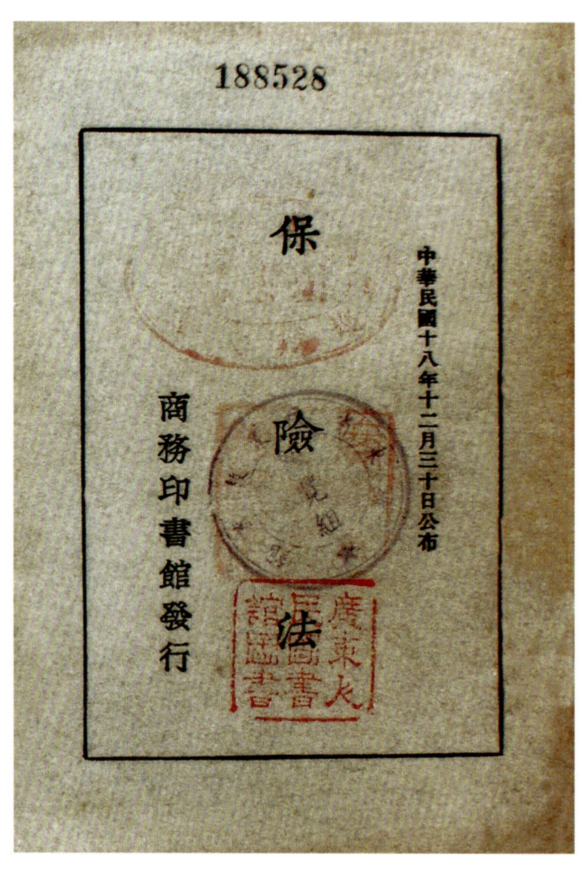

1929年12月30日，国民政府首次公布《保险法》，这是我国第一部比较完整的保险法规，共3章82条。1937年1月1日，经修订后重新公布，共四章98条。但均未公布实施日期。

Cover of the text of the *Insurance Law* (first relatively complete insurance law in China) by the Republic of China in late 1929

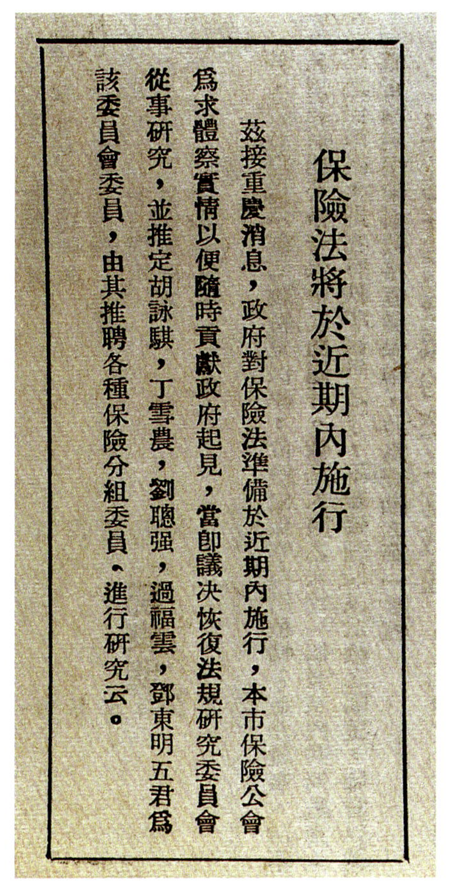

保險法將於近期內施行

茲接重慶消息，政府對保險法準備於近期內施行，本市保險公會爲求體察實情以便隨時貢獻政府起見，當即議決恢復法規研究委員會從事研究，並推定胡詠騏，丁雪農，劉聰强，過福雲，鄧東明五君爲該委員會委員，由其推聘各種保險分組委員、進行研究云。

当时媒体报道“保险法将于近期内施行”的新闻消息，但实施日期后来并未公布。
News report that the *Insurance Law* to be put in force recently, but no exact date announced afterward

行政院會議提案表

国民政府行政院提请施行的保险法、保险业法、保险业法施行法的提案（资料提供：中国第二历史档案馆）
The proposal of the Administrative Council to the government to apply the series of insurance laws

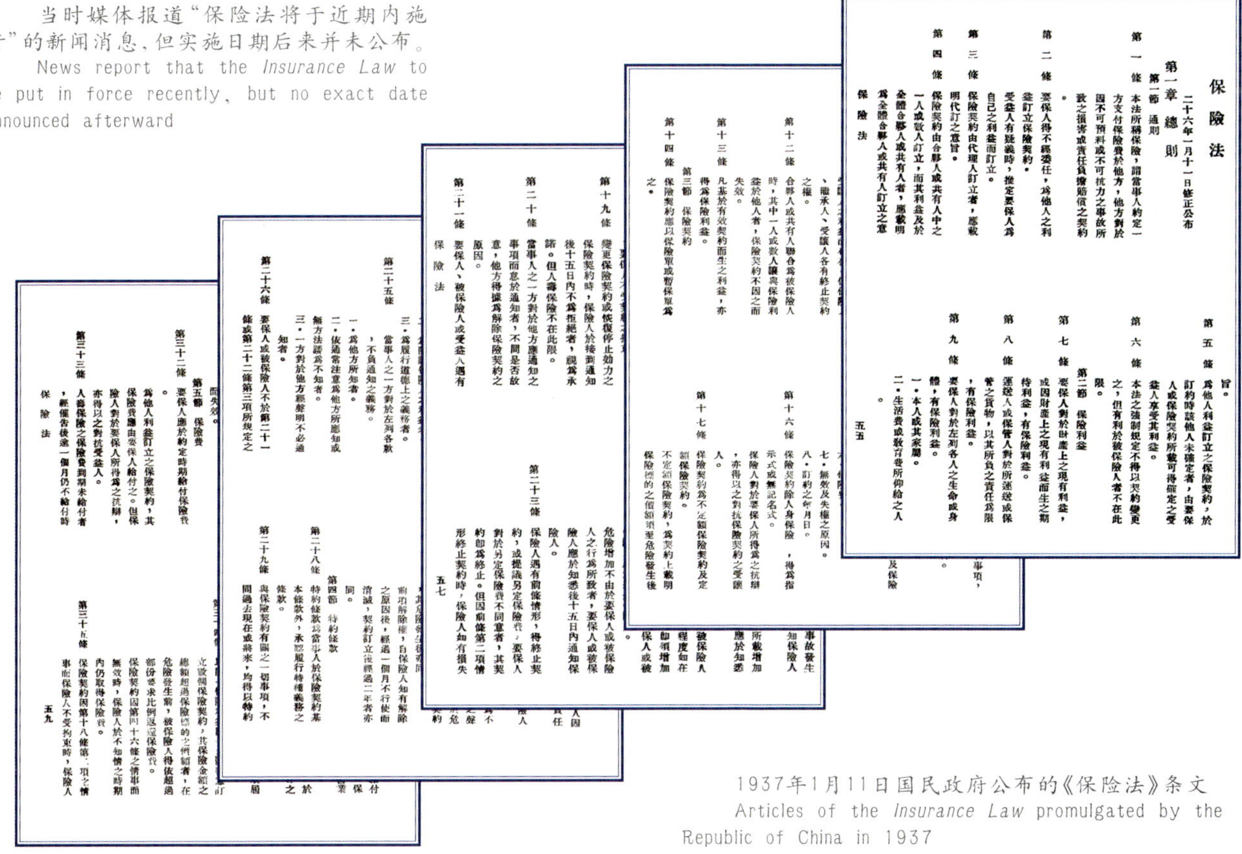

保險法

二十六年一月十一日修正公布

第一章 總則

第一節 通則

第一條 本法所稱保險，謂當事人約定一方支付保險費於他方，他方對於因不可預料或不可抗力之事故所致之損害或責任負擔賠償之契約。

第二條 要保人得不經委任，爲他人之利益訂立保險契約。受益人有疑義時，推定要保人爲自己之利益而訂立。

第三條 保險契約由代理人訂立者，應載明代訂之意旨。

第四條 保險契約由合夥人或共有人中之一人或數人訂立，而其利益及於全體合夥人或共有人者，應載明爲全體合夥人或共有人訂立之意旨。

第五條 爲他人利益訂立之保險契約，於訂約時該他人未確定者，由要保人或保險契約所載可得確定之受益人享受其利益。

第六條 本法之強制規定不得以契約變更之，但有利於被保險人者不在此限。

第二節 保險利益

第七條 要保人對於財產上之現有利益，或因財產上之現有利益而生之期待利益，有保險利益。

第八條 運送人或保管人對於所運送或保管之貨物，以其所負之責任爲限，有保險利益。

第九條 要保人對於左列各人之生命或身體，有保險利益。

一·本人或其家屬。

二·生活費或教育費所仰給之人。

保險法　五五

1937年1月11日国民政府公布的《保险法》条文
Articles of the *Insurance Law* promulgated by the Republic of China in 1937

1935年7月5日，首次公布《保险业法》。1937年1月1日修订后再次公布，共7章80条，分总则、保证金、保险公司、相互保险社、会计、罚则、附则等章节。

First promulgated on July 5, 1935, the *Insurance Industry Law*, after it's being revised, was re-promulgated on January 1, 1937. The Law was categorized in 7 chapters with 80 articles: General Rules, Insurance Company, Mutual Insurance Company, Accounting, Penalty Provisions, Supplementary Articles, etc.

The Law hadn't been put into effect due to foreign insurers' protest against it.

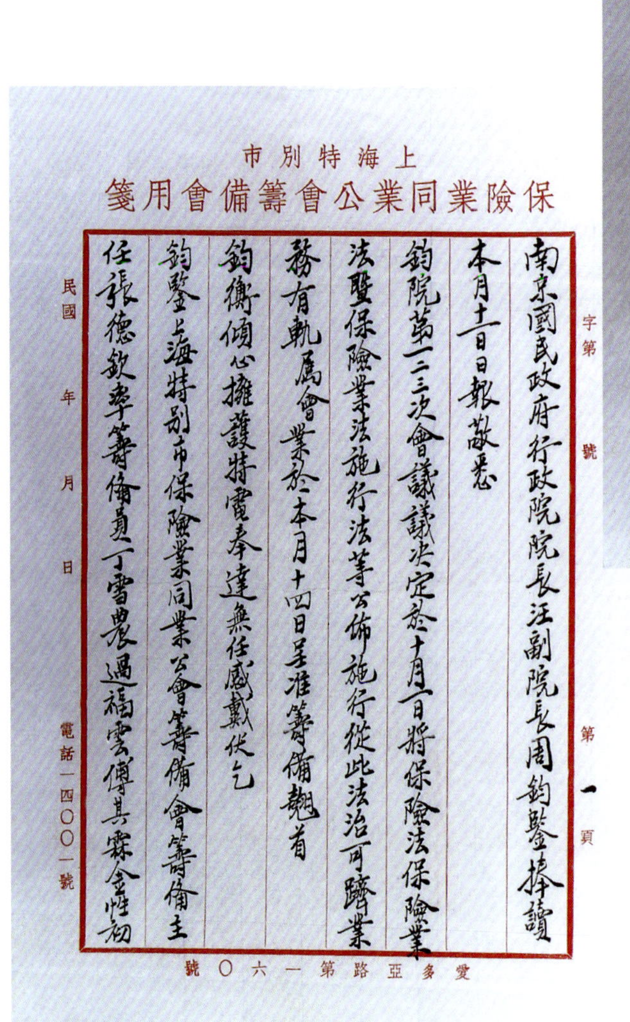

上海特別市
保險業同業公會籌備會用箋

字第 號

南京國民政府行政院院長汪副院長周鈞鑒捧讀
本月十三日報敬悉
鈞院第一二三次會議議決定於十月一日將保險法保險業
法暨保險業法施行法等公佈施行從此法治可躋業
務有軌屬會業於本月十四日呈准籌備就緒
鈞衡傾心擁護特電奉達無任感戴伏乞
鈞鑒上海特別市保險業同業公會籌備會籌備主
任張德欽李籌備員丁雪農過福雲傅其霖金性初

第一頁

民國 年 月 日

電話一四〇〇一號

愛多亞路第一六〇號

上海特別市
保險業同業公會籌備會用箋

字第 號

馬少荃郭雨東陳巳生顧文生等同叩

上海特別市保險業同業公會籌備會圖記

第二頁

民國卅一年八月二十日

電話一四〇〇一號

愛多亞路第一六〇號

1942年5月20日，上海保险同业公会筹备会委员致南京政府行政院拥护《保险法》、《保险业法》、《保险业法施行法》公布的函。（资料提供：中国第二历史档案馆）

Letter by the Preparatory Committee of Shanghai Insurance Association to support the Insurance Law in 1942.

二十二、30年代的保险市场
Insurance Market in 1930s

20世纪30年代是我国保险市场较为繁荣的时期，其主要特点：一是保险立法更加完善。除1929年公布的《保险法》，由1937年修正公布外，国民政府的其它几部主要法律如《保险业法》、《保险业法施行法》、《简易人身保险法》等也在这时期公布实施；二是外商保险公司及其代理机构在保险市场占绝对优势。到1937年，仅在上海的外商保险机构就达126家。当时中国每年流出的保险费高达235万英镑，占全国保险费的75%；三是民族保险业得到了发展壮大。据1937年《中国保险年鉴》载，到1935年国人开设的保险公司已达30余家。30年代我国保险市场的状况，正如1937年《中国保险年鉴》所说："迩来国人对于保险之需要，尤为迫切，爱国之心理日益加强，保险事业蓬蓬勃勃，一日千里，虽未能与外商颉颃，然基础渐固，信用颇坚……，尤其保险法制定，政府已有保护之法规，保险公会告成，进而有联合之组合，商人亦有团结之表现，保险事业之前途，正如雨后春笋，方兴未艾，此国人所当引为欣慰者也。"

Insurance market was flourishing in 1930s. According to China Insurance Yearbook, there were more than thirty Chinese insurers in China. In General, insurance market was still in the hands of foreign insurers.

30年代在上海开业的北美洲保险公司内景
Office of North America Insurance Co. in 1930's

30年代宏利保险公司保险单
Policy by the Manufactures Life in 1930s

30年代宏利保险公司办公室工作照
Office of the Manufactures Life Insurance Co. in 1930s

1936年《中国保险年鉴》列名的全国性保险公司
（共48家，其中国营2家，民营46家）
48 Countrywide Insurance Companies Listed in 1936's *China Insurance Yearbook*

公司名称	注册地	公司名称	注册地
上海华兴保险公司	上海	香安保险公司	香港
上海联保水火险公司	香港	珠江保险公司	广州
大华保险公司	上海	泰山保险公司	上海
太平保险公司	上海	通易信托公司保险部	上海
中一信托局保险部	上海	康年人寿保险公司	香港
中央信托局保险部	上海	康年水火保险公司	香港
中国天一保险公司	上海	陆海通人寿保险公司	香港
中国保险公司	上海	华安水火保险公司	上海
中国海上意外保险公司	上海	华安合群保寿公司	上海
中国第一信用保险公司	上海	华成经保火险公司	上海
仁济和水火保险公司	上海	华商联合保险公司	上海
永安人寿保险公司	香港	邮政储金汇业局保险处	上海
永安水火保险公司	香港	宁绍人寿保险公司	上海
永宁水火保险公司	上海	宁绍人寿保险公司	上海
四明保险公司	上海	爱群人寿保险公司	香港
安平保险公司	上海	慎平火险公司	福州
羊城保险置业公司	广州	福星人寿小保险	福州
先施人寿保险公司	香港	广州大华保险公司	广州
先施保险置业公司	香港	肇泰保险公司	上海
利华人寿小保险公司	天津	联安水火保险公司	香港
利群人寿小保险公司	福州	联泰水火保险公司	香港
均安保险公司	香港	兴华保险公司	重庆
东方人寿保险公司	北平	丰盛保险公司	上海
宏济人寿小保险公司	天津	宝丰保险公司	上海

二十三、东北伪满保险业与汪伪政府保险业

Insurance under Manchoukuo and Wang Jingwei Government

1931年“九·一八”事变后，日本占领了我国辽宁、吉林、黑龙江三省。1932年，成立傀儡政权“满洲国”，从此日本势力垄断了东北保险市场。

伪满保险业经历了两个阶段。1931至1935年为保险业发展的初期阶段。日商大量涌入东北，超过了英俄的势力。1933年，公布伪政权《满洲国经济建国纲领》，规定保险业效法日本，采取国营和民营并存的方针。于是，日商代理店改设分公司或办事处，原来未在东北经营的保险公司也相继到东北开拓，英俄被迫退出了东北市场。

1936至1945年，东北保险业为日满独占。1936年，公布《保险业法》，主要内容：“1.经营性质以股份公司为限；2.保险业实行许可制；3.保险公司不得兼营其他事业，生命保险和损害保险不得合并经营；4.设立代理店要经过许可，以一店一社为原则；5.外国保险公司在本法实施地区内设立的支店、事务所以及代表者，必须缴纳相当的保证金。”

1937年9月，伪满洲国政府交通部公布《邮政生命保险法》，规定邮政生命保险属于国营，由邮政机构办理，保险金额50–800元，分终身、养老、立业三种，投保年龄7–60岁，免体检。邮政生命保险由伪满洲国交通部主管，邮政总局下设经办机构。当年承保2.4万件，保险金额380万元法币。1945年，投保人数为400余万人。

满洲生命保险株式会社是垄断东北市场的主要保险机构。其由伪满洲国政府与日本内地30个生命保险会社团体共同出资，于1936年在长春成立，高桥康顺任理事长。到1944年底，共有遍及东北的92个分支机构。

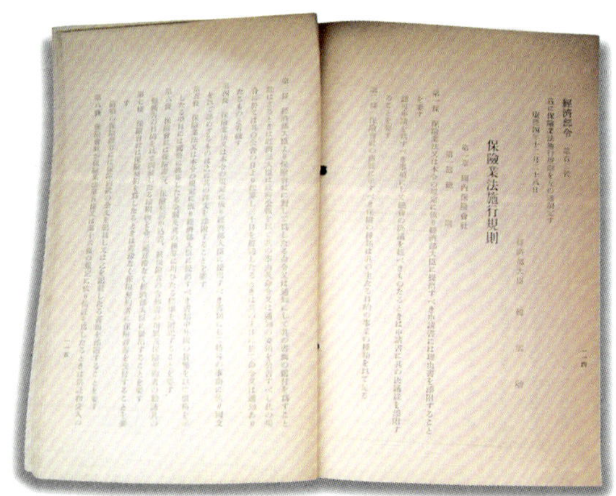

伪满洲国保险业法
Insurance Industry Law of Manchoukuo

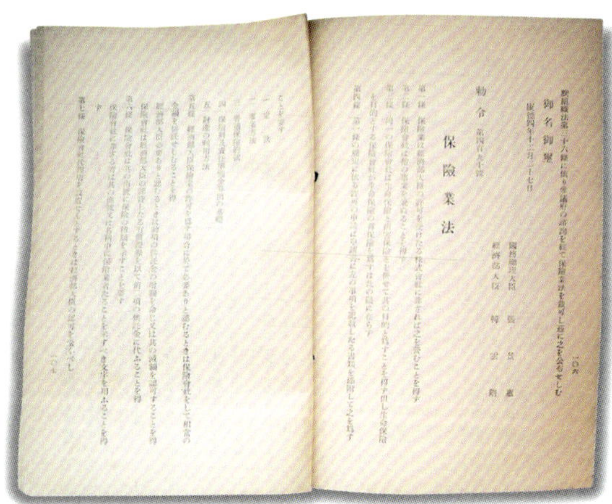

伪满洲国保险业法施行规划
Implementation plan of the *Insurance Industry Law* of Manchoukuo

40年代日本安田海上火灾保险公司广告
Ad of the Yasuda Fire & Marine Insurance Co. (Japan) in 1940's

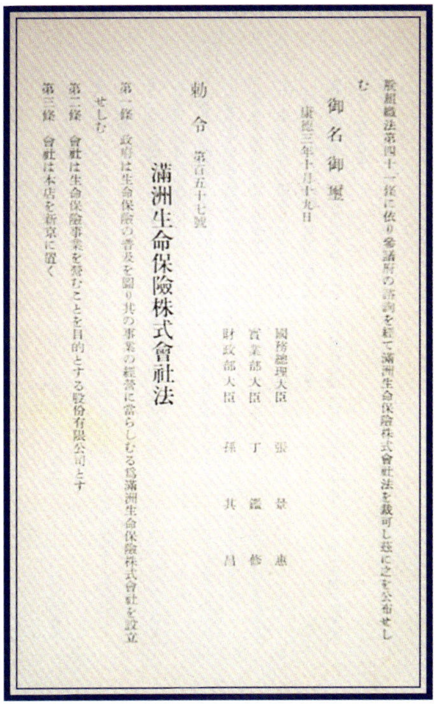

參議府官制第四十一條に依り參議府の諮詢を經て滿洲生命保險株式會社法を裁可し茲に之を公布せしむ

御名御璽

康德三年十月十九日

國務總理大臣 張景惠
實業部大臣 丁鑑修
財政部大臣 孫其昌

勅令第百五十七號

滿洲生命保險株式會社法

第一條 政府は生命保險の普及を圖り其の事業の經營に當らしむる爲滿洲生命保險株式會社を設立せしむ

第二條 會社は生命保險事業を營むことを目的とする股份有限公司とす

第三條 會社は本店を新京に置く

满洲生命保险株式会社是垄断东北保险市场的主要保险机构，图为满洲生命保险株式会社法。

Act of Manchuria Life Insurance Co.

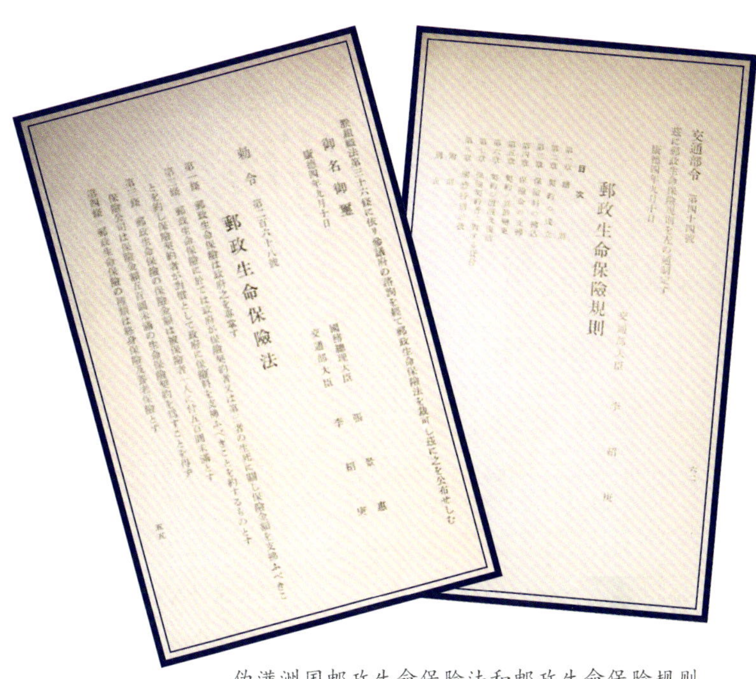

伪满洲国邮政生命保险法和邮政生命保险规则

Life Insurance Law and *Rules on Post Life Insurance* of Manchoukuo

满洲火灾海上保险株式会社是另一家著名的日本公司，成立于1937年12月，由日商与伪满洲国政府合资经营，后在大连、沈阳、哈尔滨开设分公司，另有遍布满洲的 213个代理店。1940年8月，为完善和巩固损害保险体系，扭转费率下跌局面，伪满洲国29家中外保险机构组建满洲火灾保险协会。

1942年，伪满洲国通讯社刊行《满洲经济十年史》，其中有《满洲保险业的飞跃发展》一章。

伪满保险业主要经营生命保险和损害保险。1931－1944年，保险费收入14944.7万元，支付赔款1538.5万元。1945年8月15日，抗日战争以日本投降而告终，伪满和日本在东北保险企业42家都由国民政府接管。

After the September Eighteenth Incident, Japanese established a puppet government and called it Manchoukuo in Northeast China, by which, they controlled the insurance market there, mainly dealt with life and non-life insurance. After the War of Resistance Against Japan, 42 Japanese insurance companies in Northeast China were taken over by the Kuomintang Government.

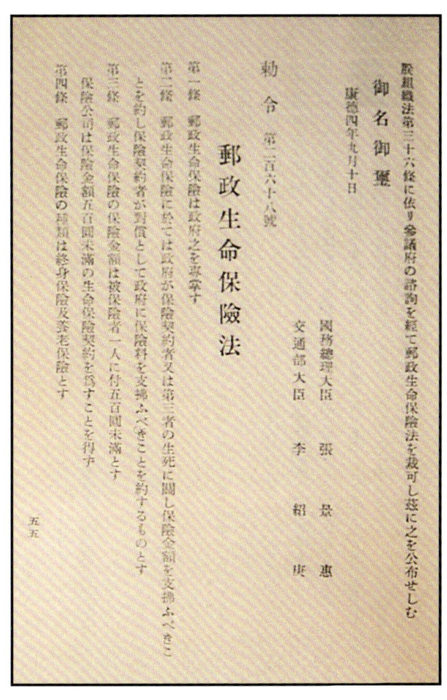

參議府官制第三十六條に依り參議府の諮詢を經て郵政生命保險法を裁可し茲に之を公布せしむ

御名御璽

康德四年九月十日

國務總理大臣 張景惠
交通部大臣 李紹庚

勅令第二百六十八號

郵政生命保險法

第一條 郵政生命保險は政府之を專掌す

第二條 郵政生命保險に於ては政府が保險契約者又は第三者の生死に關し保險金額を支拂ふべきことを約し保險契約者が對價として政府に保險料を支拂ふべきことを約するものとす

第三條 郵政生命保險の保險金額は被保險者一人に付五百圓未滿とす
保險公司は保險金額五百圓未滿の生命保險契約を爲すことを得ず

第四條 郵政生命保險の種類は終身保險及養老保險とす

五五

伪满洲国邮政生命保险法

Post Life Insurance Law promulgated by Manchoukuo

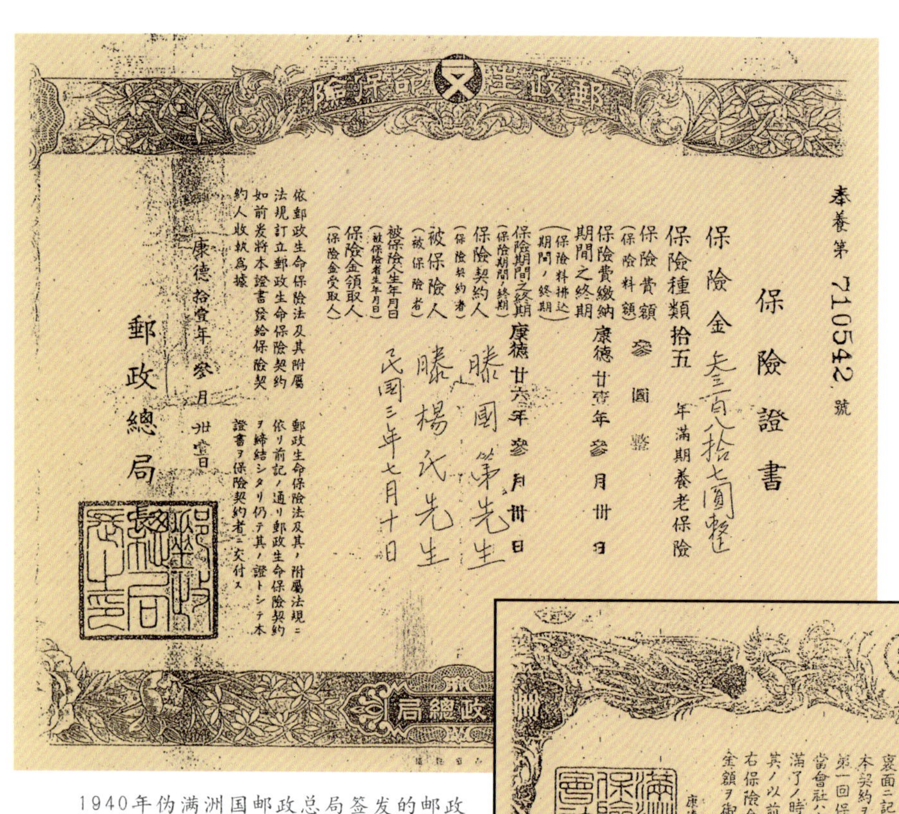

郵政生命保險

奉養第 710542 號

保險證書

保險金 叁百八拾七圓整

保險種類 拾五年滿期養老保險

保險費額（保險料額） 叁圓整

保險費繳納期間之終期（保險料拂込期間ノ終期） 康德廿壹年叁月卅日

保險期間之終期（保險期間ノ終期） 康德廿六年叁月卅日

保險契約人（保險契約者） 滕國第先生

被保險人（被保險者） 滕楊氏先生

被保險人生年月日（被保險者生年月日） 民國三年七月十日

保險金領取人（保險金受取人）

依郵政生命保險法及其附屬法規訂立郵政生命保險契約如前茲將本證書發給保險契約人收執爲據

郵政生命保險法及其ノ附屬法規ニ依リ前記ノ通リ郵政生命保險契約ヲ締結シタリ仍テ其ノ證トシテ本證書ヲ保險契約者ニ交付ス

康德拾壹年叁月卅壹日

郵政總局

1940年伪满洲国邮政总局签发的邮政生命保险保单

Post Life Insurance policy issued by the Post General Office of Manchoukuo in 1940

No 19

保險契約日 康德 年 月 日

保險契約ノ締結保險期間滿了ノ時 康德 同 年 同 月 同 日

保險料拂込方法及金額

保險料拂込期日 康德 年 月 日

保險契約者

被保險者

保險金受領者

本會社與保險契約人依本單背面記載之保險約款締結本契約於前記契約日己將第一回保險費收訖是以本會社在上開被保險人至保險期間滿了之時尚生存時或其以前死亡時即對上開保險金受領人支付前記保險金額

當會社ハ保險契約者ト此證券裏面ニ記載シタル保險約款ニ據リ本契約ヲ締結シ前記契約日ニ第一回保險料ヲ領收致候仍テ當會社ハ右被保險者カ保險期間滿了ノ時マテ生存シタルトキ又ハ其ノ以前ニ死亡シタルトキハ右保險金受領者ニ前記保險金額ヲ御支拂可致候也

康德 年 月 日 新京本店ニ於テ之ヲ作成ス

新京特別市市照光路四百壹號

滿洲生命保險株式會社

理事長

满洲生命保险株式会社签发的保险契约书

Insurance contact document issued by Manchuria Life Insurance Co.

大连满洲火灾海上保险株式会社外景

Office building of Manchuria Marine & Fire Insurance Co. in Dalian

汪伪政府时期的保险业

Insurance under Wang Jingwei Government

1940年3月，汪精卫伪政府在南京成立。汪伪政府成立后，为了加强对保险业的监督管理，采取了一系列统治措施，以期把沦陷区保险业置于它的控制下。1942年，汪伪政府重订《苏浙皖三省各埠火险保价规则》，以期统一火险费率，接着又修改了国民政府的《保险法》和《保险业法》，于1942年10月10日公布施行。并制定了《保险业登记规则草案》等法规。接着又于同月成立了保险监理局，并发布公告："凡经营保险者，均须依照法定程序呈监理局转请实业部批准，依法登记，缴纳保证金，领取营业执照始得营业。"

1944年7月1日，汪伪政府中央储备银行拨款1亿元，成立了"中央保险股份有限公司"，总公司设在上海，汪伪政府行政院副院长兼财政部长周佛海任董事长，许建屏任总经理，1944年10月1日，汪伪财政部决定撤销保险监理局，委托中央保险股份有限公司专设检查机关，办理关于保险公司的注册、监督、指挥事项，中央保险股份有限公司实际已成为汪伪政府凌驾于所有保险公司之上的权力机构。成立后一年多的时间，即伴随着日军投降、汪伪政府覆灭而告终。

After its foundation in Nanjing in March 1940, Wang Jingwei government, to enhance the supervision and control over insurance, adopted a series of governing measures to take insurance in the enemy-occupied area under its control.

In 1942, Wang's government re-revised the *Rules on Fire Insurance Premium for Ports in Jiangsu, Zhejiang, and Anhui Province*, to unify the rates of fire insurance and, in the next step, amended the *Insurance Law* and *Insurance Industry Law* by the Republic of China to promulgated and put into effect on October 10, 1942.

On July 1, 1944, the Central Reserve Bank of Wang's government made an appropriation of 100 million yuan to found the Central Insurance Co. that headquartered in Shanghai.

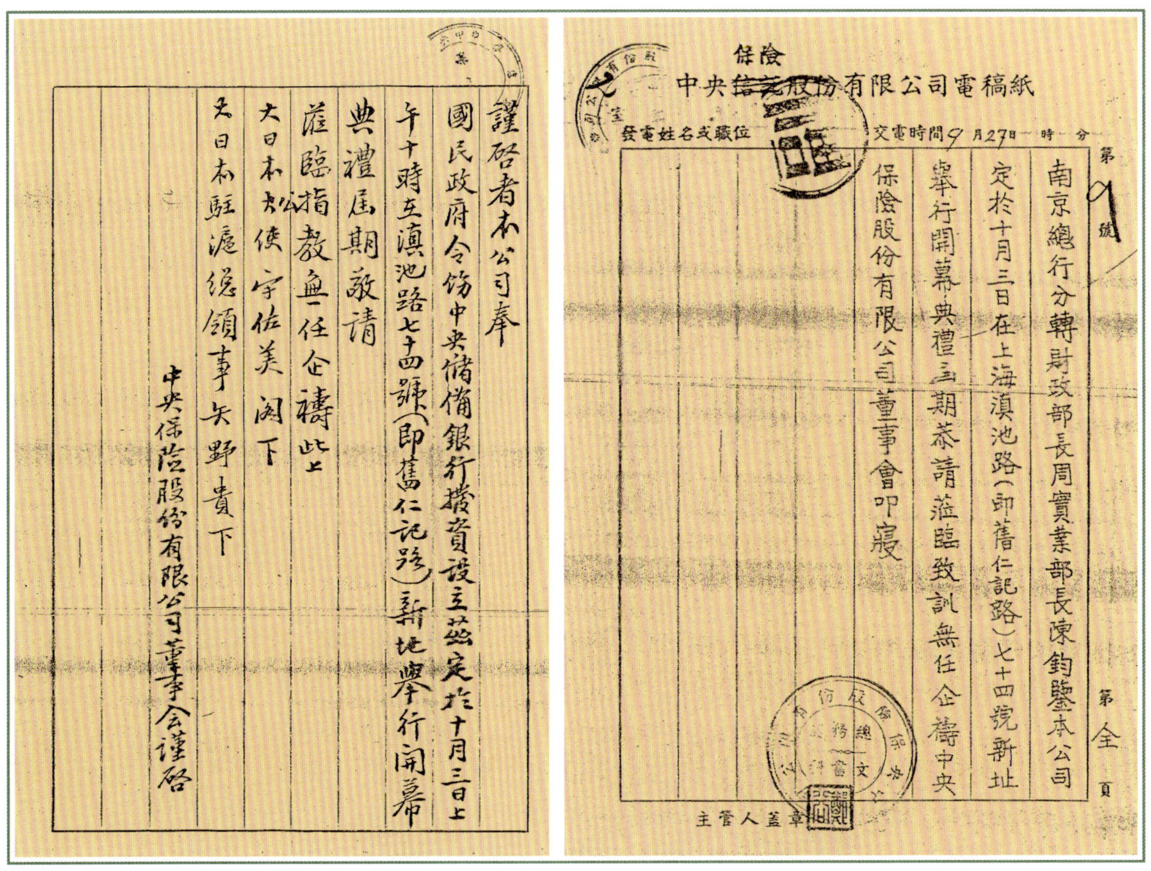

謹啓者本公司奉
國民政府令仿中央儲備銀行撥資設立茲定於十月三日上
午十時在滇池路七十四號(即舊仁記路)新址舉行開幕
典禮屆期敬請
蒞臨指教無任企禱此上
大日本大使宇佐美閣下
大日本駐滬總領事矢野貴下
中央保險股份有限公司董事會謹啓

中央保險股份有限公司電稿紙
發電姓名或職位　交電時間9月27日　時　分　第　號
南京總行分轉財政部長周實業部長陳鈞鑒本公司
定於十月三日在上海滇池路(即舊仁記路)七十四號新址
舉行開幕典禮並期恭請蒞臨致訓無任企禱中央
保險股份有限公司董事會叩寢
第全頁
主管人蓋章

汪伪政府主要保险机构中央保险公司开业典礼文件
Document of inauguration of the Central Insurance Co.

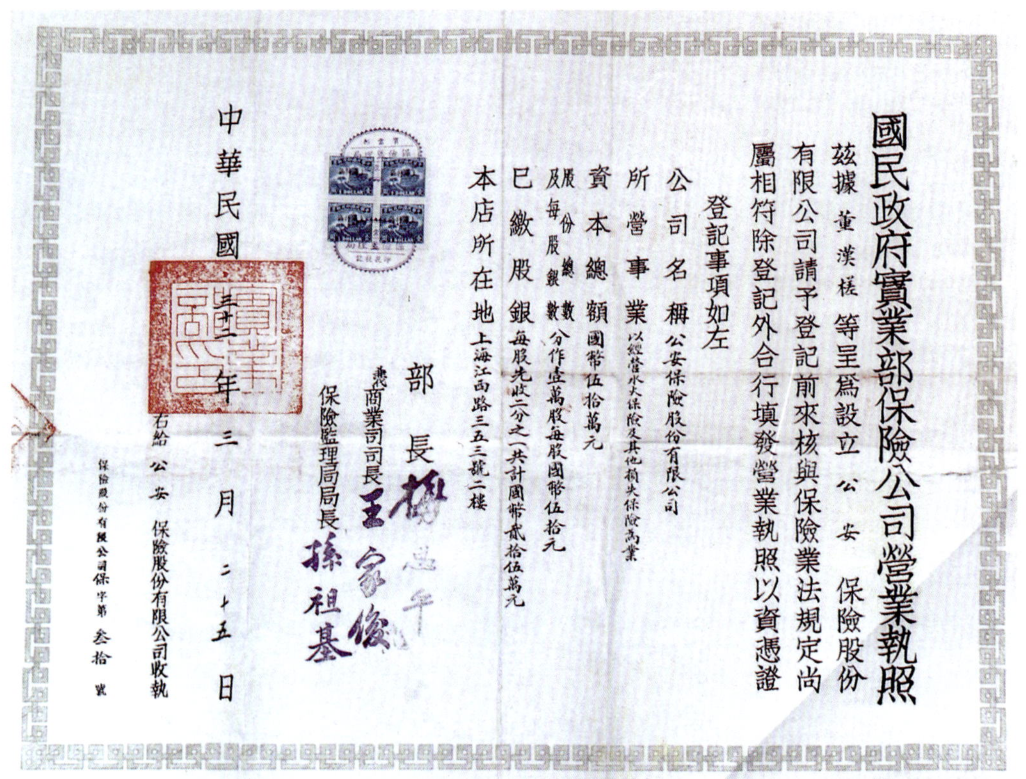
國民政府實業部保險公司營業執照

茲據董漢槎等呈爲設立公安保險股份有限公司請予登記前來核與保險業法規定尚屬相符除登記外合行填發營業執照以資憑證

登記事項如左

公司名稱 公安保險股份有限公司

所營事業 以經營水火保險及其他損失保險爲業

資本總額 國幣伍拾萬元

股份總數及每股銀數 分作壹萬股每股國幣伍拾元

已繳股銀 每股先收二分之一共計國幣貳拾伍萬元

本店所在地 上海江西路三五三號二樓

部長 梅思平

兼商業司長 王家俊

保險監理局局長 孫祖基

右給公安保險股份有限公司收執

中華民國三十二年三月二十五日

保險股份有限公司保字第叁拾號

汪伪政府签发的营业执照（资料提供：中国第二历史档案馆）

License Issued by Wang Jingwei Government

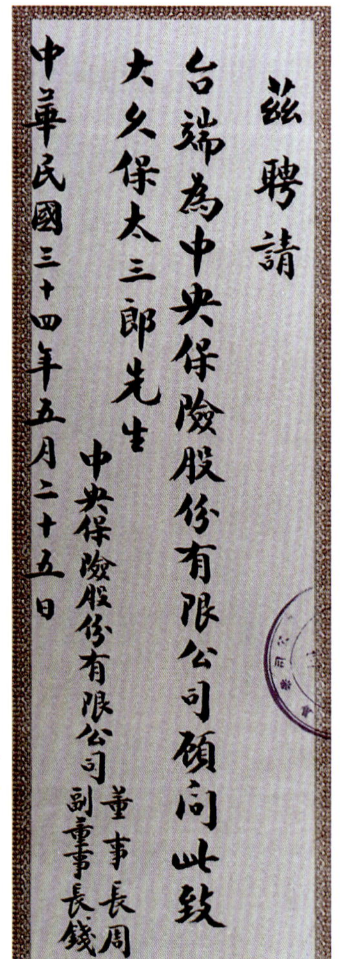
茲聘請

台端為中央保險股份有限公司顧問此致

大久保太三郎先生

中央保險股份有限公司

董事長周

副董事長錢

中華民國三十四年五月二十五日

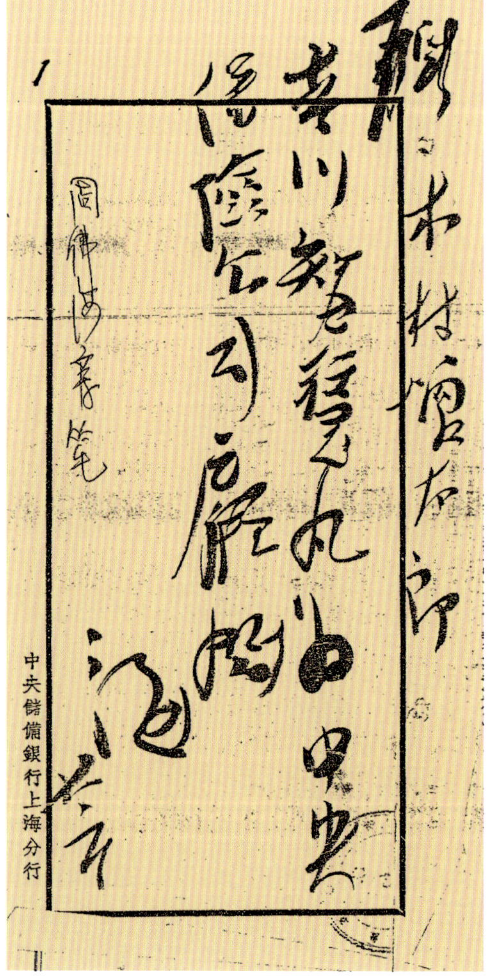

右图一：汪伪政府中央保险股份有限公司聘请日本顾问的聘书（资料提供：中国第二历史档案馆）

The Central Insurance Co.'s letter on appointing Japanese consultant (L)

右图二：汪伪政府要员周佛海关于为中央保险公司聘请日本顾问的亲笔信

Important official of Wang's government Zhou Fuhai's letter to employ a Japanese consultant for the Central Insurance Co. (R)

二十四、战后保险市场格局

Post-War-Against-Japan Insurance Situation

1945年8月，抗战胜利。战后收复的领土大部分被国民政府统治，敌伪机构全部被清理接收，官僚资本的保险机构与卷土重来的外商保险公司重新控制了保险市场。

战后，国民政府政治经济重心东移。原在抗战期间迁往重庆的如中央信托局产物保险处、中央信托局人寿保险处、中国产物保险公司、中国人寿保险公司以及后来在重庆成立的官僚资本保险机构，如太平洋产物保险公司、中国农业保险公司、资源委员会保险事务所和一些民营保险公司都复业或返沪。太平洋战争期间被迫停业的上海外商保险公司又卷土重来，最先复业的是美商美亚代理保险公司，其他如英商於仁保安、凤凰、老公茂康记产物保险公司，美商北美洲联合产物保险公司、大美保险公司等也陆续复业。与此同时，集中在上海的游资涌向工商业，保险业也成为竞相投资的热点。新的保险公司骤然增多。随着时局变化，金融市场重心由大后方转向上海，上海又成为全国保险业的中心。

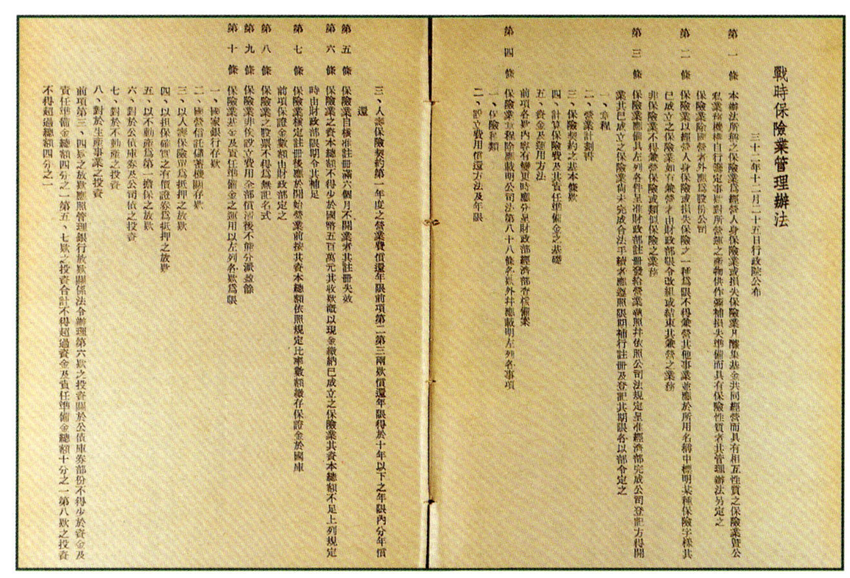

戰時保險業管理辦法

三十二年十二月二十五日行政院公布

第一條 本辦法所稱之保險業為經營人身保險業或損失保險業凡醵集基金共同經營而具有相互性質之保險業暨公私業務機構自行籌定事款對所營運之產物供作彌補損失準備而具有保險性質者其管理辦法另定之

保險業除國營者外應為股份公司

第二條 保險業以經營人身保險或損失保險之一種為限不得兼營其他事業並應於所用名稱中標明某種保險字樣其已成立之保險業如有兼營者由財政部限令改組或結束其兼營之業務

非保險業不得兼營保險或類似保險之業務

第三條 保險業應備具左列各件呈准財政部註冊發給營業執照并依照公司法規定呈准經濟部完成公司登記方得開業其已成立之保險業尚未完成合法手續者應遵照限期補行註冊及登記其期限各以部令定之

一、章程

二、營業計劃書

三、保險契約之基本條款

四、計算保險費及其責任準備金之基礎

五、資金及運用方法

前項各款內容有變更時應分呈財政部經濟部查核備案

第四條 保險業章程除應載明公司法第八十八條各款外并應載明左列各事項

一、保險種類

二、設立費用償還方法及年限

三、人壽保險契約第一年度之營業費償還年限前項第二第三兩款償還年限得於十年以下之年限內分年償還

第五條 保險業自核准註冊滿六個月不開業者其註冊失效

第六條 保險業之資本總額不得少於國幣五百萬元其收款應以現金繳納已成立之保險業其資本總額不足上列規定時由財政部限期令其補足

第七條 保險業核定註冊後應於開始營業前按其資本總額依照規定比率數額繳存保證金於國庫

前項保證金數額由財政部定之

第八條 保險業之股票不得為無記名式

第九條 保險業非俟設立費用全部償清後不能分派盈餘

第十條 保險業基金及責任準備金之運用以左列各款為限

一、國家銀行存款

二、國營信託儲蓄機關存款

三、以人壽保險單為抵押之放款

四、以担保確實之有價證券為抵押之放款

五、以不動產為第一擔保之放款

六、對於公債庫券及公司債之投資

七、對於不動產之投資

八、對於生產事業之投資

前項第三、四款之放款應照管理銀行放款關係法令辦理第六款之投資關於公債庫券部份不得少於資金及責任準備金總額四分之一第五、七款之投資合計不得超過資金及責任準備金總額十分之一第八款之投資不得超過總額四分之一

1937年，抗日战争全面爆发，重庆逐渐成为大后方的政治、经济、文化中心。华商保险业大批迁渝，实业界和国民党四大家族的投资，形成了官僚垄断的保险体系。1943年12月25日，国民党政府颁布《战时保险业管理办法》，自公布之日起施行，共25条。

Office Procedure of wartime Insurance by the Kuomintang government

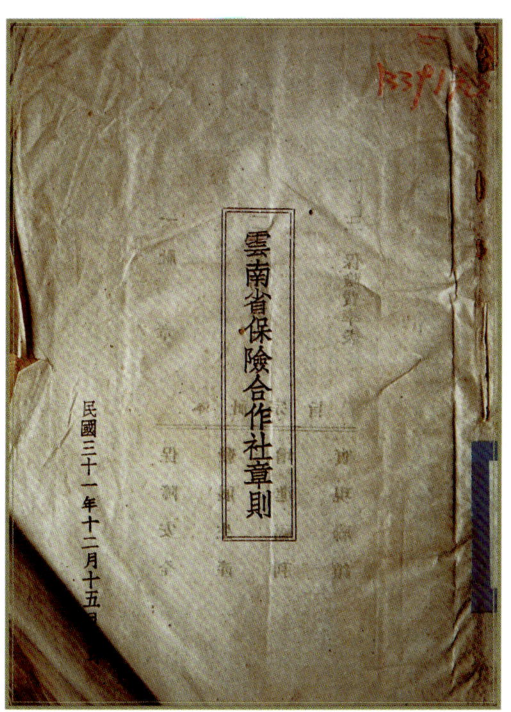

1942年12月，云南省保险合作社章则。

Articles of Yunnan Mutual Insurance Society

时局转折之际，敌伪金融机构接收清理工作和收复区保险机构的复业问题急需解决。国民政府财政部为此于1945年9月28日，公布《收复区商营保险公司复员办法》，规定不同类型的保险机构复业办法和一些主要手续。同年10月23日，财政部公告，饬令敌伪政府核准设立的保险公司一律停业清理。同盟国及中立国保险公司在抗战时期停止营业者，均依照收复区商营金融机关清理办法规定，由财政金融特派员先行接收。公告后，上海、南京有57家保险公司清理改组后获准营业。

Insurance companies run by bureaucrat and foreign capital controlled the insurance market again in 1915 after the war against Japanese aggression. All main insurers, such as China Life Insurance Co. and China Agriculture Insurance Co. moved back to Shanghai, where became the insurance centre of China again.

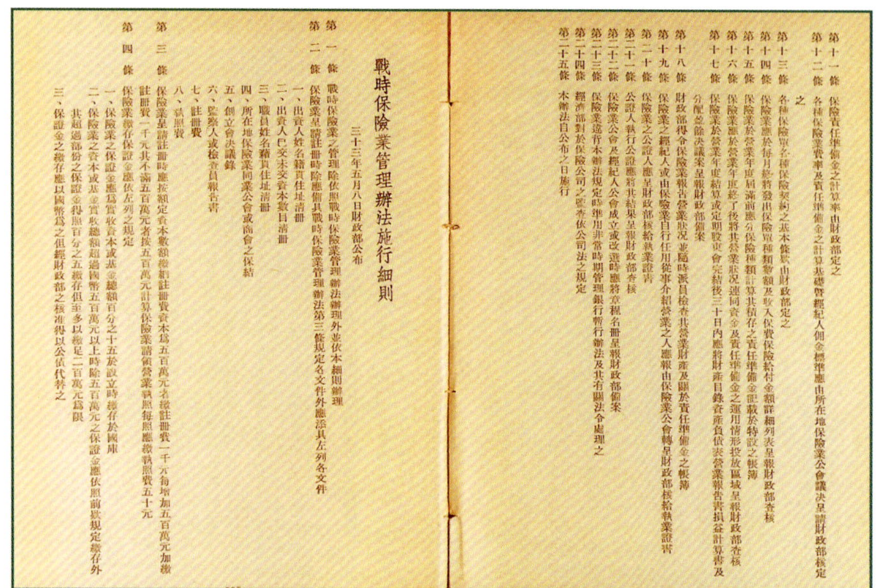

戰時保險業管理辦法施行細則

三十三年五月八日財政部公布

第一條 戰時保險業之管理除依照戰時保險業管理辦法辦理外並依本細則辦理

第二條 保險業呈請註冊時除應備具戰時保險業管理辦法第三條規定各文件外應添具左列各文件

一、出資人姓名籍貫住址清冊

二、出資人已交未交資本數目清冊

三、職員姓名籍貫住址清冊

四、所在地保險業同業公會或商會之保結

五、創立會決議錄

六、監察人或檢查員報告書

七、註冊費

八、執照費

第三條 保險業呈請註冊時應按額定資本數額繳納註冊費資本爲五百萬元者繳註冊費一千元每增加五百萬元加繳註冊費一千元其不滿五百萬元者按五百萬元計算保險業請領營業執照每照應繳執照費五十元

第四條 保險業繳存保證金應依左列之規定

一、保險業之保證金應爲實收資本或基金總額百分之十五於設立時繳存於國庫

二、保險業之資本或基金實收總額超過國幣五百萬元以上時除五百萬元之保證金應依照前款規定繳存外其超過部份之保證金得照百分之五繳存但至多以繳足二百萬元爲限

三、保證金之繳存應以國幣爲之但經財政部之核准得以公債代替之

第十一條 保險責任準備金之計算率由財政部定之

第十二條 各種保險業費率及責任準備金之計算基礎暨經紀人佣金標準應由所在地保險業公會議決呈請財政部核定之

第十三條 各種保險單各種保險契約之基本條款由財政部定之

第十四條 保險業應於每月終將發出保險單種類數額及收入保費保險給付金額詳細列表呈報財政部查核

第十五條 保險業於營業年度屆滿前應分保險種類計算其積存之責任準備金記載於特設之帳簿

第十六條 保險業應於營業年度終了後將其營業狀況連同資金及責任準備金之運用情形投放區域呈報財政部查核

第十七條 保險業於營業年度結算或定期股東會完結後三十日內應將財產目錄資產負債表營業報告書損益計算書及分配盈餘決議案呈報財政部備案

第十八條 財政部得令保險業報告營業狀況並隨時派員檢查其營業財產及關於責任準備金之帳簿

第十九條 保險業之經紀人或由保險業自行任用從事介紹營業之人應報由保險業公會轉呈財政部核給執業證書

第二十條 保險業之公證人應呈財政部核給執業證書

第二十一條 公證人執行公證應將其結果呈報財政部查核

第二十二條 保險業公會及經紀人公會成立或改選時應將章程名冊呈報財政部備案

第二十三條 保險業違背本辦法規定時準用非常時期管理銀行暫行辦法及其有關法令處理之

第二十四條 經濟部對於保險公司之監查依公司法之規定

第二十五條 本辦法自公布之日施行

为保证《战时保险业管理办法》的实施，1944年5月8日，国民党政府财政部公布《战时保险业管理办法施行细则》，共15条，自公布三日起施行。

Implementing Rules of the Office Procedure of wartime Insurance promulgated by the Finance Ministry of the Republic on May 8, 1944

为使外商与华商接受统一管理，财政部规定外商保险公司应依照1944年公布的《战时保险业管理办法施行细则》及《公司法》补办注册手续。外商依法履行手续后注册的保险公司有50家，其中美22家，英13家，法3家，瑞士3家，古巴1家，加拿大1家，并包括在香港设立的7家。

1945年第四季度起，上海市陆续增设了保险机构。依申请加入同业公会的中外会员数统计，到1946年11月止，有133家，其中华商124家、外商9家；到1947年5月止增至147家，其中华商138家，外商仍为9家，因有一批外商尚待完备注册手续而未计入。至1948年止，上海市保险机构猛增为241家，其中华商178家、外商63家（不包括部分外商代理机构），达到空前程度。

To administrate foreign insurers in the same way as it did to Chinese insurers, the Finance Ministry of the Republic of China stipulated that foreign insurers should re-register in light of the *Implementing Rules of the Office Procedure of wartime Insurance* and the *Corporation Law* as well.

From the fourth quarter of 1945 to 1948, the number of insurance institutions in Shanghai had soared up to an unprecedented 241, including 178 Chinese companies and 63 foreign ones excluding partial foreign agencies).

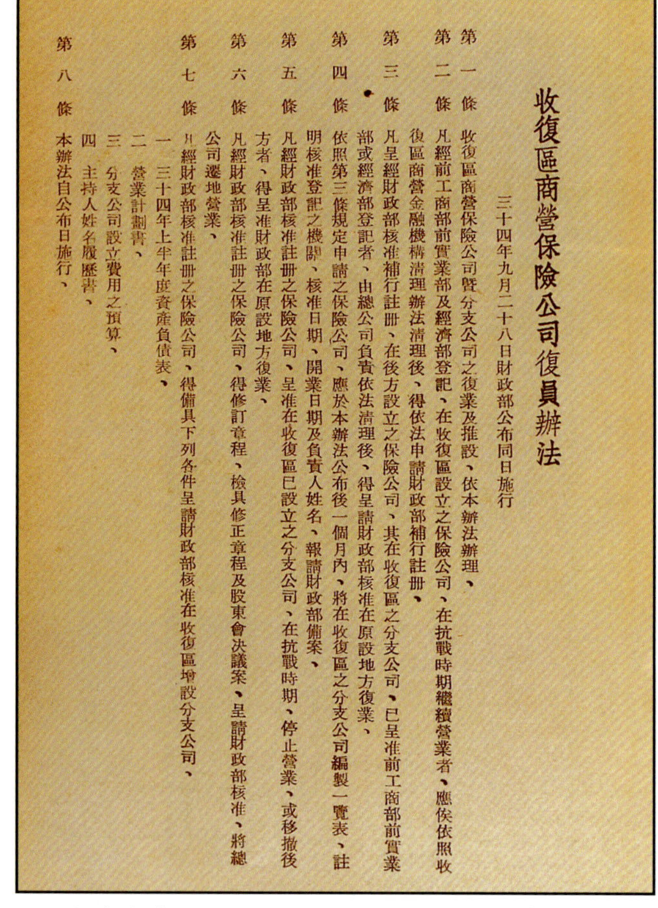

收復區商營保險公司復員辦法

三十四年九月二十八日財政部公布同日施行

第一條 收復區商營保險公司暨分支公司之復業及推設、依本辦法辦理、

第二條 凡經前工商部前實業部及經濟部登記、在收復區設立之保險公司、在抗戰時期繼續營業者、應俟依照收復區商營金融機構清理辦法清理後、得依法申請財政部補行註冊、

第三條 凡呈經財政部核准補行註冊、在後方設立之保險公司、其在收復區之分支公司、已呈准前工商部前實業部或經濟部登記者、由總公司負責依法清理後、得呈請財政部核准在原設地方復業、

第四條 依照第三條規定申請之保險公司、應於本辦法公布後一個月內、將在收復區之分支公司編製一覽表、註明核准登記之機關、核准日期、開業日期及負責人姓名、報請財政部備案、

第五條 凡經財政部核准註冊之保險公司、呈准在收復區已設立之分支公司、在抗戰時期、停止營業、或移撤後方者、得呈准財政部在原設地方復業、

第六條 凡經財政部核准註冊之保險公司、得修訂章程、檢具修正章程及股東會決議案、呈請財政部核准、將總公司遷地營業、

第七條 凡經財政部核准註冊之保險公司、得備具下列各件呈請財政部核准在收復區增設分支公司、

一 三十四年上半年度資產負債表、

二 營業計劃書、

三 分支公司設立費用之預算、

四 主持人姓名履歷書、

第八條 本辦法自公布日施行、

抗战胜利后，1945年9月28日，国民政府财政部颁布了《收复区商营保险公司复员办法》，共8条，自公布之日起施行。

Methods on Demobilizing Commercial Insurers in Reoccupation Regions Issued by the Kuomintang government in 1945

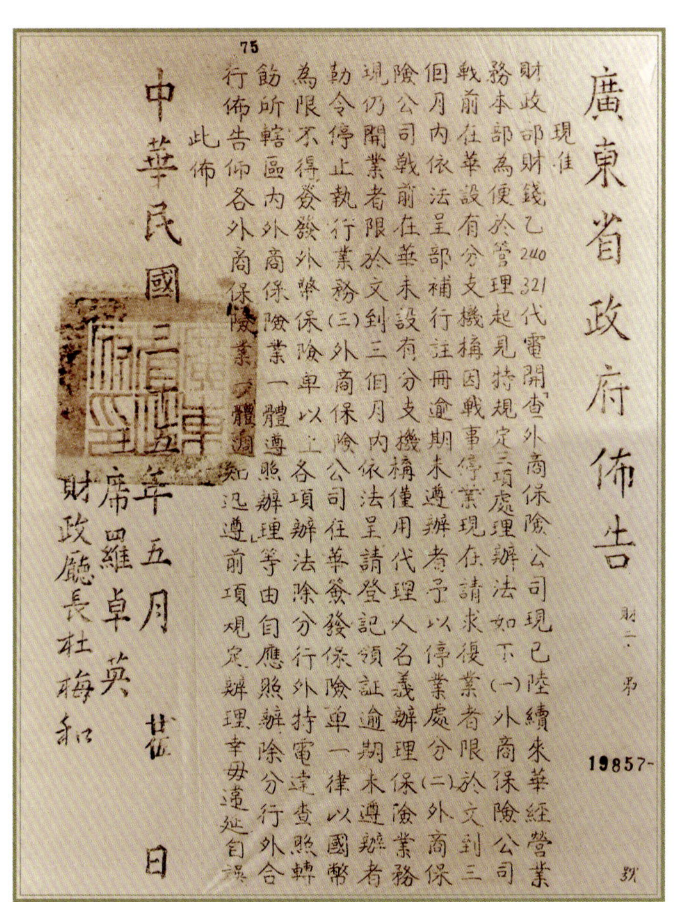
廣東省政府佈告

財二字第19857號

現准
財政部財錢乙240321代電開「查外商保險公司現已陸續來華經營業務本部為便於管理起見特規定三項處理辦法如下(一)外商保險公司戰前在華設有分支機構因戰事停業現在請求復業者限於文到三個月內依法呈部補行註冊逾期未遵辦者予以停業處分(二)外商保險公司戰前在華未設有分支機構僅用代理人名義辦理保險業務現仍開業者限於文到三個月內依法呈請登記領証逾期未遵辦者勒令停止執行業務(三)外商保險公司在華簽發保險單一律以國幣為限不得簽發外幣保險單以上各項辦法除分行外持電達查照轉飭所轄區內外商保險業一體遵照辦理」等由自應照辦除分行外合行佈告仰各外商保險業一體週知迅遵前項規定辦理幸毋違延自誤

此佈

中華民國三十五年五月 日

主席 羅卓英

財政廳長 杜梅和

1946年5月，广东省政府就恢复保险业的管理发布布告。(资料提供：广州市档案馆)

Notice on Insurance Recovery issued by Guangdong provincial government in 1946

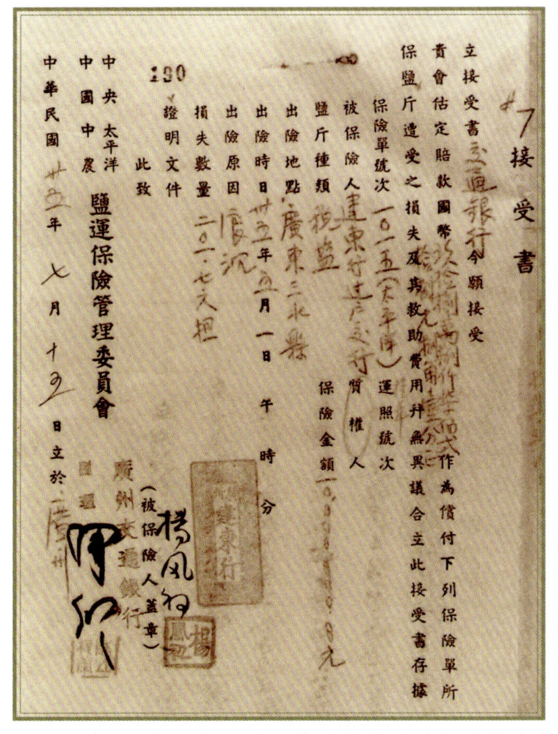
#7

接受書

立接受書交通銀行今願接受
責會估定賠款國幣[illegible]作為償付下列保險單所
保鹽斤遭受之損失及其救助費用并無異議合立此接受書存據

保險單號次 一〇一五(太平洋) 運照號次
被保險人 建東行 質權人
鹽斤種類 粗鹽 保險金額 [illegible]元
出險地點 廣東三水縣
出險時日 卅五年五月一日 午 時 分
出險原因 擱沉
損失數量 二〇一.七×担
證明文件

此致
中央 太平洋 中國 中農 鹽運保險管理委員會

中華民國卅五年七月十五日立於廣州

(被保險人蓋章) 楊鳳和
廣州交通銀行

1946年7月盐运保险管理委员会签发的出险接受书

Acceptance of insured items signed by Yien Yieh Transportation Committee

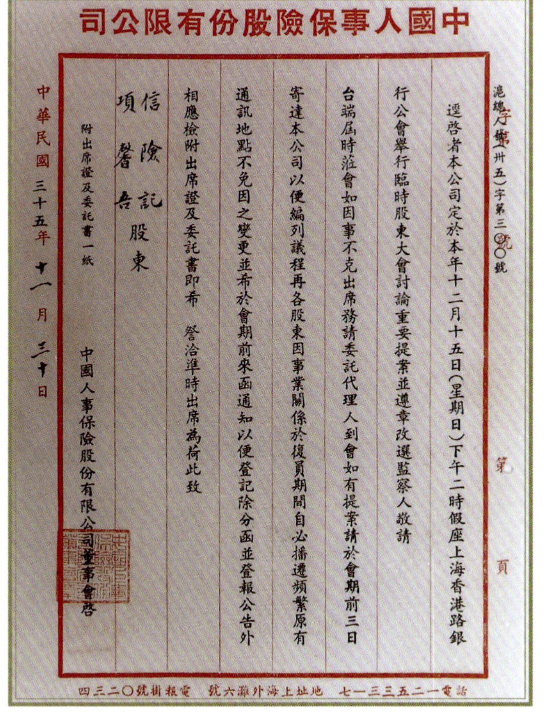
中國人事保險股份有限公司

港總字(卅五)字第三〇〇號

逕啓者本公司定於本年十二月十五日(星期日)下午二時假座上海香港路銀行公會舉行臨時股東大會討論重要提案並遵章改選監察人敬請
台端屆時蒞會如因事不克出席務請委託代理人到會如有提案請於會期前三日寄達本公司以便編列議程再各股東因事業關係於復員期間自必播遷頻繁原有通訊地點不免因之變更並希於會期前來函通知以便登記除分函並登報公告外相應檢附出席證及委託書即希 詧洽準時出席為荷此致

信險記股東
項馨台

附出席證及委託書一紙

中國人事保險股份有限公司董事會啓

中華民國三十五年十一月三十日

第 頁

電話一二五三三一七 地址上海外灘六號 電報掛號〇二三四

1946年11月中国人事保险股份有限公司公函

Official letter of China Personnel Matters Insurance Co. in 1946

抗战胜利后，以蒋宋孔陈四大家族为首的官僚资本，因其与国家政权结合，又与外国资本密切联系，已形成国家金融垄断势力。保险业随着金融重心东移上海后，国民政府官僚资本保险机构的势力也明显扩大。它们依仗政治后台，凭借雄厚资力，包揽了大部分保险业务。战后的官僚资本保险机构，除重庆、昆明等城市外，在上海的已有24家，其中包括中央信托局产物保险处、中央信托局人寿保险处、中国产物保险公司、中国人寿保险公司、太平洋产物保险公司、中国农业保险公司、资源委员会保险事务所、中国航联产物保险公司、中国航联意外责任保险公司、中国纺织建设公司保险事务所、台湾产物保险公司、交通产物保险公司等。这些规模大小不一的机构，控制了企业财产、船舶、货物运输、人寿及再保险等业务，形成了官僚资本保险集团的网络。

1943年12月8日，太平洋保险公司在重庆成立。国民政府官僚资本控制下的交通银行为主要投资者，公司的领导成员大部分也由交通银行派员担任。该公司实际上成为交通银行的附属机构。太平洋保险公司成立后即在昆明、贵阳、兰州、西安、成都等地设立分支机构，经理一般由交通银行经理兼任。太平洋保险公司的主要业务来源是交通银行的投资，押汇、放款、财产等。1945年，抗战胜利后总部迁回上海。

The Bank of Communications established the Pacific Insurance Company in 1943 in Chongqing. Later it set up branches in many cities in China. Head Office of the Pacific Insurance Company moved to Shanghai in 1945.

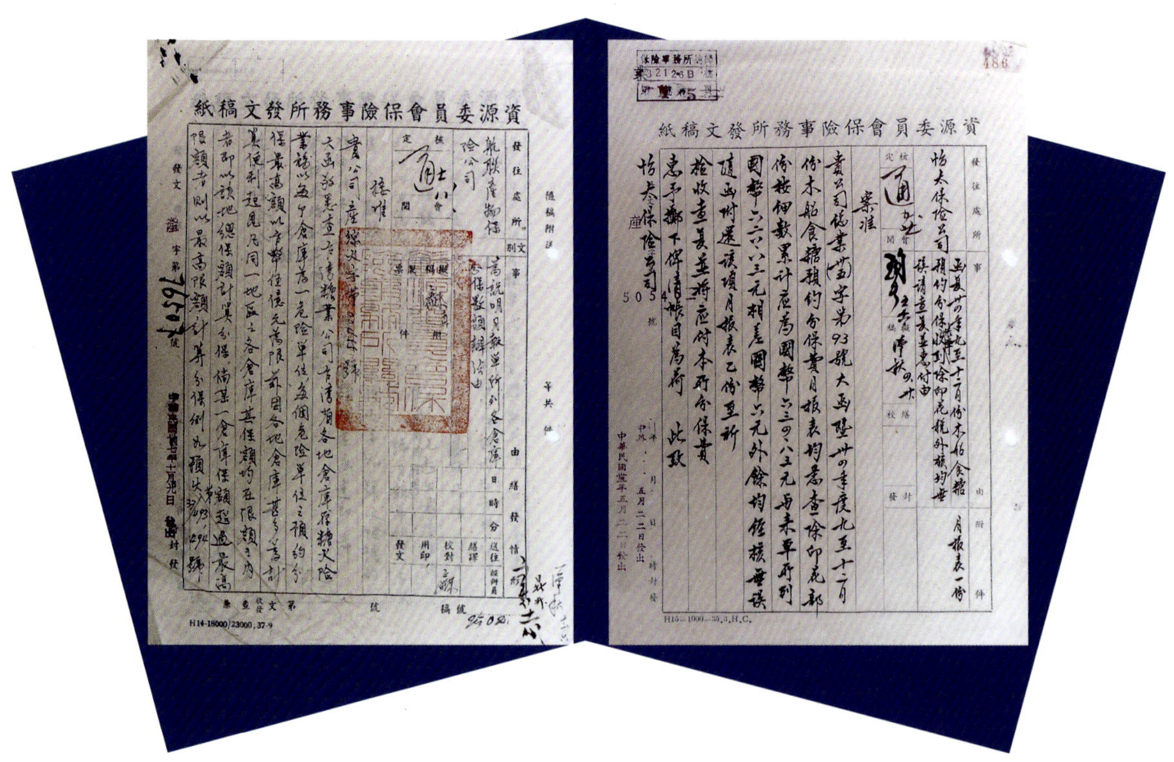
資源委員會保險事務所發文稿紙

資源委員會保險事務所發文稿紙

1946年资源委员会保险事务所致航联产物保险公司和怡太保险公司的业务函
Business letters of the Insurance Office of the Resource Committee in 1946

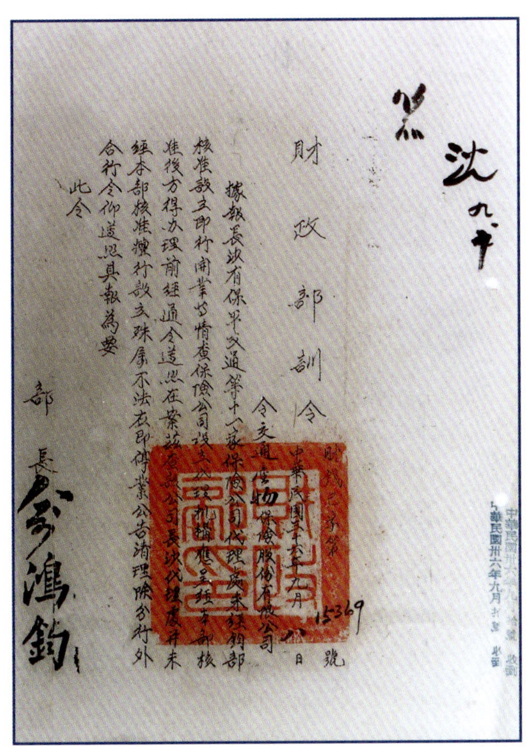
財政部訓令
財錢乙字第15369號
中華民國三十六年九月 日
令交通產物保險股份有限公司
據報長沙有保平交通等十八家保險公司代理處未經核准設立即行開業等情查保險公司設立分支機構應呈經本部核准後方得辦理前經通令遵照在案茲查該公司長沙代理處并未經本部核准擅行設立殊屬不法應即停業並將清理情形具報為要
合行令仰遵照具報為要
此令
部長 俞鴻鈞

1947年9月，民国政府财政部就11家保险公司代理处未经许可开业发部训令。
Mandate by the Finance Ministry in 1947 on 11 insurers' opening without its authorisation

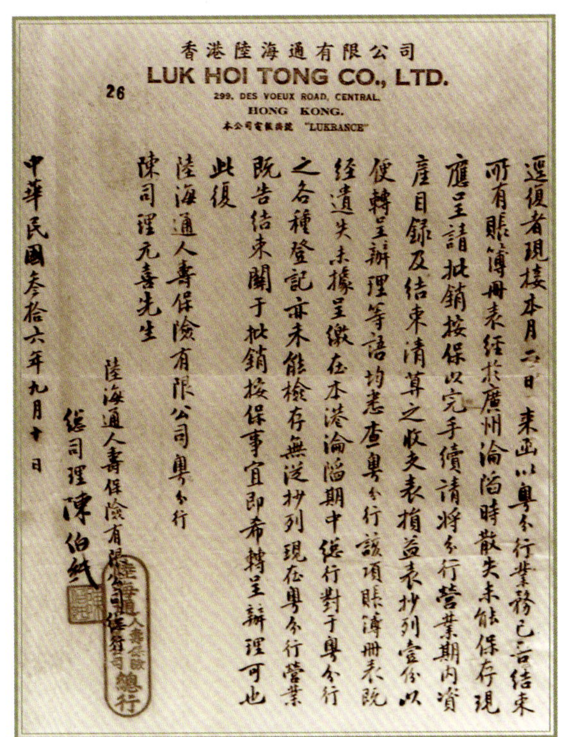
香港陸海通有限公司
LUK HOI TONG CO., LTD.
26
299, DES VOEUX ROAD, CENTRAL,
HONG KONG.
本公司電報掛號 "LUKRANCE"

逕復者現接本月二日來函以粵分行業務已告結束所有賬簿冊表經在廣州淪陷時散失未能保存現應呈請批銷按保以完手續請將分行營業期內資產目錄及結束清算之收支表損益表抄列壹份以便轉呈辦理等語均悉查粵分行該項賬簿冊表既經遺失未據呈繳在本港淪陷期中總行對于粵分行之各種登記亦未能檢存無從抄列現在粵分行營業既告結束關于批銷按保事宜即希轉呈辦理可也
此復
陸海通人壽保險有限公司粵分行
陳司理元喜先生
陸海通人壽保險有限公司
總司理 陳伯紙
中華民國叁拾六年九月十日

1947年，香港海陆通保险公司的业务复函。
Business letter of Luk Hoi Tong Co. Ltd. (Hongkong) in 1947

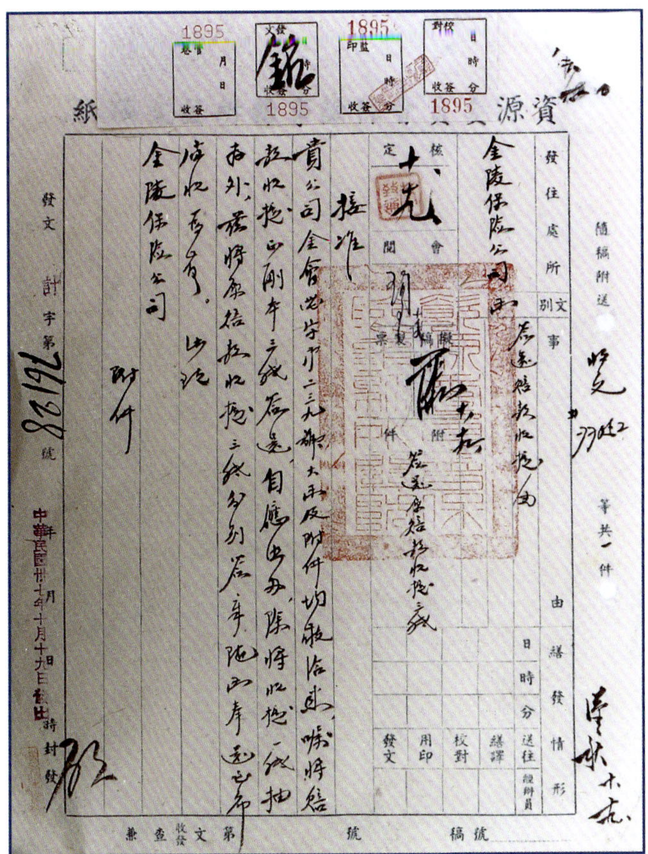
資源（ ）紙
1895
發文 附件 第 號
發往處所：金陵保險公司
事由：為送陸拾收據由
貴公司全會... 附件均敬悉 ... 收據 ... 此致
金陵保險公司
中華民國卅七年十月十九日 封發
附送 件 共一件

1948年10月19日，南京金陵保险公司业务函。
Business letter of Nanjing Jinling Insurance Co in 1948

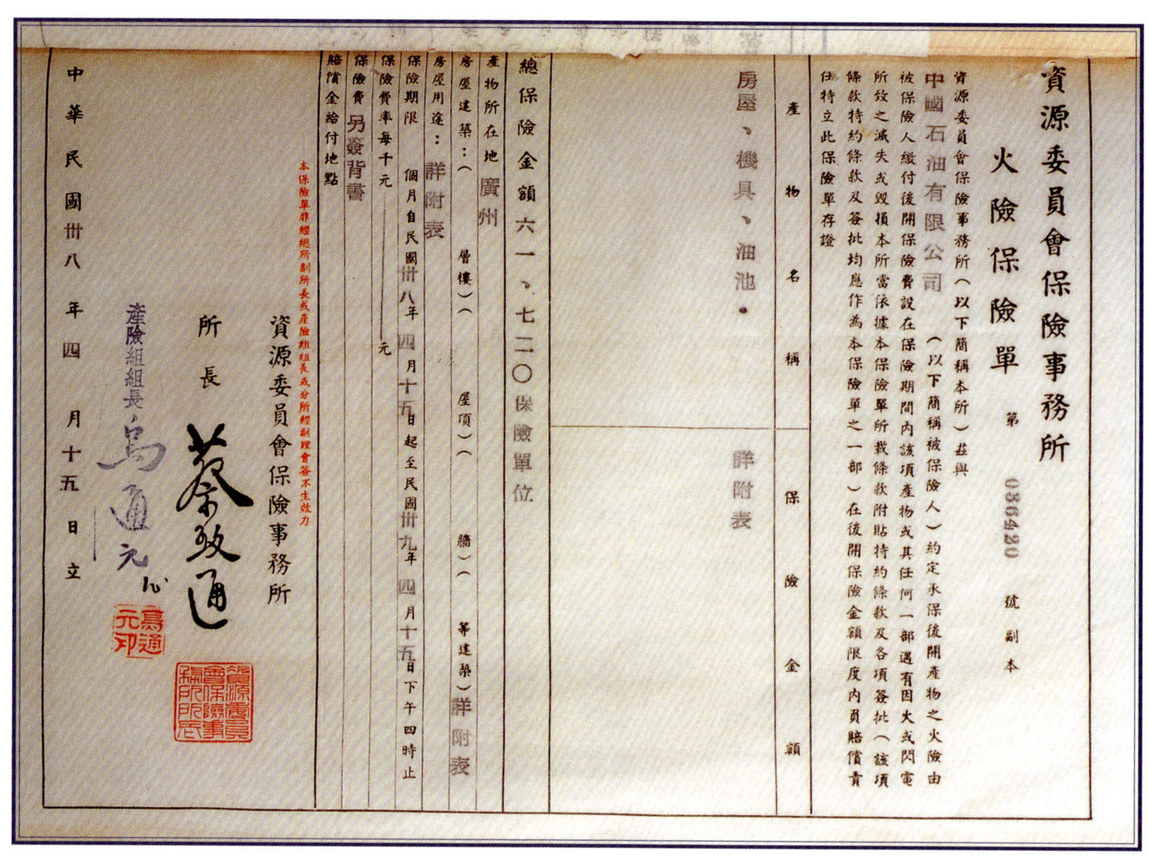

資源委員會保險事務所

火險保險單

第 036420 號 副本

資源委員會保險事務所（以下簡稱本所）茲與中國石油有限公司（以下簡稱被保險人）約定承保後開產物之火險由被保險人繳付後開保險費設在保險期間內該項產物或其任何一部遇有因火或閃電所致之滅失或毀損本所當依據本保險單所載條款附貼特約條款及各項簽批（該項條款特約條款及簽批均應作為本保險單之一部）在後開保險金額限度內負賠償責任特立此保險單存證

產物名稱	保險金額
房屋、機具、油池。	詳附表

總保險金額 六一、七二〇保險單位

產物所在地 廣州

房屋建築：（ 層樓）（ 屋頂）（ 牆）（ 等建築）詳附表

房屋用途：詳附表

保險期限 個月自民國卅八年四月十五日起至民國卅九年四月十五日下午四時止

保險費率每千元 元

保險費 另發背書

賠償金給付地點

本保險單非經總所副所長或產險組組長或分所經副理會簽不生效力

資源委員會保險事務所

所長 蔡致通

產險組組長 馬通元

中華民國卅八年四月十五日立

1949年4月5日，資源委员会保险事务所签发火险保险单。
Fire Insurance Policy by the Insurance Office of the Resource Committee in 1949.

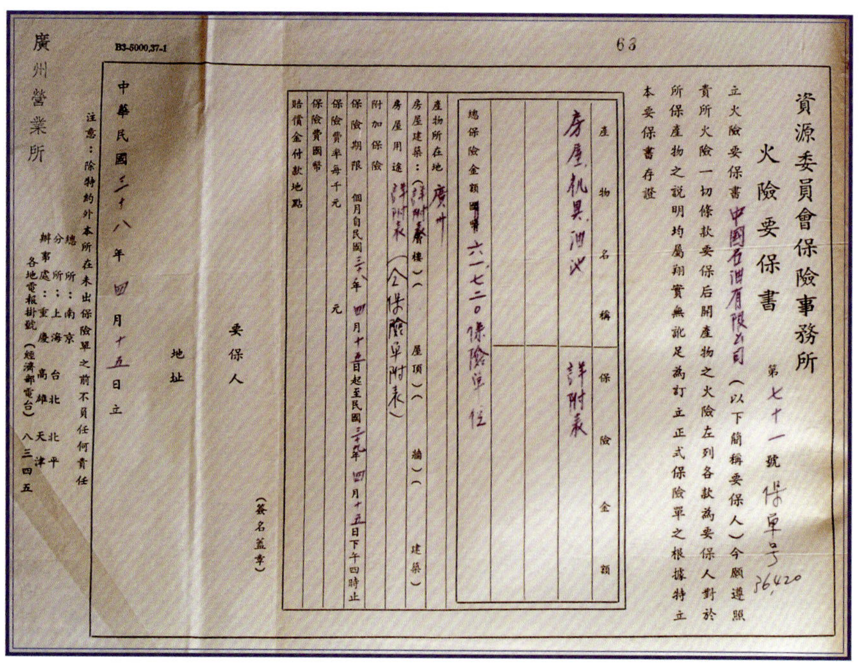

廣州營業所

B3-5000,37-1

63

資源委員會保險事務所

火險要保書

第七十一號 保單号36420

立火險要保書中國石油有限公司（以下簡稱要保人）今願遵照貴所火險一切條款要保后開產物之火險並列各款為要保人對於所保產物之說明均屬翔實無訛足為訂立正式保險單之根據特立本要保書存證

產物名稱	保險金額
房屋机具油池	詳附表

總保險金額國幣六一、七二〇保險單位

產物所在地 廣州

房屋建築：（詳附表 層樓）（ 屋頂）（ 牆）（ 建築）

房屋用途 詳附表（公保險單附表）

附加保險

保險期限 個月自民國三八年四月十五日起至民國三九年四月十五日下午四時止

保險費率每千元 元

保險費國幣

賠償金付款地點

要保人 （簽名蓋章）

地址

中華民國三十八年四月十五日立

注意：除特約外本所在未出保險單之前不負任何責任

1949年4月15日，資源委员会保险事务所签发的火险要保书。
Fire insurance proposal by the Insurance Office of the Resource Committee in 1949.

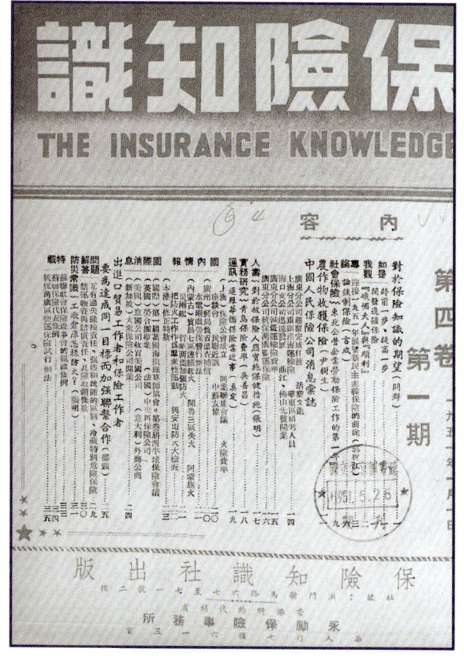

保險知識

THE INSURANCE KNOWLEDGE

第四卷第一期

內容

保險知識社出版

40年代末创办的《保险知识》杂志，解放后迁到香港。
The Insurance Knowledge launched in late 1940s. (moved to Hongkong after liberation)

交通银行行长、太平洋保险公司常务董事、总经理钱新之。

Qian Xinzhi: President of the Bank of Communications, and the Standing Director and General Manager of the Pacific Insurance Co.

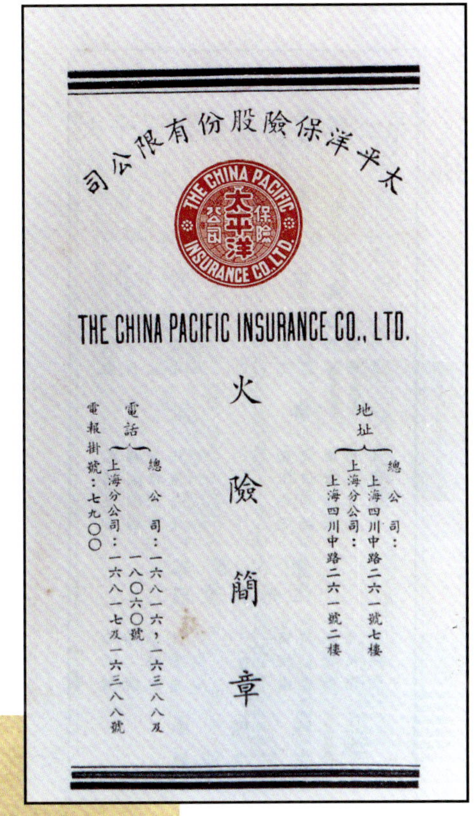

太平洋保險股份有限公司

THE CHINA PACIFIC INSURANCE CO. LTD.
太平洋保險公司

THE CHINA PACIFIC INSURANCE CO., LTD.

火險簡章

地址 總公司：上海四川中路二六一號七樓
上海分公司：上海四川中路二六一號二樓

電話 總公司：一六八一六，一六三八八及一八〇六〇號
上海分公司：一六八一七及一六三八八號

電報掛號：七九〇〇

太平洋保险公司火险简章

The China Pacific Insurance Co. (CPIC)'s general regulations on fire insurance

1945年，中国交通银行总行迁至上海，太平洋保险公司也随迁沪。图为上海交通银行总行办公大楼。

Building of the head office of the Bank of Communications in Shanghai

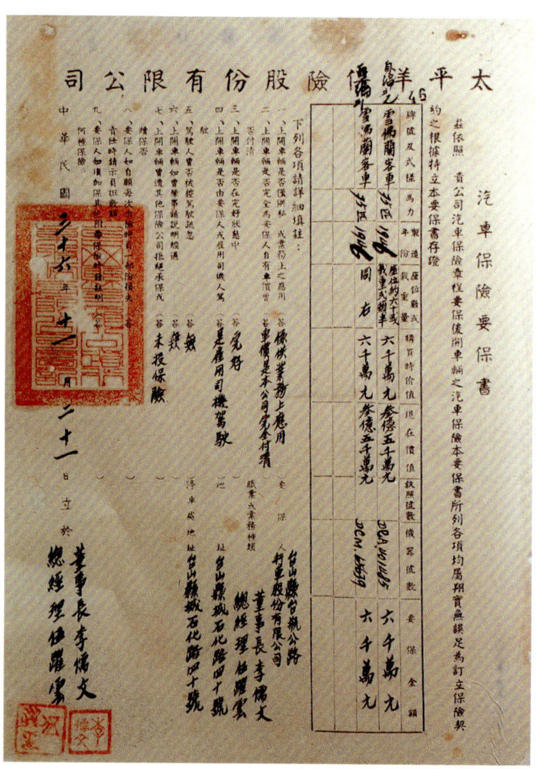

太平洋保險股份有限公司

汽車保險要保書

太平洋保险公司汽车保险要保书

Auto insurance proposal by the CPIC

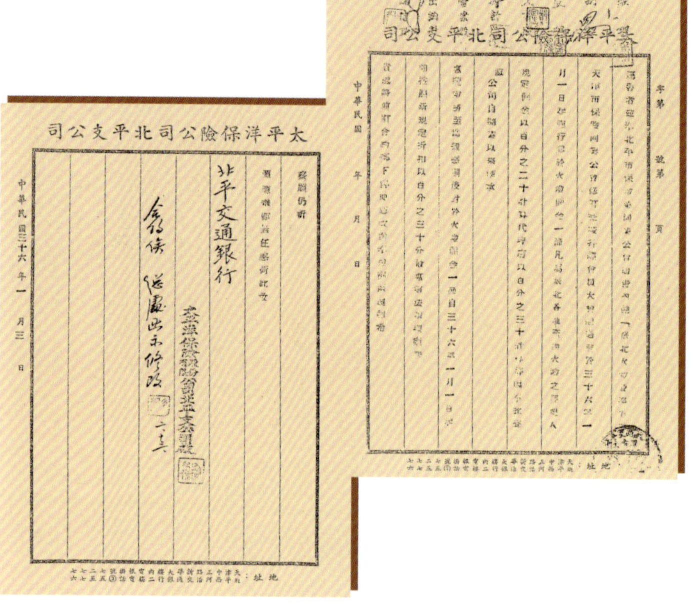

太平洋保險公司北平支公司

北平交通銀行

1947年1月3日，太平洋保险公司北平支公司业务函。

Business letter of the CPIC Peiping (Beijing) in 1947.

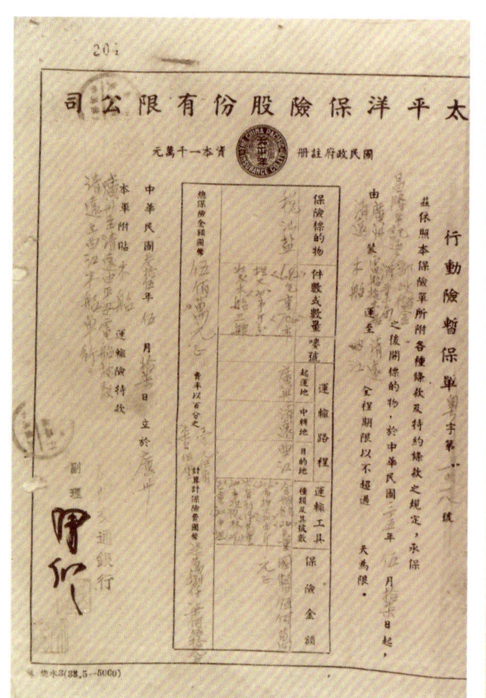

太平洋保險股份有限公司

行動險暫保單

太平洋保险公司行动险暂保单

Cover note of action insurance by the CPIC

1947

太平洋保險股份有限公司

CAPITAL $100,000,000

資本金國幣壹億圓

THE CHINA PACIFIC INSURANCE CO. LTD.

董事會

董事長 王正廷先生

常務董事

錢新之先生 杜月笙先生

盧作孚先生 劉航琛先生

[illegible]先生 王志莘先生

董事

趙棣華先生 湯筱齋先生

[illegible]心雅先生 王伯衡先生

莊叔豪先生 劉潤深先生

黃筱彤先生 張叔毅先生

監察人會

[illegible]文翰先生

徐國懋先生 [illegible]先生

[illegible]先生 [illegible]先生

[illegible]先生 [illegible]先生

總經理

錢新之先生

協理

[illegible]心雅先生 王伯衡先生

總公司：上海四川中路二六一號

1947年，太平洋保险公司董事会名单。

List of directorate of the CPIC in 1947.

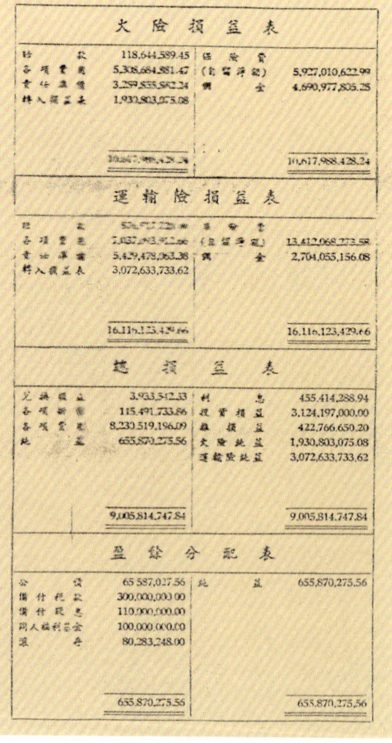

火險損益表

賠款	118,644,589.45	保險費（自留淨額）	5,927,010,622.99
各項費用	5,308,684,881.47	[illegible]金	4,690,977,805.25
責任準備	3,259,535,982.24		
轉入損益表	1,930,803,075.08		
	[illegible]		10,617,988,428.24

運輸險損益表

賠款	[illegible]	保險費（自留淨額）	13,412,068,273.58
各項費用	[illegible]	[illegible]金	2,704,055,156.08
責任準備	5,429,478,063.38		
轉入損益表	3,072,633,733.62		
	16,116,123,429.66		16,116,123,429.66

總損益表

兌換損益	3,933,542.33	利息	455,414,288.94
各項折舊	115,491,733.86	投資損益	3,124,197,000.00
各項費用	8,230,519,196.09	雜損益	422,766,650.20
純益	655,870,275.56	火險純益	1,930,803,075.08
		運輸險純益	3,072,633,733.62
	9,005,814,747.84		9,005,814,747.84

盈餘分配表

公積	65,587,027.56	純益	655,870,275.56
備付稅款	300,000,000.00		
備付股息	110,000,000.00		
同人福利基金	100,000,000.00		
滾存	80,283,248.00		
	655,870,275.56		655,870,275.56

1947年，太平洋保险公司资产负债表。

Balance sheet of the CPIC in 1947.

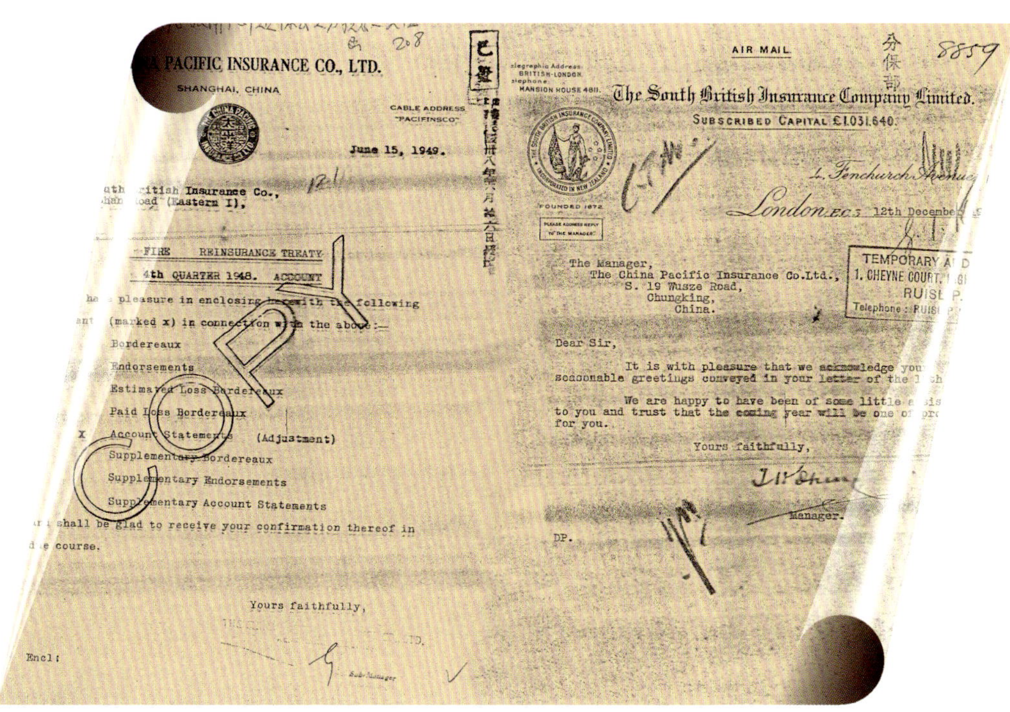

PACIFIC INSURANCE CO., LTD.
SHANGHAI, CHINA

CABLE ADDRESS "PACIFINSCO"

June 15, 1949.

...th ...itish Insurance Co.,
... ...oad (Eastern I),

FIRE REINSURANCE TREATY
4th QUARTER 1948. ACCOUNT

... pleasure in enclosing herewith the following ... (marked x) in connection with the above:—

Bordereaux
Endorsements
Estimated Loss Bordereaux
Paid Loss Bordereaux
X Account Statements (Adjustment)
Supplementary Bordereaux
Supplementary Endorsements
Supplementary Account Statements

... shall be glad to receive your confirmation thereof in due course.

Yours faithfully,

Sub-Manager

Encl:

COPY

AIR MAIL

Telegraphic Address: BRITISH-LONDON
Telephone: MANSION HOUSE 4811.

The South British Insurance Company Limited.
SUBSCRIBED CAPITAL £1,031,640.

FOUNDED 1872

PLEASE ADDRESS REPLY TO THE MANAGER

4, Fenchurch Avenue
London, E.C.3 12th December ...

The Manager,
The China Pacific Insurance Co.Ltd.,
S. 19 Wusze Road,
Chungking,
China.

TEMPORARY A... D...
1. CHEYNE COURT, ...
RUISLIP.
Telephone: RUISL...

Dear Sir,

It is with pleasure that we acknowledge your seasonable greetings conveyed in your letter of the 1...

We are happy to have been of some little assis... to you and trust that the coming year will be one of pro... for you.

Yours faithfully,

Manager.

DP.

1949年，太平洋保险公司与英国伦敦南不列颠保险公司业务联系函。
Business letter between the CPIC and the South British Insurance Co.

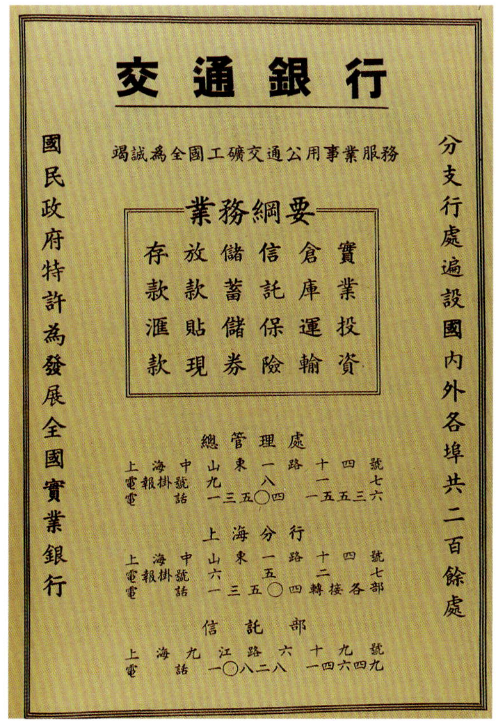

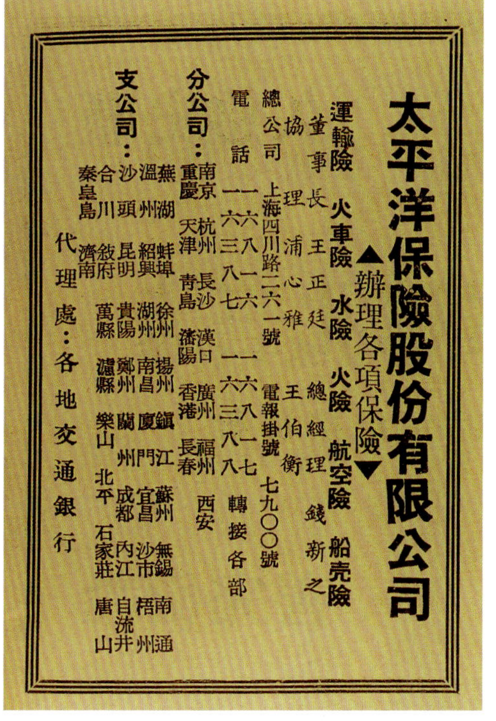

交通银行与太平洋保险公司广告
Ads of the Bank of Communications and the CPIC (R)

与太平洋保险公司同为官僚资本控制的中国农业保险公司，是1943年由中国农业银行投资建立。公司最高权力机构为董事会，总经理顾翊群。1945年，抗日战争胜利后，随中国农业银行迁沪。该公司在成立之前，主要由中国农业银行代理中央信托局的保险业务，其基本业务除农行贷款保险外，主要是从中国保险公司内争取农本局(后改为花纱布管理局)投保。公司成立后，除独家承办农本局投保这项巨大保险业务外，还承办了盐载保险和茧纱保险。茧纱保险是公司迁沪后独家经营的巨额业务之一。公司在重庆时，还在北碚小面积试办了一些耕牛和猪的保险，并对与农业有关的各种保险规章制度，进行了调查研究。

Founded by China Agriculture Bank in 1943, China Agriculture Insurance Co., in addition to be an agency of the Central Trust Co., operate loan and silkworm & cocoon insurance. Moreover, it had run a pilot scheme of livestock insurance in some Beibei of Chongqing, Sichuang Province.

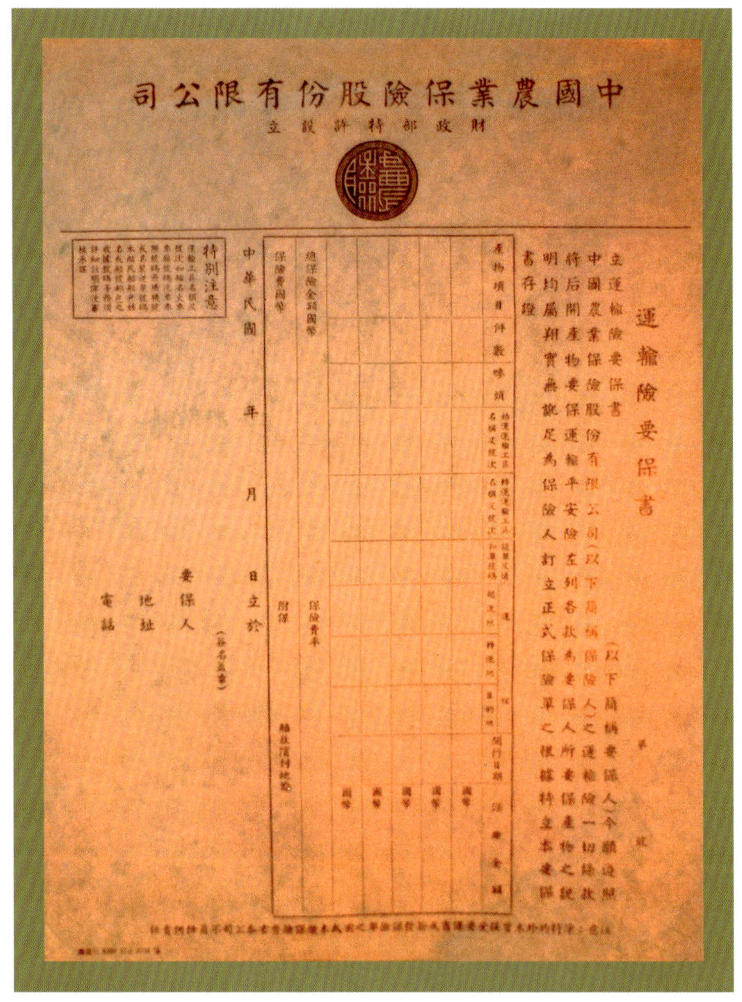

中國農業保險股份有限公司

財政部特許設立

運輸險要保書

立運輸險要保書　　(以下簡稱要保人)今願遵照中國農業保險股份有限公司(以下簡稱保險人)之運輸險一切條款特后開產物要保運輸平安險左列各款為要保人所要保產物之說明均屬翔實無訛足為保險人訂立正式保險單之根據特立本要保書存證

貨物項目　件數　保險金額

總保險金額國幣

保險費國幣

保險費率

附保

中華民國　年　月　日立於

要保人　(簽名蓋章)

地址

電話

特別注意

40年代，农业保险公司天津市分公司使用的运输险要保书。
Transportation insurance proposal by China Agriculture Insurance Co. in 1940s

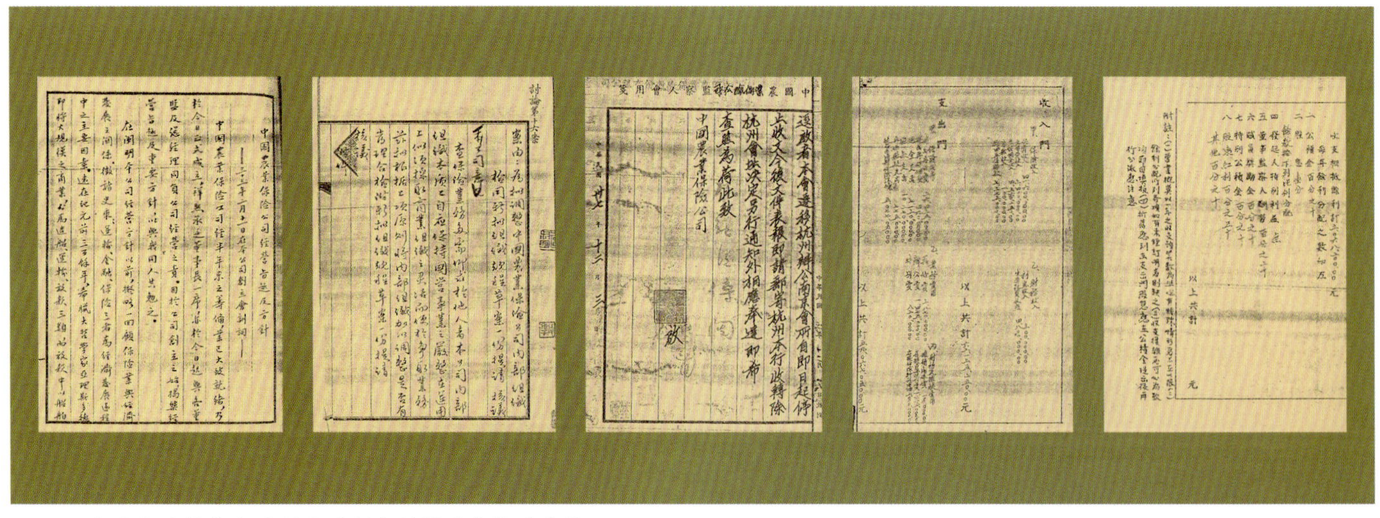

中国农业保险公司创立时制定的经营宗旨及方针
Objects & guidelines of China Agriculture Insurance Co when it's founded

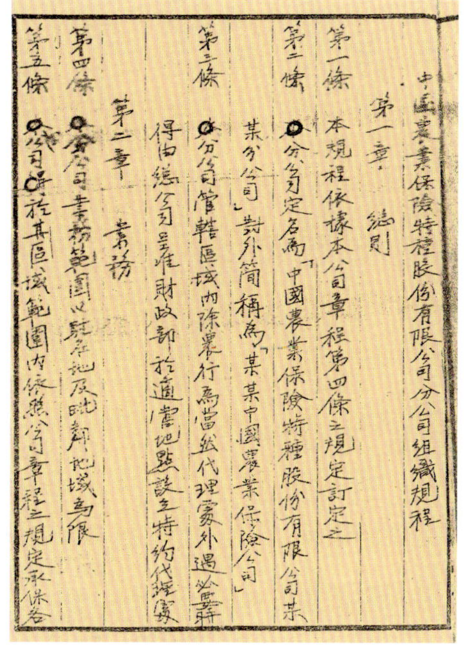

中国农业保险特种股份有限分公司组织规程

Organization rules of China Agriculture Insurance Speciality Co.

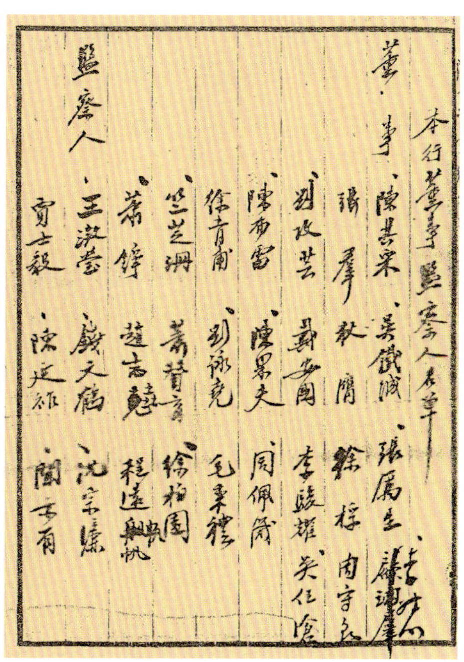

中国农业保险公司董、监事名单

Directors and Supervisors of China Agricultural Insurance Co.

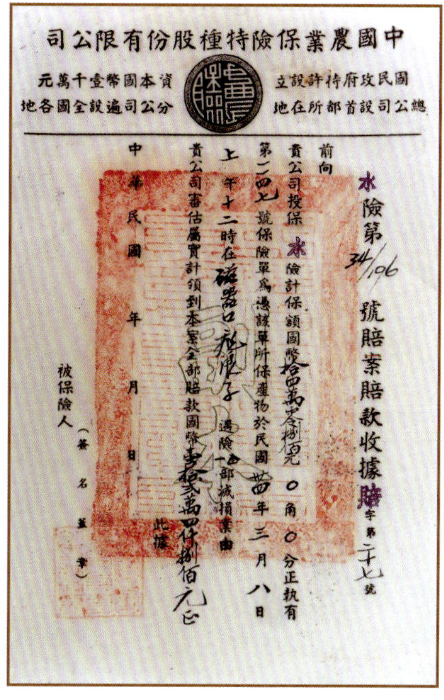

中国农业保险特种股份有限公司水险赔案赔款收据

Marine—insurance Indemnity receipt of China Agriculture Insurance Speciality Co.

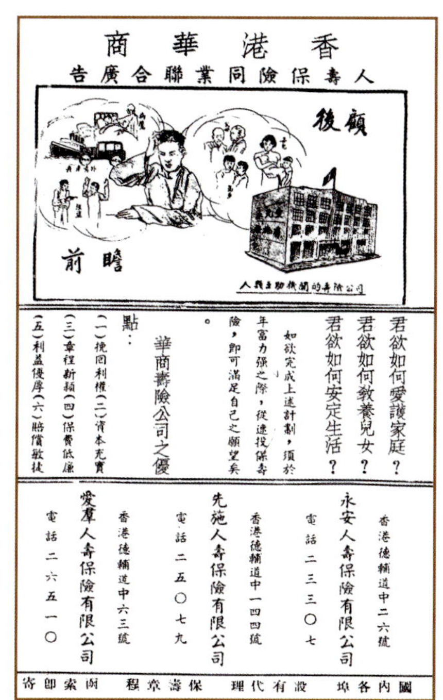

香港华商人寿保险同业联合会广告

Ad of Hongkong Chinese Life Insurance Association

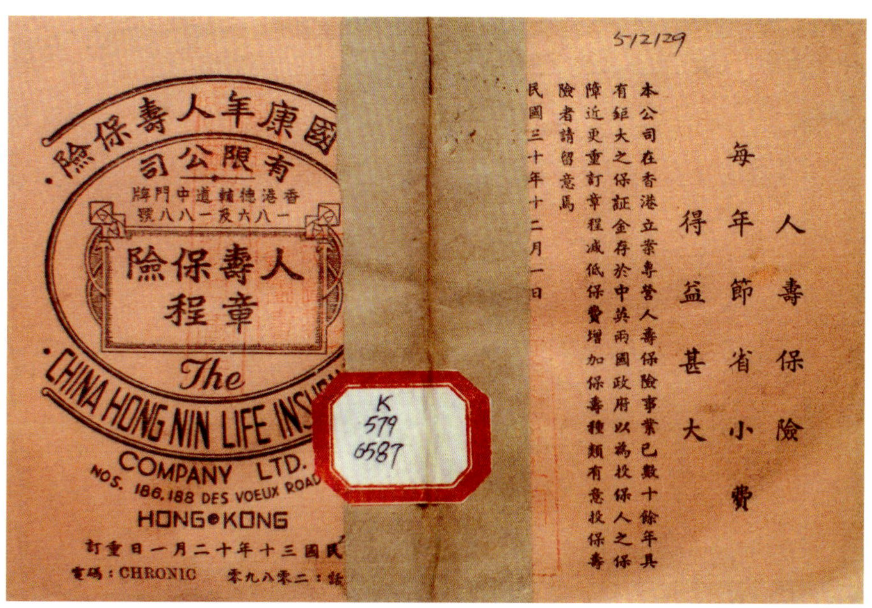

中国康年人寿保险公司章程

Rules of China Hong Nin Life Insurance Co.

中华民国保险商业同业公会
The Insurance Association of the Republic of China

中华民国保险商业同业公会联合会，是1946年7月15日在上海成立的全国性保险业联谊机构，罗北辰为理事长，丁雪农、过福云、董汉槎、毛啸岑等九人为常务理事。并设立了人身保险、火灾保险、运输保险、保险法规和保险学术研究五个专门委员会。由于当时国内经济形势混乱，国民政府濒临崩溃的边缘，因此该组织基本上未能进行正常活动，处于名存实亡的状态，到1949年初即自行解体。

Acting as a nationwide insurance fellowship, the Insurance Association of the Republic of China (IARC) was founded on July 15, 1946 in Shanghai, which set up 5 special committees concerning personal, fire, transportation insurance, insurance laws & regulations, and insurance academic research. Because of the chaos in the domestic economic situation, the Kuomintang government was at the edge of collapse, basically the association hadn't been able to engage in its activities and disassembled of its own accord.

中华民国保险商业保险同业公会理事长中央信托局人寿保险处经理罗北辰
Luo Beichen: director general of the IARC/manager of the Life Insurance Office of the Central Trust Co.

中华民国保险商业同业公会常务理事安平保险公司经理董汉槎
Dong Hancha: standing dirctor of the IARC/manager of Ping'an Insurance Co.

一九四九年華商保險公會春節聯歡同寅留影

1949年华商保险公会春节联欢会同仁合影
Members of the IARC attending the Spring Festival Party in 1949

二十五、社会保险的发展
Evolution of Social Insurance

备荒赈济的仓储制度是社会保险的雏型。春秋战国以后已逐步形成了仓储制度，如汉代的"常平仓"、隋朝的"义仓"、宋朝的"社仓"。

清乾隆年间(1736–1790)，清宫萧乾等91名太监自发建立了互助保险组织——万寿兴隆寺养老义会。其章程规定，凡入会太监在"退休"前三年必须缴银百两，年老时方可到养老义会所属寺院养老。其组织形式具有现代"养老保险年金"的性质，是中国养老保险的萌芽。

During the reign of Qianlong of Qing Dynasty (1736-1790), Xiao Qian and other eunuchs totalled 91, of themselves, established a mutual insurance institution, named Wanshouxinglong Society the organizational form of which had the quality of modern named Wanshouxinglong Society endowment-insurance annuity; it's the bud of Chinese endowment insurance.

位于北京北长街35号的清代万寿兴隆养老义会旧址
Site of Wanshouxinglong Society

民国初期，以孙中山为首的国民党开始着力提倡社会保险。1920年，孙中山在《地方自治开始实行法》中提出地方自治团体开展保险合作的主张。1924年，孙中山在其颁布的《工会条例》中规定：工会的职责之一是组织劳动保险和储蓄。1926年，国民党第二次全国代表大会通过关于设置劳动保险的决议案。

In the early Republic of China, Kuomintang, under the lead of Sun Zhongshan, began to embark on advocating social insurance.

国民党元老于佑任为社会保险题词
Senior statesman Yu Youren's inscription on social insurance

孙中山大力提倡社会保险，他认为社会保险可以提高劳动生产率。
Sun Zhongshan who greatly advocated social insurance

1926年，国民党二大代表合影，此次会议通过了劳动保险的决议案。
Delegates attending the 2nd Congress of Kuomintang that passed the labour-insurance resolution.

1931年，由张法尧编写的中国最早的社会保险专著《社会保险要义》出版，该书向国人介绍了世界各国社会保险制度，阐明了社会保险的意义和可借鉴的模式。

Published in 1931, the *Substance of Social Insurance*, compiled by Zhang Farao, is the earliest monograph on social insurance in China, which introduced Chinese social insurance system of countries of the world by clarifying the significance of social insurance and the modes that can be taken for reference.

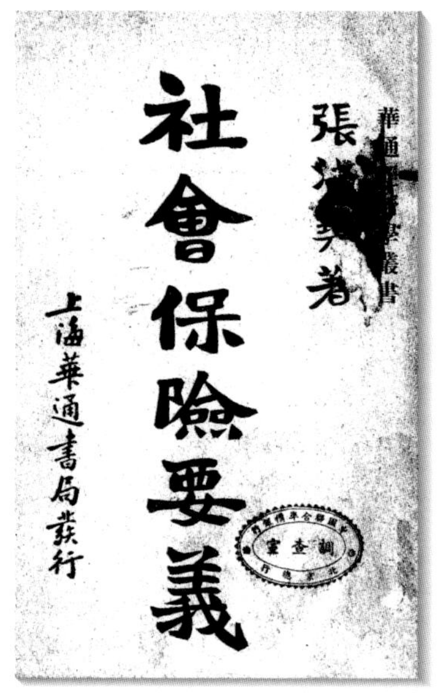

1931年出版的《社会保险要义》，张法尧著。

Substance of Social Insurance by Zhang Farao, published in 1931

王宠惠(1881—1958)，曾任北洋政府总理、国民政府委员、外交部长等职。

Wang Chonghui: premier of the North government; commissioner/foreign-affairs minister of the Republic.

保險制度至近世而始發達而社會保險視
其他保險尤為重要誠今日所宜詳加研究
者也無論何國社會其以工作為生活之人實
居大多數此種勞工恃工資為餬口絕少積
蓄以備不虞一旦不幸遇有疾病傷殘衰老
死亡或失業時其於經濟上之需要尚必異常
急迫既有保險以資救濟則個人或其家族
庶可無後顧之憂質言之社會保險之施
行實解決民生問題之最要辦法也張君
法堯近以所著社會保險要義見示研究
具有心得而所述各國社會保險制度尤為
言簡而賅按社會保險制度或為強制
或為任意各國在法律上業有規定而
強制保險適用於工業國已成為近今立
法之趨向此種制度德國實始施行之其後
歐美各國暨日本亦均次第倣效不惟載
諸法律且有規定之於憲法者如德意志
聯邦憲法第一六一條波蘭共和國憲法第
一〇二條其尤顯著者也吾國
國民政府注重人民經濟亟謀完善之措
置最近提出國民會議之約法草案內於
保險一事亦經列有條文將來此種制度
果能實施張君是書庶幾喚起社會之注
意而為研究此問題者參考之資料殆可
卜也
中華民國二十年五月王寵惠序

王宠惠为《社会保险要义》写的序

Prologue by Wang Chonghui for the *Substance of Social Insurance*

中华苏维埃中央执委会第一次会议
The First Session of the Chinese Soviet Central Executive Committee

30年代，中国共产党在其各个根据地开始推行社会劳动保险和失业保险。1930年，江西革命根据地召开的苏维埃第一次全国代表大会通过了《劳动法草案》，其中第六章为《社会保险》。同年，中华苏维埃第一次全国工农兵代表大会通过《中华苏维埃共和国劳动法》，其中第八章、第十章为《劳动保险》和《社会保险》。1934年，中央苏区召开第二次全国工农兵代表大会，再次主张创立社会保险制度和国家失业津贴制度。

1947年6月26日，国民政府成立了中央社会保险局，包华国为局长。同年10月31日，国民政府颁布《社会保险法原则草案》。

In 1930s, the Communist Party of China began to push social labour insurance and unemployment insurance in its revolutionary bases. In 1930, the *Draft of Labour Law* was passed at the First Session of the Chinese Soviet Congress of Workers at the revolutionary base in Jiangxi Province; the sixth chapter of the Draft was titled Social Insurance.

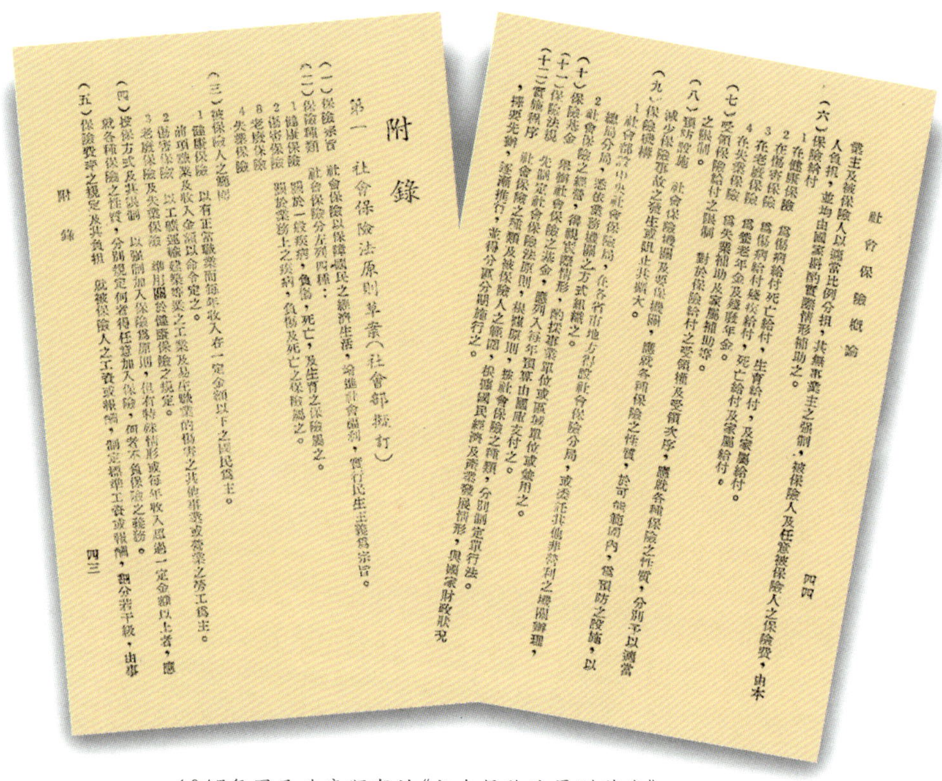

附錄

第一 社會保險法原則草案（社會部擬訂）

（一）保險宗旨 社會保險以保障國民之經濟生活，增進社會福利，實行民生主義為宗旨。

（二）保險種類 社會保險分左列四種：

1 健康保險 關於一般疾病，負傷，死亡，及生育之保險屬之。

2 傷害保險 關於業務上之疾病，負傷及死亡之保險屬之。

3 老廢保險

4 失業保險

（三）被保險人之範圍

1 健康保險 以有正當職業而每年收入在一定金額以下之國民為主。

前項職業及收入金額以命令定之。

2 傷害保險 以工礦運輸建築等業之工業及易生職業的傷害之其他事業或營業之勞工為主。

3 老廢保險及失業保險 準用關於健康保險之規定。

（四）投保方式及其限制 以強制加入保險為原則，但有特殊情形或每年收入超過一定金額以上者，應就各種保險之性質，分別規定何者得任意加入保險，何者不負保險之義務。

（五）保險費率之規定及其負擔 就被保險人之工資或報酬，制定標準工資或報酬，劃分若干級，由事

附錄 四三

社會保險概論 四四

業主及被保險人以適當比例分擔，其無事業主之強制，被保險人及任意被保險人之保險費，由本人負擔，並均由國家斟酌實際情形補助之。

（六）保險給付

1 在健康保險 為傷病給付死亡給付，生育給付，及家屬給付。

2 在傷害保險 為傷病給付殘疾給付，死亡給付及家屬給付。

3 在老廢保險 為養老年金及殘廢年金。

4 在失業保險 為失業補助及家屬補助等。

（七）受領保險給付之限制 對於保險給付之受領權及受領次序，應就各種保險之性質，分別予以適當之限制。

（八）預防設施 社會保險機關及要保機關，應就各種保險之性質，於可能範圍內，為預防之設施，以減少保險事故之發生或阻止其擴大。

（九）保險機構

1 社會部設中央社會保險局，在各省市地方得設社會保險分局，或委託非營利之機關辦理，總局分局，悉依業務機關之方式組織之。

2 社會保險之經營，得視實際情形，酌採事業單位或區域單位或並用之。

（十）保險基金 先設定社會保險之基金，應列入每年預算由國庫支付之。

（十一）保險法規 先制定社會保險法原則，根據原則，按社會保險之種類，分別制定單行法。

（十二）實施程序 社會保險之種類及被保險人之範圍，根據國民經濟及產業發展情形，與國家財政狀況，擇要先辦，逐漸推行，並得分區分期施行之。

1947年国民政府颁布的《社会保险法原则草案》
Draft of Principles on Social Insurance Law promulgated by the Kuomintang government in 1947

中华苏维埃第一次全国工农兵代表大会通过《中华苏维埃共和国劳动法》
Labour Law of the Soviet Republic of China passed at the First Session of the Chinese Soviet Congress of Workers

二十六、民国保险人物
Big Names During the Republic of China

傅其霖
Fu Qilin

傅其霖，浙江镇海县人。在民国之前即潜心从事保险，除了过福云，就要数傅其霖了。傅其霖早年供职于上海最早的华商保险公司——华兴水火保险公司，不久升任该公司水险部主任。由于他天资聪慧，颇多建树，深得公司董事会倚仗。一战爆发后，外商航运大受打击，而我国航运业则发展迅速，傅连续为三北、宁绍、鸿安三家轮船公司及国营招商局扩大经营水险计划，成绩卓著，后升任副经理。

当时因保险业者未能通力合作，所以对于巨额再保险业务极感困难。他极力倡导同业合作，并邀请华商保险公司组建了保险公会，傅被推举为董事、执行委员，为维护同业的利益贡献巨大，深得同业推崇。后华安水火保险公司经理沈仲礼逝世，董事会力邀傅出任经理，经过10余年发展奋斗，公司各项业务欣欣向荣，傅又升任公司常务董事兼总经理。

对于水火险合作的方法，傅倡议极多，他集合同业创建华商分保团，后又正式成立船舶保险联合会，傅任委员，聘请工程专家及验船师办理修理救助事宜，此外又联络上海航政局组织评判及审定船员资格，博得各界赞誉。后来与华商同业组建华商联合保险公司专营再保险务，傅任常务董事并一度兼任董事长。

Fu Qilin, who involved in insurance as early as before the Republic of China, worked as vice manager in an earliest Chinese insurance company Huaxing Marine & Fire Insurance Co. in its early career and, later on invitation, took up the post of manger of Hua'an Marine & Fire Insurance Co. and finally was promoted to be standing director and managing director of the company.

丁雪农，江苏扬州人。青年时代留美，归国后任交通银行青岛分公司经理。因在美求学时专攻保险，回国后耳闻目睹中国保险业的落后，于是在1930年创办了太平保险公司并自任经理。不到10年，太平保险公司已成为当时规模最大的一家保险公司，分支机构遍布全国，并在新加坡设立分公司。1935年，太平、安平、丰盛三家公司合并，成立太安丰总经理处，丁雪农任协理，并任上海市保险业同业公会常务委员兼华洋联合委员会委员，并组建了华商联合分保公司，这是华商自办的第一家再保险公司。他还曾任上海人力车夫团体保险委员会主席，并倡导体育，是华东体育会创办人之一，并任该会会长。

1949年上海解放后，他积极参与筹组民联分保交换处，1951年去香港，1962年在台湾病逝。

Dong Xuenong, born in Jiangsu Province, worked as manager for the Bank of Communications Qingdao Branch after he came back from the United State. In 1930, Ding launched Taiping Insurance Co. and held the position of manager. In less a decade after its foundation, Taiping developed to be one of the largest companies among its peers. In 1935, Ding organized the Chinese United Reinsurance Co., the first Chinese-operated reinsurance company. Furthermore, he had been president of Shanghai Rickshaw-Driver Group Insurance Committee.

丁雪农
Ding Xuenong

任硕宝
Ren Shuobao

任硕宝，福建闽侯人。1918年，他从福州格致书院毕业后，进入保险界服务。他先是在法商保太保险公司任视察专员，在各地视察各代理处业务状况，颇受公司赏识。组建友邦水火保险公司时，任被聘为经理。后又兼任美亚保险公司中国各口岸水险部经理。1932年，上海实业界、金融界巨头联合组建华商泰山保险公司，聘任为水火险部经理。这是脱离洋商进入华商保险的开始。任专心于公司的业务与管理，重要事务，必亲自料理，公司业务日渐兴隆，根基也日趋稳定。

此外，任对社会公益事业也极为热心，曾任上海市保险业同业公会的估价委员、兵险委员会主席、火险查勘研究班委员等。任还任华洋联合委员，及统一保价委员会中方主席，对于华商火险保价问题潜心研究，制成火险保价表，以供同业参考。

Ren Shuobao, born in Fujian Province, set foot in insurance in 1918. He was employed as manager when the American Asiatic Underwriters was under organization; later concurrently took up the post of marine department of each port for AAU. In 1932, he was employed as manager of marine & fire department of Taishan Insurance Co.

朱如堂，浙江吴兴人。1921年，专攻商业管理，获得MBA学位后归国。1924年，任暨南大学商学院院长。1926年，进入保裕保险公司服务。1931年，与几个爱好保险的友人筹措开办宝丰保险公司，同年担任上海市保险业同业公会执行委员，1935年，被推任为常委。

朱如堂对我国保险业早期的发展功绩颇丰。1933年，中英文火险保单标准条款与格式的制定与实行，他出力良多。其后，公会又设保险单译文委员会，他任常委之一，先后审定了火险、汽车险等保单译文。1935年，中外保险机构为密切联系，他出任华商公会方面的代表，为华商同业谋求利益，他据理力争，不辱使命。1936年，上海实施火险经纪人规章，这是我国保险史上划时代的一笔。这项规章的提议、起草、讨论、修正以至实施，费了许多人的时间及心血，朱如堂便是其中最重要的一人。

Zhu Rutang, born in Zhejiang Province, came back to China after his overseas study with degree of MBA. In 1926, he entered Baoyu Insurance Co. to work on business; in 1931, with several friends loving insurance together, he prepared to erect Baofeng Insurance Co and, in the same year, he shouldered the executive commissioner of Shanghai Insurance Association and was recommended to be the standing committee member of the association.

朱如堂
Zhu Rutang

陈干青
Chen Ganqing

冯佐芝，广东宝安县人。17岁毕业于香港皇仁书院，辛亥革命暴发前，同李煜堂等联合创办联保保险公司。随后担任上海分公司经理，曾两任华洋联合会华方代表，并任广肇公所，广东医院董事，曾热心帮助上海青年会征求队。

Feng Zuozhi, born in Guangdong, jointly founded the United Insurance Co. with Li Yitang, etc. before the Revolution of 1911; then, he assumed the office of manger of the company, twice Chinese representative for Sino-Foreign United Federation, etc.

陈干青，上海崇明人。中学毕业后考入南洋大学航海科，后进入民国交通部商船专门学校，毕业后进北轮埠公司，逐渐升任升安轮船长，后历任升利、德兴、肇兴轮船公司总船长。期间训练出不少航海人才。1928年，他同肇兴轮船公司总经理李子初先生商议创立肇泰保险公司，承保国内商船船舶保险，兼任该公司协理8年。1932年，他联合同行数人，出资创立了中国海上意外保险公司，自任经理，后该公司加入上海保险同业公会，并且兼营水火险。1935年，担任上海市保险同业公会执行委员。他曾出席1920年日内瓦第十三届国际劳工大会，曾任中国商船驾驶员联合会会长、中国商船驾驶总会主席委员、上海船业公会执行委员、招商局高级船员遇险责任审查委员会委员、海损理算师和船货估计师、中国海上意外保险公司经理等职。

Chen Ganqing, from Shanghai, negotiated with Li Zichu, general manger of Zhaoxing Shipping House, to found Zhaotai Insurance Co. to underwrite vessel insurance for inland traders; he concurrently took up the post of assistant manager of the company for 8 years. In 1932, with his peers, he funded to found China Marine Accident Insurance Co.; he acted as manager.

冯佐芝
Feng Zuozhi

郭琳天
Guo Lintian

陈鹤，字鸣，浙江定海人。1924年毕业于圣约翰大学，归国后，在上海法商保太保险公司工作达18年之久。1943年，任民安产物保险公司协理。1947年，上海同业成立民联分保交换处，任副主任委员、上海民安产物保险公司总经理等职。

Chen He, born in Zhejian, had worked for a French insurer for as long as 18 years since he came back to China after his graduation in 1924 from St. John University. In 1943, he assumed the office of assistant manager of Min'an Property Insurance Co., and in 1947, the vice chairperson of the Reinsurance Exchange Office founded in the same year by Shanghai Insurance Association, and the managing director of Shanghai Min'an.

郭琳天，广东中山人。1911年毕业于北京大学，任上海永安人寿保险公司总经理。在银行保险、法律、经济等方面有较深造诣。在任总经理期间，对保险法规，一般业务方面均有贡献，才华横溢，只因积劳成疾，死时年仅33岁。

Guo Lintian, from Guangdong, occupied general manager of Shanghai Yong'an Life Insurance Co. after he graduated from Beijing University in 1911, with outstanding attainments in bancassurance, law, and economy, etc. During his career in Yong'an, he contributed much to insurance laws & regulations, and general business, which owed to his great talent. Breaking down from constant overwork, he passed away when he was only 33 years old.

陈鹤
Chen He

严福堂
Yang Futang

金通明，上海人。1933年毕业东吴大学法科，1934年进入中国银行服务，1937年6月调入中国保险总公司。抗战暴发后，调任中国保险公司香港分公司经理，负责创办事宜，并使香港分公司业务蒸蒸日上。

Jin Tongming, born in Shanghai, had worked in the Bank of China since 1934 till in June 1937 was sent to the head office of China Insurance Co., and after the war against Japanese aggression, was sent to be the manager of China Insurance Co. Hongkong Branch, contributing much to the thriving of the branch's business.

严福堂，浙江余姚人。18岁时就从事保险业，工作于英商洋行保险部，历任水险部大写，洋行买办。1920年，中央信托公司开业，严福堂担任保险部主任，他在公司中拟订营业方针，调整人员，增设分公司及代理处，并担任保险公会董事，闸北救火会董事等职，深得保险界人士信赖。宋汉章是他的挚友，在中国保险公司筹备阶段，他们常常一起商讨，贡献颇多，晚年还担任中一信托公司襄理等职。

Yan Futang, from Zhejiang Province, began to work for the insurance department of a British company when he was just 18 years old. He acted as director of the Insurance Department of the Central Trust Co. when the company started business. Also, he was a director of the Insurance Association, etc., greatly relied by persons of insurance sector. In his old age, he undertook the post of assistant manager of Zhongyi Trust Co.

金通明
Jin Tongming

Bicentenary chinese Insurance
中国保险业二百年(1805-2005)

新中国保险业(1949-2005)
Insurance in the people's Republic of China (1949-2005)

新中国成立使中国保险业掀开了新的一页。1949年前后，军管会接管了国民政府运营的保险企业；同时，为恢复经济、发挥保险业经济补偿的职能，中央政府批准了组建国内唯一的保险公司——中国人民保险公司。1958年末，在武汉召开的全国金融会议决定立刻停止国内保险业务，自此，新中国保险业滑入了低谷。

1979年4月，中央政府做出了逐步恢复国内保险业务的重大决定，国内保险业务开始复苏。伴随着中国社会经济的快速发展，中国保险业进入了一个崭新的发展时期。20多年来，人民的保险意识日益增强，保险的社会功能日益完善，保险的社会影响力渗透到了每一个角落。保费总量年均增长超过30%，市场主体从唯一的中国人保增加到44家中资保险公司、41家外资保险公司，以及1200多家保险中介机构。截至2005年1月，保险总资产达到1.2万亿元。

目前，国有保险公司的股份制改革已取得了很大进展，股份制保险公司的运营机制在逐步提高，资金使用体制改革已稳步推进，条款费率管理制度改革在顺利进行。随着社会主义市场经济的不断完善，保险业的体制改革也进入了新的发展阶段。

建立和落实科学发展观，做大做强保险业已成为当前中国保险业发展的航标，中国保险业又迎来一个战略机遇。

After the founding of the People's Republic of China, the Military Commission of control took over the insurance enterprises run by Kuomintang government. Meanwhile, the Central Government approved the founding of the unique nationwide insurance company PICC, in order to recover the economy and give the role of economic considerations of insurance to play. Since then, Chinese insurance marked a brand new stage. In late 1958, Chinese insurance, under the background of the Great Leap Movement, lost its soil for existence – the finance conference of the whole country held in Wuhan concluded a determination to immediately stop the domestic insurance business and, from then on, new China's insurance slid in a winter.

During the over 2 decades starting from the recovery, a world-shaking change had occurred in Chinese domestic insurance: yearly average growth in office premium exceeded 30 per cent; the number of market entities had been added from the exclusive PICC to 44 Sino-funded insurers, 41 foreign-funded insurers, and over 1,200 insurance intermediaries; the assets of the insurance totaled 1.2 trillion yuan by January 2005.

Presently, a significant progress has been made in the share-holding reform of state-owned insurance companies, the operational mechanism of joint-stock insurance company has been improved step by step, structural reform of capital-applying management has been steadily pushed, reform of managerial system on terms & rates has been smoothly evolved. Along with the constant improvement in the socialist market economy system, the restructuring of insurance has entered a new phase.

It has been the orientation for Chinese insurance on the stage to erect and fulfil the scientific concept of development and to boost the sector. China is entering in a key, strategic era full of opportunities.

一、新中国保险事业的筹备

Preparation for the Establishment of PICC

人民解放战争的节节胜利，使人们看到了新中国的曙光，创建统一的国家保险机构提上了议事日程。

创建国家保险机构的设想首先源于苏联的理论和经验，其次是源于恢复国民经济、平衡财政收支的现实需要。在1949年8月由陈云主持的上海财经会议上，统一了设立中国人民保险公司的思想。1949年9月17日，中国人民银行总行正式拟文中央人民政府政务院财政经济委员会，呈请核准设立中国人民保险公司。9月21日，财委会就中国人民保险公司的成立向中央报批。

The tentative plan to establish a national insurance institution firstly derived from the theory and experience of the Soviet and secondly from the actual demand to restore the national economy and balance financial revenue and expenditure. On September 17, 1949, head office of the People's Bank of China (PBOC) officially draft the document to the Finance & Economy Committee of the Government Administration Council of the Central Government for setting up the People's Insurance Company of China (PICC); four days later, the committee reported to the Central Government in terms of the establishment of PICC.

中国人民银行第一任总经理南汉宸

Nan Hanchen: first general manager of the PBOC

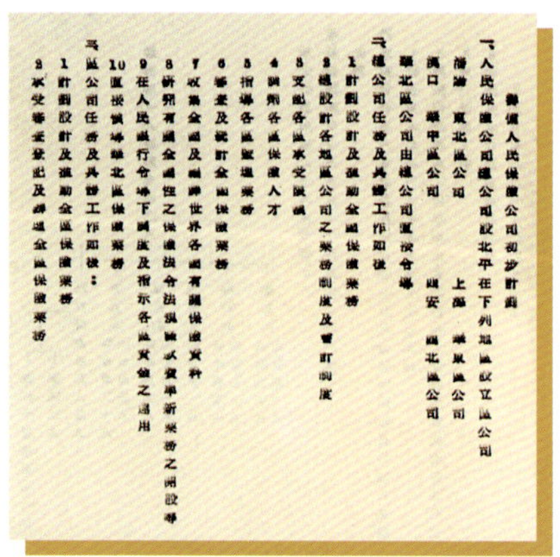

1949年8月，上海财经会议上提交的"筹备人民保险公司初步计划"。

Primary plan on preparation of PICC from the Shanghai Finance Conference in August 1949

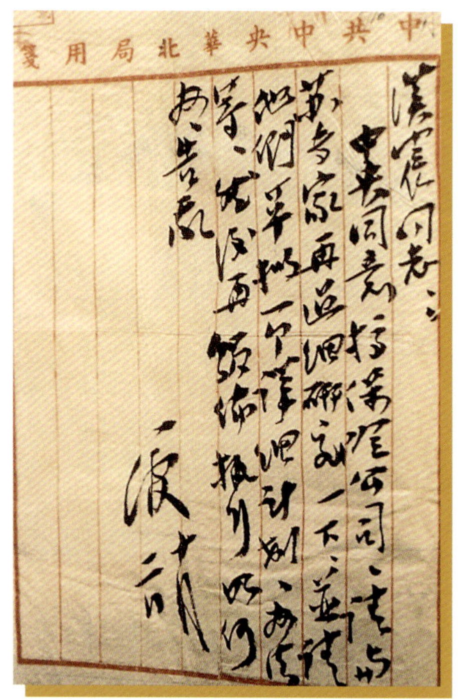

汉宸同志：
中央同意搞保险公司，……

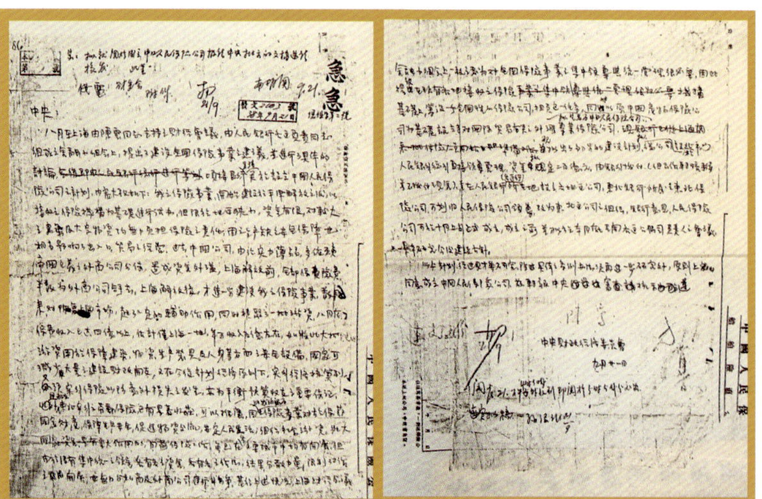

1949年9月21日中央财政经济委员会就中国人民保险公司成立事宜写给中央的报告

The report on founding PICC by the Finance & Economy Committee on September 21, 1949

1949年9月25日至10月6日，由中国人民银行总行组织的第一次全国保险工作会议在北京举行。会议期间，薄一波亲笔函告南汉宸总经理"中央同意搞保险公司"，极大地鼓舞了与会者。

Bo Yibo's letter to Han Nanchen that the Central Government approved to operate insurance business

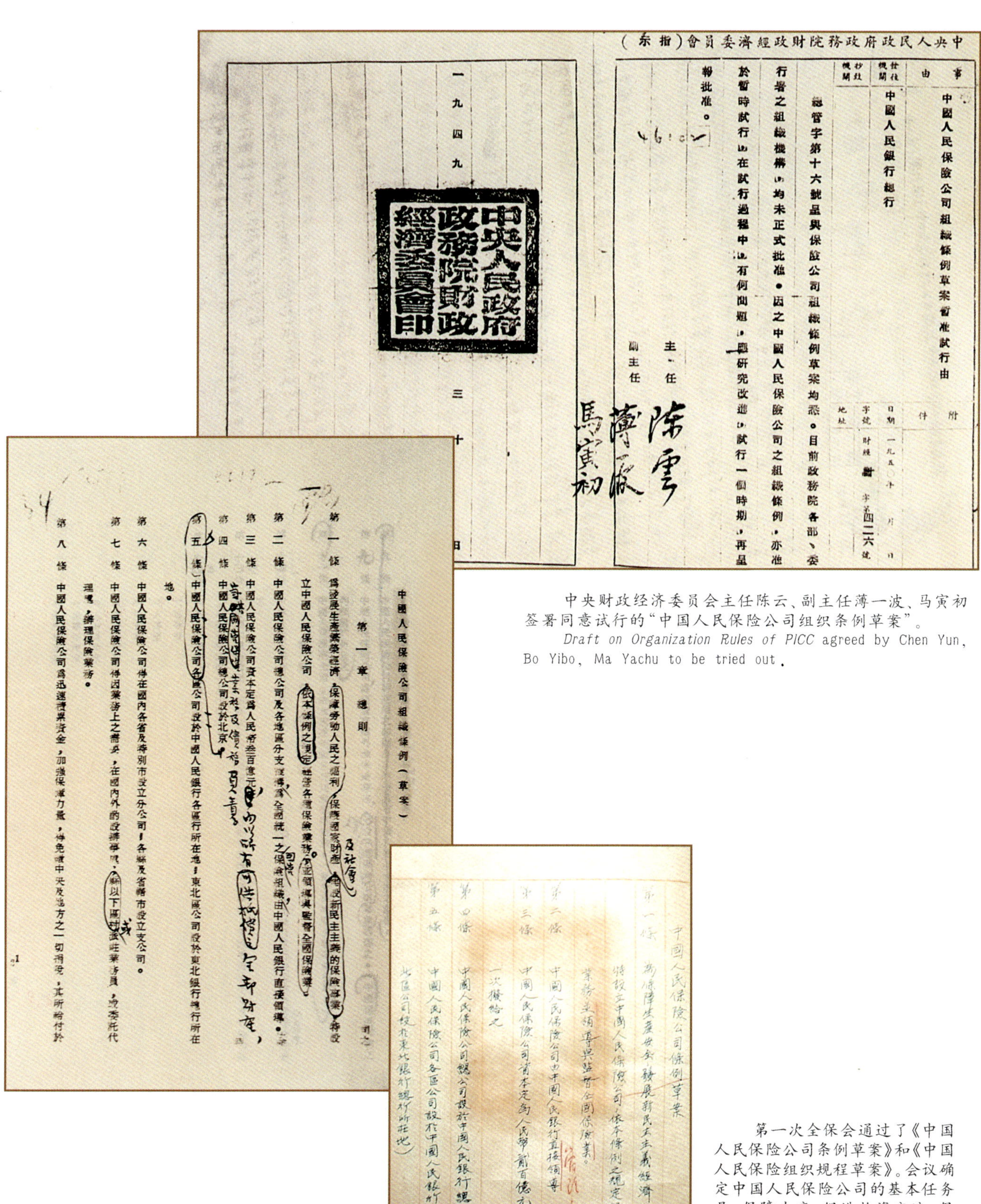

中央人民政府政務院財政經濟委員會(指示)

事由：中國人民保險公司組織條例草案暫准試行由

發往機關：中國人民銀行總行

抄致機關：

總管字第十六號呈與保險公司組織條例草案均悉。目前政務院各部、委行署之組織機構，均未正式批准。因之中國人民保險公司之組織條例，亦准於暫時試行，在試行過程中，有何問題，應研究改進，試行一個時期，再呈報批准。

主任 陳雲

副主任 薄一波 馬寅初

附件：

日期：一九五〇年 月 日

字號：財經 字第四二六號

地址：

中央人民政府政務院財政經濟委員會印

中國人民保險公司組織條例（草案）

第一章 總則

第一條 為發展生產繁榮經濟，保障勞動人民之福利，保護國家財產，建設新民主主義的保險事業，特設立中國人民保險公司，依本條例之規定經營各種保險業務，並領導與監督全國保險業。

第二條 中國人民保險公司總公司及各地區分支機構，為全國統一之保險組織，由中國人民銀行直接領導。

第三條 中國人民保險公司資本定為人民幣叁百億元。

第四條 中國人民保險公司總公司設於北京。

第五條 中國人民保險公司各區公司設於中國人民銀行各區行所在地；東北區公司設於東北銀行總行所在地。

第六條 中國人民保險公司得在國內各省及特別市設立分公司；各縣及省轄市設立支公司。

第七條 中國人民保險公司得因業務上之需要，在國內外的設辦事處、縣以下區設駐在業務員，或委託代理處，辦理保險業務。

第八條 中國人民保險公司為迅速積累資金，加強保障力量，俾免除中央及地方之一切捐稅，其所給付於

中國人民保險公司條例草案

第一條 為保障生產安全，發展新民主主義經濟，安定人民生活，特設立中國人民保險公司，依本條例之規定經營各種保險業務。

第二條 中國人民保險公司由中國人民銀行直接領導。

第三條 中國人民保險公司資本定為人民幣貳百億元，由中國人民銀行一次撥給之。

第四條 中國人民保險公司總公司設於中國人民銀行總行所在地。

第五條 中國人民保險公司各區公司設於中國人民銀行各區行所在地（東北區公司設於東北銀行總行所在地

中央财政经济委员会主任陈云、副主任薄一波、马寅初签署同意试行的“中国人民保险公司组织条例草案”。

Draft on Organization Rules of PICC agreed by Chen Yun, Bo Yibo, Ma Yachu to be tried out.

第一次全保会通过了《中国人民保险公司条例草案》和《中国人民保险组织规程草案》。会议确定中国人民保险公司的基本任务是：保障生产，促进物资交流，保护国家财产，提高劳动人民福利。

Draft on Rules of PICC and *Draft on Organization Rules of PICC* passed at the first National Insurance Work Conferenco

第一次全国保险工作会议结束时，苏联专家库图佐夫介绍了苏联保险的基本原则，与会者受到很大启示。会后，以原北京产物保险公司为基础，建立中国人民保险公司总公司营业部。第一次全国保险工作会议的圆满结束，标志着中国人民保险公司筹备阶段的完成，中国保险历史翻开了新的一页。

After the First Insurance Conference of China, based on the original Beijing Property Insurance Co., the business office of the headquarters of PICC was founded. The consummation of the conference marked the completion of the preparation of PICC and a new page of Chinese insurance history.

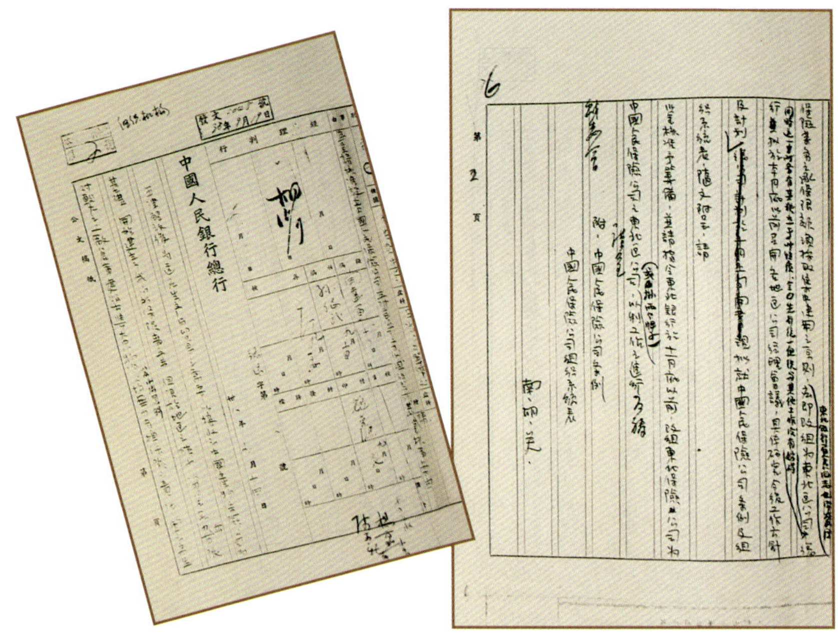

中國人民銀行總行

1949年9月14日，中国人民银行总行呈请设立中国人民保险公司的报告。
The report for establishment of PICC, by the People's Bank of China.

新中国第一次全国保险工作会议于1949年9月25日至10月6日在北京召开。这次会议决定成立中国人民保险公司（总公司设在北京）、中国保险公司（总公司设在上海），分别经营国内保险业务和国外保险业务。参加会议的领导来自中央、北京、上海、天津、武汉及东北地区。前排左起第5人（搂小孩者）为中国人民保险公司第一任总经理胡景沄。
Participants of the First National Insurance Work Conference in Beijing from September 25 to October 6, 1949

1949年10月，中华人民共和国政务院批准成立中国人民保险公司。
Hands raising of members of the Government Administration Council for the founding PICC in October, 1949.

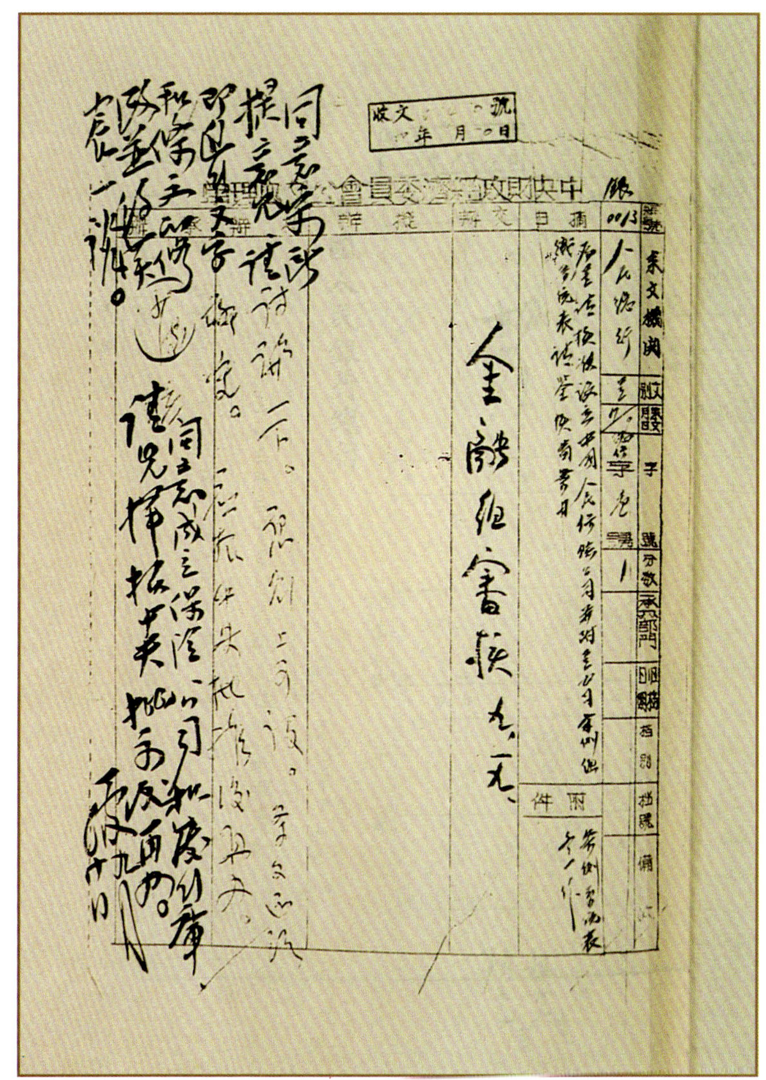

中央財政經濟委員會公文處理單

1949年9月10日，薄一波对中国人民银行总行关于设立中国人民保险公司报告的批复。
Bo Yibo's written reply on setting up PICC by the PBOC on Sep. 10, 1949.

二、中国人民保险公司成立

Foundation of PICC

1949年10月20日上午9时半，中国人民保险公司总公司和直属营业部在北京西交民巷108号正式开业。中国人民保险公司的成立标志着新中国统一的国家保险机构的诞生。

成立之初，中国人民保险公司不仅是一个经营各种保险业务的经济实体，而且是兼有领导与监督全国保险业职能的行政管理机构。从1950年1月下旬起，保险监理业务改由人民银行金融管理部门负责，“人保”从此向完全的金融企业转变。

第一次全保会议议定中国人民保险公司资本为200亿元（旧人民币，下同）。1949年11月3日由中国人民银行批准为300亿元。1949年12月1日，政务院财经委员会批准增资为600亿元，并以全部财产对其业务和债务负责。

中国人民保险公司初设四室一会，即秘书室、业务室、监理室、会计室和设计委员会。为适应业务发展的需要，根据1950年1月4日颁布的《中国人民保险公司组织条例》（草案），总公司机构改为十室。

On October 20, 1949, PICC, located at 108, Xijiaominxiang, was founded in Beijing; then it branched into all over the country. By early 1950s, there had been 564 agencies of PICC.

In its early time, PICC was not only an enterprise, but also an administrative department to lead and supervise insurance of the whole country. PICC began to walk into a transformation of a pure financial enterprise, since the late January 1949 when the business of insurance regulating had been taken over by the PBOC.

1949年10月20日，中国人民保险公司天津分公司与总公司同日成立，天津分公司全体人员在公司所在地花园路3号与来宾合影留念。前排左起第8人为经理赵步崇，第7人为第一副经理王佩璋，第3人为第二副经理龚作霖。（照片提供：张通福）

Participants of the inauguration of PICC Tianjin Branch on Oct. 20, 1949.

中国人民保险公司第一任总经理胡景沄
Hu Jingyun: First General Manager of PICC

中国人民保险公司

- 秘书室
- 人事室
- 检查室
- 财产保险室
- 人身保险室
- 农业保险室
- 国外业务室
- 理赔室
- 会计室
- 设计室

1950年中国人民保险公司机构设置图
Structural establishment of PICC in 1950

中国人民保险公司在北京西交民巷108号办公场景(照片提供:叙一飞)
PICC's office at 108, Xijiaominxiang

中国人民保险公司成立后，在地方政府的支持下，成立了华东区、东北区、华中区、西北区和西南区等五大区公司。到1950年6月，除五大区公司外，还有分公司31个，支公司8个，办事处75个，营业部及派驻所4个。

By June 1950, besides sub companies in east, Northeast, central, northwest, and southwest China, PICC had also set up 31 branches, 8 subsidiaries, 75 offices, and 4 sales departments and agencies as well.

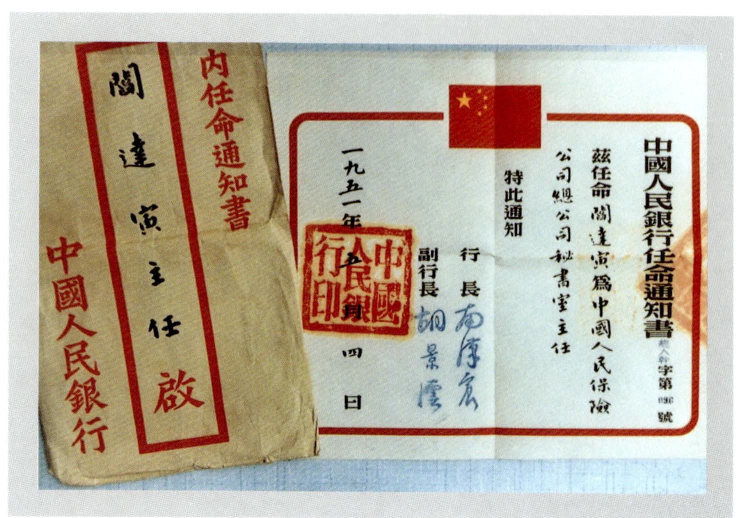

内任命通知書

閻達寅主任啟

中國人民銀行

中國人民銀行任命通知書

茲任命閻達寅為中國人民保險公司總公司秘書室主任

特此通知

行長 南漢宸

副行長 胡景澐

一九五一年 月 四日

中国人民银行任命通知书
Notice of appointment by the PBOC

中國共產黨天津市人民保險公司支部新黨員入黨宣誓紀念 一九五三年三月廿七日

1949年10月20日中国人民保险公司天津分公司成立时就设立了中国共产党的党小组，当时有党员4人，1951年4月设立党支部，支部书记为杜天荣。图为1953年发展新党员的情景，右起第6人为杜天荣书记。（照片提供：张通福）
New Members of the Communist Party of China in Tianjin Branch in 1949

50年代中国人民保险公司北京分公司部分员工合影(照片提供:郭贵忠)
Some employees in PICC Beijing Branch in 1950s

1954年中国人民保险公司宁夏分公司全体员工合影(照片提供:罗石平、张海峰)
Staff of PICC Ningxia Branch in 1954

50年代中国人民保险公司西南区公司营业部青年团员组织生活合影(照片提供:何光远、唐国纲)
Members of the Communist Youth League of Southwest China Sub-company of PICC in 1950s

1952年川西人民保险公司部分青年员工在重庆银行学校培训后合影(照片提供:吕战虎)
Some young employees of PICC West Sichuan Branch participating in the training in Chongqing Banking School in 1952

50年代中国人民保险公司重庆分公司员工合影(照片提供:何光远、唐国纲)
Staff of PICC Chongqing Branch in 1950s

50年代初，中国人民保险公司各地的代理处已达564个，其中有385个为人民银行各地分支机构。保险从业人员已有2000多人。从业人员中主要为调干和青年学生。为了提高从业人员素质，各地纷纷开设了保险干部培训班，培训干部1000多人。

In early 1950s, PICC had 564 agencies all over China, of which, 385 were branches, with more than 2,000 insurance practitioners.

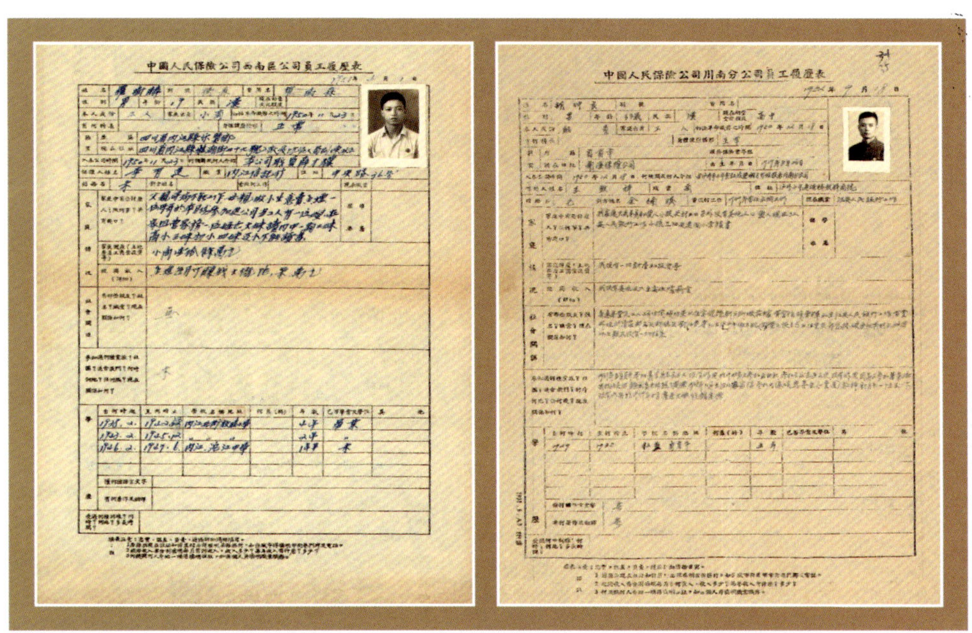

中国人民保险公司西南和川南第一代保险职工履历表（资料提供：曹明科）

Resume of the first-generation employees of PICC Southwest China and South Sichuan Branch

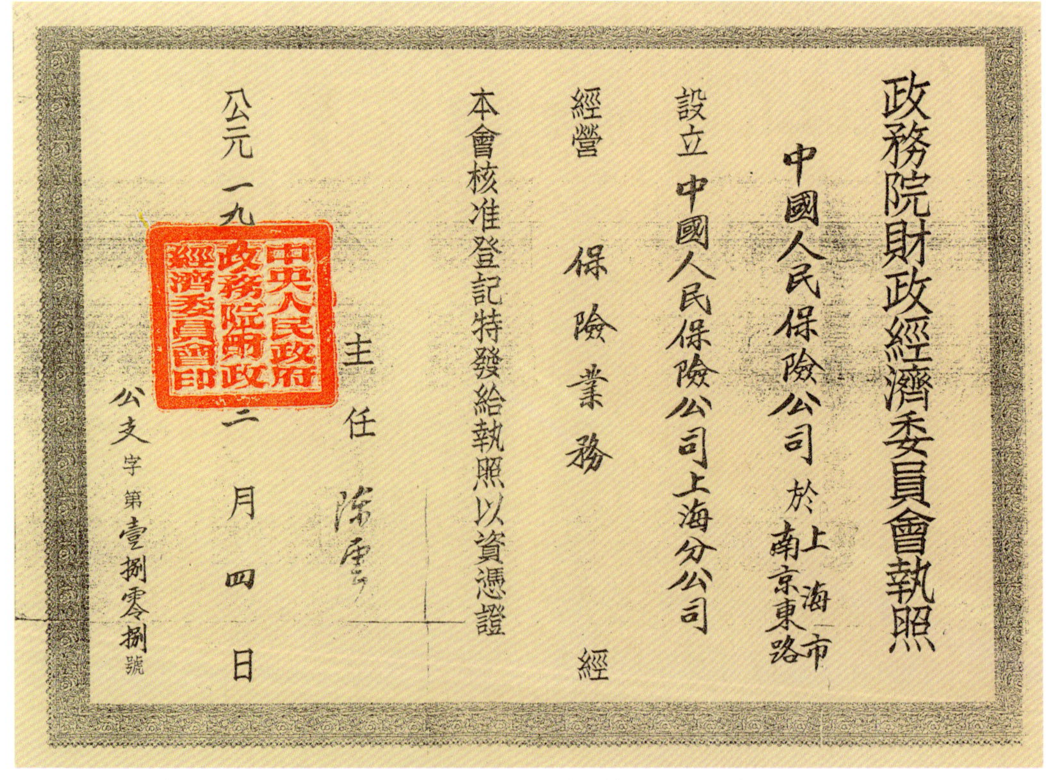

政務院財政經濟委員會執照

中國人民保險公司 於 上海市南京東路

設立 中國人民保險公司上海分公司

經營 保險業務

本會核准登記特發給執照以資憑證

主任 陳雲

公元一九　二月四日

中央人民政府政務院財政經濟委員會印

公支字第壹捌零捌號

經

1953年中国人民保险公司上海分公司经营执照（资料提供：吴越）

Business license of PICC Shanghai Branch in 1953

三、保险市场的改造

Transformation of the Insurance Market

新中国成立后，为了打破外商和私营保险公司对中国保险市场的垄断，开始有步骤、有组织、有分别地对旧中国的保险业进行了整顿改造。主要措施有：1.接管和清理官僚资本保险公司；2.整顿和改造民族保险业；3.对外资保险公司切断保险业务来源，使得洋商在中国市场难以生存，自动撤出中国保险市场。

After the foundation of the People's Republic of China, the Central Government began to trim and transform the insurance in old age, in order to break the monopolization by foreign and private-owned insurance companies.

1949年至1952年外商保险公司保费收入百分比

Percentage of Premium Revenue of Foreign Insurers (1949 – 1952)

年份（年）	1949	1950	1951	1952
外商保费收入占全国保费收入百分比	62%	9.8%	0.4%	0.1%

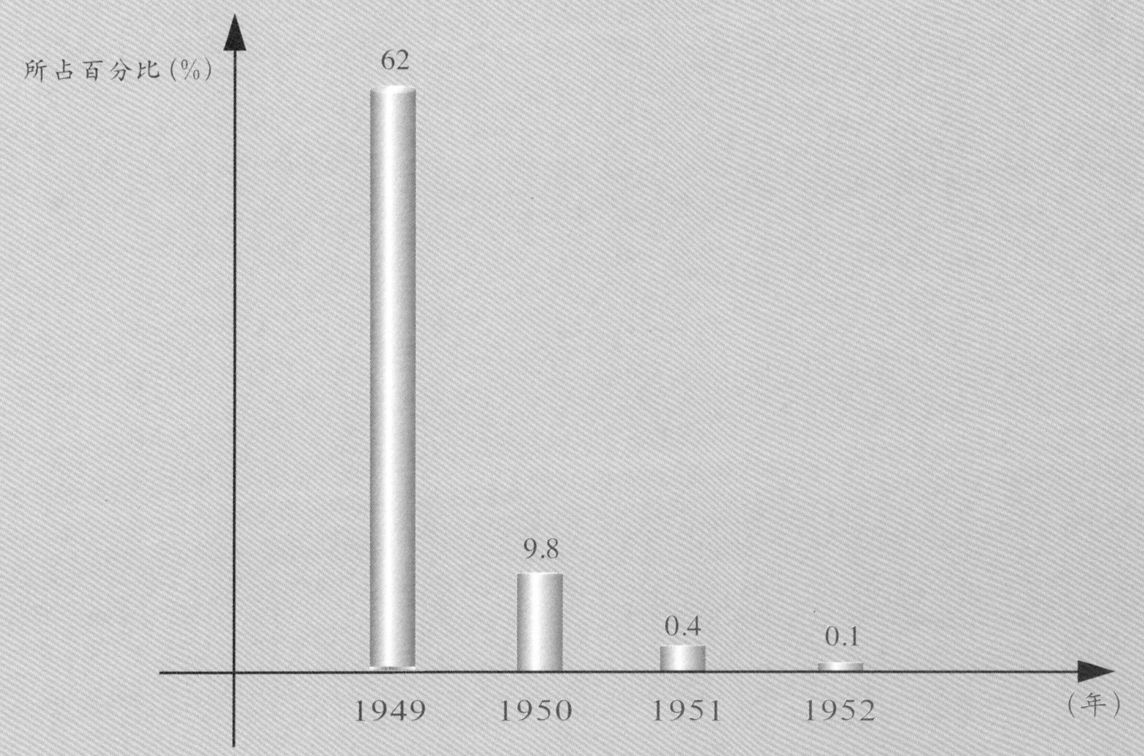

1950年外资保险公司情况表

Condition of Foreign Insurers in 1950

地区	公司名称	总公司资本额	代理处	备注
天津	海龙产物		百利洋行保险部	
	伦　兰		太古公司保险部	
	皇家交易		太古公司保险部	英汇保险
	英国海外		太古公司保险部	
	保　益		太古公司保险部	家定保险
	海　洋		太古公司保险部	
	英商於仁保安	威信洋行保险部		
	福美产物	威信洋行保险部		
	巴噜士产物	百利洋行保险部		
	巴噜士水险	百利洋行保险部		
青岛	伦　兰		太古公司保险部	
	英　汇		太古公司保险部	
	英国海外		太古公司保险部	
	家　定		太古公司保险部	
	海　洋		太古公司保险部	
重庆	海龙产物代理处			
广州	海龙产物		美亚代理保险公司	
	福美产物			
	商务意外损害			
	友宁产物			
	英商美国友邦产物			
	古巴美联产物			
	瑞士业兴产物			
	瑞士联宁产物			
上海	巴噜士产物	瑞士法郎12000000	罗德洋行	瑞士
	巴噜士水险	百利有限公司		
	保太产物	法郎31500000		
	英商鹰星	英镑3350000	上海保险行	
	英商惠斯登	英镑287670	上海保险行	
	英商声天雷	英镑900000	上海保险行	
	巴勒产物	英镑3468760		
	公裕 太阳产物	英镑6200000		
	贸兴水上	英镑100000		
	保裕产物	英镑384772		
	老公茂惠记产物	英镑3750000		
	南英保泰	英镑2000000		
	英商皇家产物	英镑6000000		
	伦　兰	英镑5000000	太古公司保险部	
	英　汇	英镑2000000	太古公司保险部	
	家　定	英镑2175000	太古公司保险部	
	海　洋	英镑500000	太古公司保险部	
	英　外	英镑1340000	太古公司保险部	
	香港产物	港币10000000	怡和公司保险部	
	爱兰司产物	英镑5450000	怡和公司保险部	
	谏当产物	港币10000000	怡和公司保险部	
	泰斯顿产物	罗比2300000	怡和公司保险部	
	昆士伦产物	澳镑1000000	怡和公司保险部	
	平克司产物	澳镑1000000	怡和公司保险部	
	乌思伦产物	乌思伦镑1500000	怡和公司保险部	
	利物浦产物	英镑2655250	怡和公司保险部	
	英商於仁保安	英镑2000000		
	北美洲	美金15000000		
	美国好望	美金15000000		
	海龙产物	美金4000000	美亚代理保险公司	
	福美产物	美金9397690	美亚代理保险公司	
	商业意外损害	美金1000000	美亚代理保险公司	
	友宁产物	美金1100000	美亚代理保险公司	
	英商美国友邦产物	英镑140000	美亚代理保险公司	
	古巴美联产物	比沙100000	美亚代理保险公司	
	瑞士兴业产物	法郎2000000	美亚代理保险公司	
	瑞士联宁产物	法郎1750000	美亚代理保险公司	

REGULATIONS GOVERNING REGISTRATION OF INSURANCE COMPANIES OWNED BY FOREIGNERS PROMULGATED

外商保險公司登記辦法

1949年9月6日，为统一了解天津市外商保险公司业务情况，军管会金融处颁布《外商保险公司登记办法》。图为刊登在天津《华北汉英报》上的相关报道及《办法》条例。

Registration Rules for Foreign Insurers by the Finance Department of the Military Commission of Control and related report in 1949

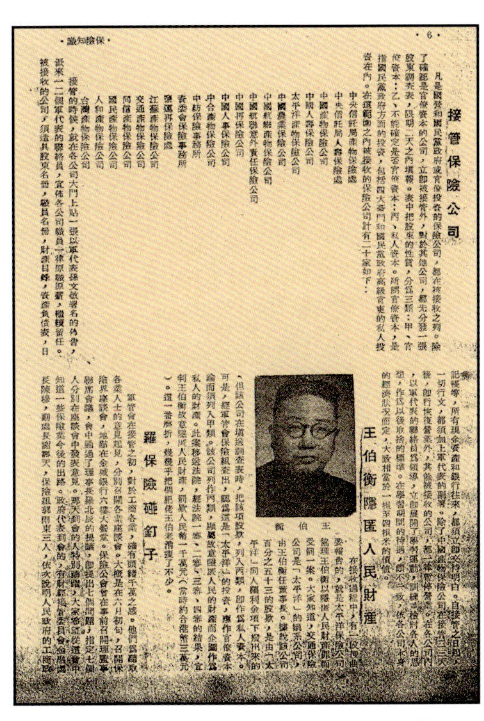
接管保險公司

1949年5月上海解放后，上海军管会接管了21家官僚资本保险公司，并对两家与官僚资本合资的保险公司实行监管。

Report on 21 bureaucratic-capital insurers and 2 insurers jointed funded with bureaucratic capital taken over by Shanghai Military Commission of Control in 1949

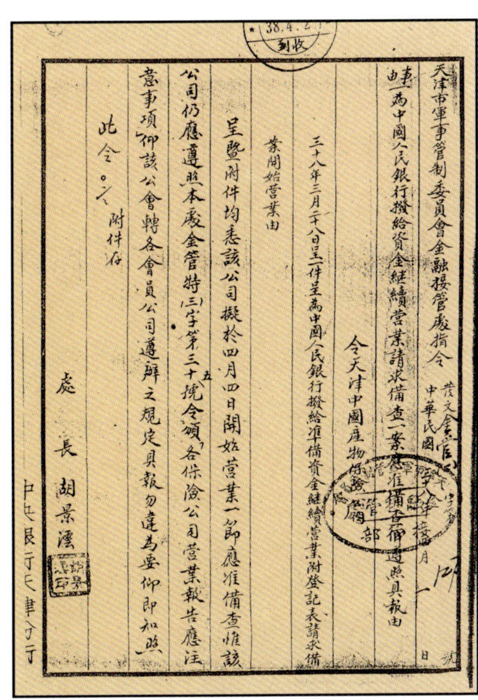
天津市軍事管制委員會金融接管處指令

1949年1月15日天津解放后，天津市军事管制委员会金融接管处接管了旧中国银行、新华信托投资银行、中国保险公司、太平洋保险公司、中国农业保险公司等官僚资本金融机构。3月20日，接管处指令原负责人龚作霖重新组织“天津中国产物保险公司”。图为4月1日、天津军管会金融接管处关于天津中国产物保险公司4月4日开业的指令。

Dictate by Tianjin Military Commission of Control on the open of Tianjin Property Insurance Co. in Apr.1, 1949

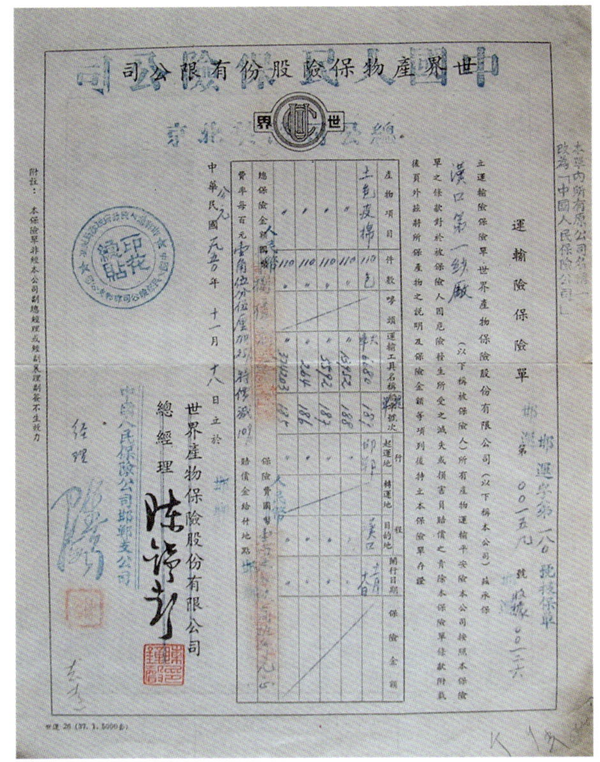
世界產物保險股份有限公司

運輸險保險單

解放后，国民党官僚资本创办的保险公司划归中国人民保险公司管理。图为1950年11月18日，中国人民保险公司邯郸支公司改用原世界产物保险公司保险单签发的运输保险单。（资料提供：成继跃）

Transportation insurance policy issued by PICC Handan Subsidiary in 1950 in original World Property Insurance Co.'s form

对复业的私营保险公司进行的改造措施先是切断他们与外资保险公司的分保关系，在津沪两地成立了47家民族保险公司参加的“民联分保交换处”，严禁中资保险公司向外国保险公司办理分保业务。1951年，将继续营业的28家私营保险公司合并为“新丰”和“太平”两家保险公司，并改造为公私合营的保险公司，1956年又将两家合并为太平保险公司，专营海外保险业务。

In 1951, the 28 continuously operated private-owned insurers were integrated into two: Xinfeng and Taiping Insurance Co. transformed to be state-private incorporated later. In 1956, the two companies were merged into Taiping Insurance Co. to specialize in overseas insurance business.

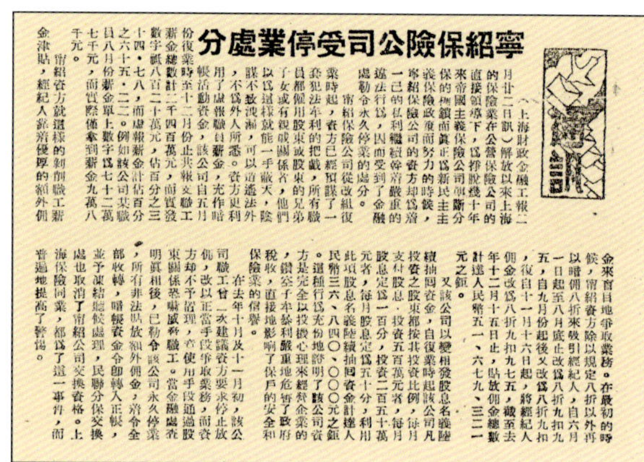

寧紹保險公司受停業處分

（上海財政金融工報二月廿二日訊）解放以來上海的保險業在公營保險公司的直接領導下，爲擺脫幾十年來帝國主義保險公司壟斷保的枷鎖而眞正爲新民主主義保險政策而努力的時候，寧紹保險公司的資方却爲着一己的私利繼續幹着嚴重的違法行爲，因而受到了金融處勒令永久停業的處分。

甯紹保險公司從改組復業時起，資方已經預謀了一套犯法牟利的把戲，所有職員都僱用股東或股東的兄弟子女或有親戚關係者，他們以爲這樣就能一手蔽天，陰謀不致洩漏，可以逍遙法外，不爲外人所悉。資方更利用了虛報職員薪金，充作暗帳活動資金，該公司自五月份復業時至十二月份止共報支職工薪金總數計二千四百萬元，而實發數字祇八百二十萬元，佔百分之三十四・七八，而虛報薪金計佔百分之六十五・二二。例如該公司某職員八月份薪金單上數字爲七十二萬七千元，而實際僅拿到薪金九萬八千元。

甯紹資方就這樣的剝削職工薪金津貼，經紀人藉資優厚的額外佣金來肓目地爭取業務。在最初的時候，甯紹資方除以規定八折以外再以暗佣八折來吸引經紀人，自六月一日起至八月底止改爲八折九扣九五，自九月份起後又改爲八折九扣，復自十一月十六日起，將經紀人佣金改爲八折九扣九七五，截至去年十二月十五日止，貼放佣金總數計達人民幣五一、六七九、三二一元之鉅。

又該公司以變相發股息名義陸續抽回資金，自復業時起該公司凡投資之股東都按其投資比例，每月支付股息，投資五百萬元者，每月股息定爲一百分，投資二百五十萬元者，每月股息定爲五十分，利用此項股息名義陸續抽回資金計達人民幣三六、八四〇、〇〇〇元之鉅。這種行爲充份地證明了該公司資方是完全以投機心理來經營企業的，鑽空子牟暴利嚴重地危害了政府稅收，直接地影響了保戶的安全和保險業的信譽。

在去年十月及十一月初，該公司職工曾一次建議資方要求停止放佣，改以正當手段爭取業務，而資方却不予置理，並使用手段通過股東關係恐嚇威脅職工。當金融處查明眞相後，已勒令該公司永久停業，所有非法貼放額外佣金，責令全部收轉，暗帳資金令即轉入正帳，並予凍結聽候處理，民聯分保交換處也取消了甯紹公司交換資格。上海保險同業，都爲了這一事件，而普遍地提高了警惕。

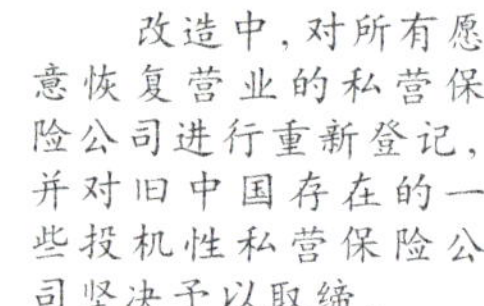

改造中，对所有愿意恢复营业的私营保险公司进行重新登记，并对旧中国存在的一些投机性私营保险公司坚决予以取缔。

The report on punishment of shutout to Ningshao Insurance Co.

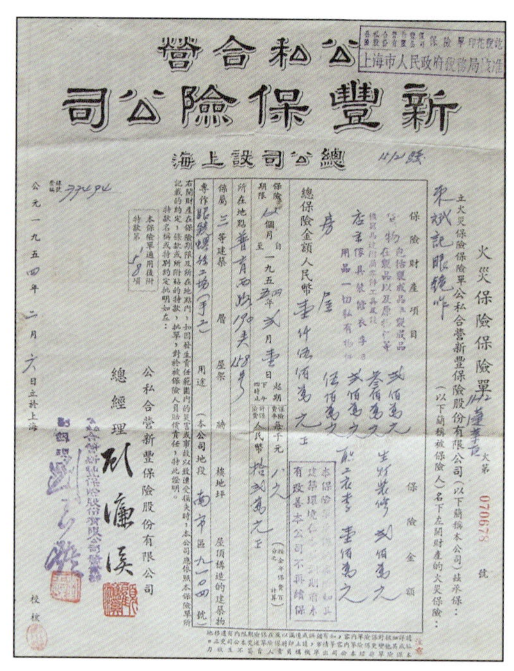

公私合營
新豐保險公司
總公司設上海
火災保險保單
公私合營新豐保險股份有限公司
總經理

新丰保险公司签发的火险保单（资料提供：成继跃）

Fire insurance policy issued by Xinfeng insurance Co. in 1954

1949年2月1日，东北银行哈尔滨分行根据形势需要，与哈尔滨市政府联合成立新丰保险公司。同年3月，原哈尔滨联合保险公司并入新丰保险公司，为我国第一家公私合营的保险公司。图为新丰保险公司旧址及经理王雨田。

Site of Xinfeng Insurance Co.(1949) and its manager Wang Yutian

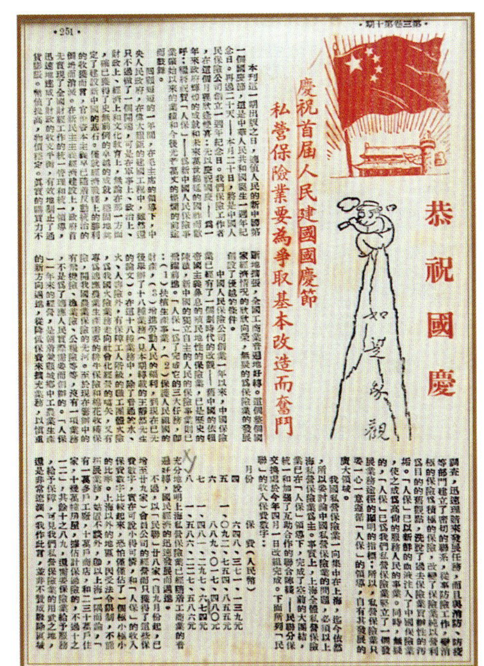

恭祝國慶

慶祝首屆人民建國國慶節 私營保險業要為爭取基本改造而奮鬥

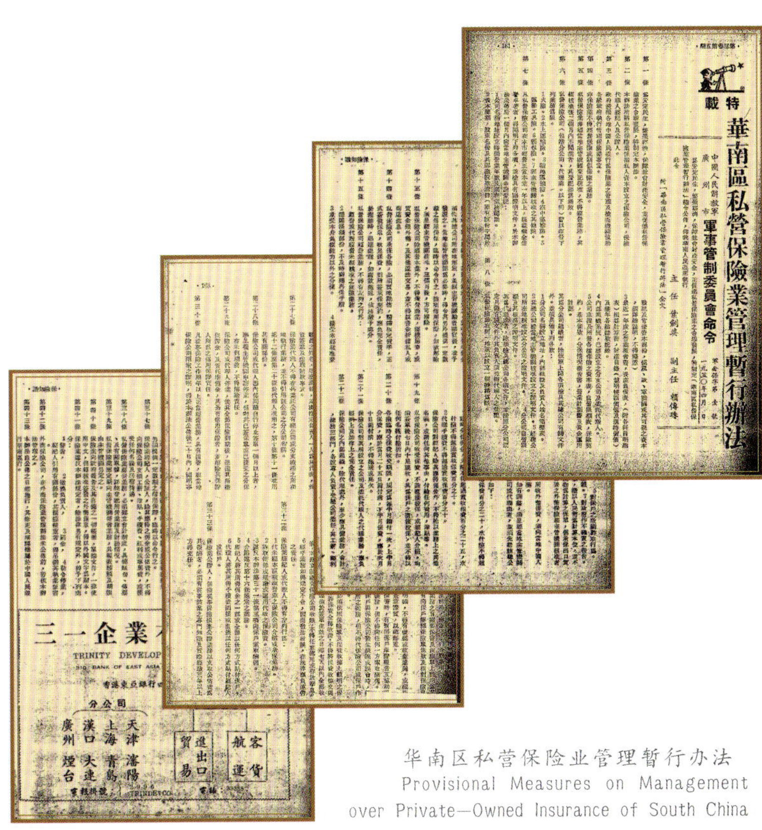

特載

華南區私營保險業管理暫行辦法

中國人民解放軍廣州市軍事管制委員會命令

三一企業

華南区私营保险业管理暂行办法

Provisional Measures on Management over Private-Owned Insurance of South China

50年代太平保险公司员工合影

Staff of Taiping Insurance Co. in 1950s

公私合营的太平保险公司总经理林震峰

Lin Zhenfeng: general manager of Taiping Insurance Co. when operated by both the state and private

副总经理金瑞琪

Jin Ruiqi: Vice General Manager of Taiping Insurance Co.

1956年8月1日

解放日报

公私合營太平新丰保險公司联合啓事

1956年8月1日

我兩公司自1951年11月和1952年1月先后公私合營以來，在中國人民保險公司領導下，不断改善經营管理，業务有較快的進展。茲为進一步接受社会主义改造，更好地發揮对社会主义建設的積極作用，需要合并經营，以利充实内部和加强对國外業务的管理，經我兩公司董事会决議，并呈奉上級主管部門核准，自1956年8月1日起，我兩公司合并为公私合營太平保險公司，并將合并后的总机構迁移北京办公。兩公司原在上海的机構自同日起撤銷，所有上海地区的保險業务及未滿期保單責任，統請中國人民保險公司上海市分公司按原保險單所載事項繼續負責，并代为处理一切未了事务。特此通知。

北京地址：北京阜成門外天寧寺路路东

1956年8月1日刊登在《解放日报》的公私合营太平、新丰保险公司联合启事。

Common announcement by Taiping and Xinfeng Insurance Co. in *Jiefang Daily* in 1956

四、早期保险业务

Early Insurance Business

火灾保险是国家保险机构成立后最早承办的一项业务。从1951年起，中国人民保险公司制定实行了新的全国统一的普通火灾保险办法，扩大了保险责任，增加了地震、地陷、爆炸等责任，降低了费率，比解放前低了65%。

Fire insurance is the first business that operated by PICC after its foundation. From 1951, PICC formulated and implemented new, coincident measures on general fire insurance, enlarging the range of insurance liabilities while adding earthquake, land-collapse, and explosion insurance, etc. in and declining the rate by 65 per cent lower than that before the liberation.

人保初创时期员工佩带的保徽
Badge of early PICC

1950年10月20日，中国人民保险公司天津市分公司制作的周年纪念册。
Memorial brochure for the Anniversary of PICC Tianjin Branch in 1950

从1951年开始办理公民财产保险；东北区公司也从本年开始开办小额简易火灾保险，这个险种开办时间较长。从1949年10月到1952年底，中国人民保险公司火灾保险保费收入达到4300余亿元，赔付289亿元(旧币)。

Property insurance for citizens had been started since 1951; PICC Northeast China Branch initiated to deal with groat postal fire insurance, which lasted a relatively long time.

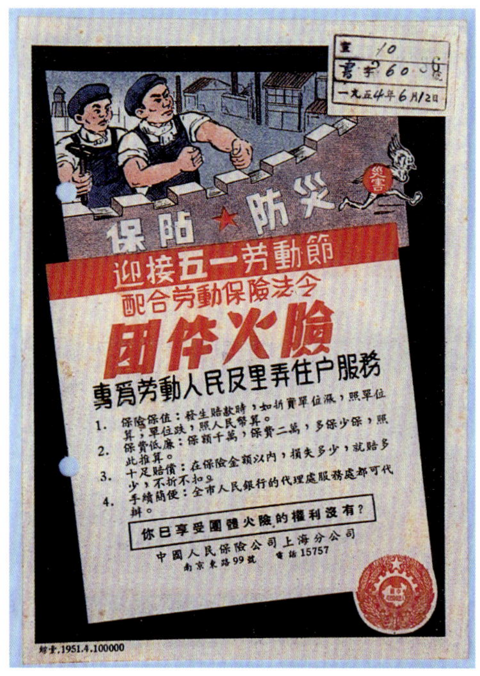

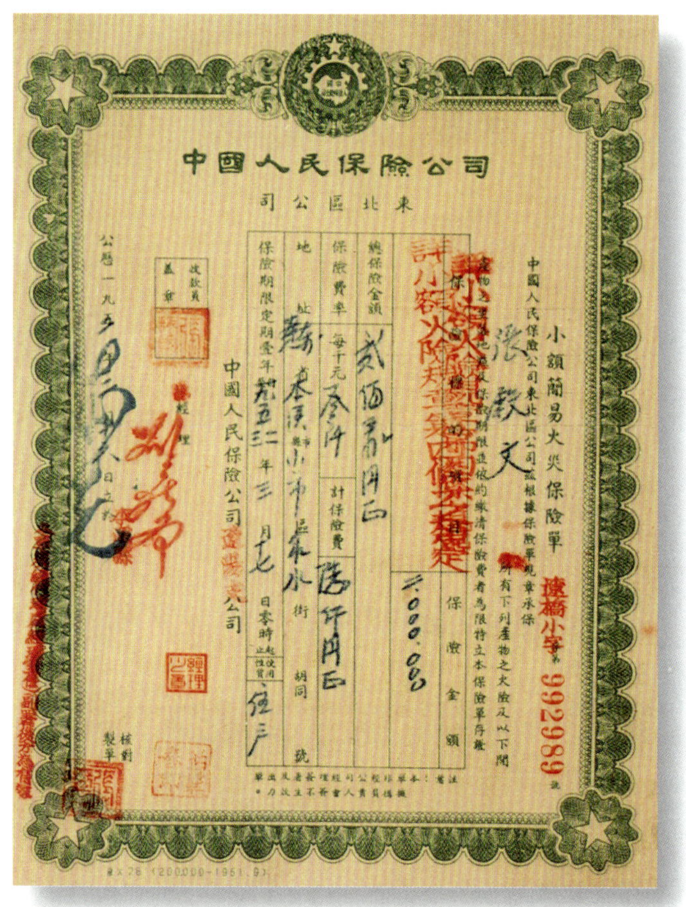

50年代火险保单
Fire Policy in 50s

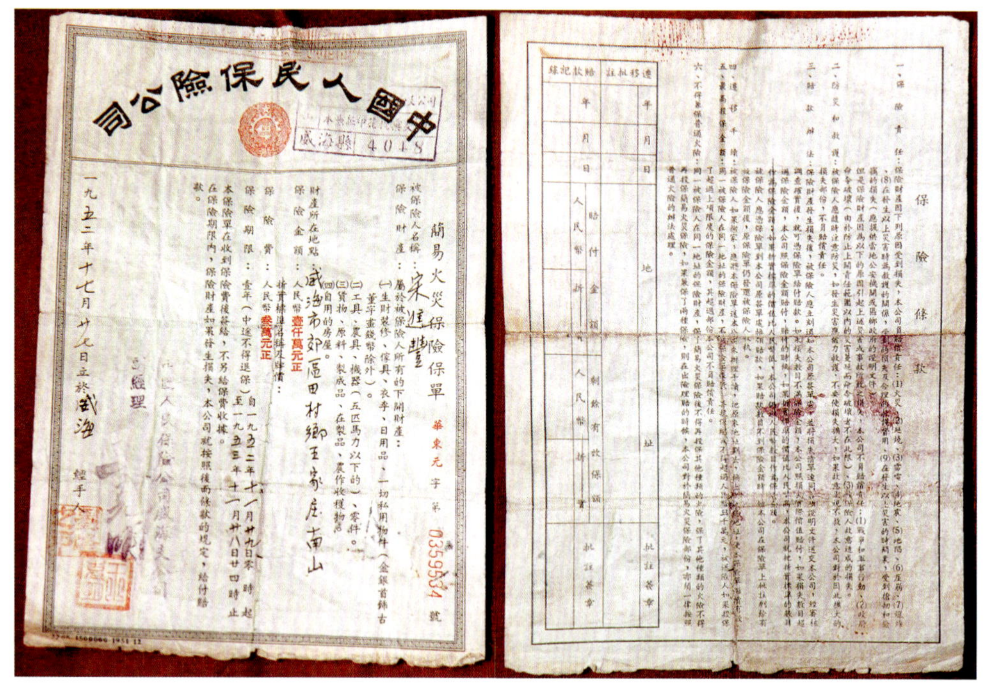

中国人民保险公司威海支公司1952年简易火灾保险保单
Postal fire insurance policy by PICC Weihai Branch in 1952

50年代初期，企业和个人两者通用的火险保单，除基本条款外，还在保单上附贴了各种相关的特约条款。

Special clauses attached to fire insurance policy for both enterprises and individuals in early 1950s

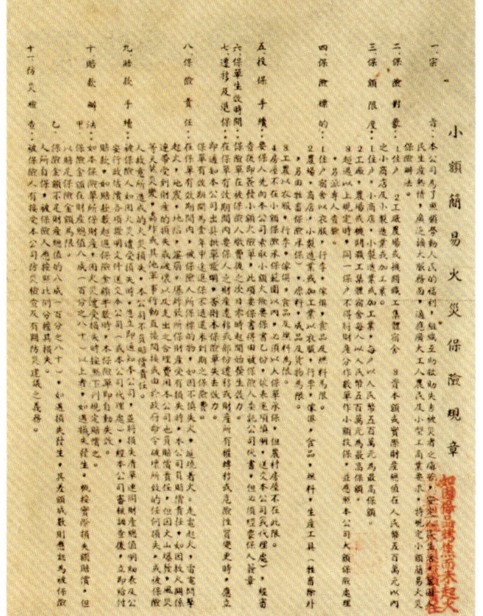

小額簡易火災保險規章

一、宗　　旨：本公司為了照顧勞動人民的福利，組織互助救助失吉被災者之痛苦，安定人民生產熱情，廣泛擴大服務面，適應廣大工人農民及小型工商業要求，特規定小額簡易火災保險辦法。

二、保險對象：1住戶　2工廠農場或機關職工集體宿舍　3資本額或實際財產總值在人民幣五百萬元以內之小商店及小製造業或加工業。

三、保額限度：1住戶，小商店，小製造業或加工業，每戶以人民幣五百萬元為最高保額。2工廠，農場或機關職工集體宿舍每人以人民幣五百萬元為最高保額。3超過以上規定時，同一保戶不得將財產分作數單作小額投保，並應照本公司大額保險處理，另出專人查勘。

四、保險標的：1住戶宿舍以衣服，行李，傢俱，食品及燃料為限。2農場，商店，小製造業或加工業以衣服，行李，傢俱，食品，燃料，生產工具（牲畜除外，另由牲畜保險承保），原料，成品及貨物為限。3工農以衣服，行李，傢俱，食品及燃料為限。4房屋不在小額保險承保範圍以內，必須以大保單承保，但農村房屋不在此限。

五、投保手續：要保人先向本公司索取小額火險要保書乙份，依表逐項填明，送交本公司或代理處，經查後即簽發小額火險單，此項要保書得由被保險人委託公司代書，但必須經要保人簽章。

六、保單生效時間：保險單在被保險人繳費後之次日零時起開始發生效力。

七、遷移及退保：在保單有效期間內要保人之財產遷移或部份遷移或財產所有權轉移或危險性質變更時，應立即通知本公司出具批單證明，否則本保險單失去效力。保單有效期間為壹年中途退保不退還未到期之保險費。

八、保險責任：在保單有效期間內，被保險人所保標的物，如因不慎失火，延燒著火，走電起火，雷電閃擊起火，地震，地陷，塌陷，爆炸或所保財產受有損失時，本公司負賠償責任，如因救火關係連帶受到財產的損失或破壞以及支出之合理費用本公司也負賠償責任，但因火山爆發，風災等天然災變，戰爭或其他軍事行動直接間接或由於政府命令破壞所致的任何損失，或被保險人故意所造成的火災損失，本公司不負賠償責任。

九、賠款手續：被保險人如因火災遭受損失時，應立即通知本公司，並將損失清單連同財產總值明細表及公安行政法償各項證明文件送交本公司或本公司代理處，經本公司審核調查後，立即給付賠款，如賠款數超過保險金額半數時，本保險單即自動失效。

十、賠款辦法：甲、如本保險單所保財產，因火災遭受損失時按照下列規定賠償之。保險金額在財產總值八成一百分之八十一以上者，如遇損失發生，概按實際損失額賠償，但以賠足保險金額為限。乙、保險金額不足財產總值的八成一百分之八十一，如遇損失發生，其差額成數則應認為被保險人所自保，被保險人應按照比例分擔其損失。

十一、防災檢查：被保險人有接受本公司防災檢查及有關防災建議之義務。

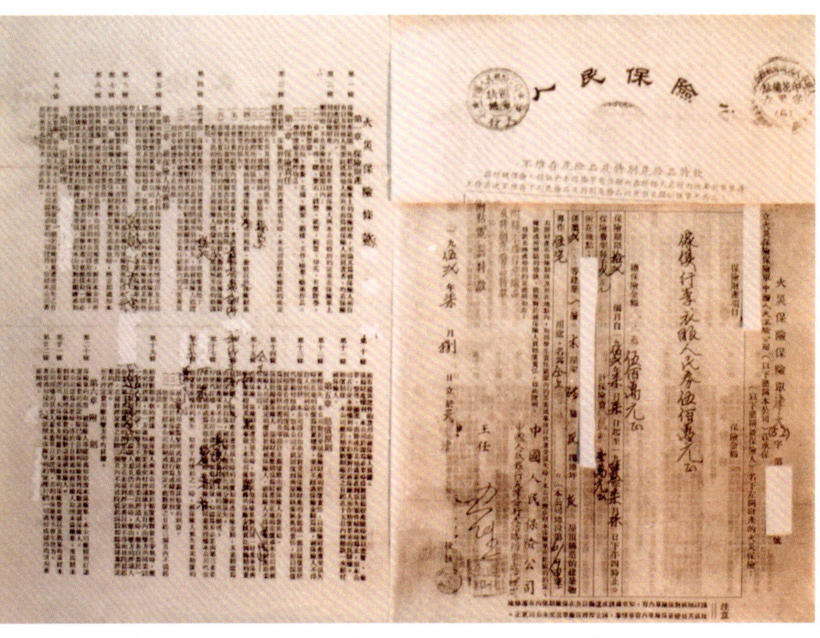

1952年中国人民保险公司天津分公司签发的火险保单

Fire Policy Signed By PICC Tianjin Branch In 1952

物资运输保险是城市财产自愿保险业务的主体，主要承保轮船、木船、火车、汽车、驿运、航运六种运输保险及其附加险(主要是沿海匪盗险和破碎渗漏险)。物资运输保险主要承保国营企业在运输过程中的物资。针对投保单位以国营企业为主的特点，该保险采取了预约保险合同的投保办法。伴随国民经济的恢复和发展，此险种业务迅速增长，若以1950年的保费数字为基数100，则1951年为269，1952年为345，1953年为449。

运输工具保险主要有汽车保险、木船保险和海洋渔船保险三种。其中，木船保险和海洋渔船保险均为解放后创办的险种。

Transportation insurance developed fast, as it's the backbone of voluntary insurance business of city properties while mainly underwriting ship, wooden vessels, trains, automobiles, post-horse transportation, and shipping as well as the additional insurance mainly referred to coast bandit insurance and crash & leakage insurance.

紀念中國共產黨三十一週年
及成渝鐵路全綫勝利通車
大家用實際行動來慶賀：增加生產，厲行節約，以支持中國人民志願軍！
中國人民保險公司川西分公司
1952.7.1
業務項目
—強制保險—
財產保險
鐵路車輛保險
船舶保險
旅客意外傷害保險
—自願保險—
火災保險
運輸保險
運輸工具保險
人身保險
農業保險
保險結合防災
確保祖國財產
生產安全第一
促進經濟建設
地址：成都市中新街　電話：275　電報掛號：42001
支公司：溫江·新津·郫縣·眉山·綿陽·金堂·夾江
特約代理處：遍設各地人民銀行內

1952年中国人民保险公司川西分公司在报刊上刊登的广告
Ad of PICC West Sichuan Branch in 1952

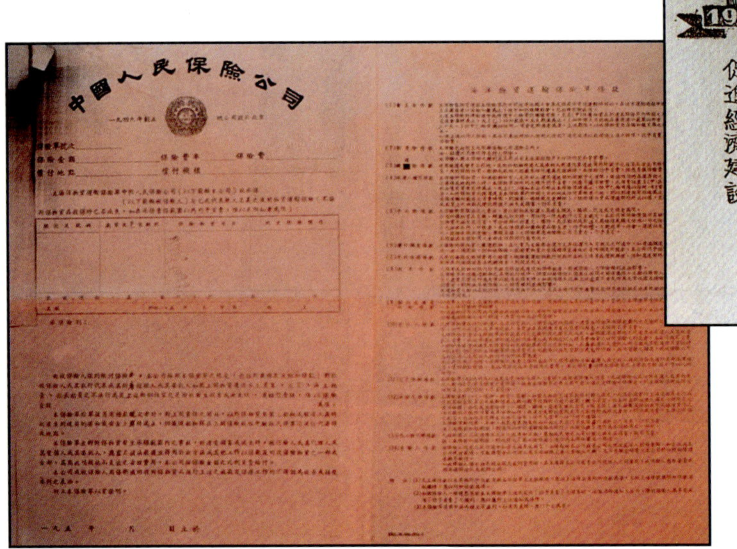

1951年中国人民保险公司海洋运输保险保险单
Marine Shipping Policy Signed By PICC In 1951

特載
中國人民保險公司輪船運輸保險條款

中国人民保险公司轮船运输保险条款
Clauses of Shipping Insurance Signed By PICC

在国民经济恢复时期，人身自愿保险完全由中国人民保险公司经营。人身自愿保险共分两类，一是集体方式投保的设有储蓄性质的人身保险。1949年底在上海市试办职工团体人身保险后，于次年起陆续在全国推行。二是个人方式投保的、带储蓄性质的人身保险，主要是简易人身保险。从1951年开办到1952年底，全国约有10万人参加此类保险。

In the period of the recovery of the national economy, personal voluntary insurance was exclusively operated by PICC, while it's classified into two: one was the personal insurance carrying the quality of deposits insured in the way of group; the other was that by in the way of individual. From 1951 when the insurance was started to late 1952, approximately 100 thousand people of the country had been covered by the insurance.

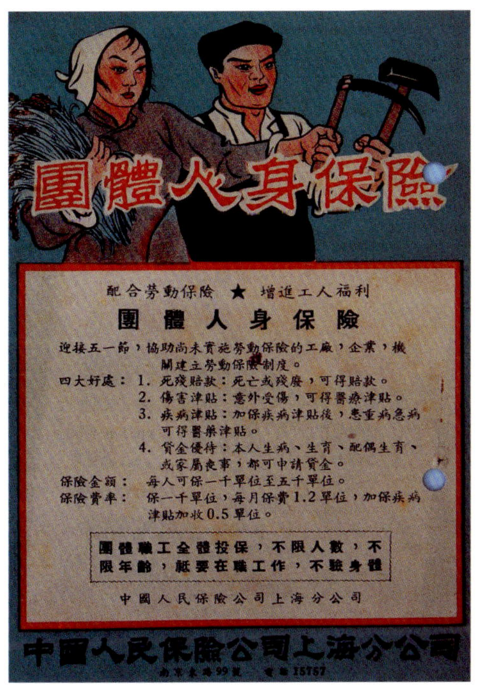

50年代人保上海分公司团体人身险宣传单
Handbill on group life insurance by PICC Shanghai Branch in 1950s

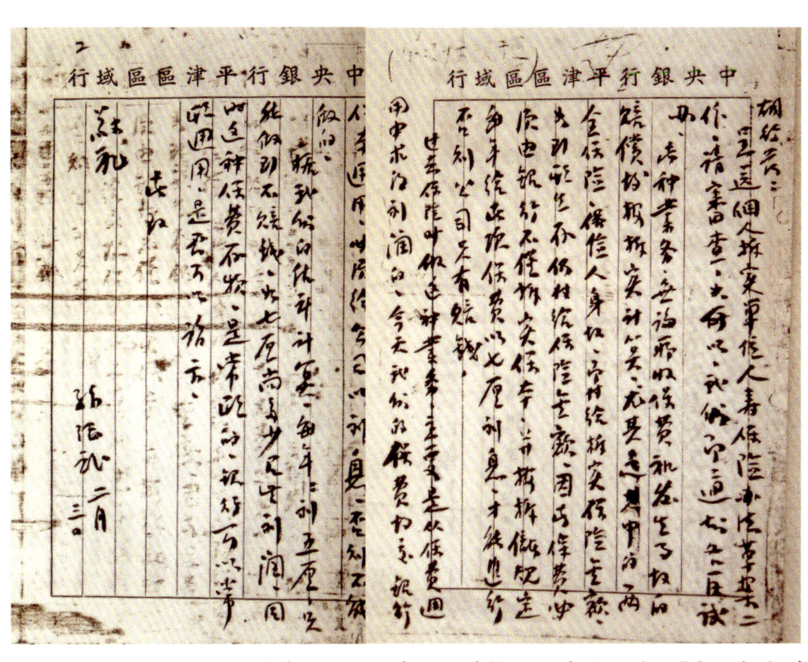

中国人民保险公司副总经理孙继武写给总经理胡景法的关于"个人折实单位人寿保险办法草案"的审批函
Vice general manager of PICC Sun Jiwu's letter to general manager Hu Jingyun on the approval & examination to the *Draft of the Measures on adjusted payment by privates in accordance with that for companies for life insurance*

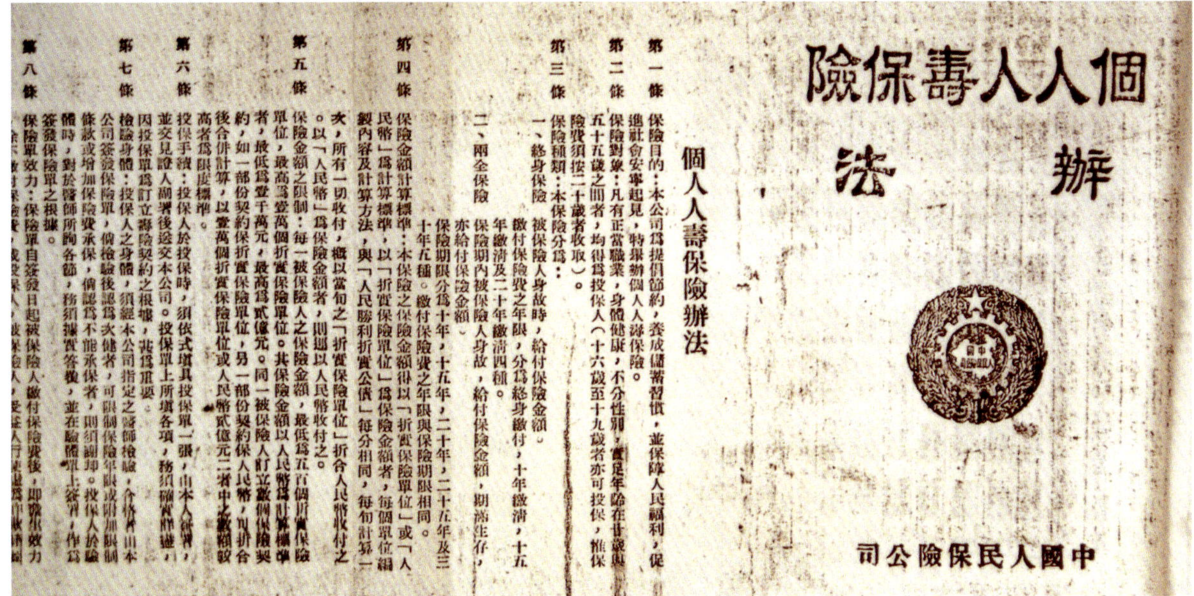

個人人壽保險辦法

中國人民保險公司

個人人壽保險辦法

第一條 保險目的：本公司爲提倡節約，養成儲蓄習慣，並保障人民福利，促進社會安寧起見，特舉辦個人人壽保險。

第二條 保險對象：凡有正當職業，身體健康，不分性別，實足年齡在廿歲與五十五歲之間者，均得爲投保人（十六歲至十九歲者亦可投保，惟保險費須按二十歲者收取）。

第三條 保險種類：本保險分爲：

一、終身保險　被保險人身故時，給付保險金額。繳付保險費之年限，分爲終身繳付，十年繳清，十五年繳清及二十年繳清四種。

二、兩全保險　保險期內被保險人身故，給付保險金額，期滿生存，亦給付保險金額。保險期限分爲十年，十五年，二十年，二十五年及三十年五種。繳付保險費之年限與保險期限相同。

第四條 保險金額計算標準：本保險之保險金額得以「折實保險單位」或「人民幣」爲計算標準，以「折實保險單位」爲保險金額者，每個單位組織內容及計算方法，與「人民勝利折實公債」每分相同，每旬計算一次，所有一切收付，概以當旬之「折實保險單位」折合人民幣收付之。以「人民幣」爲保險金額者，則逕以人民幣收付之。

第五條 保險金額之限制：每一被保險人之保險金額，最低爲五百個折實保險單位，最高爲壹萬個折實保險單位。其保險金額以人民幣爲計算標準者，最低爲壹千萬元，最高爲貳億元。同一被保險人訂立數個保險契約，如一部份契約保折實保險單位，另一部份契約保人民幣，則折合後合併計算，以壹萬個折實保險單位或人民幣貳億元二者中之數額較高者爲限度標準。

第六條 投保手續：投保人於投保時，須依式填具投保單一張，由本人簽署，並交見證人簽署後逕交本公司。投保單上所填各項，務須確實詳盡，因投保單爲訂立壽險契約之根據，甚爲重要。

第七條 檢驗身體：投保人之身體，須經本公司指定之醫師檢驗，合格者由本公司簽發保險單，倘檢驗後認爲次健者，可限制保險年限或附加限制條款或增加保險費承保，倘認爲不能承保者，則須謝却。投保人於檢驗時，對於醫師所詢各節，務須據實答覆，並在驗體單上簽署，作爲簽發保險單之根據。

第八條 保險單效力：保險單自簽發日起被保險人繳付保險費後，即發生效力 [illegible]

中国人民保险公司《个人人寿保险办法》条例
Regulations on Measures on Individual Life Insurance by PICC

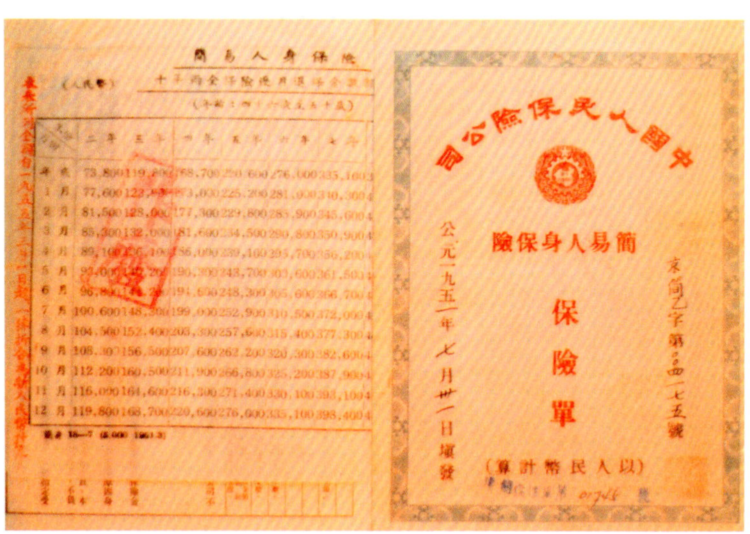
中國人民保險公司

簡易人身保險

保險單

（以人民幣計算）

公元一九五一年七月廿一日填發

1951年7月21日，中国人民保险公司天津分公司签发的《简易人身保险保险单》。

Industrial Life Policy Issued by PICC Tianjin Branch in 1951

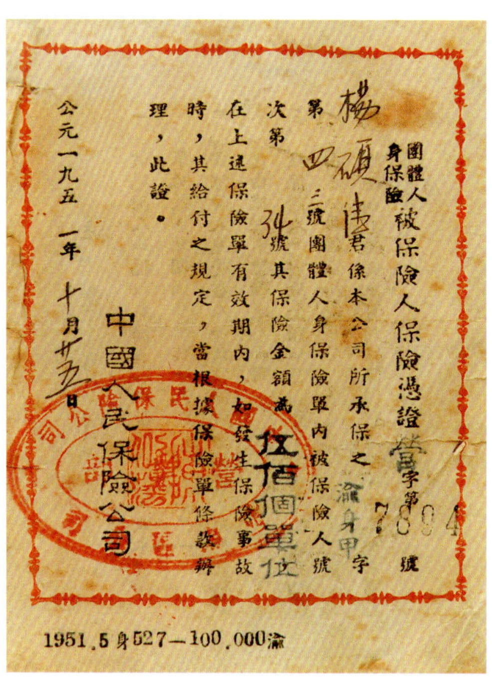
團體人身保險被保險人保險憑證　字第7894號

君係本公司所承保之第　號團體人身保險單內被保險人

在上述保險單有效期內，如發生保險事故時，其給付之規定，當根據保險單條款辦理，此證。

中國人民保險公司

公元一九五一年十月廿五日

1951.5 身527—100,000渝

中国人民保险公司西南区公司1951年团体人身保险分户保险凭证，以折实单位计算保额，此法可起到一定的保值作用。

Insurance Certificate Used by the Southwest Branch

中國人民保險公司

簡易人身保險

保險單

（以人民幣計算）

003031

1952年中国人民保险公司邵阳支公司的《简易人身保险单》

Industrial Life Policy Issued By PICC Shaoyang Branch In 1952

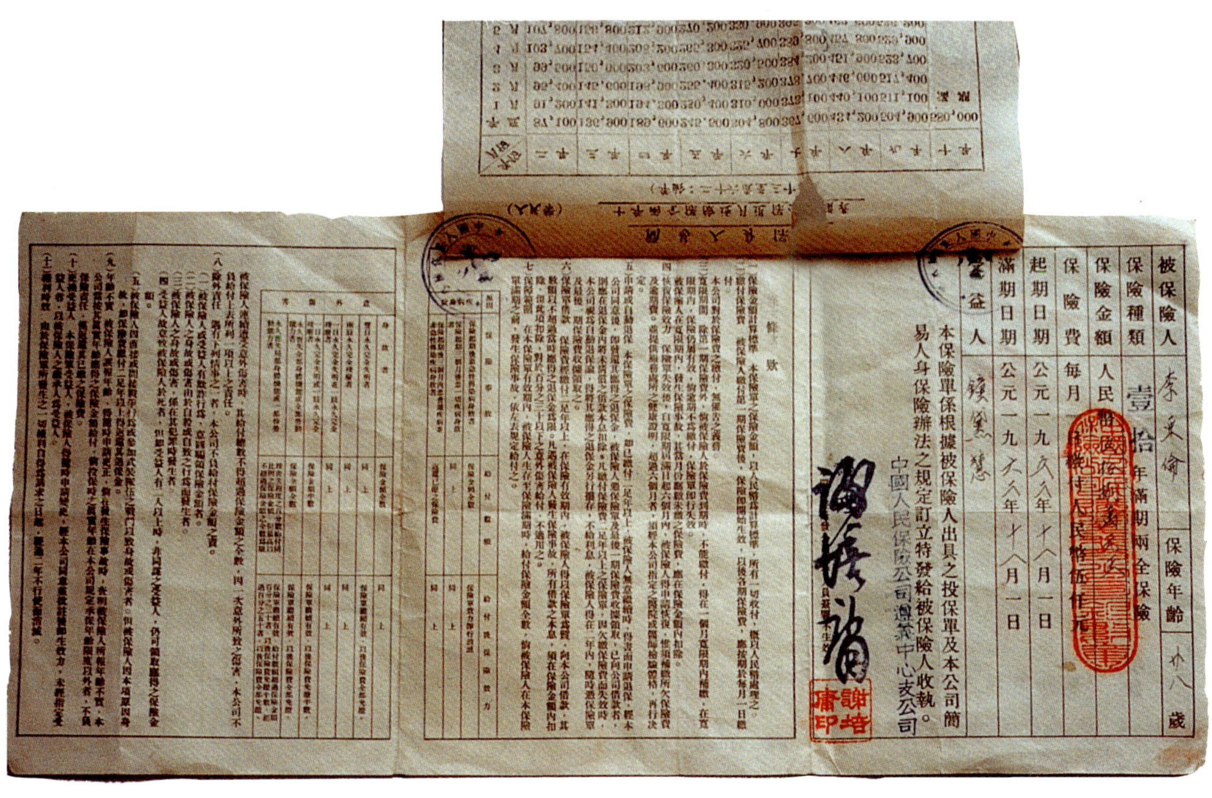

被保險人 李亞倫
保險年齡 卄八歲
保險種類 壹拾年滿期兩全保險
保險金額 人民幣伍仟元
保險費 每月
起期日期 公元一九[illegible]年十一月一日
滿期日期 公元一九[illegible]年十一月一日
受益人 [illegible]

本保險單係根據被保險人出具之投保單及本公司簡易人身保險辦法之規定訂立特發給被保險人收執。
中國人民保險公司遵義中心支公司

1952年11月25日中国人民保险公司遵义中心支公司签发的《简易人身保险单》
Industrial Life Policy Issued by PICC Zunyi Branch in 1952

中國人民保險公司
簡易人身保險
保險單
(以人民幣計算)
字第044號
公元一九五[illegible]年十一月[illegible]日填發

1998年，中保人寿保险公司贵州省分公司兑现这张46年前的保单，副总经理左宗立将保险金交付被保险人李亚伦手中。
Payment Forty-six Years Later By Guizhou Branch to the insured in 1998

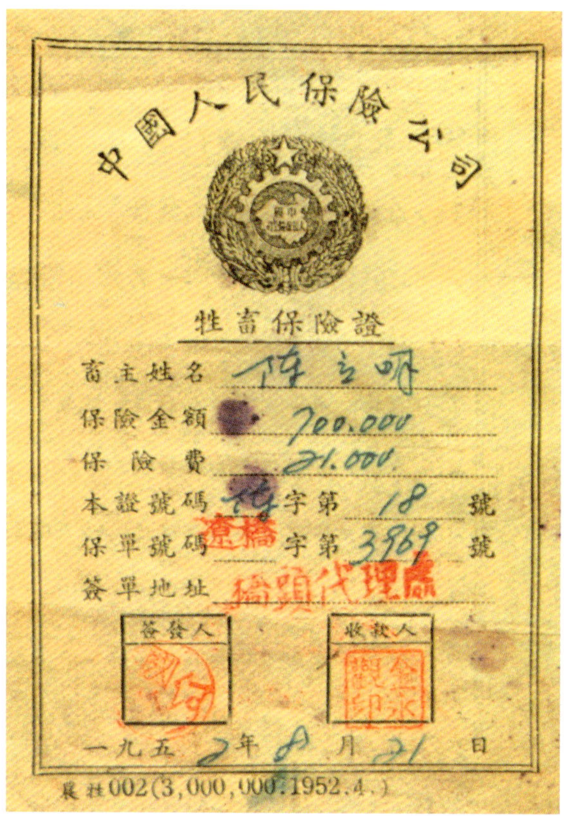

中國人民保險公司

牲畜保險證

畜主姓名

保險金額 700,000

保險費 21,000

本證號碼 字第 18 號

保單號碼 遼橋 字第 3869 號

簽單地址 橋頭代理處

簽發人 收款人

一九五2年8月21日

農社002(3,000,000:1952.4.)

牲畜保险证
Livestock Insurance Certificate of PICC

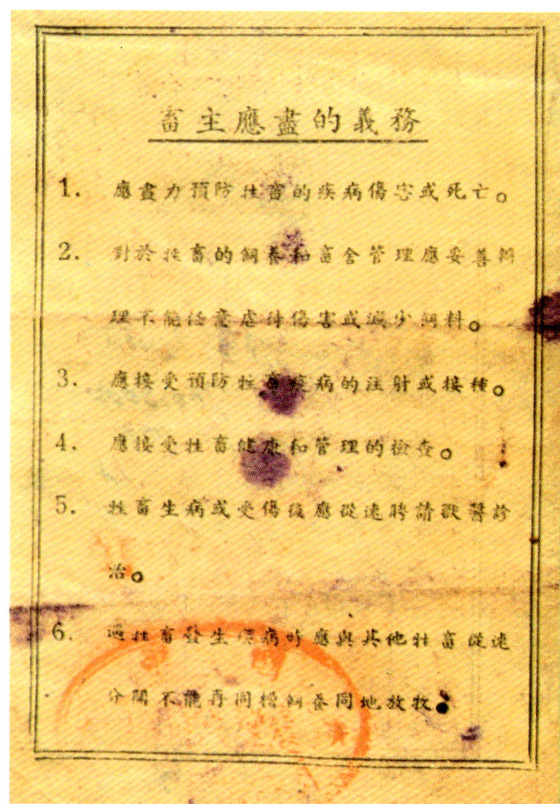

畜主應盡的義務

1. 應盡力預防牲畜的疾病傷害或死亡。
2. 對於牲畜的飼養和畜舍管理應妥善料理不能任意虐待傷害或減少飼料。
3. 應接受預防牲畜疾病的注射或接種。
4. 應接受牲畜健康和管理的檢查。
5. 牲畜生病或受傷後應從速聘請獸醫診治。
6. 遇牲畜發生傳染病時應與其他牲畜從速分開不能再同槽飼養同地放牧。

畜主应尽的义务
Stockowner's obligations

中国人民保险公司早期对农村保险业务采取自愿投保方式，承保集体和个人所有的生产和生活资料，先后开展了牲畜保险和农作物保险。

1950年春，牲畜保险业务开始在山东、四川、北京等省、市重点试办。1951年后开始在全国范围内推广。到1952年，承保数量达1400万头，其中40万头牲畜在死亡后获得赔偿。

1951年至1952年保险公司在若干地区重点试办农作物保险，先后在山东、苏北、陕西、山西、四川、江西、河北等省及北京、西安等市共36个地点试办了棉花保险。另外，还试办了小麦、水稻、甘蔗、烟草、芝麻、葡萄等农作物保险和个体农民的财产火灾保险。

从1950年到1952年，农业保险保费收入4800多亿元（旧人民币，下同），赔付1800多亿元。

1953年3月，在中国人民保险公司第三次全国会议上，决定立即停办当前并非迫切需要的农业保险业务。1953年5月10日，财政部向中央提交《关于第三次全国保险会议情况及结束农村保险业务的综合报告》。到1953年底，各地基本上结束了停办工作。停办时，全国有效保险牲畜1480万头，退保约500余万头，退还农民保险费400多亿元。

Early, PICC adopted the way of voluntarily buying insurance to develop its countryside insurance business; it underwrote the production and livelihood means owned by collectivities and individuals, while carrying out livestock and crop insurance in succession. But all the businesses were stopped in 1953 by the decision made at the 3rd nationwide conference of PICC.

中国人民保险公司早期业务发展的同时，机构也在不断向全国扩展。

Simultaneously with the development of business in its early period, PICC also constantly branched widely to the whole country.

中国人民保险公司早期营业及办公地点位于天安门广场西侧西交民巷108号，图为当时营业部干部合影。
Cadres of the Sales Department of early PICC on the west side of the Tian'anmen Square

1950年7月中国人民保险公司筹建宁夏分公司的曹镛、杨庆、行寄高、钱德芳、吴松林同志合影。
Members preparing PICC Ningxia Branch in July 1950

中国人民保险公司万县中心支公司旧址，地处重庆市万州区二马路217号，1950年7月1日至1959年1月公司在此办公营业。

Site of central subsidiary of PICC Wanxian County in Chongqing (1950—1959)

1952年益阳地区保险公司全体团员合影

Staff of PICC Yiyang Branch in 1952

1951年国庆节湖南益阳地区保险公司全体工作人员合影

Staff of PICC Yiyang Branch on National Day of 1951

1952年中国人民保险公司察哈尔分公司干部合影
Cadres of PICC Chahaer (into Hebei Province and Inner Mongolia Branch now) Branch in 1953

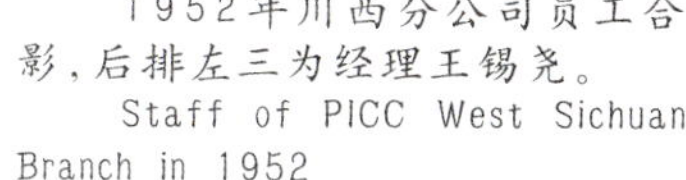

1952年川西分公司员工合影，后排左三为经理王锡尧。
Staff of PICC West Sichuan Branch in 1952

50年代初期，西南区公司防灾理赔科全体同志合影，他们胸前都佩带司徽。
Staff with company-badge of Dicaster Prevention Claim Division of PICC Southwest China Branch in early 1950s

五、强制保险的推行

Push of Mandatory Insurance

1951年2月3日，中央人民政府政务院作出《关于实行国家机关、国营企业、合作社财产强制保险及旅客强制保险的决定》，规定“国家机关、国营企业及合作社因保险而支出之费用，准编入预算报销，或列入成本计算”。同时，“指定中国人民保险公司为办理强制保险的法定机关”。1951年4月24日，政务院财经委员会发出《关于颁布财产强制保险等条例的命令》，批准公布中国人民保险公司拟定的《财产强制保险条例》、《船舶强制保险条例》、《铁路车辆强制保险条例》、《轮船旅客意外伤害强制保险条例》、《铁路旅客意外伤害强制保险条例》和《飞机旅客意外强制保险条例》。1951年2月13日，《人民日报》发表《必须实行强制保险》的社论，统一对强制保险的认识。由此，中国人民保险公司在全国的各分支机构积极推行强制保险。

On April 24, 1951, the Finance & Economy Committee of the Government Administration Council of the Central Government promulgated a series of regulations on mandatory insurance and then PICC embarked on mandatory insurance across the country from late 1952; since then, almost all state-owned enterprises purchased the related property mandatory insurance in the same year. The Communication Department then was also an agency of PICC to sell passenger accidental insurance.

人民日報

漢江南岸敵傷亡慘重 我軍士氣旺盛準備全線反攻

周總理明日演說

全國各大城市中蘇友好協會 籌備慶祝中蘇同盟一週年

中央人民政府政務院 關於實行國家機關、國營企業、合作社財產强制保險及旅客强制保險的決定

南京等五大城市人民遊行示威 堅決反對美國重新武裝日本

社論 必須實行强制保險

記燕京大學的大喜事

1951年2月13日，《人民日报》发表《必须实行强制保险》的社论

Editorial on mandatory insurance by *People Daily* in Feb. 1951

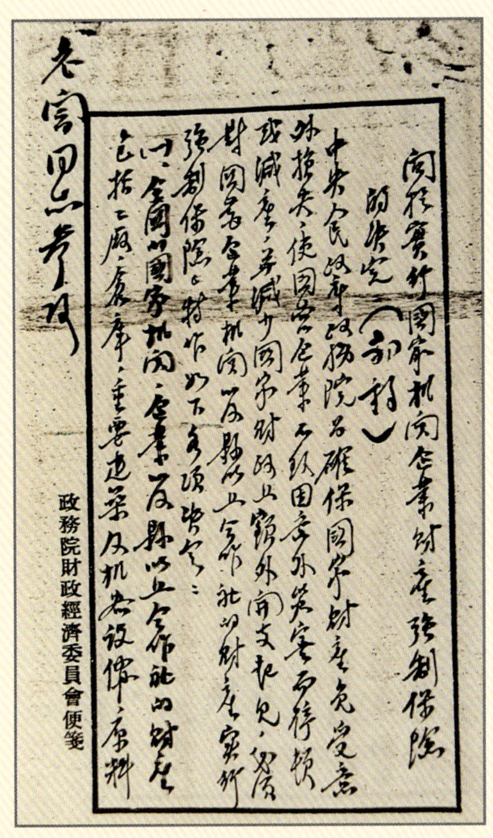

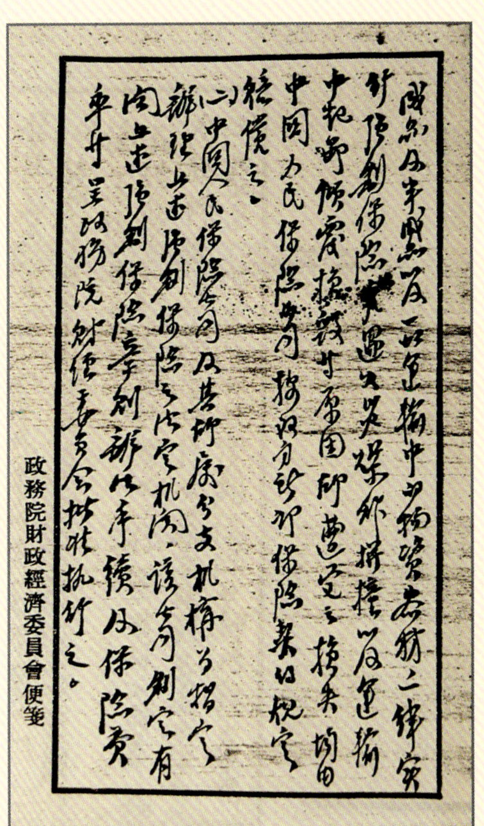

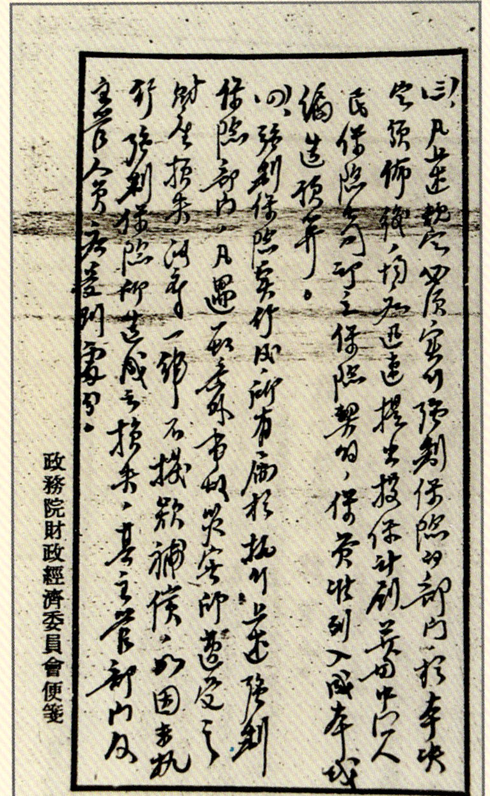

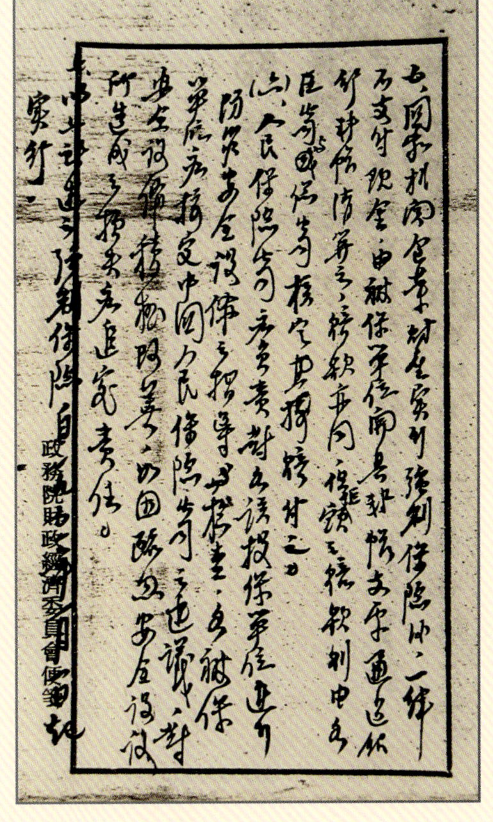

政务院关于实行国家机关企业财产强制保险的决定初稿(手稿)
First manuscript by the Government Administration Council on the decision of implementing property mandatory insurance for state organs and state-owned enterprises

到1952年底，全国国营企业、合作社的财产已全部投保，县以上国家机关财产的绝大部分也已投保，财产及运输工具的强制保险保费收入达7700亿元（旧人民币，下同），赔付1200亿元。强制保险的推行充分发挥了经济保障的作用，为国民经济的恢复和发展作出了贡献。

铁路、轮船和飞机旅客意外伤害强制保险，由中国人民保险公司委托交通部门代办。保险费由运输部门在售票时随票价附收，然后按月交国家保险机构。铁路和飞机旅客意外伤害强制保险从1951年7月起在全国实施。由于私营航运业的存在，加之航线的分散，致使轮船旅客意外伤害强制保险推迟到1951年9月才在全国推行。

三种旅客意外伤害强制保险规定，每一旅客的保险金额不分席位、仓位的等次，也不分全票、半票和免票，一律为人民币1500万元。旅客凡是由于意外事故受伤需治疗时，保险公司均按实际需要在1500万元的限额内给付医疗费用。

所有的强制保险业务均在1957年停办。

However, all mandatory insurance businesses were stopped in 1957.

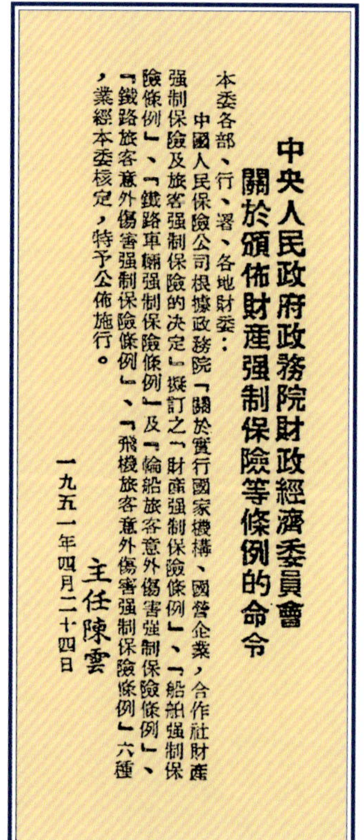

中央人民政府政務院財政經濟委員會
關於頒佈財產强制保險等條例的命令

本委各部、行、署、各地財委：

中國人民保險公司根據政務院「關於實行國家機構、國營企業，合作社財產强制保險及旅客强制保險的決定」擬訂之「財產强制保險條例」、「船舶强制保險條例」、「鐵路車輛强制保險條例」及「輪船旅客意外傷害强制保險條例」、「鐵路旅客意外傷害强制保險條例」、「飛機旅客意外傷害强制保險條例」六種，業經本委核定，特予公佈施行。

主任陳雲

一九五一年四月二十四日

1951年4月24日中央人民政府政务院关于颁布六种强制保险条例的命令

Mandate by the Government Administration Council on promulgation of the rules of the six mandatory insurances in Apr. 1951

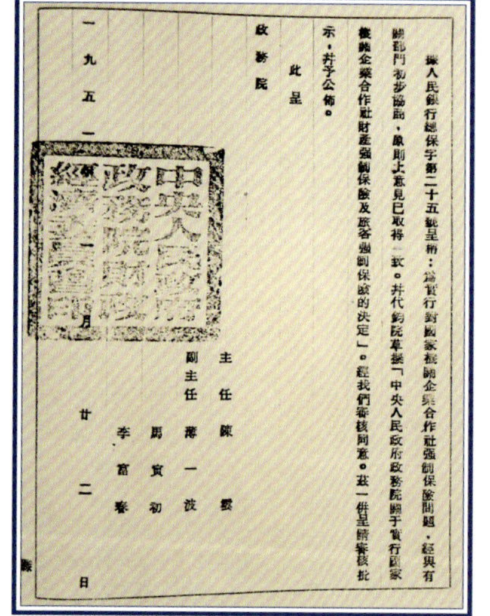

據人民銀行總保字第二十五號呈稱：為實行對國家機關企業合作社强制保險問題，經與有關部門初步協商，原則上意見已取得一致。并代鈞院草擬「中央人民政府政務院關于實行國家機關企業合作社財產强制保險及旅客强制保險的決定」。經我們審核同意。茲一併呈請審核批示，并予公佈。

此呈

政務院

主任 陳雲

副主任 薄一波 馬寅初 李富春

一九五一年二月廿二日

中央人民政府政务院财政经济委员会批准实施各种强制保险的函

Letter by the Government Administration Council to approve the implementation of various mandatory insurances

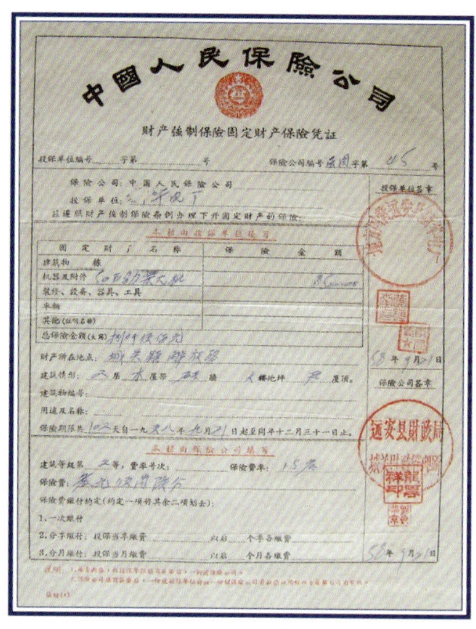

中國人民保險公司

财产强制保险固定财产保险凭证

1958年9月21日中国人民保险公司颁发的财产强制保险凭证。（资料提供：成继跃）

Warrant of mandatory insurance issued by PICC in Sep. 1958

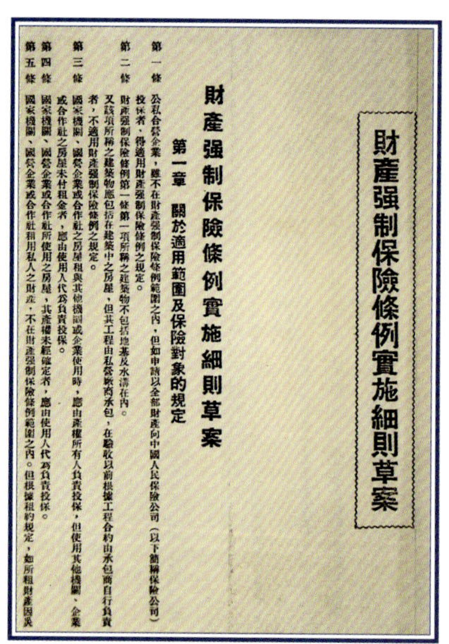

財產强制保險條例實施細則草案

財產强制保險條例實施細則草案

第一章 關於適用範圍及保險對象的規定

第一條 公私合營企業，雖不在財產强制保險條例範圍之內，但如申請以全部財產向中國人民保險公司（以下簡稱保險公司）投保者，得適用財產强制保險條例之規定。

第二條 財產强制保險條例第一條第一項所稱之建築物不包括地基及水溝在內。又該項所稱之建築物應包括在建築中之房屋，但其工程由私營廠商承包，在驗收以前根據工程合約由承包商自行負責者，不適用財產强制保險條例之規定。

第三條 國家機關、國營企業或合作社之房屋租與其他機關或企業使用時，應由產權所有人負責投保，但使用其他機關、企業或合作社之房屋未付租金者，應由使用人代為負責投保。

第四條 國家機關、國營企業或合作社所使用之房屋，其產權未經確定者，應由使用人代為負責投保。

第五條 國家機關、國營企業或合作社租用私人之財產，不在財產强制保險條例範圍之內。但根據租約規定，如所租財產因災

财产强制保险条例实施细则草案

Draft on the Detailed Rules for Implementation of Property Mandatory Insurance

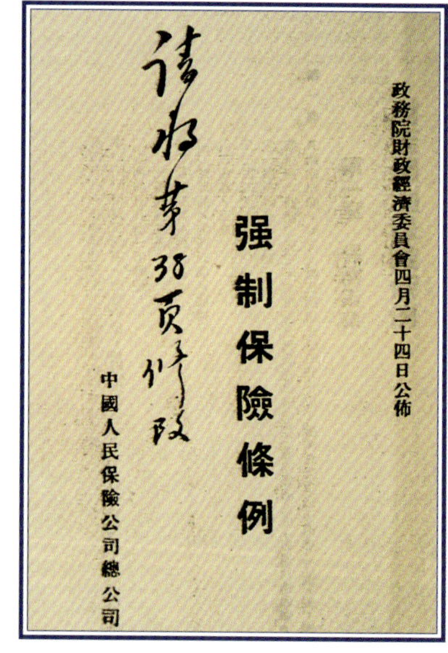

政務院財政經濟委員會四月二十四日公佈

强制保險條例

中國人民保險總公司

强制保险条例

Regulations on Mandatory Insurance

50年代初中国保险公司宴请外国保险交流代表团
Banquet treating delegation of foreign insurance exchange by China Insurance Company in 1950s

50年代初中国保险公司从上海迁入北京。图为部分工作人员合影。
Part of employees with China Insurance Co. after they moved to Beijing from Shanghai in 1950s.

中国保险公司办公大楼
Office Building of China Insurance Company

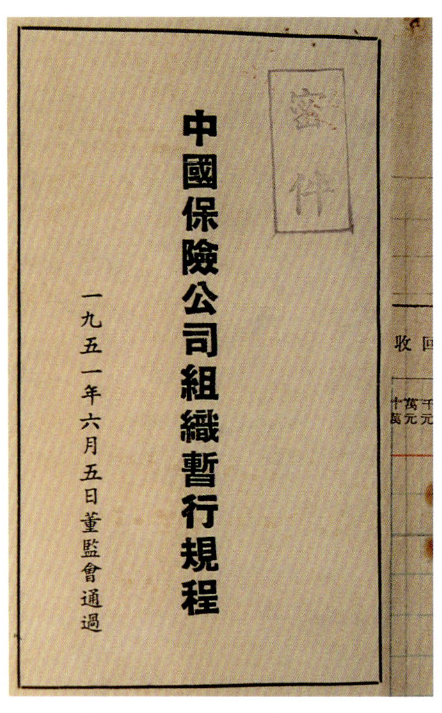
密件

中國保險公司組織暫行規程

一九五一年六月五日董監會通過

中国保险公司组织暂行规程
Temporary Organizational Rules of China Insurance Company

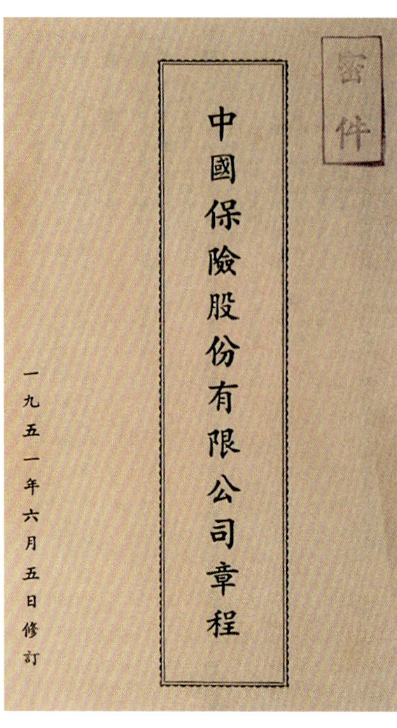
密件

中國保險股份有限公司章程

一九五一年六月五日修訂

中国保险股份有限公司章程
Statute of China Insurance Company

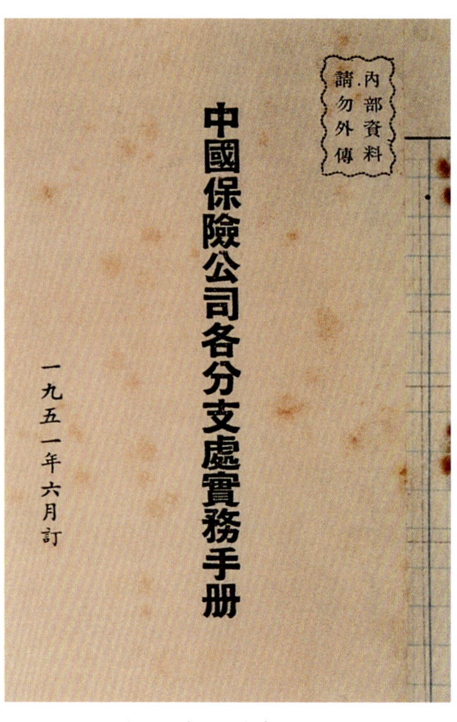
內部資料 請勿外傳

中國保險公司各分支處實務手冊

一九五一年六月訂

1951年6月制订的中国保险公司各分支处实务手册
Practice brochure for branches worked out in Jun. 1951

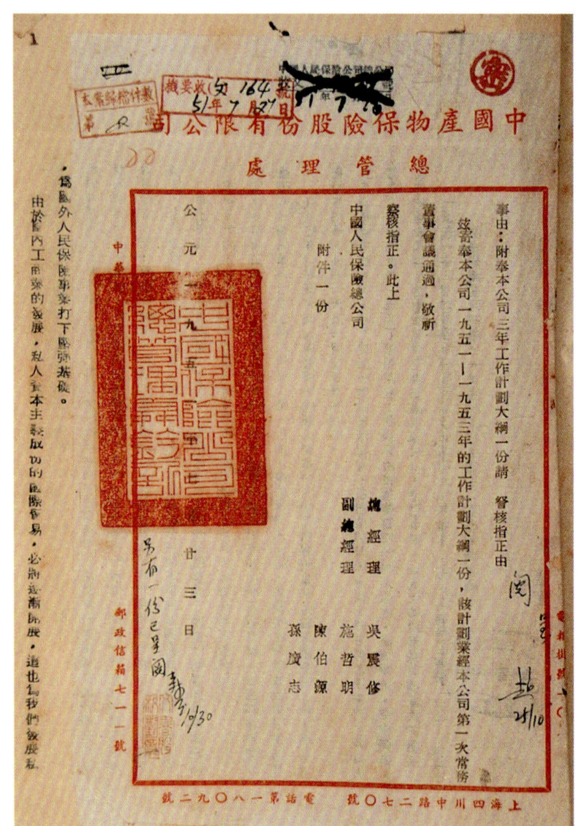
中國產物保險股份有限公司
總管理處

事由：附奉本公司三年工作計劃大綱一份請 督核指正由

茲寄奉本公司一九五一—一九五三年的工作計劃大綱一份，該計劃業經本公司第一次常務董事會議通過，敬祈
察核指正。此上
中國人民保險總公司

附件一份

總經理 吳震修
施哲明
副總經理 陳伯源
孫廣志

公元一九五一年七月廿三日

上海四川中路二七〇號 電話第一八〇九二號 郵政信箱七一一號

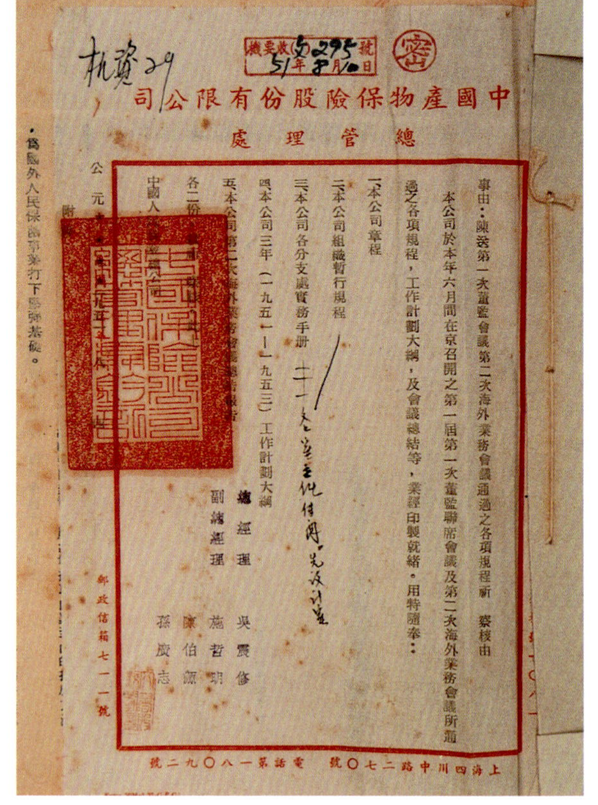
中國產物保險股份有限公司
總管理處

事由：陳送第一次董監會議第二次海外業務會議通過之各項規程祈 察核由

本公司於本年六月間在京召開之第一屆第一次董監聯席會議及第二次海外業務會議所通過之各項規程，工作計劃大綱，及會議總結等，業經印製就緒。用特隨奉：

一、本公司章程
二、本公司組織暫行規程
三、本公司各分支處實務手冊
四、本公司三年（一九五一—一九五三）工作計劃大綱
五、本公司第二次海外業務會議總結報告

各二份

總經理 吳震修
施哲明
副總經理 陳伯源
孫廣志

上海四川中路二七〇號 電話第一八〇九二號 郵政信箱七一一號

中国保险公司公函。左为向中国保险公司报告《本公司三年工作计划大纲》的函，右为该公司《第一次董监事会和第二次海外业务会议通过的各项规程》的报告。
Letter of 3-Year Blueprint reported to China Insurance Company (L); report on regulations passed at the 1st directorate and board of supervisors and 2nd conference of overseas business (R)

七、50年代后期的保险业务

Insurance Business in Late 1950s

到1952年底，国民经济的恢复任务完成。从1953年起，中国经济进入了第一个五年计划时期，配合国民经济的发展，保险业相应有所发展，同时经历了整顿、巩固到稳步发展的过程。

根据1953年3月中国人民保险公司第三次全国保险会议确定的“整顿城市业务，停办农村业务，整顿机构，在巩固的基础上稳步前进”的方针，整顿和收缩是1953年保险工作的重心。经过调整，农村业务基本停办，保险公司机构得以精简，从1783个减少到1057个，人员由51000多人减到32000多人。1953年全国保险收入18567亿元（旧人民币，下同），支付赔款5412亿元。

By late 1952, the recovery of the national economy had been completed; from 1953, Chinese economy entered the first 5-year-scheme period. To keep up with the development in the national economy, Chinese insurance had developed to a certain extent, and meanwhile, it experienced the phases of being trimmed, consolidated, and stable development.

中國人民保險公司

團體火險

分戶憑證

保險單第 20265 號第 362 分號

分戶姓名：

保 品：(一)傢具、衣服及行李、日常用品。(二)房屋（以自建自用且非營業性者爲限）。

保險金額：(一)壹佰伍拾萬元整 (二)

保險截止日期：至一九五三年 月 日 下午四時止。

中国人民保险公司团体火险分户凭证
Certificate of group fire insurance of PICC

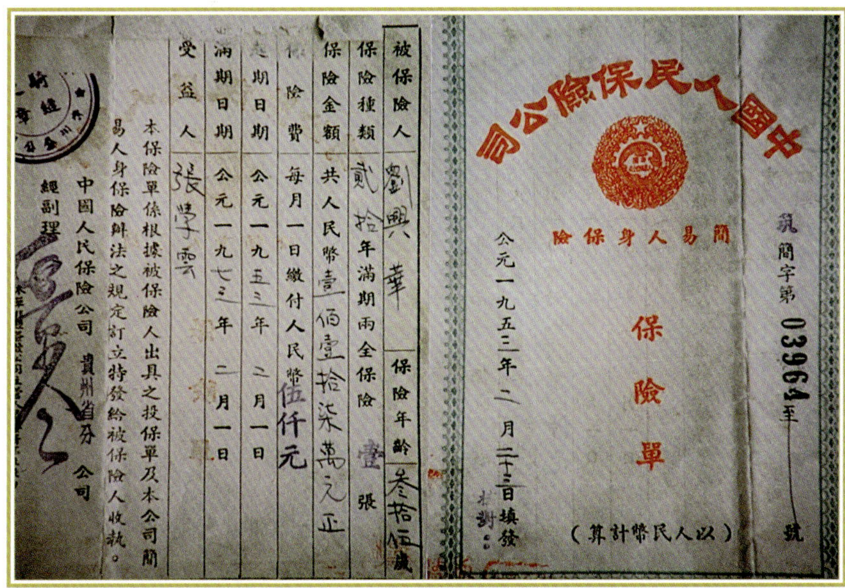

中國人民保險公司

簡易人身保險

保險單

筑簡字第 03964 號

（以人民幣計算）

公元一九五三年二月二十三日填發

被保險人	劉興華
保險年齡	叁拾伍歲
保險種類	貳拾年滿期兩全保險
保險金額	共人民幣壹佰壹拾柒萬元正
保險費	每月一日繳付人民幣伍仟元
起期日期	公元一九五三年二月一日
滿期日期	公元一九七三年二月一日
受益人	張學雲

本保險單係根據被保險人出具之投保單及本公司簡易人身保險辦法之規定訂立特發給被保險人收執。

中國人民保險公司貴州省分公司

總副理

1953年中国人民保险公司贵州分公司简易人身保险单
Postal personal insurance policy by PICC Guizhou Branch in 1953

1953年西北区保险公司处级干部及西北五省公司经理合影
Division-level Cadres of PICC Northwest China Branch with Managers of branches in 5 northwest provinces in 1953

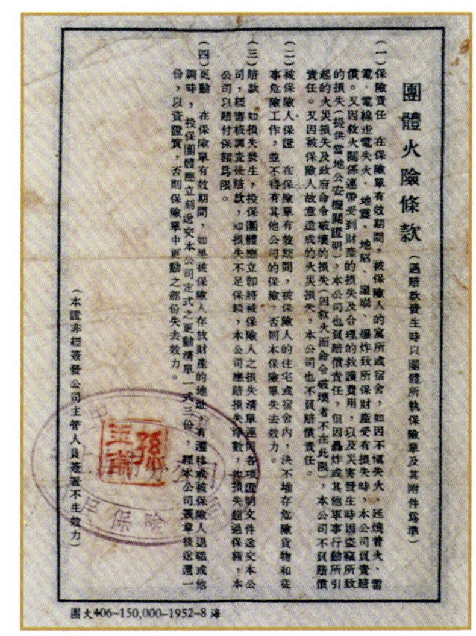

團體火險條款（遇賠款發生時以團體所執保險單及其附件爲準）

（一）保險責任 在保險單有效期間，被保險人的寓所或宿舍，如因不慎失火、延燒着火、雷電、電線走電失火、地震、地陷、崖崩、爆炸致所保財產受有損失時，本公司負責賠償。又因救火關係連帶受到財產的損失及合理的救護費用，以及災害發生時因盜竊所致的損失（投保當地公安機關證明），本公司也負賠償責任，但因轟炸或其他軍事行動所引起的火災損失及政府命令破壞的損失（因救火而命令破壞者不在此限），本公司不負賠償責任。又因被保險人故意造成的火災損失，本公司也不負賠償責任。

（二）被保險人保證 在保險單有效期間，被保險人的住宅或宿舍內，決不堆存危險貨物和從事危險工作，並不得有其他公司的保險，否則本保險單失去效力。

（三）賠款 如損失發生，投保團體應立即將被保險人之損失清單連同各項證明文件送交本公司，經審核調查後賠款，如損失不足保額，本公司照賠損失淨數，如損失超過保額，本公司以賠付保額爲限。

（四）更動 在保險單有效期間，如果被保險人存放財產的地址，有遷移或被保險人退職或他調時，投保團體應立刻送交本公司定式之更動清單一式三份，經本公司簽章後送還一份，以資證實，否則保險單中更動之部份失去效力。

（本證非經簽發公司主管人員簽署不生效力）

團火406-150,000-1952-8 滬

1953年“人保”上海分公司团体火险条款
Clauses of group fire insurance of PICC Shanghai Branch in 1953

1954年全国尤其是长江、淮河流域发生百年未遇的洪水灾害，保险公司及时赔付，充分发挥了保险的经济补偿职能。保险机构进一步精简，全国分支机构的工作人员由年初的25846人，减少到年底的20406人。

In 1954, the whole country, especially Yangtze, Huaihe River valley suffered from a rare flood; insurers handled the claims and benefits in time, fully exerting the function of economic considerations of insurance.

Also, insurance institutions were further cut, resulted in the decrease of employees of the branches from 25,846 in early 1954 to 20,406 in late the year.

1954年人保防火宣传车
A car of PICC to propagandize fire prevention in 1954

1954年重庆九龙坡区消防演习场地。人保在消防演习场地悬挂保险防火宣传横幅。
Fire Drill Ground in Chongqing in 1954

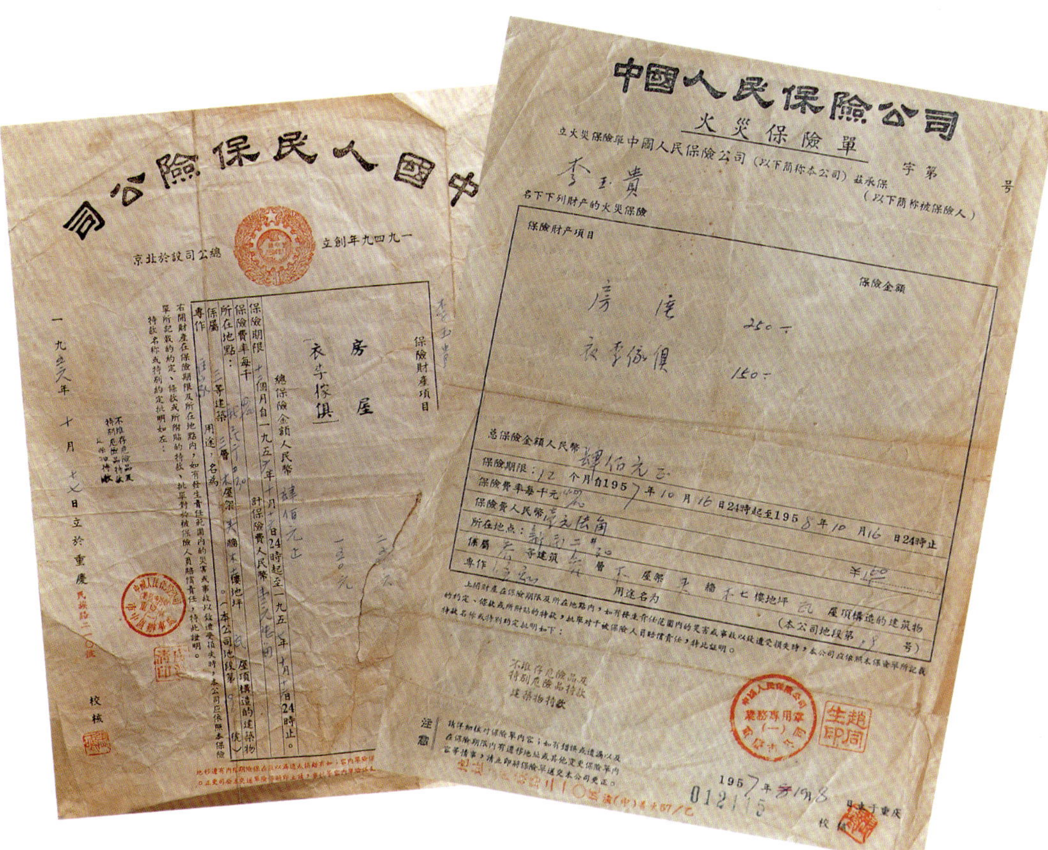
中國人民保險公司
一九四九年創立
總公司設於北京

中国人民保险公司
火灾保险單

1956、1957年中国人民保险公司重庆分公司火灾保险保险单
Fire policies by PICC Chongqing Branch in 1956, 1957

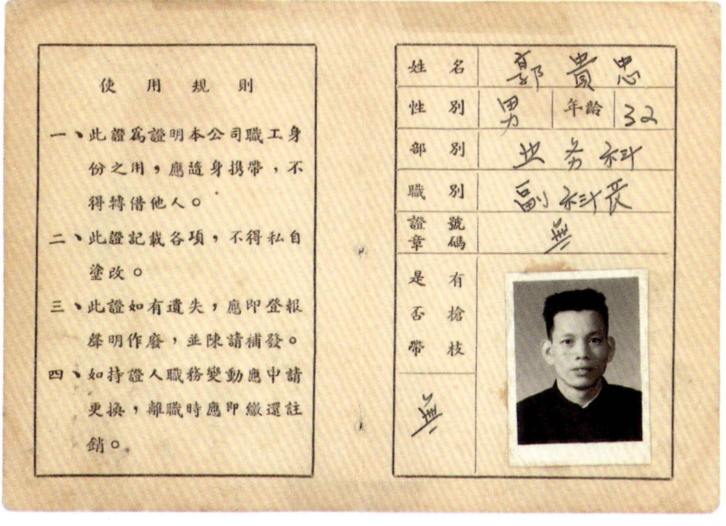
使用規則

一、此證爲證明本公司職工身份之用，應隨身携帶，不得轉借他人。

二、此證記載各項，不得私自塗改。

三、此證如有遺失，應即登報聲明作廢，並陳請補發。

四、如持證人職務變動應申請更換，離職時應即繳還註銷。

姓名	郭貴忠		
性別	男	年齡	32
部別	業务科		
職別	副科長		
證章號碼	無		
是否有帶槍枝	無		

当时中国人民保险公司北京分公司职工工作证(资料提供：郭贵忠)
An employee's card of PICC Beijing Branch at that time

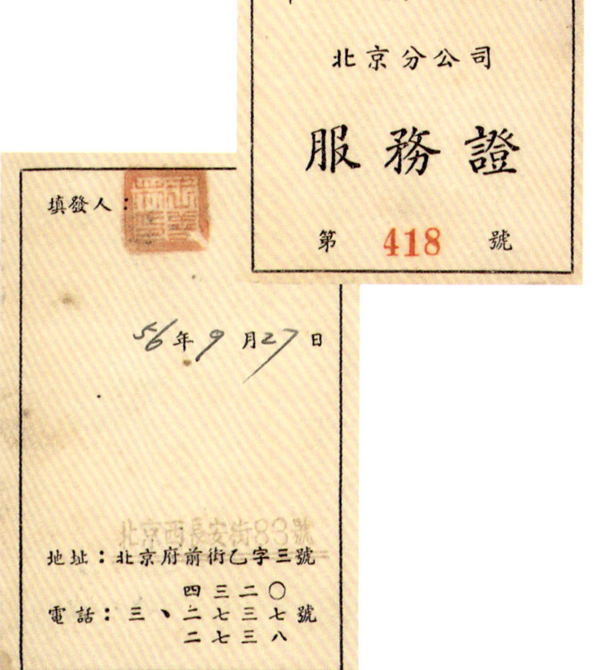
中國人民保險公司
北京分公司
服務證
第 418 號

填發人：
56年9月27日

地址：北京府前街乙字三號
電話：三、四三二〇 二七三七 二七三八號

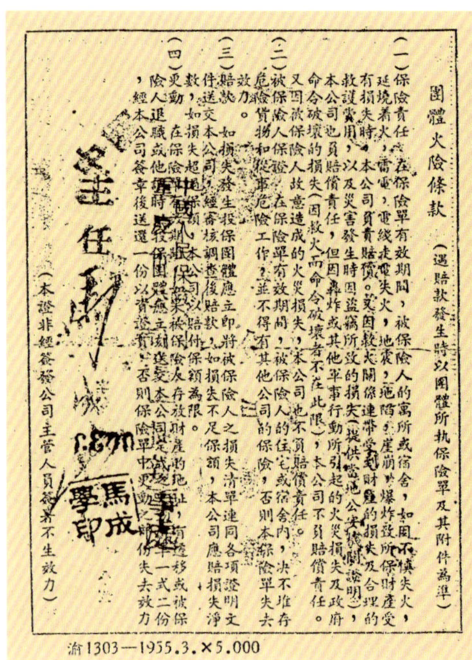

團體火險條款（遇賠款發生時以團體所執保險單及其附件為準）

（一）保險責任：在保險單有效期間，被保險人的寓所或宿舍，如因不慎失火，延燒着火，雷電，電綫走電失火，地震，地陷，崖崩，爆炸致所保財產受有損失時，本公司負責賠償。又因救火關係連帶受到財產的損失及合理的救護費用，以及災害發生時因盜竊所致的損失（提供當地公安機關證明），本公司也負賠償責任，但因轟炸或其他軍事行動所引起的火災損失及政府命令破壞的損失（因救火而命令破壞者不在此限），本公司不負賠償責任。

（二）又因被保險人故意造成的火災損失，本公司也不負賠償責任。被保險人在保險單有效期間，被保險人的住宅或宿舍內，決不准存危險貨物和從事危險工作，並不得有其他公司的保險，否則本保險單失去效力。

（三）賠款：如損失發生投保團體應立即將被保險人之損失清單連同各項證明文件送交本公司，經審核調查後賠款，如損失不足保額，本公司應賠損失淨數，如損失超過保額以保額為限。

（四）變動：如被保險人在保險財產的地址有遷移或被保險人退職或他調時，投保團體應立刻填送變動通知一式二份經本公司簽章後送還一份以資證實，否則保險單中變動之一份失去效力

（本證非經簽發公司主管人員簽章不生效力）

渝1303—1955.3.×5.000

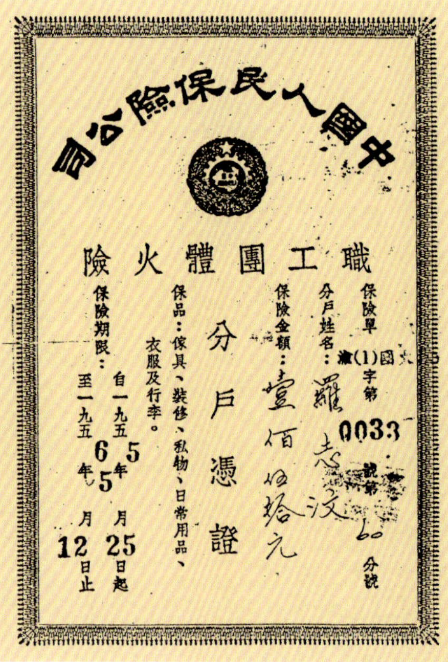

中國人民保險公司

職工團體火險分戶憑證

保險單 渝(1)團火字第 0033 號

分戶姓名：羅志汶 60 分號

保險金額：壹佰捌拾元

保品：傢具、裝修、私物、日常用品、衣服及行李。

保險期限：自一九五5年5月25日起
至一九五6年5月12日止

1955年中国人民保险公司重庆分公司职工团体火险分户凭证

Certificate of employee's group fire insurance by PICC Chongqing Branch in 1955

小額簡易火災保險規章

一、保險責任：……

二、保險對象：……

三、保額限度：……

四、保險財產：……

五、投保手續：……

六、保單生效時間：……

七、遷移或退保……

八、賠款辦法：……

九、防災和救護：……

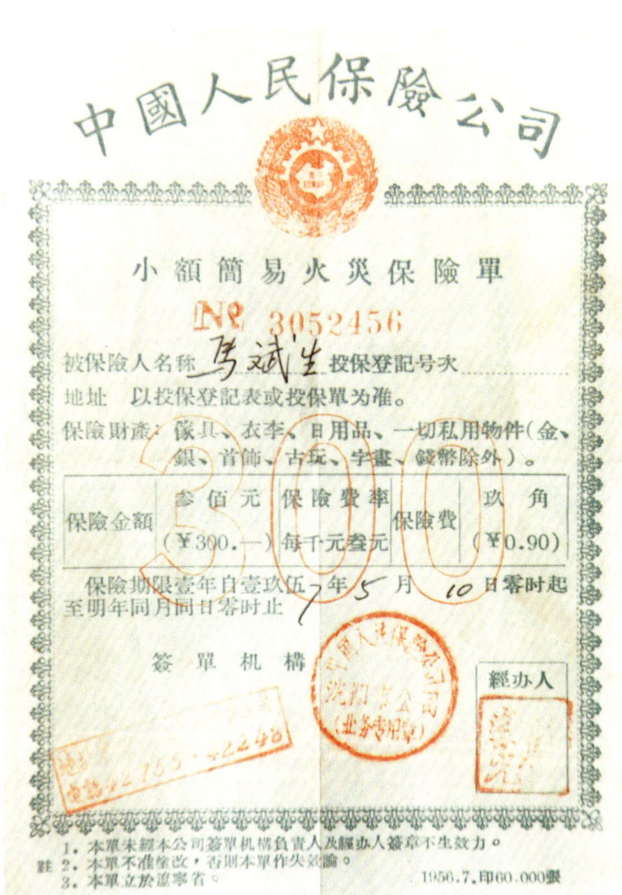

中國人民保險公司

小額簡易火災保險單

№ 3052456

被保險人名稱 馬斌生 投保登記號次

地址 以投保登記表或投保單為准。

保險財產：傢具、衣李、日用品、一切私用物件（金、銀、首飾、古玩、字畫、鈔幣除外）。

保險金額	叁佰元（¥300.—）	保險費率 每千元叁元	保險費	玖角（¥0.90）

保險期限壹年自壹玖伍7年5月10日零时起
至明年同月同日零时止

簽單机構　　經办人

注 1. 本單未經本公司簽單机構負責人及經办人簽章不生效力。
2. 本單不准塗改，否則本單作失效論。
3. 本單立於[illegible]者。

1956.7.印60.000張

1957年中国人民保险公司沈阳市分公司小额简易火灾保险单（资料提供：王伟）

Groat postal fire insurance policy by PICC Shenyang Branch in 1957

保险业务的整顿引发了人们对农村保险业务的反思，认识到农村保险还是需要的。于是总公司组织翻译了《苏联国家保险》等作为全公司上下学习的材料，借鉴苏联经验，恢复重办农村业务的信心。

1954年11月，第四次全国保险会议通过《农村保险工作四年总结》等重要文件，检讨了停办阶段清理整顿工作的缺点和不足。确定1955年的工作是：停办部分国营企业强制保险业务，重点恢复农村保险业务，稳定推展城市业务。这样从1955年起，开始停办铁道、粮食、邮电、地质、水利、交通等六个系统的财产、铁路车辆和船舶强制保险。旅客意外伤害强制保险自1955年起作为经办公司业务，不再作为代总公司办理的业务。

正值全国农业合作化高潮之时，1956年2月全国第五次保险会议召开，为配合全国上下对保险工作的呼声，会议决定将业务的重点转向农村。这样在“一·五”的最后两年，保险业获得了稳步发展的机会。到1957年，全国有26个省（市）恢复办理了牲畜保险。

Insurance business trimming ignited the people's meditation and they realized that insurance was needed to cover countryside. Therefore, the headquarters of PICC organized the translation of *Insurance in Soviet Nation* as the material for the whole company to learn. With reference to the experience of Soviet Union, they regained the confidence in recovering insurance in countryside.

According to the resolution by the 4th National Insurance Work Conference in 1954, insurance for countryside had been recovered step by step and, at the same time, the mandatory insurance wouldn't be handled by the head office of PICC.

In Feb. 1956, the 5th National Insurance Work Conference was held and the decision to shift the stress of insurance business to countryside was made in the conference.

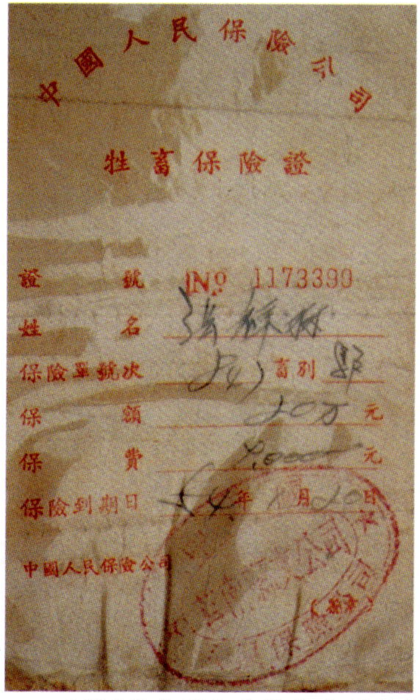

中國人民保險公司

牲畜保險證

證　　號 No 1173390
姓　　名
保險畜號次　　畜別
保　　額　　元
保　　費　　元
保險到期日　　年　月　日

中國人民保險公司

更改事項

實收保費記錄

月　　日實收　　元
月　　日實收　　元

1954年中国人民保险公司莒南县支公司牲畜保险证
Livestock insurance certificate by PICC Ju'nan Branch in 1954

1956年江西省第一期农业保险训练班上饶专区全体学员合影
Students from Jiangxi attending the first training class on agro insurance in 1956

1958年1月召开了第六次全保会议，进一步明确了保险工作方针，并布置了当年的保险工作。同年5月，中共中央召开的“八届二中全会”，使前期制定的下放方案尚未来得及实施，中国保险业即已跨上了“大跃进”的快车。同年12月29日，由财政部、人民银行联合签发，国务院批准停办了国内保险业务。

In December 1958, the government decided to stop the domestic insurance business under the background of the Great Leap Movement

1958年，中国人民保险公司在全国各地遍设分支公司，全国保险工作人员达5万多人。图为中国人民保险公司北京市分公司西城区办事处1958年国庆节职工合影。

Employees of Xicheng Dist. Office of Beijing Branch of PICC at National Day of 1958

中国人民保险公司

城市公民财产保险凭証

公财 字第 00070 号

保户姓名：楊碩清

保险财产项目及保险金额	房屋和附属的装修設备	元
	家庭财产 300	元
	專业性質的器具設备	元
	手工工具、原料、商品	元
总保险金额人民币 叁佰元正		
建筑等级 三 等	保险費率：4‰	
总保险費人民币 壹元贰角正		
保险财产所在地：新华路97		
保险期限：一年自1958年 月 日24时起 至1959年4月30日24时止		
备註		

本公司承保上列财产，在保险有效期内如发生保险責任范圍内的災害或事故致所保财产遭受损失时，依照四川省城市公民财产保险办法之規定負賠偿責任。

中国人民保险公司

公元19 年 月 日立

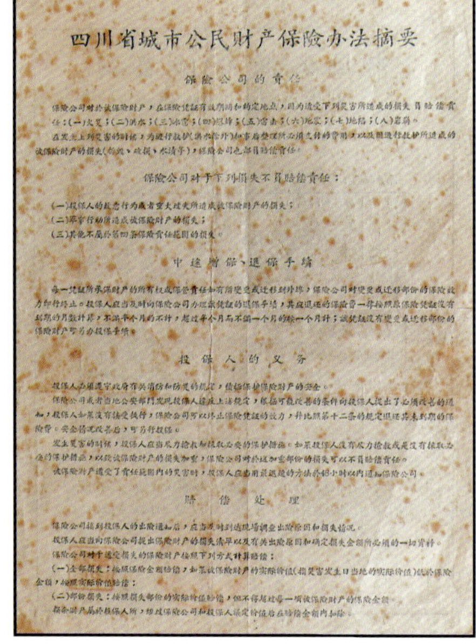

四川省城市公民财产保险办法摘要

保险公司的責任

保险公司对于下列損失不負賠偿責任：

(一)投保人的故意行为或者重大过失所造成被保险财产的損失；

(二)军事行动所造成被保险财产的損失；

(三)其他不屬於第四条保险責任範圍的損失。

中途增保、退保手續

投保人的义务

賠偿处理

“大跃进”初期，在农村保险业务高发展的同时，城市保险业务也有了很大发展。图为1958年“人保”重庆市分公司城市财产保险凭证。

City property insurance certificate by PICC Chongqing Branch in 1958

中國人民保險公司

强制保險保險費單據 字第 號

第一聯 保險費收據 58年2月6日

朱居全 台鑒

今收到你處所投保之 强制保險 保險憑證保險公司編號 字第 號

批改憑證保險公司編號 字第 號應繳 保險費計 壹角伍分

此據 ¥0.75

代理收款銀行簽章處		保險公司簽章處	

强會1 ⅓

注意：本收據須經中國人民銀行及保險公司正式蓋章齊全後方爲有效。

1958年中国人民保险公司秦皇岛支公司火灾强制保险费单据

Premium receipt by PICC Qinhuangdao Branch in 1958

中國人民保險公司

簡易人身保險

保險單

上饒(58)字第 098 号

公元一九58年 7月1日填发

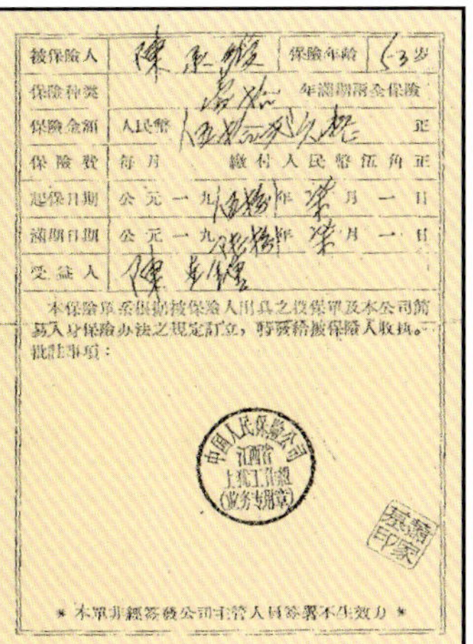

被保險人	陳	保險年齡	53岁
保險种类		年滿期兩全保險	
保險金額	人民幣		正
保險費	每月	繳付人民幣伍角	正
起保日期	公元一九 年 月 一 日		
滿期日期	公元一九 年 月 一 日		
受益人	陳		

本保險單系根據被保險人出具之投保單及本公司簡易人身保險办法之規定訂立，特簽給被保險人收執。

批註事項：

中国人民保險公司江西省上饒工作組(业务专用章)

＊本單非經簽發公司主管人員簽署不生效力＊

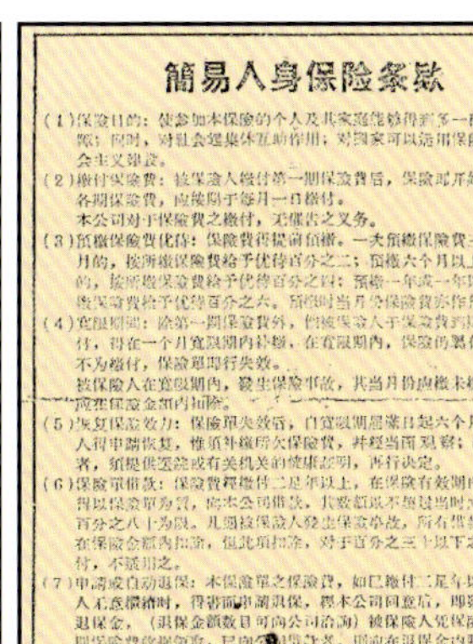

簡易人身保險条款

1958年简易人身险投保人已发展到180万人。图为人保江西上饶工作组签发的简易人身险保险单单据。
Bill of postal personal insurance policy by PICC Shangrao Branch in 1958

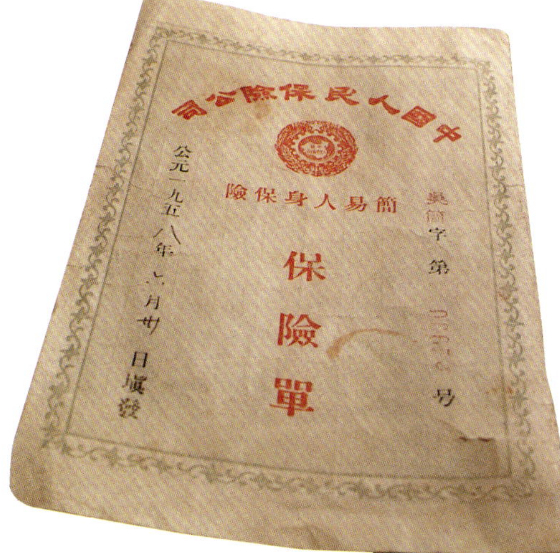

中國人民保險公司

簡易人身保險

保險單

吴简字第 号

公元一九五八年六月卅日填發

1958年6月30日中国人民保险公司吴忠市支公司签发的简易人身保险保险单。右图为1998年4月10日，中保人寿保险宁夏吴忠市支公司向被保险人胡清荷(右一)兑现该张保单。

Postal personal insurance policy by PICC Wuzhong Branch in 1958; PICC Life Insurance Co. Wuzhong cashing in the policy for the insured in Apr. 1998.

八、国内保险业务的停办

Domestic Insurance Suspended

1958年5月，中共"八届二中全会"正式提出了"鼓足干劲，力争上游，多快好省地建设社会主义"的总路线，揭开了"大跃进"的序幕。宏观环境的巨变使得全国第六次保险会议1958年1月的决议还未来得及实施，就卷入了"大跃进"的漩涡。从此开始了中国保险业的坎坷历程。

"大跃进"初期，保险业一度在数量上迅猛发展。农村保险业务尤其是保险和防疫、治疗相结合的养猪保险，更是效果显著。同时，城市的人身保险业务也取得较大的发展。与此同步，1958年全国保险工作人员已逾5万。

人民公社的规模不断扩大，人们日益感到公社的社会保险形式可以代替国家保险形式。于是，1958年10月西安财贸会议正式作出了"人民公社化以后，保险工作的作用已经消失，除国外业务必须继续办理外，国内保险业务应立即停办"的决议。

随后，1958年12月武汉全国财政会议正式作出"立即停办国内保险业务"的决定。1959年1月第七次全国保险会议开始布置善后清理工作。中国人民保险公司留下4亿准备基金，其中各省市400－600万元，国外业务留下5000万元，其余上缴各级财政。这样，经过短暂的发展高峰后，国内保险业务走入了最低谷。

The Great Leap Movement starting from May 1958 marked the frustration in insurance; finally the domestic insurance had been suspended since Dec. 1959.

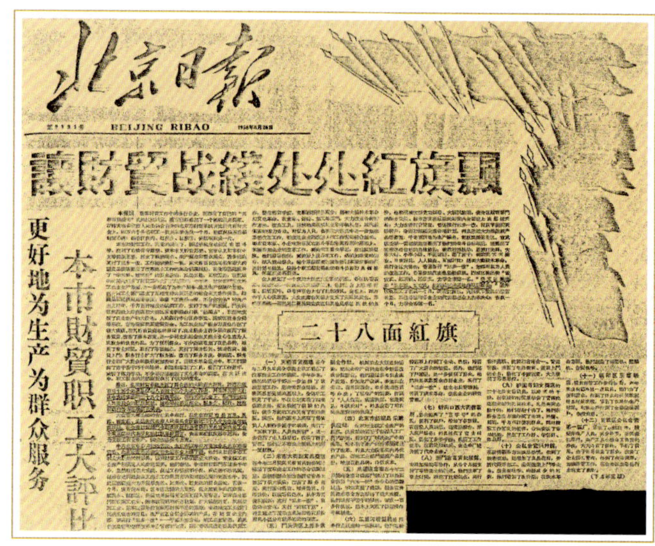

北京日報

BEIJING RIBAO

讓財貿战綫处处紅旗飄

本市財貿職工大評比

更好地为生产为群众服务

二十八面紅旗

"大跃进"初期，保险业务一度在数量上迅猛发展。

Report on the once rapid increase in quantity of insurance business in early Great Leap Movement

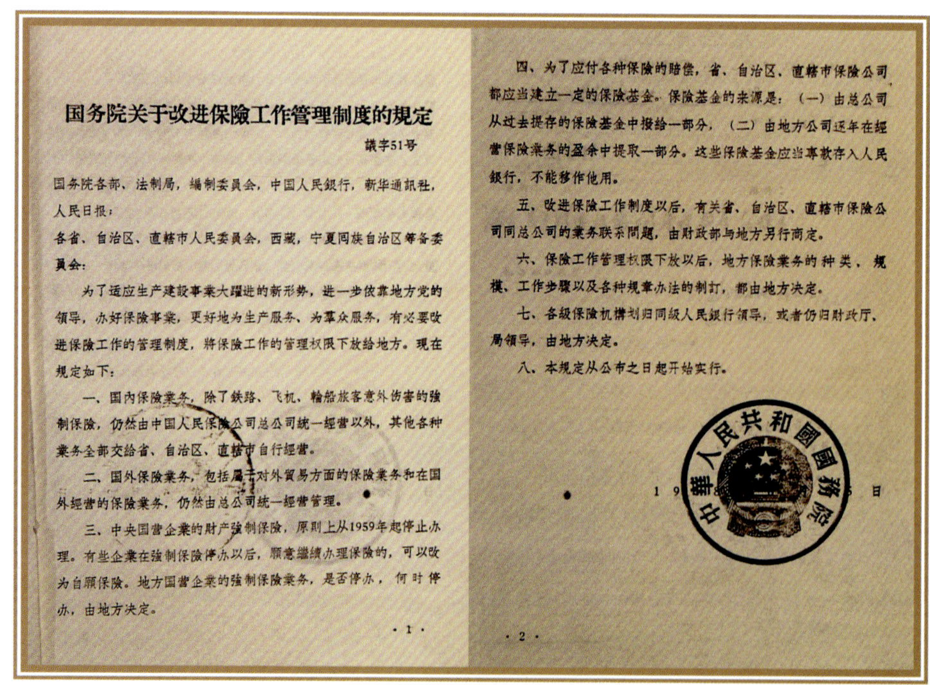

国务院关于改进保险工作管理制度的规定

議字51号

国务院各部、法制局，编制委員会，中国人民銀行，新华通訊社，人民日报：

各省、自治区、直轄市人民委員会，西藏，宁夏回族自治区筹备委員会：

为了适应生产建設事業大躍进的新形势，进一步依靠地方党的領导，办好保險事業，更好地为生产服务、为羣众服务，有必要改进保險工作的管理制度，将保險工作的管理权限下放給地方。现在規定如下：

一、国内保險業务，除了鉄路、飞机、輪船旅客意外伤害的強制保險，仍然由中国人民保險公司总公司統一經营以外，其他各种業务全部交給省、自治区、直轄市自行經营。

二、国外保險業务，包括屬于对外貿易方面的保險業务和在国外經营的保險業务，仍然由总公司統一經营管理。

三、中央国营企業的財产強制保險，原則上从1959年起停止办理。有些企業在強制保險停办以后，願意繼續办理保險的，可以改为自願保險。地方国营企業的強制保險業务，是否停办，何时停办，由地方决定。

·1·

四、为了应付各种保險的賠償，省、自治区、直轄市保險公司都应当建立一定的保險基金。保險基金的来源是：（一）由总公司从过去提存的保險基金中撥給一部分，（二）由地方公司逐年在經营保險業务的盈余中提取一部分。这些保險基金应当專款存入人民銀行，不能移作他用。

五、改进保險工作制度以后，有关省、自治区、直轄市保險公司同总公司的業务联系問題，由財政部与地方另行商定。

六、保險工作管理权限下放以后，地方保險業务的种类、規模、工作步驟以及各种規章办法的制訂，都由地方决定。

七、各級保險机構划归同級人民銀行領导，或者仍归財政厅、局領导，由地方决定。

八、本規定从公布之日起开始实行。

中華人民共和國國務院

1 9 日

·2·

1958年国务院《关于改进保险工作管理制度的规定》提出将保险工作的管理权限下放给地方，并提出了中央国营企业的财产强制保险与地方企业强制保险业务的停办意见。

Provisions on Improving the Managerial System of Insurance Work by the State Council in 1958

1958年，大跃进年代投保的木船于洪水期间在长江里翻船，所载生铁沉入江底。当时中国人民保险公司重庆市分公司组织员工打捞生铁220吨。图为报喜时抬横幅的情景。

PICC Chongqing Branch's employees carrying a banner celebrating the successful salvage of 220 tons of pig iron sank in Yangtze River in 1958

人保北京市分公司西城区办事处获市财贸系统28面红旗之一（照片提供：郭贵忠）

PICC Beijing Branch Xicheng Dist. Office's employees won one of the 28 red flags from the finance & trade authority

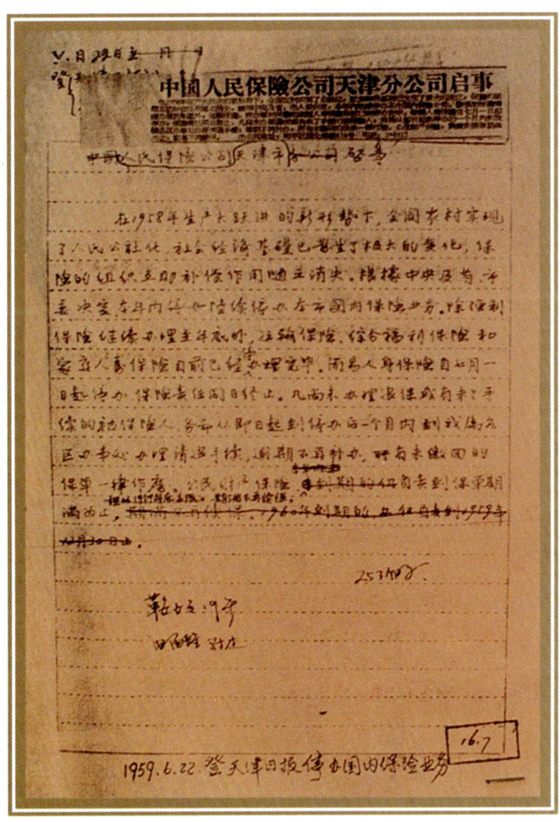
中国人民保险公司天津分公司启事

在1958年生产大跃进的新形势下，全国农村实现了人民公社化，社会经济基础已发生了极大的变化，

1959.6.22 登天津日报停办国内保险业务

1959年6月22日刊登在《天津日报》上的“中国人民保险公司天津分公司启事”原稿。该启事的内容是根据上级决定年内停止办理国内保险业务。

Draft of the Notice by Tianjin Branch on *Tianjin Daily* in 1959 that insurance business to be stopped

中国人民保险公司北京市分公司领导参加修建十三陵水库义务劳动。图中前排左起汪抱和（副经理）、张钟祥（副经理）、莫新吾（经理）

Senior Officers of Beijing Branch Participating in Voluntary Labor

中華人民共和國財政部發文稿紙

簽發：　部外會簽：　部内會簽：

核稿：

標題(事由)：

主办單位和拟稿人：

主送机关：

抄送机关：

附件：

打印　校对：

發文　字第　号　年　月　日封發

1958年国内业务停办前中国人民保险公司工作人员在公司大楼门前合影

Employees of PICC at the eve of insurance business stopping in 1958

中华人民共和国财政部、中国人民银行联合报告

关于国内保险业务停办的善后清理工作和国外保险业务一律由中国人民银行接办的报告

国务院五办：

10月西安财贸会议讨论通过的关于农村人民公社财政管理问题的意见中提出：人民公社化以后，保险工作的作用已经消失，除国外保险业务必须继续办理以外，国内保险业务应即停办。在停办过程中要贯彻群众路线的方法，妥善地做好善后工作。停办的具体步骤和做法，由各省（市、自治区）人民委员会自行决定。停办后的清理工作，由中国人民银行接办。现在根据我們的了解，各地自西安财贸会議以后，都已經对停办国内保险业务問題作了研究和布置。一部份地区經过研究，认为只要对群众做好宣传解释工作，立即停办，問題不大。有的在今年年内即可办理結束。有的准备在明年年初办理結束。一部份地区认为立即停办还有困难，准备明年再过渡一年，将各项短期保险业务保到期满后再办理結束。各地的保险公司机构，有的已經由财政部門交給人民銀行接管，有的还没有交。为了做好国内保险业务停办的善后清理工作和继續办好国外保险业务，现在經我們共同商量，拟再作如下安排：

一、关于国内保险业务，我們同意各地所作的布置，凡是立即停办問題不大的，即于今年年内或明年年初办理結束；凡是立即停办还有困难的，也可以再过渡一年。以上都由各省（市、自治区）人民委員会自行

财政部、中国人民银行联合起草的《关于国内保险业务停办后的善后清理工作和国外保险业务一律由中国人民银行接办的报告》。

Report on the Redress of the Insurance Business Stopping & Foreign Insurance Business to be Handled by the PBOC by the Finance Ministry and the PBOC

1958年底国内保险业务停办后，重庆市相应成立了业务清理组，主要办理未到期简易人身险退费工作。为了对被保险人负责，该组一直坚持到1959年10月。这是清理组全体人员合影。

Redress force in Chongqing in 1959 after domestic insurance stopping

九、中国保险业的低潮时期(1959–1979)

Decline of Chinese Insurance (1959 – 1979)

1958年10月国务院召开的财贸会议认为，人民公社化以后，除国外业务必须办理外，国内业务应立即停办，以此为标志，中国保险业进入低潮时期。中国人民保险公司专营涉外保险业务后，主要经营进出口货物运输保险、远洋船舶保险、国际航线飞机保险、再保险和海外业务。

1961年中国人民保险公司机构精简。文化大革命期间，保险从业人员减少到13人。

With the sign of domestic insurance stopping, Chinese insurance slid in a winter. PICC began to specialize in some overseas business and, in 1961, the number of practitioners of PICC were cut to 13 during the Cultural Revolution.

1963年中国人民保险公司副总经理施哲明（右）访问越南
PICC's vice general manager Shi Zheming (R) visiting Vietnam in 1963

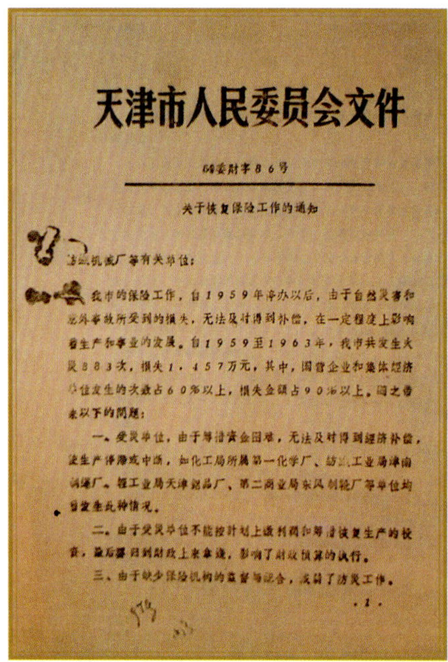

天津市人民委员会文件

64委财字86号

关于恢复保险工作的通知

[illegible]纺织机械厂等有关单位：

我市的保险工作，自1959年停办以后，由于自然灾害和意外事故所受到的损失，无法及时得到补偿，在一定程度上影响着生产和事业的发展。自1959至1963年，我市共发生火灾883次，损失1，457万元，其中，国营企业和集体经济单位发生的次数占60%以上，损失金额占90%以上。因之带来以下的问题：

一、受灾单位，由于筹措资金困难，无法及时得到经济补偿，使生产停滞或中断，如化工局所属第一化学厂、纺[illegible]工业局津南[illegible]厂、轻工业局天津[illegible]品厂、第二商业局东风[illegible]厂等单位均曾发生此种情况。

二、由于受灾单位不能按计划上缴利润和筹措恢复生产的投资，最后都归到财政上来拿钱，影响了财政预算的执行。

三、由于缺少保险机构的监督与配合，减弱了防灾工作。

·1·

财产强制保险條例
及費率規章

天津市保險公司
一九六四年十一月

1964年9月，天津市人民委员会决定组建“天津市保险公司”，在天津恢复办理国内保险业务。天津市保险公司于1965年1月1日恢复办理财产强制保险和自愿货物运输保险。1967年受“文化大革命”影响，天津市保险公司停办了保险业务。左图为天津市人民委员会文件，右图为天津市保险公司的费率规章。

File of Tianjin Municipal People's Committee (L); *Rules on Premium Rate of PICC Tianjin Branch* (R).

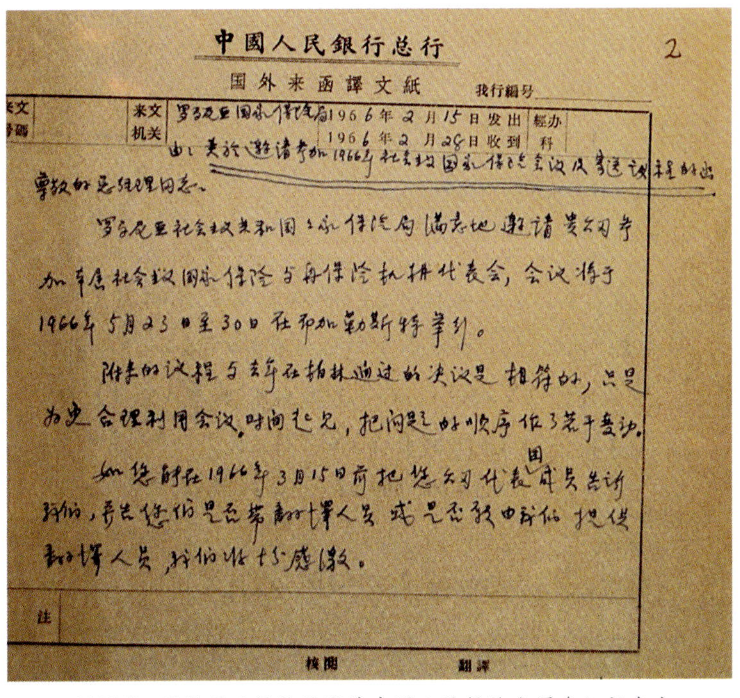

中國人民銀行总行 2

国外来函譯文紙 我行編号

来文号码

来文机关：罗马尼亚国家保险局 1966年2月15日发出 1966年2月28日收到 經办科

由：关於邀请参加1966年社会主义国家保险会议及寄送议程的函

事致的总经理同志。

罗马尼亚社会主义共和国国家保险局满意地邀请贵公司参加本届社会主义国家保险与再保险机构代表会，会议将于1966年5月23日至30日在布加勒斯特举行。

附来的议程与去年在柏林通过的决议是相符的，只是为更合理利用会议时间起见，把问题的顺序作了若干变动。

如您能在1966年3月15日前把您公司代表团成员告诉我们，并告您们是否带翻译人员或是否需由我们提供翻译人员，我们将十分感激。

注

核閱 翻譯

1966年，罗马尼亚保险局邀请中国人民保险公司参加社会主义国家保险会议及寄送议程的函电。

Letters from Romania to invite PICC to attend the Insurance Conference of Socialism states in 1966.

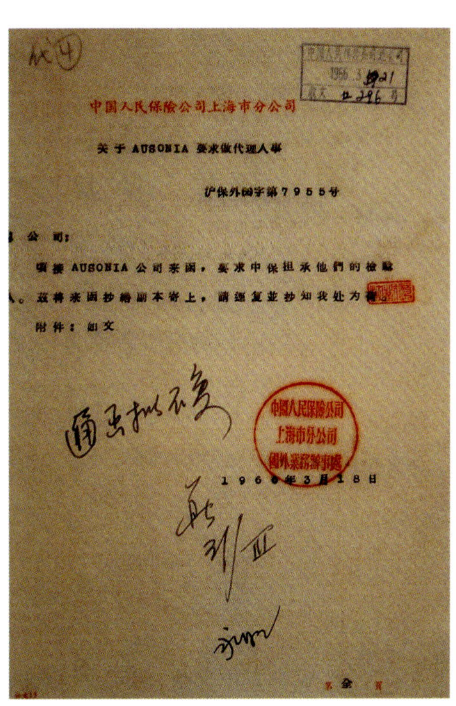

中国人民保险公司上海市分公司

关于AUSONIA要求做代理人事

沪保外66字第7955号

总公司：

顷接AUSONIA公司来函，要求中保担承他們的檢驗人。兹將来函抄錄副本寄上，請速复並抄知我处为荷。

附件：如文

1966年3月18日

1966年，AUSONIA公司要求中国人民保险公司上海分公司做代理人。图为上海分公司致总公司的请示。

Instruction requesting by Shanghai Branch to PICC on the intention to be Ausonia's agency

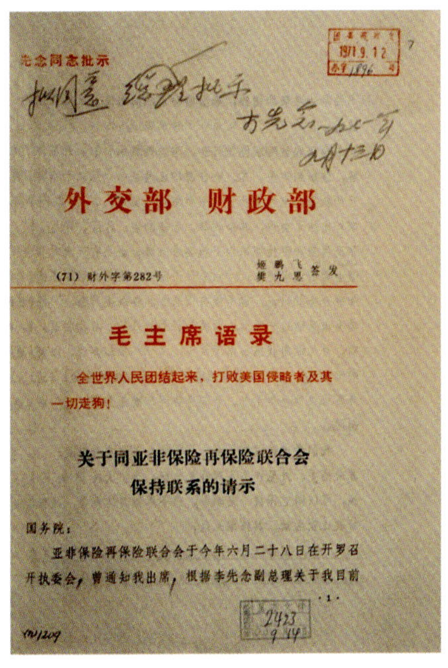

先念同志批示

1971.9.12

外交部 财政部

(71) 财外字第282号

姬鹏飞
樊九思 签发

毛主席语录

全世界人民团结起来，打败美国侵略者及其一切走狗！

关于同亚非保险再保险联合会保持联系的请示

国务院：

亚非保险再保险联合会于今年六月二十八日在开罗召开执委会，曾通知我出席，根据李先念副总理关于我目前

·1·

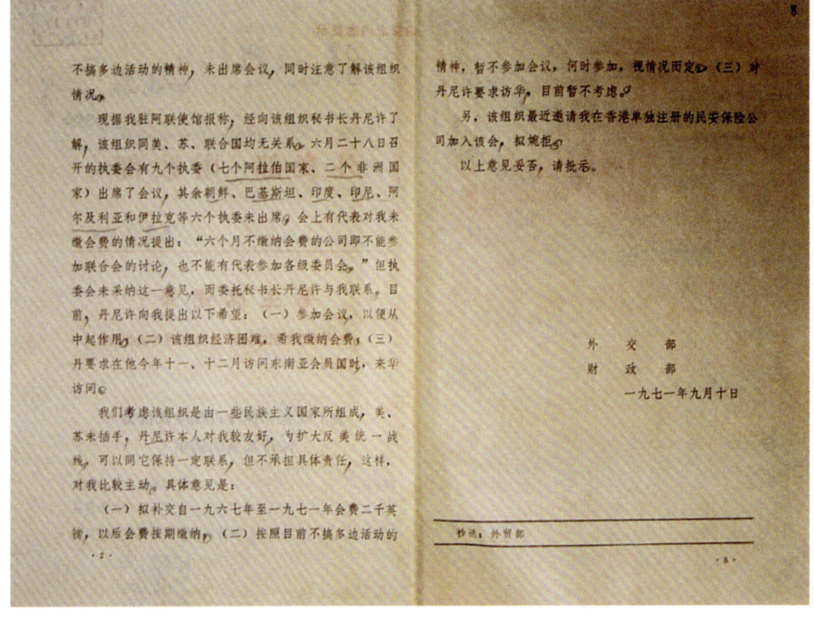

不搞多边活动的精神，未出席会议，同时注意了解该组织情况。

现据我驻阿联使馆报称，经向该组织秘书长丹尼许了解，该组织同美、苏、联合国均无关系。六月二十八日召开的执委会有九个执委（七个阿拉伯国家、二个非洲国家）出席了会议，其余朝鲜、巴基斯坦、印度、印尼、阿尔及利亚和伊拉克等六个执委未出席。会上有代表对我未缴会费的情况提出：“六个月不缴纳会费的公司即不能参加联合会的讨论，也不能有代表参加各级委员会。”但执委会未采纳这一意见，而委托秘书长丹尼许与我联系。目前，丹尼许向我提出以下希望：（一）参加会议，以便从中起作用；（二）该组织经济困难，希我缴纳会费；（三）丹要求在他今年十一、十二月访问东南亚会员国时，来华访问。

我们考虑该组织是由一些民族主义国家所组成，美、苏未插手，丹尼许本人对我较友好，为扩大反美统一战线，可以同它保持一定联系，但不承担具体责任，这样，对我比较主动。具体意见是：

（一）拟补交自一九六七年至一九七一年会费二千英镑，以后会费按期缴纳；（二）按照目前不搞多边活动的

·2·

精神，暂不参加会议，何时参加，视情况而定；（三）对丹尼许要求访华，目前暂不考虑。

另，该组织最近邀请我在香港单独注册的民安保险公司加入该会，拟婉拒。

以上意见妥否，请批示。

外交部
财政部
一九七一年九月十日

抄送：外贸部

·3·

停办国内保险业务期间，我国仍保持着与国外保险组织的联系。图为文革期间外交部、财政部关于同亚非保险再保险联合会保持联系的请示。

Instruction requesting by the Ministry of Foreign Affairs and Finance Ministry on keeping in touch with Asia-Africa Reinsurance Federation

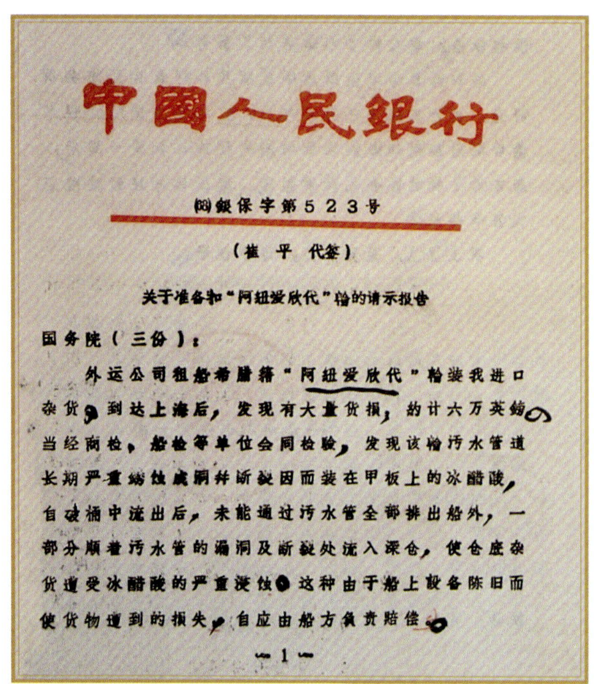

中国人民银行

(68)银保字第523号

（崔平代签）

关于准备扣"阿纽爱欣代"轮的请示报告

国务院（三份）：

外运公司租船希腊籍"阿纽爱欣代"轮装我进口杂货，到达上海后，发现有大量货损，约计六万英镑。当经商检，船检等单位会同检验，发现该轮污水管道长期严重锈蚀腐烂并断裂因而装在甲板上的冰醋酸，自破桶中流出后，未能通过污水管全部排出船外，一部分顺着污水管的漏洞及断裂处流入深舱，使舱底杂货遭受冰醋酸的严重浸蚀。这种由于船上设备陈旧而使货物遭到的损失，自应由船方负责赔偿。

—1—

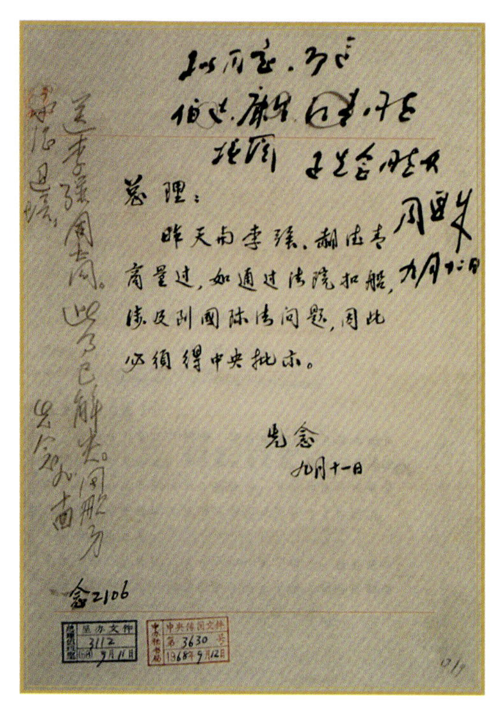

总理：

昨天同李强、胡明专商量过，如通过法院扣船，涉及到国际法问题，因此必须得中央批示。

先念

九月十一日

1968年，我国外运公司租用的希腊籍"阿纽爱欣代号"轮装满进口杂货，到达上海后发现损失严重。有关部门提出船方应负责赔偿部分损失，并建议中国人民保险公司通过国际分保组织向有关方面提出约合人民币20万元的索赔。在未获得赔偿前暂时扣留船只。上右图为李先念报请周恩来批示，并有陈伯达、康生、江青圈阅的报告。此事引起了周恩来、李先念等对进口货物自办保险的重视。在另一次进口铂金货物发生丢失损失事件后，周恩来亲自批示恢复了业已停办的进口货物运输保险。

Report by PBOC to the State Council on a severe shipping loss in 1968 (L); report by Li Xiannian to Zhou Enlai for his instructions (R)

"史无前例"的文化大革命使国民经济遭受了严重破坏。这期间的保险业也受到重创。1969年，我国国内保险业务停办期间，涉外业务也受到了很大的冲击。中国人民保险公司机构被精简，86名在职干部大部分被下放到河南淮滨"五七"干校劳动。国外业务的清理和收尾工作由一个名为9人、实际工作为13人的"保险业务小组"负责。保险业务小组自1969年4月成立，到1971年9月为止。

With Chinese national economy together, the national insurance was badly destroyed in the Cultural Revolution. An insurance Business Team was organized in 1969 to deal with insurance business during the period.

"保险业务小组"副组长于葆忠

Yu Baozhong: vice section chief of the Insurance Business Team

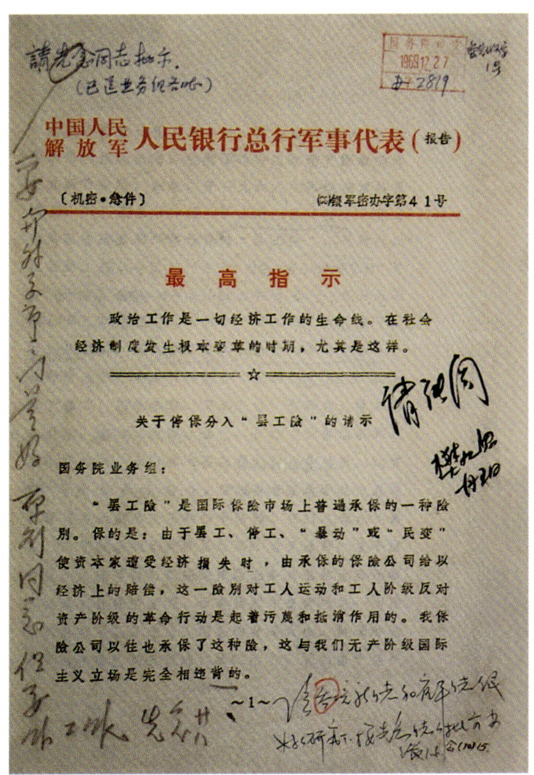

中国人民解放军人民银行总行军事代表(报告)

(机密·急件) 69银军密办字第41号

最 高 指 示

政治工作是一切经济工作的生命线。在社会经济制度发生根本变革的时期，尤其是这样。

☆

关于停保分入"罢工险"的请示

国务院业务组：

"罢工险"是国际保险市场上普遍承保的一种险别。保的是：由于罢工、停工、"暴动"或"民变"使资本家遭受经济损失时，由承保的保险公司给以经济上的赔偿，这一险别对工人运动和工人阶级反对资产阶级的革命行动是起着污蔑和抵消作用的。我保险公司以往也承保了这种险，这与我们无产阶级国际主义立场是完全相违背的。

~1~

1969年，驻人民银行总行"军代表"以分入罢工险"对工人阶级反对资产阶级的革命行动是起着污蔑和抵消作用"为名报告国务院业务组，要求中国人民保险公司停止分入"罢工险"。李先念在当时情况下批示："要与外交部商量好，原则同意，但要作好工作。"后在周恩来、李先念等同志的过问下，很快(1971年)纠正了这种"左"的错误。

An instruction requesting by the People's Liberation Army's Military Delegation of PBOC

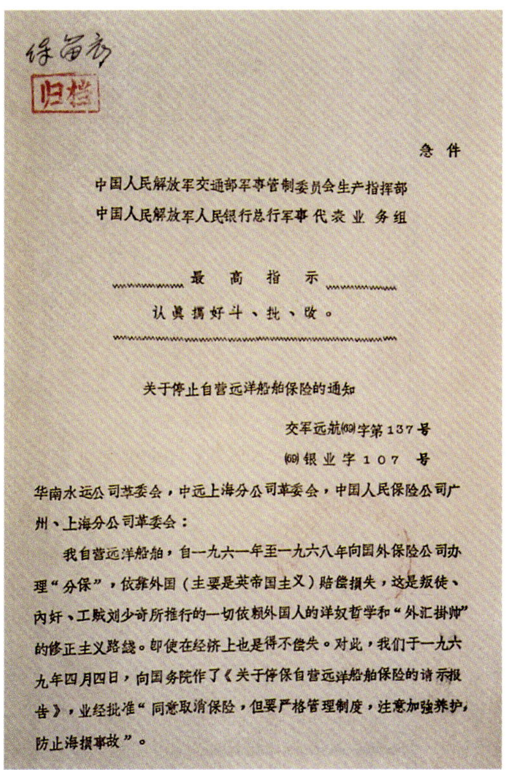

归档

急 件

中国人民解放军交通部军事管制委员会生产指挥部
中国人民解放军人民银行总行军事代表业务组

最 高 指 示

认真搞好斗、批、改。

关于停止自营远洋船舶保险的通知

交军远航(69)字第137号
(69)银业字107号

华南水运公司革委会，中远上海分公司革委会，中国人民保险公司广州、上海分公司革委会：

我自营远洋船舶，自一九六一年至一九六八年向国外保险公司办理"分保"，依靠外国（主要是英帝国主义）赔偿损失，这是叛徒、内奸、工贼刘少奇所推行的一切依赖外国人的洋奴哲学和"外汇挂帅"的修正主义路线。即使在经济上也是得不偿失。对此，我们于一九六九年四月四日，向国务院作了《关于停保自营远洋船舶保险的请示报告》，业经批准"同意取消保险，但要严格管理制度，注意加强养护，防止海损事故"。

在"左"的思想指导下，我国自办远洋船舶保险业务已一度停办。在周恩来总理的亲自过问下，这项业务得到恢复和维持。

Written reply by the government on the strike reinsurance in 1969

1973年中国人民保险公司总经理耿道明(左)与外国保险同行交谈

PICC general manager Geng Daoming interviewing with a foreign peer in 1973

十、国内保险业的恢复
Recovery of Domestic Insurance

1978年，中国共产党中央召开十一届三中全会，决定“把全党工作的着重点和全国人民的注意力转移到社会主义现代化建设上来”。中国保险业终于迎来了新曙光。

1979年2月召开的中国人民银行全国分行行长会议决定恢复国内保险业务，国务院在1979年第99号文件批转的《中国人民银行分行行长会议纪要》中指出：“为了使企业和社队发生意外损失时能及时得到补偿，而又不影响财政支出，要根据为生产服务，为群众服务和自愿的原则，通过试点，逐步恢复国内保险。”

Chairmen Conference of Branches of the PBOC was convened in February 1979 in Beijing, according to the decision of which, the domestic insurance was decided to recover in China.

1979年李先念副总理与海外银行保险公司经理会议全体代表合影
Vice premier Li Xiannian with managers attending the conference of overseas banks & Insurers in 1979

1979年12月17日中国人民银行上海市分行在大光明电影院举行的"贯彻国务院决定'恢复国内保险'大会"
The Conference of Insurance Recovery by POBC Shanghai Branch in Dec. 1979

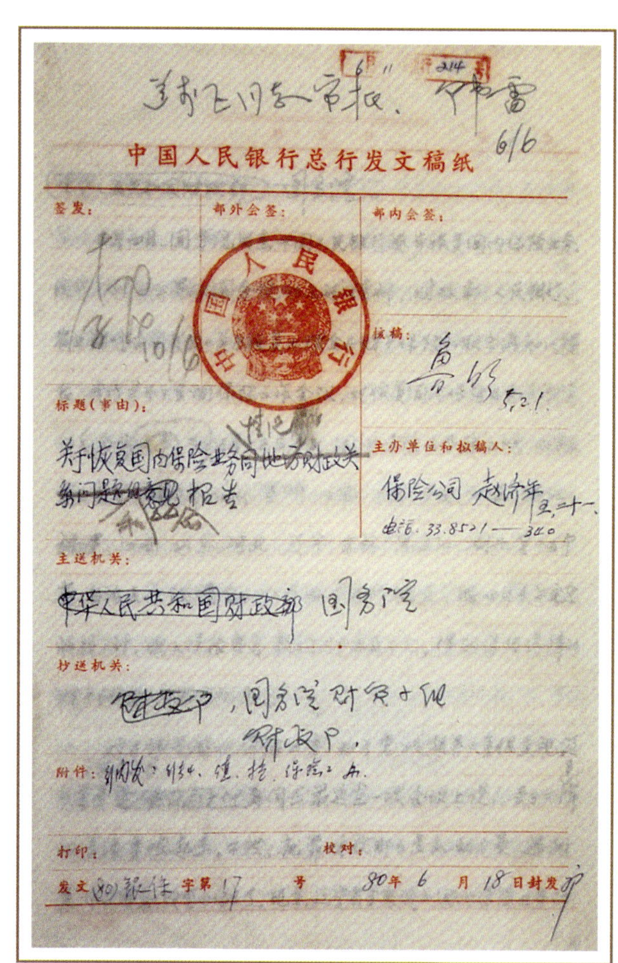

中国人民银行总行发文稿纸

签发：

部外会签：

部内会签：

核稿：

标题（事由）：关于恢复国内保险业务情况和意见的报告

主办单位和拟稿人：保险公司

主送机关：国务院

抄送机关：

附件：

打印：　　校对：

发文（80）银保字第17号　80年6月18日封发

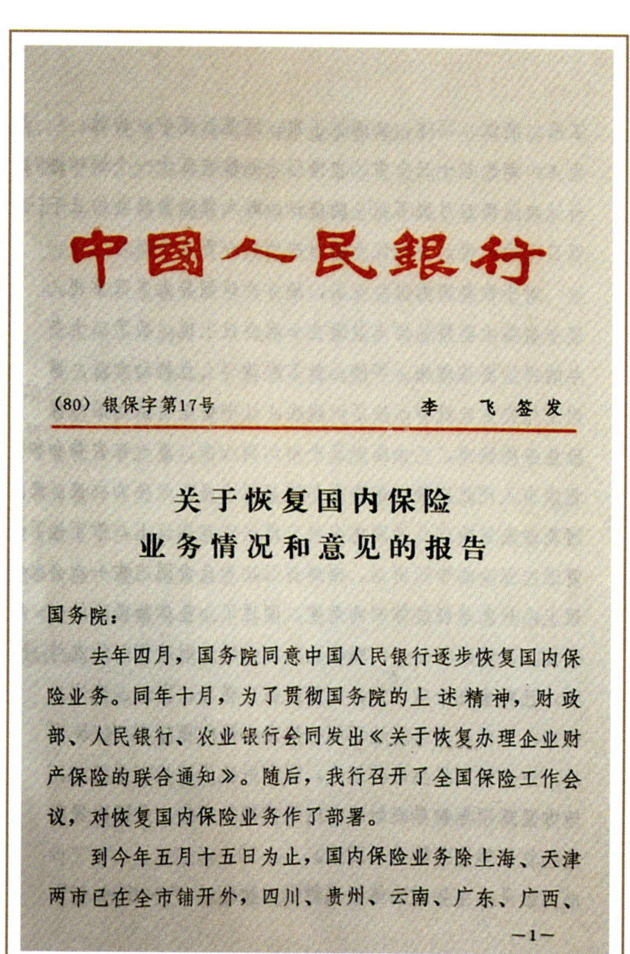

中國人民銀行

（80）银保字第17号　　李　飞　签发

关于恢复国内保险
业务情况和意见的报告

国务院：

去年四月，国务院同意中国人民银行逐步恢复国内保险业务。同年十月，为了贯彻国务院的上述精神，财政部、人民银行、农业银行会同发出《关于恢复办理企业财产保险的联合通知》。随后，我行召开了全国保险工作会议，对恢复国内保险业务作了部署。

到今年五月十五日为止，国内保险业务除上海、天津两市已在全市铺开外，四川、贵州、云南、广东、广西、

—1—

1980年6月中国人民银行写给国务院的《关于恢复国内保险业务情况和意见的报告》

Report on the Conditions of Advices of Recovering Domestic Insurance by PBOC to the State Council in 1980

薄一波副总理接見全国保险工作

1980年6月中国人民保险公司在上海召开国内保险业务座谈会，研究恢复国内保险业务后的有关问题。
Symposia on domestic insurance business by PICC in Shanghai in 1980

1979年薄一波副总理接见全国保险工作会议代表
Vice premier Bo Yibo with delegates attending the National Insurance Work Conference in 1979

中国人民保险总公司第一期经理轮训班结业留念 81.12.24

1981年12月中国人民保险公司举办的第一期经理轮训班结业合影
Participants of the first alternate training class for managers by PICC in 1981

金融教师进修学院国内保险师训班
1981.9.

1981年9月在金融教师进修学院举办的国内保险师训班人员合影
Trainees of the inland insurance practitioner training class by Financial Teacher Training Institute in 1981

十一、恢复时期的PICC及其业务

PICC during the Recovery

1983年7月宋国华任中国人保公司总经理
Song Guohua, General Manager in 1983.

1984年11月秦道夫被任命为中国人民保险公司董事长兼总经理
Qin Daofu, Chairman and General Manager in 1984

1982年12月17日，国务院批复中国人民银行《关于成立中国人民保险公司董事会的报告》，并批准《中国人民保险公司章程》。根据《章程》规定：中国人民保险公司是中华人民共和国的国营企业，是经营保险业务的专业公司。经营范围包括各种财产保险、人身保险、责任保险、信用保险、农业保险以及再保险等业务。1983年7月，中国人民保险公司成立董事会和监事会，尚明任董事长，童赠银任首席监事，宋国华任总经理。1983年9月，经国务院批准，中国人民保险公司升格为国务院直属局级经济实体，独立行使职权进行业务活动。从1984年1月1日起，中国人民保险公司正式从中国人民银行中分立出来，但仍接受中国人民银行的领导、管理、监督和稽核。1984年12月，秦道夫被任命为中国人民保险公司董事长兼总经理。

1985年中国人民保险公司进行经营体制改革，将原来的总公司一级核算，改为总、分公司两级核算。

财产保险作为保险业务的主干，恢复后获得了迅速发展，险种由企财险、货运险，汽车险几项增加到1989年的200多种。保费收入连年上升。

1982年，停办了24年的我国农业保险开始恢复，首先在江西、黑龙江、山东等地试办牲畜保险。然后扩大到农作物保险。

The *Rules of PICC* was promulgated by the State Council in 1982 and, in July 1983, the board of directors and supervisors were set up by PICC. Tow years later, PICC began to reform its managerial system in 1985.

After the recovery, property insurance, a major business of PICC, developed at a rather fast pace.

In 1982, Chinese agro insurance, which had been suspended for 24 years, was first recovered in Jiangxi, Heilongjiang, and Shandong province, where livestock insurance was done as a pilot scheme.

1984年中国人民保险公司董、监事会合影
Directors and Supervisors of PICC In 1984

中国人民保险公司(PICC)国内财产险业务情况(单位：万元)

Figures of Property Insurance of PICC (1980 – 1986)

年度	保费收入	赔款支出
1980	29216	621
1981	53232	15440
1982	74677	26224
1983	100421	40355
1984	143047	59271
1985	215903	123289
1986	310111	170066

1982–1990年农业保险业务收入(单位：万元)

Figures of Agro Insurance of PICC (1982 – 1990)

项目 年度	种植业			养殖业		
	保 费	增长率	赔付费	保费	增长率	赔付率
1982	4	200	19	73.68		
1983	51	1175.0	149.02	122542.1	128.69	
1984	362	609.8	88.95	645428.7	62.84	
1985	1765	387.6	83.85	2567	298.0	147.49
1986	3346.5	89.6	193.19	4378.7	70.56	160.80
1987	5409.9	61.66	103.15	4618.5	5.48	152.08
1988	6627.1	22.50	46.41	4906.7	6.24	73.12
1989	9032.4			6311		
1990	12562			6635.7		
合计	39069.9			29903.6		

1979年，经国务院批准，恢复了停办20年的国内保险业务。

1982年3月召开的全国保险工作会议决定试办职工团体人身保险和人身意外伤害保险。

根据国务院批转中国人民保险公司的《关于加快发展我国保险业务的报告》，保险公司从1984年起承办城镇集体企业职工的法定养老金保险。

另外，为配合我国计划生育政策，在农村地区还开办了计划生育养老保险。随着社会经济的发展需要，人身保险业务也不断拓宽领域，险种日益丰富，如母婴安康保险、医疗保险、婚姻保险等。到1990年底，全国参加各种人身保险的人数已达2.1921亿人次，开办险种70多个。

Group life insurance for employees and personal accident injury insurance were run as a pilot scheme in 1982. Additionally, birth-control endowment insurance was also operated in line with the policy of birth-control of China.

1984年中国人民邮政发行的"人民保险"邮票是我国发行的第一枚保险邮票

First insurance—related stamp the *People's Insurance* issued by the People's Post of China in 1984

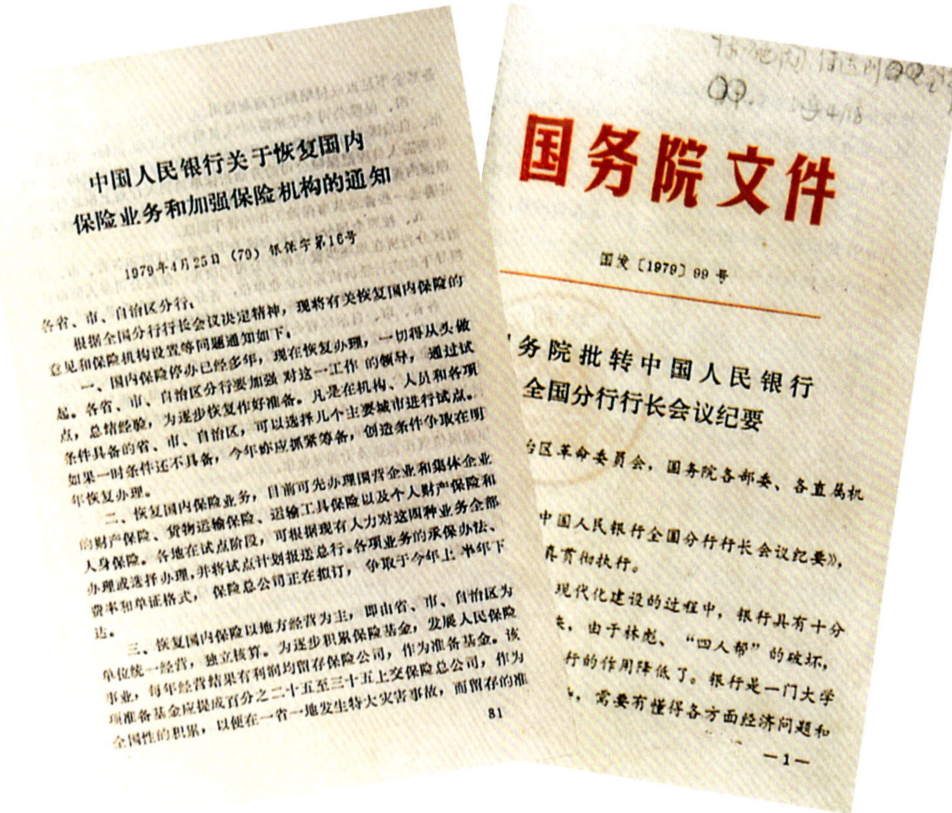

中国人民银行关于恢复国内保险业务和加强保险机构的通知

1979年4月25日 (79) 银保字第16号

各省、市、自治区分行：

根据全国分行行长会议决定精神，现将有关恢复国内保险的意见和保险机构设置等问题通知如下：

一、国内保险停办已经多年，现在恢复办理，一切得从头做起。各省、市、自治区分行要加强对这一工作的领导，通过试点，总结经验，为逐步恢复作好准备。凡是在机构、人员和各项条件具备的省、市、自治区，可以选择几个主要城市进行试点。如果一时条件还不具备，今年亦应抓紧筹备，创造条件争取在明年恢复办理。

二、恢复国内保险业务，目前可先办理国营企业和集体企业的财产保险、货物运输保险、运输工具保险以及个人财产保险和人身保险。各地在试点阶段，可根据现有人力对这四种业务全部办理或选择办理，并将试点计划报送总行。各项业务的承保办法、费率和单证格式，保险总公司正在拟订，争取于今年上半年下达。

三、恢复国内保险以地方经营为主，即由省、市、自治区为单位统一经营，独立核算。为逐步积累保险基金，发展人民保险事业，每年经营结果有利润均留存保险公司，作为准备基金。该项准备基金应提成百分之二十五至三十五上交保险总公司，作为全国性的积累，以便在一省一地发生特大灾害事故，而留存的准

81

国务院文件

国发〔1979〕99号

务院批转中国人民银行全国分行行长会议纪要

区革命委员会，国务院各部委、各直属机

中国人民银行全国分行行长会议纪要》，

真贯彻执行。

现代化建设的过程中，银行具有十分

，由于林彪、"四人帮"的破坏，

行的作用降低了。银行是一门大学

，需要有懂得各方面经济问题和

—1—

1979年国务院批转的中国人民银行全国分行行长会议纪要

Summary of the conference of Chairmen of Branches of PBOC endorsed by the State Council in 1979

1986年，中国人民保险公司迁到北京阜成门内大街410号办公。该办公楼（左图）后成为中国保险监督管理委员会地址。2005年4月25日，中国保险监督管理委员会由此迁入北京西城区金融街15号（右图）。

In 1986, PICC moved to 410, Fuchengmennei Avenue, Beijing, (L) where located the CIRC; later in April 2005, the CIRC moved to 15, Finance Street, Xicheng Dist., Beijing (R).

1984年，中国人民保险公司衡阳市公司的职工为群众办理投保手续

Working employees of PICC Hengyang Branch in 1984

为世界第一大水电工程——长江三峡工程项目保险
Biggest hydropower project: the project of the Three Gorges of Yangtze River insured by PICC

全国最大的财产保险项目——广东大亚湾核电站的各项保险均由中国人民保险公司深圳分公司承保
Largest property insurance project: Guangdong Dayawan Nuclear Power Plant insured by PICC Shenzhen Branch

1995年7月，吉林省桦甸市被特大洪水淹没在一片汪洋中。图为中国人民保险公司的员工在解救灾民。
Employees of PICC rescuing victims from a superflood in Jinlin Province in 1985

按照国际惯例，中国人民保险公司从1980年起开办卫星保险。自1980年到1993年，中国人民保险公司承保卫星14颗，收入保费5110万元，支付赔款7500多万元。
PICC started to insure satellites from 1980 on.

1990年10月，厦门航空公司一架波音737飞机落地时被撞，获得中国人民保险公司赔偿。
Crashed Boeing 737 of Xiamen Airlines in 1990 insured by PICC

1987年大兴安岭发生特大森林火灾，中国人民保险公司共支付赔款1.18亿元。
Fire in the Great Xing'an Maintains in 1987, for which, an indemnity of 118 m paid by PICC.

中国人民保险公司成立50年以来，一直得到党和国家领导人的亲切关怀和热情支持。图为1956年12月周恩来、朱德、邓小平、李富春等党和国家领导人接见金融保险界代表。
Zhou Enlai, etc. interviewing delegates of finance and insurance sector in 1956.

1995年冬，江泽民主席接见出席中国银行、中国人民保险公司海外机构总经理会议的代表。
Jiang Zemin interviewing participants of the conference for general managers of overseas branches of Bank of China (BOC) and PICC in 1995

人民保險
造福于民
江澤民
一九九四年
十月一日

1994年中共中央总书记、国家主席江泽民为中国人民保险公司成立45周年题词。
Jiang Zemin's inscription for PICC's 45th anniversary in 1994

1991年9月7日，国务院总理李鹏在中南海紫光阁前接见中国人民保险公司、中国银行海外机构总经理会议代表并发表讲话。

Li Peng giving speech to delegates attending the conference for general managers of BOC and PICC's branches aboard in 1991.

发展人民保险事业

李鹏

一九九四年七月

1994年7月国务院总理李鹏为中国人民保险公司成立45周年题词

Li Peng's inscription for PICC's 45th anniversary in 1994

1996年7月，中国保险集团在北京宣布成立，大会之前朱镕基接见会议代表并讲话。
Zhu Rongji giving lecture before the conference of the establishment of PICC Group in 1996

十二、保险竞争初现

Competition Emerged in Insurance

恢复保险业后，中国人民保险公司独家垄断中国保险市场，1985年市场发生变化。1985年3月3日国务院发布了《保险企业管理暂行条例》，该条例规定只要符合一定的要求，即可设立新的保险公司。

1986年7月15日，中国人民银行根据中央8号文件关于“农场要积极试行农牧业保险制度，动员小农场参加保险”的精神，按《保险企业管理暂行条例》的规定，首先在新疆批设了“新疆生产建设兵团农牧业生产保险公司”，专门经营新疆生产建设兵团农场内部的种养两业保险，1988年经中国人民银行批准开始经营除法定保险和外币保险的所有保险业务。1992年该公司更名为“新疆兵团保险公司”。2002年10月18日，公司被批准成为全国性财产保险公司，更名为“中华联合财产保险公司”，并先后在全国（除新疆外）设立16家分支机构，经营财险业务。2004年，公司保费收入65亿元，在全国十几家产险公司中位列第4。

PICC exclusively operated insurance business in China until in 1988 when some new insurers were erected up. Xinjiang Constructing Corps. Farming & Stockbreeding Insurance Co. was set up in 1986, which specialized in planting and breeding insurance within the corps.'s internal farming area. With the approval from the PBOC, it had started to handle all insurance operations except legal and forex insurance since 1988. It's renamed to Xinjing Corps Insurance Co. in 1992.

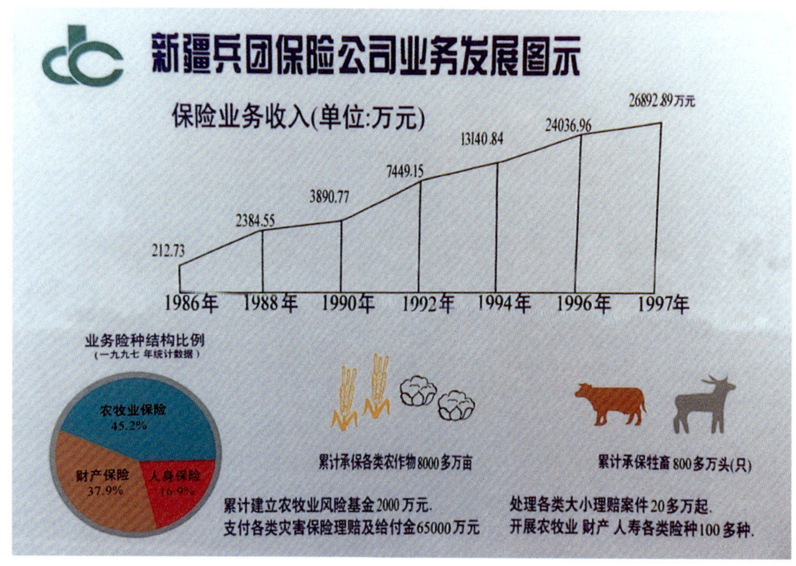

新疆兵团保险公司业务发展图示
Business Illustration of Xinjiang Corps Insurance Co.

2002年10月18日，兵保公司易名中华联合财产保险公司，中国保监会副主席冯晓增（左）和新疆自治区党委常委陈德敏出席揭牌仪式。（照片提供：李建杰）
CIRC vice chairman Feng Xiaozeng and Xinjiang Autonomous Region standing committeeman of Party Committee Chen Demin presenting the plate-unveiling ceremony of China United Property Insurance Company on October 18, 2002.

中国太平洋保险公司第一届第一次董事会议
Directors of China Pacific Insurance Co. attending the first board conference

1987年，经国务院和中国人民银行批准，恢复后的交通银行及其分支机构开设保险部，经营保险业务。1991年4月26日，经中国人民银行批准，交通银行在其保险业务部的基础上组建了中国太平洋保险公司，这是继中国人民保险公司成立后的第二家全国性商业综合性保险公司。

The Bank of Communications established the Insurance Department in 1987 and the China Pacific Insurance Co., Ltd. (CPIC) in 1991, the second national comprehensive insurance company in China.

中国太平洋保险公司暨上海分公司开业典礼
China PACIFIC Insurance Co., Ltd. & it's Shanghai branch

1988年3月，中国人民银行又在深圳批准设立了一家区域性保险公司——平安保险公司。这是新中国第一家股份制保险公司。公司成立之初，主要在沿海和特区开办保险业务。1992年6月，经国务院同意，中国人民银行批准，平安保险公司更名为中国平安保险公司，1997年1月，国家工商局核定公司名称为“中国平安保险股份有限公司”。这是继太保之后，中国第三家全国综合性保险公司。

With the approval of the People's Bank of China (PBOC), Ping An Insurance Co., the first regional insurer in China, was established in 1988 in Shenzhen; in 1992 it was renamed as China Ping An Insurance Co., Ltd., which is the third national comprehensive insurance company in China.

1988年5月27日平安保险公司在深圳蛇口成立
Open Ceremony of the Ping An Insurance Co. In 1988

1995年9月中共中央政治局委员、全国人大副委员长田纪云视察平安保险公司
Tian Jiyun Inspecting China Ping An in 1995.

中国平安保险公司办公大楼
Office building of China Ping An Insurance Co.

十三、再度崛起的保险中心：上海

Shanghai: Re-rising Insurance Hub

上海是中国改革开放后，保险市场发展最快的城市，从保险业恢复后的1980年开始由中国人民保险公司垄断市场，到1987年的交通银行设立保险业务部，1991年的中国太平洋保险成立，再到1991年平安保险的强势进入。1992年，根据中国对外开放的总体要求，中国保险市场首选上海对外开放，美国友邦保险公司（AIA）在上海设立了分公司。1994年9月，日本东京海上火灾保险公司也在上海成立了分公司，这是进入中国市场的第二家外国保险公司。1994年10月中国首家由企业出资组建的股份制、区域性产险公司——天安保险股份有限公司在上海成立。1995年1月，与之相似的大众保险股份有限公司也在上海成立。1995年底，中国人民银行批准加拿大宏利人寿保险公司在上海设立合资保险公司，为中国首家中外合资保险公司。其后，又有20多家独资、合资保险公司将其总部设在上海，使上海成为名副其实的“中国保险之都”。

Since China's reform and opening, Shanghai has been the marketplace where domestic insurance develops fastest. A great number of insurers have established their operations in Shanghai: PICC, CPIC, China Ping An Insurance Co., Dazhong Insurance Co., Tian'an Insurance Co., AIG, Tokyo Marine & Fire Insurance Co., and Manulife-Sinochem, hence Shanghai the insurance hub of China.

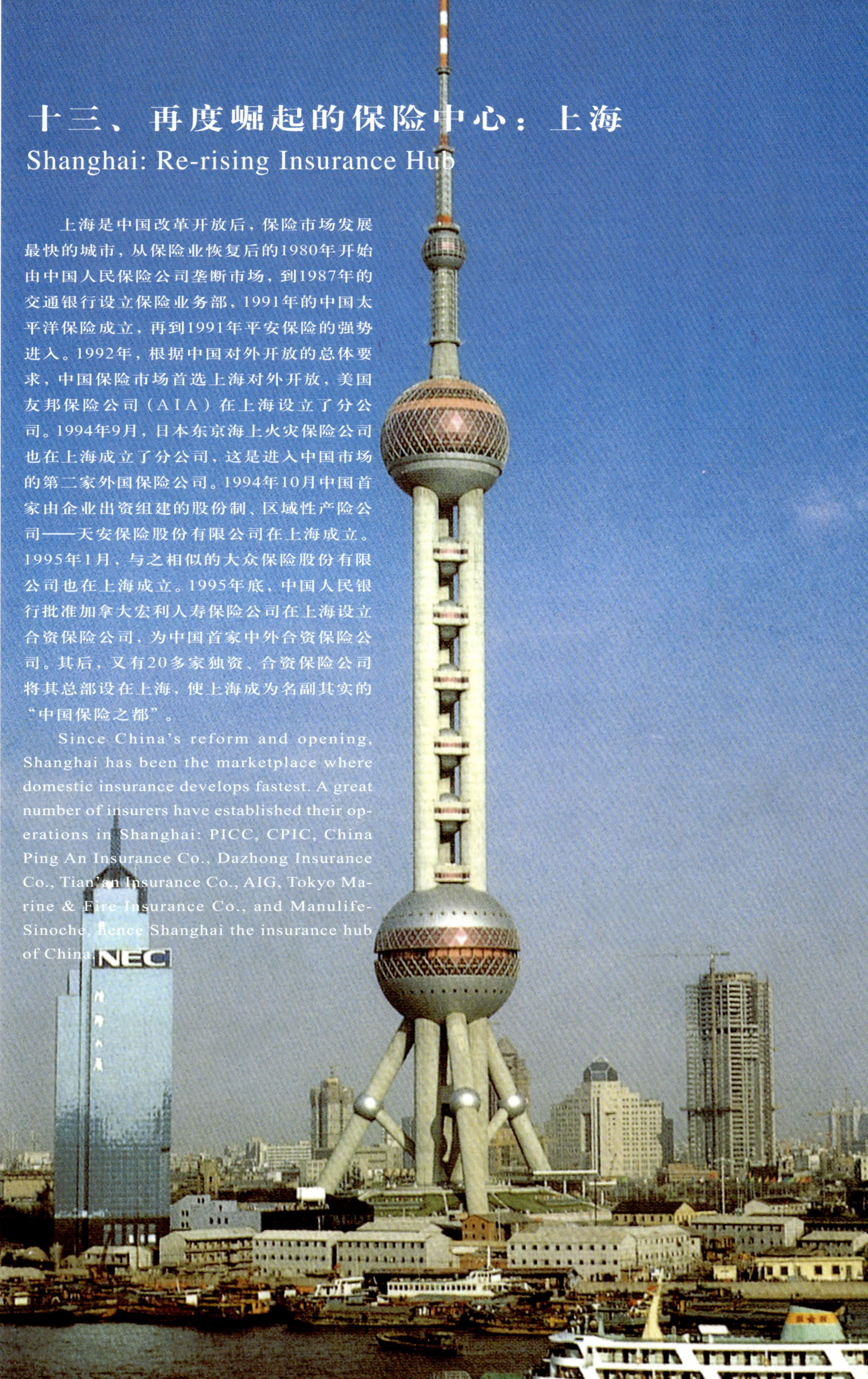

至2004年底总部设在上海的保险公司一览表

Insurance Companies Headquartered in Shanghai by Late 2004

中国太平洋保险（集团）有限公司	中保康联人寿保险有限公司
中国太平洋财产保险股份有限公司	恒康天安人寿保险有限公司
中国太平洋人寿保险股份有限公司	海尔纽约人寿保险有限公司
太平人寿保险有限公司	海康人寿保险有限公司
中国大地财产保险股份有限公司	广电日生人寿保险有限公司
天安保险股份有限公司	美国友邦保险有限公司
大众保险股份有限公司	东京海上火灾保险公司
生命人寿保险股份有限公司	丰泰保险（亚洲）有限公司
东方人寿保险股份有限公司	皇家太阳联合保险有限公司
中宏人寿保险有限公司	美国联邦保险股份有限公司
太平洋安泰人寿保险有限公司	三井住友海上火灾保险公司
安联大众人寿保险有限公司	韩国三星火灾海上保险公司
金盛人寿保险有限公司	

上海财险市场2003年保费一览

Premium in Shanghai's Property Insurance Market in 2003

（单位：人民币百万元）

人保	2377.99	太保	931.41	平安	759.35	天安	367.68
大众	390.07	华泰	121.81	太平	135.82	中华联合	150.00
华安	42.96	美亚	206.85	东京海上	164.00	丰泰	70.11
皇家太阳	37.39	美国联邦	12.47	三星火灾	60.12	三井住友	71.31

合　计：5899.34

上海寿险市场2003年保费一览

Premium in Shanghai's Life Insurance Market in 2003

（单位：人民币百万元）

国寿	6644.00	太保	2022.00	平安	8396.02	泰康	644.38
新华	1082.04	太平人寿	1204.75	美国友邦	1726.21	中宏	474.00
太平洋安泰	609.00	安联大众	166.56	金盛	125.00	中保康联	37.62
恒康天安	46.62	海尔纽约	81.80	海康	6.25	广电日生	0.23
生命	4.44						

合计：23270.92

中国第一家企业出资组建的股份制产险公司：天安保险股份有限公司

Tian'an Insurance Co.: China's First Property Insurer Funded by Enterprises

天安保险股份有限公司是1994年10月22日经中国人民银行批准成立的，它由上海及江苏、浙江、安徽等省20多家大型企业合资组建的股份制、区域性财产保险公司，总部设在上海浦东，办理长江三角洲区域内人民币、外币的各种财产、责任、信用、机动车辆、飞机、船舶、货运、健康保险及其再保险和法定保险业务。2004年，公司保费收入50亿元，创业10年来保费年增长率高达53.91%。

Tian'an Insurance Co., Ltd., a joint-stock, regional property insurer, was established in 1994, with the approval from the PBOC.

天安保险股份有限公司开业典礼
Open ceremony of Tian'an Insurance Co.

经中国人民银行批准，大众保险股份有限公司于1995年1月26日在上海隆重开业。图为座落在上海市北京西路860号的公司总部。(照片提供：孙环民)

Office Building of Dazhong Insurance Co. Ltd, Set Up In 1995 In Shanghai.

十四、中国保险市场的对外开放

Opening of Chinese Insurance Market

1980年至1992年，是中国保险业对外开放的准备阶段，一些外国保险公司在华设立代表处，其职能为：沟通母公司与中国保险业的联系；对中国保险市场进行考察、调研；为中国保险公司培训人员；支持中国保险教育事业。从1992年到加入世贸组织之前，这是我国保险业对外开放的试点阶段，其标志是国务院选择上海作为第一个保险对外开放的试点城市。随后，外资保险的经营区域也逐渐扩大到广州等地，经营范围包括境外企业的各项保险和境内外商投资企业的财产及相关责任险，外国人和境内个人缴费的人身保险业务，以及上述两项业务的再保险。截至2004年底，中国内地共有外资保险公司41家，其中，中外合资保险公司19家，外国保险公司22家。10年间，外资保险公司业务得到了较快发展，保费收入从1992年的29.5万元增加到2004年的98亿元。

Some foreign insurers set up representative offices in China during from 1980 to 1992, the preparatory period for Chinese insurance to open. From 1992 till China's accession into the WTO, Chinese insurance was in the pilot stage of opening. By late 2001, China's mainland had a total of 29 foreign insurers.

改革开放后中国第一家外资保险公司：美国友邦保险

AIA: the First Foreign Insurer in China after the Reform and Opening

在中国保险市场对外开放的过程中，美国国际集团进入中国别具历史意义。1992年10月，美国友邦获准在上海经营寿险及非寿险业务，成为改革开放后第一家进入中国保险市场的外资保险企业。目前，美国国际集团下属的友邦、美亚公司已在上海、广州、北京、深圳、苏州等地经营保险业务。

美国友邦保险是第一家将个人营销理念带入中国的保险企业。友邦为中国寿险市场培养出了第一代寿险营销员。随后，寿险个人营销之风席卷中国大陆，中国寿险业发生了历史性的革命。

1998年5月12日中国总理朱镕基会见AIG董事长格林伯格(左)
Premier Zhu Rongji with Evan G. Greenberg, president of AIG, in 1998

上海友邦大厦内的培训中心，这里培训出中国第一代寿险个人营销员。
Training Center of AIA Shanghai Branch

AIA (the American International Assurance Co., Ltd.) got the license to run life and non-life insurance within Shanghai in 1992. AIA is the first among foreign insurers to enter China and the first introduced individual marketing ideology into China. So far it has set up Shanghai and Guangzhou Branch in China.

中国第一家中外合资人寿保险公司：中宏人寿保险公司

Manulife-Sinoche Insurance Co.: China's First Sino-Foreign Life Insurer

中宏人寿由加拿大宏利人寿保险公司和中国对外经济贸易信托投资公司（中化集团成员）合资组建，1996年11月26日在上海正式成立。

2004年，中宏人寿保费收入5.976亿元，在全国28家寿险公司中排名第13位。

Manulife-Sinochem jointly founded by Canadian biggest life insurer Manulife Financial Group and SinoChem Corporation was established in Shanghai in 1996.

原中国总理李鹏和加拿大总理克雷蒂安主持开业典礼
Li Peng and Canadian premier attending the open ceremony of Manulife—Sinoche

第一家境内设立的境外资本保险公司：香港民安保险深圳分公司

Min An Insurance Co. (Chinese) Ltd. Shenzhen Branch: First Overseas-Capital-Funded Insurer in China

香港民安保险深圳分公司1981年12月4日正式成立，并于1982年1月9日在深圳特区开业。香港民安保险作为香港注册的中资保险机构，把深圳作为“窗口”，引进国际保险的承保办法、条款和先进经验，为迁入内地投资的香港企业提供保险的跟进服务，同时也向企业和个人提供保险服务。香港民安在内地设立了深圳、海口两家分公司和厦门代表处。2004年5月，香港民安保险深圳分公司成为全国第一家获准子公司化改造的保险公司在全国范围经营保险业务。

Min An Insurance Co.(Chinese) Ltd. Shenzhen Branch was founded in 1981 and opened in Shenzhen in 1982.

经中国人民银行总行批准，香港民安保险有限公司于1997年10月6日在厦门成立代表处。图为厦门市人民政府朱亚衍副市长、中国人民银行厦门市分行陈辉煌副行长、中保财产保险有限公司厦门市分公司赵一平总经理、中保人寿保险有限公司厦门市分公司黄仲达总经理及香港民安保险有限公司萧亦煌副董事长兼总经理共同主持剪彩仪式。
Open Ceremony of Xiamen Representative Office of Min An Insurance Co. Ltd in 1997

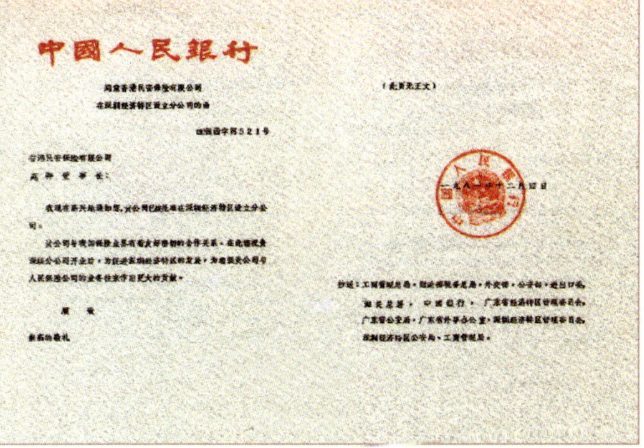

中國人民銀行

十五、《中华人民共和国保险法》颁布

Promulgation of *Insurance Law of PRC*

早在新中国刚刚成立时的1949年10月25日，中国人民银行总行就成立了"法规编审委员会"。其中第六组为"保险章则组"。在此基础上中国人民保险公司委托华东区分公司成立了新中国第一个保险业专门研究机构——保险法规研究会。该机构曾召集大学教授及保险从业人员等30余人协力起草了《保险法(草案)》和《保险业管理条例(草案)》，但受当时政治与经济环境的影响，两"草案"未能施行。

1979年国内保险业务恢复后的十几年里，保险业和保险公司的规范主要依据《保险企业管理暂行条例》(1985)、《中华人民共和国经济合同法》(1981)和《中华人民共和国财产保险合同条例》(1983)。这些法规对传统计划经济下刚刚起步的保险市场的发展起到了积极的规范和促进作用，但随着中国保险市场的发展，这些法规已经不适应市场经营管理的需要。1991年10月19日，经中国人民银行研究决定，保险法起草小组成立，由10人组成。

1995年6月30日，《保险法》在八届全国人大常委会第十四次会议上获得通过，同年10月1日起实施。这是建国以来的第一部保险法，它的实施，从根本上结束了我国长期以来保险立法支离破碎、很多方面无法可依的局面，对规范保险活动、保护当事人的合法权益、加强对保险业的监督、促进保险业健康发展起到了十分重要的作用。《保险法》的颁布实施是中国保险法制史上一个具有分水岭意义的事情。为配合《保险法》的施行，中国人民银行相继制定了一系列配套的规章制度，特别是1998年11月中国保监会正式成立后，相继出台了一系列规章和规范性文件。

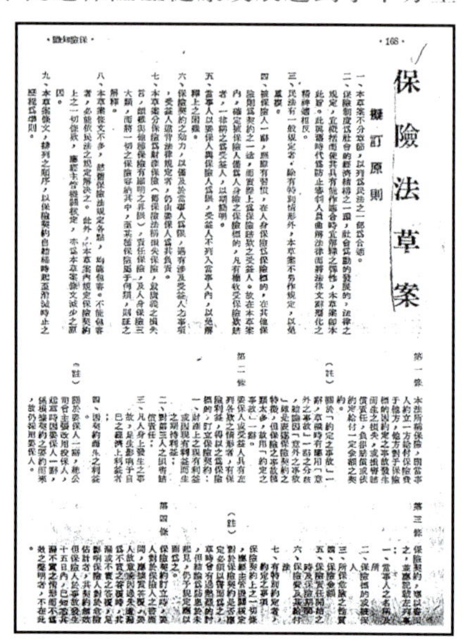

保險法草案

擬訂原則

解放初期，《保险知识》刊登的《保险法草案》

Draft of Insurance Law in the *Insurance Knowledge* in Chinese early liberation

中国保险报
保险法出台适逢其时
石头落地
南方部分地区暴雨成灾
向好干部许照约同志学习
二季度国家统计产品合格率上升
中华人民共和国保险法

中国人民银行副行长殷介炎在中国保险报社主办的“保险法与中国保险业的发展”研讨会上发言

PBOC's vice president Yin Jieyan giving speech at the Seminar on Insurance Law & China Insurance Development in 1995

保险法颁布后，各地保险界人士纷纷举行座谈会。

One of Symposiums on the *Insurance Law*

The *insurance law* of the People's Republic of China was promulgated on June 30, 1995 at the 14th Session of the Standing Committee of the 8th National People's Congress of China. Before the *Insurance Law*, the *Draft Insurance Law* and the *Draft Insurance Industry Law* were worked out in early liberation, but were implemented for special economic and political situation. There had been several insurance legal rules in China since 1979, exp., *Property Insurance Contract Regulations* in 1983. In order to push the development of insurance, an insurance draft team was organized in 1991;through their hard and careful work, the *Insurance law* was completed in 1995.

第二十三条 本条例自颁布之日起施行。

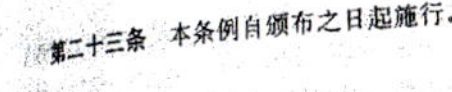
保险企业管理暂行条例

1985年3月3日国务院发布

第一章 总 则

第一条 为了加强国家对保险企业的管理，促进保险事业的发展，维护被保险方（在保险单或保险凭证中称被保险人）的利益，发展保险的经济补偿作用，以利于社会主义现代化建设和人民生活的安定，特制定本条例。

第二条 本条例适用于经营各种保险业务的企业。

第三条 凡在中华人民共和国境内的国家、集体和个人的财产如需保险，应向中国境内的保险企业投保。

第四条 国家保险管理机关是中国人民银行。

国家保险管理机关的职责是：拟定保险事业的方针、政策，批准保险企业的设立，指导、监督保险企业的业务活动，审定基本保险条款和保险费率，检查保险企业的会计帐册和报表单据，并对保险企业在经营业务中违反国家法律、法规、政策，或者损害被保险方的合法利益的行为，给予经济制裁，直至责令其停业。

第五条 国家鼓励保险企业发展农村业务，为农民提供保险服务。保险企业应支持农民在自愿的基础上集股设立农村互助保险合作社，其业务范围和管理办法另行制定。

第二章 保险企业的设立

第六条 设立保险企业，经营保险业务，必须得到国家保险管理机关的批准并向工商行政管理机关申请营业执照。无营业执照

· 507 ·

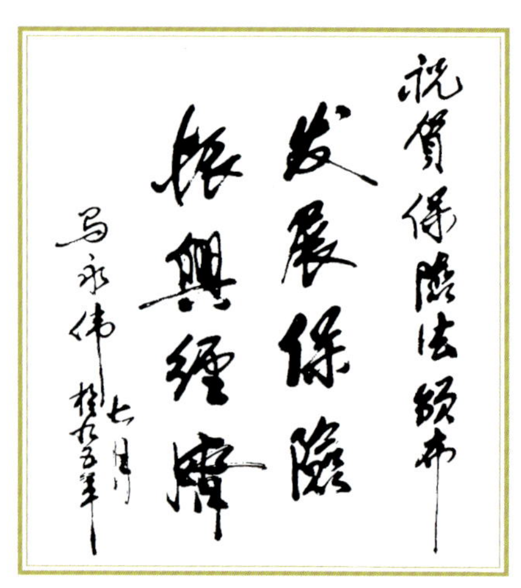

中国保险学会会长马永伟题词
Chairman of the Insurance Institute of China Ma Yongwei's inscription for the promulgated *Insurance Law*

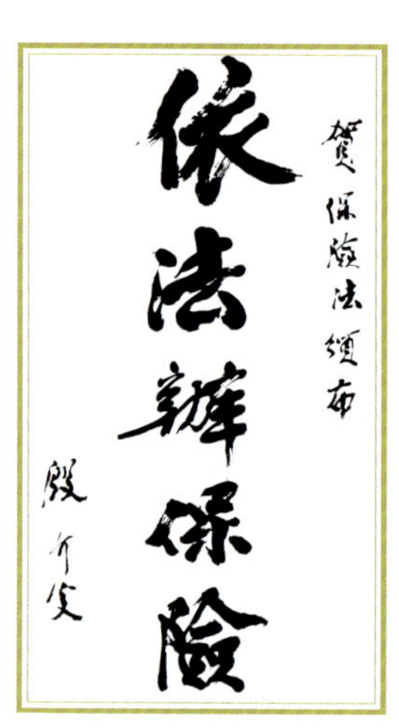

中国人民银行副行长殷介炎题词
POBC's vice chairman Yin Jieyan's inscription for the promulgated *Insurance Law*

《中华人民共和国保险法》起草小组成员名单

Members Drafting the *Insurance Law of PRC*

组　长	秦道夫	中国人民保险公司前董事长兼总经理
副组长	夏利平	中国人民银行金融管理司副司长
副组长	王恩韶	中国保险(英国)有限公司前董事长兼总经理
成　员	李嘉华	国务院参事、人保法律顾问
成　员	刘福寿	人行条法司
成　员	傅安平	人行金管司
成　员	邢　伟	人行金管司
成　员	王　建	人保总公司法律研究室主任
成　员	封智君	中国太平洋保险公司北京分公司
成　员	骆　鹏	中国平安保险公司北京代表处首席代表

十六、中国第一张生命表

Chinese First Experience Life Table

1992年，当时的保险监管部门中国人民银行保险司委托中国人民保险公司编制中国第一张经验生命表。人保公司精算处具体承担了这项工作，并成立了编制小组，李政怀任组长，组员有詹肇岚、范平和崔正宇。人民银行保险司傅安平负责项目立项和实施。

1992年下半年编制小组开始研究编制生命表的可行性。第二年，生命表总体设计方案和编制程序完成，并于年底获主管部门批准。1994年方案全面启动：4—6月资料收集试点工作在北京、上海、辽宁和山东进行。随后数据收集工作在全国展开，并于年底完成。1995年1月底数据上报工作结束。3月，数据库建立与数据检验工作完成。4月，小组开始数据处理。7月底，中国第一张经验生命表——“中国人寿保险经验生命表（1990—1993）”诞生。

1996年6月，中国人民银行下发通知：从1997年4月1日起，中国境内开发的所有人寿保险险种都必须以该表为保单定价、计算退保金和准备金的依据。从此，中国寿险业保险费率制定及准备金评估有了科学依据，从而奠定了中国寿险精算发展的基础。

In 1992, the Insurance Division of the People's Bank of China (PBOC), the insurance watchdog of that time entrusted PICC to work out Chinese first experience life table. In the late half of 1992, the feasibility for the performance of the table was researched; next year, the general design scheme and procedures had been completed, which also received the approval from competent authorities. After the all-round startup in 1994 and eventually in late July 1995, Chinese first experience life table (1990 – 1993) came to the world.

中国经验生命表研制小组组长李政怀向专家顾问组及监管部门领导介绍CL(1990—1993)的研制过程与模型
Li Zhenghuai demonstrating to the expert group the establishment process and design of CL (1990—1993)

十七、中国保险市场的五路新军

Five Vigorous Newcomers to Chinese Insurance Market

为进一步推动中国保险业市场化进程，1996年8月中国人民银行又正式批准五家国内保险公司开业。这五家公司是《中华人民共和国保险法》颁布实施后成立的首批商业性、股份制的保险企业。新华人寿、泰康人寿的成立，打破了我国人身保险市场三家主体垄断经营的局面；而随着华泰、华安、永安等股份制保险公司在北京、深圳、西安的设立，以及一批外资财险公司的开业和发展，一个以国有制为主体，中外保险公司并存，多家保险公司竞争的保险市场多元化格局初步形成。

Five insurance companies were established in 1996 with the approval of the PBOC, namely Huatai Property Insurance Co., Ltd., New China Life Insurance Co., Ltd., Taikang Life Insurance Co., Ltd., Yong An Insurance Co., Ltd., and Sinosafe Insurance Co., Ltd. The appearance of new insurers intensifies the competition in the market of China.

新华人寿保险股份有限公司开业于1996年9月6日，由15家国有大型企业和大型股份制企业依法发起设立。是股份制、全国性的人寿保险企业，具有独立法人资格。经营范围包括各类人民币、外币的人身保险业务，其中包括各类人寿保险、健康保险、意外伤害保险等保险业务。可在中国境内外设立分支机构、代表机构及附属机构。为境内外的保险机构代理保险、检验、理赔、开展保险咨询业务等。图为该公司在人民大会堂举行的开业庆典暨向老运动员赠送保险仪式。

Open ceremony of New China Life Insurance Co. in 1996

1996年8月22日，泰康人寿保险股份有限公司在北京成立，该公司是由16家国有大中型企业发起组建的全国性、专业化的股份公司，注册资本6亿元。图为泰康首界股东大会暨首届董事会成员合影。

Directorate Members of Taiking Life Insurance Co., Ltd. at the First Shareholder's Conference in Beijing in 1996

董事长关国亮，2002年8月荣获“北京市优秀青年企业家”称号；2004年6月荣获“世界经理人CEO成就奖”；2004年10月入选“最具世界影响力的中国企业领袖”。

Board chairman Guan Guoliang: titled “Beijing excellent young entrepreneur” in August 2002; award winner of “world managing agent CEO achievements” in June 2004; selected as “most internationally influential Chinese entrepreneur” in October 2004.

新华人寿保险股份有限公司成立于1996年8月，是一家国际化大型股份制专业寿险公司，经营范围包括各类人寿保险、健康保险和人身意外伤害保险业务。

目前，新华人寿保险公司在全国拥有34家省级分公司，152家地市级中心支公司，584家营销服务部，内外勤员工达14万人，2004年度保费收入近200亿元，市场份额位居寿险市场前列。成立九年来，新华保险在业界建立了良好的品牌和成熟的企业文化。“立信于心，尽责至善”成为公司每一位员工的品牌宣言，“发展观”是公司的世界观，“责任”是公司的核心价值观。

2004年9月底，新华保险控股股份有限公司经中国保监会批准筹建。控股公司下设寿险、财险、健康险、年金、资产管理公司、代理公司、经纪公司等专业子公司，将为客户提供更为全面、优质的风险保障和投资理财服务。

Founded in August 1996, New China Life Insurance Co., Ltd., as an internationalized professional life insurer, mainly operates various life, health, and personal accident injury insurance business. Presently, New China Life, with its 34 provincial branches, 152 city-level branches, 584 marketing outlets and staff totaled 140 thousand, holds the leading position in Chinese insurance market; in 2004, its annual premium came to almost 20 billion yuan.

新华人寿保险公司于2004年8月上榜中国企业500强，名列第102位；2004年10月入选“最具世界影响力的中国著名企业”；2004年11月荣获“中国保险行业最具影响力品牌年度大奖”；2004年12月荣登“北京百强企业”龙虎榜；2005年1月被评为“最受信赖的保险公司”。

New China Life: ranked 102nd of the top 500 Chinese enterprises in August 2004; selected as “Chinese famed enterprise with most international influence” in October 2004; annual award winner of “most influential brand in Chinese underwriting” in November 2004; ascended in the list of “Beijing Top 100 Enterprises”; estimated as “most reliable insurer” in January 2005.

华安财产保险股份有限公司于1996年10月18日正式创立。图为该公司在创立暨第一届股东大会上董事会成员及人行深圳分行的有关负责人合影。

Members Attending the First Shareholders Conference, Sinosafe Insurance Co.

永安财产保险股份有限公司于1996年9月28日设立，总部设在陕西西安。该公司的营业范围和机构设置区域为重庆、四川、山西、陕西、新疆、甘肃、青海、宁夏。主要办理国内和涉外各类财产保险、责任保险、信用保险、农业保险、保证保险和上述各项保险业务的再保险业务。公司注册资本金为3.1亿元，董事长为邱森贵，总经理为汪海洋。图为永安公司与国外保险界同行交流。

Business Meeting of General Re and Yong An Insurance Co. in 1998.

1996年9月26日，华泰财产保险股份有限公司举行开业仪式，并同时向河北灾区捐建华泰希望小学。图为华泰第一任领导班子及全体员工合影。

Staff Attending the Open ceremony & That of Endowing Huatai Hope Primary School in 1996.

华安保险公司李光荣董事长
Li Guangrong: board chairman of Sinosafe

华安财产保险股份有限公司是经中国人民银行批准，于1996年10月18日正式创立的一家专业性保险公司，总部设于深圳，主要经营各种财产险、责任险、信用保证险、农业险及其上述保险的再保险。2003年初，经中国保监会批准，公司开始经营意外伤害险和短期健康险业务。

2004年，华安经中国保险监督管理委员会批准，已开设北京、上海、深圳、广东、湖南、福建、广西、江苏、四川、浙江、大连11家省级分公司和200余家下设机构，成为全国性的专业保险公司。2005年，华安又经中国保监会批准，筹建山东、重庆、云南、陕西、辽宁、江西、山西、天津、安徽、湖北、河南、宁波等12家分公司，初步完成了全国战略布局。

华安保险公司自从2002年7月股权变更之后，大胆转变经营思路，连续两年实现跨越式发展。2004年7月，华安在全国首家推出“利率联动”的产品——华安金龙收益联动性家庭财产保险，在全国率先对利率上调做出回应，引起了各界的广泛关注。2005年2月，华安又在全国推出为餐饮业主度身定做的一揽子综合保险产品，该产品为政府分摊责任，为餐饮业主转嫁风险、为食客提供安全保障，一经推出就引起了政府、卫生部门、餐饮业主和广大食客的关注和肯定。

Founded on October 18, 1996 with the approval from PBOC, Sinosafe Insurance Co., Ltd., as a specialized insurer headquartered in Shenzhen, mainly operates various property, liability, credit security, agriculture insurance and reinsurance for the above-mentioned insurance. Sinosafe, authorized by the CIRC, has begun to set foot in accident injury and short-term health insurance since early 2003; the next year, Sinosafe was upgraded to be a countrywide insurer with 11 provincial branches and 200-plus subordinate organs approved by the commission.

十八、中国人民保险公司机构体制改革

Structural Reform of PICC

1996年，在中国保险市场占主导地位的中国人民保险公司机构体制发生了重大改革，中国人民保险公司改制成立中国人民保险(集团)公司(简称中保集团)。中保集团下设中保财产保险有限公司、中保人寿保险有限公司、中保再保险有限公司三个子公司。

1998年10月，根据国务院对中国保险业整体改革的方案，与中国保监会筹备相对应，中保集团完成历史使命，其属下三个子公司更名后成为独立法人。

PICC was reorganized into PICC Group in 1996, which had 3 sub companies: PICC Property, PICC Life, and PICC Reinsurance Co., Ltd. According to the restructuring proposal for PICC; PICC Group was put down and its three subsidiaries were reorganized into independent companies in 1998.

1996年7月23日中国人民保险(集团)公司成立
Inauguration of PICC (Group) Corporation in 1996

国务院副秘书长周正庆(中)、中国人民银行行长戴相龙(右)、原中保集团董事长兼总经理马永伟(左)为中保集团成立揭幕。
Zhou Zhengqing, Secretary General of the State Council, Dai Xianglong, President of the PBOC, and Ma Yongwei, Chairman/General Manger of PICC Group at the inauguration of PICC Group

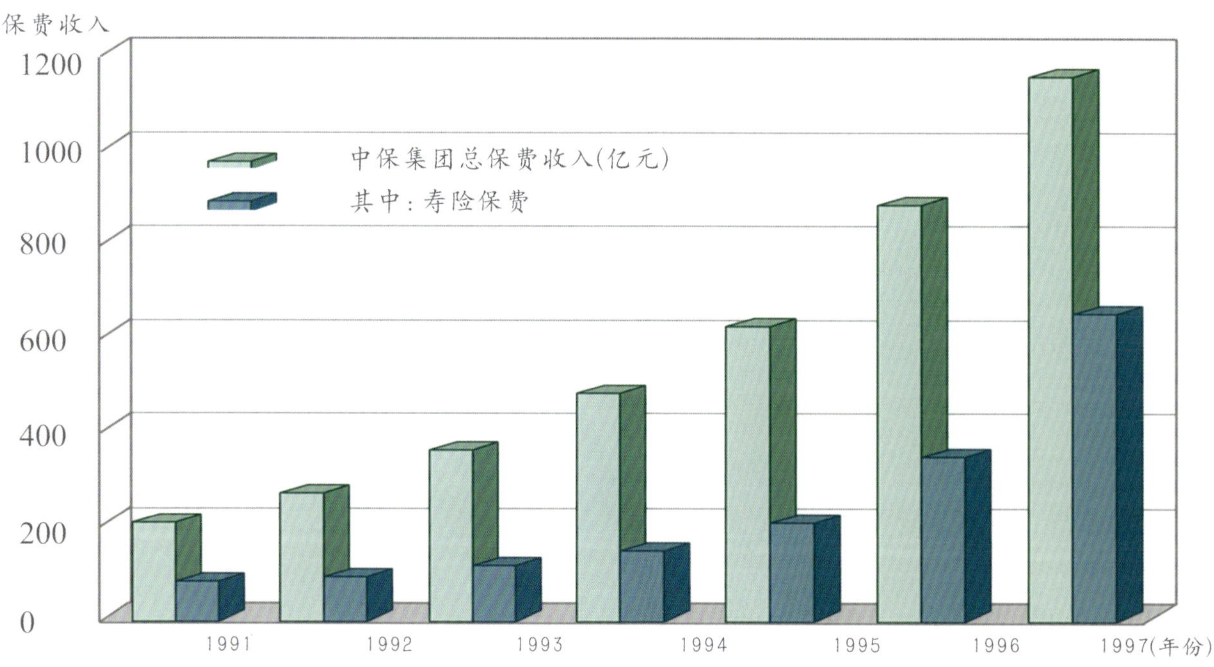

中保人寿保险有限公司总经理王宪章
Wang Xianzhang: General Manager of PICC Life

中保财产保险有限公司更名为中国人民保险公司，在全国设分支机构4000余家，系统从业人员10万多人，承接了原中国人民保险公司经营的除人寿保险以外的全部业务，险种达200多种。

中保人寿保险有限公司更名为中国人寿保险公司。在全国设立分支机构4000余家，公司员工4万多人，个人代理人66万余人。

中保再保险有限公司更名为中国再保险公司。公司注册资本20亿元人民币。中国再保险公司的成立，填补了中国保险史上没有独立的专业再保险公司的空白，完善了中国保险市场，为中国保险业迅猛发展提供了可靠的保障。

专业再保险公司接受法定分保和部分商业分保，直接保险公司可以接受商业分保业务，人民币分保机制初步形成，国内商业分保趋于活跃，再保险业务有了很大的发展。

PICC Property Insurance Company Ltd. was renamed as the People's Insurance Company of China specializing in non-life insurance with 4,000 branches across China; PICC Life was reorganized into China Life Insurance Company and PICC Reinsurance was reorganized into China Reinsurance Company which is the first insurer specializing in reinsurance.

原中保再保险有限公司领导及各部门负责人
Former leadership and senior department principals of PICC Reinsurance

中保财险办公楼成为中国人民保险公司办公地
Office building of PICC (of PICC Property Co. before)

十九、中国保险监督管理委员会成立

China Insurance Regulatory Commission

在新中国成立的初期，中国人民银行和财政部对保险业行使领导和管理职能。1995年6月《保险法》颁布，该法对保险业的经营规则和监督管理制订了专门规定。为贯彻落实《保险法》，中国人民银行于1995年7月设立保险司，专门负责对中资保险公司的监督，对外资保险的监管由外资金融机构管理司保险处负责。从1995年至1998年，我国保险监管主要以市场行为监管为主，并开始探索偿付能力监管。

随着保险业的发展和银行业、证券业、保险业的分业经营，国务院于1998年11月18日批准设立中国保险监督管理委员会。保监会的成立，标志着我国保险监管走向了专业化、规范化的新阶段。

China Insurance Regulatory Commission (CIRC) was founded on November 18, 1998 in Beijing. Ma Yongwei was appointed chairman of the commission. It marked the standardization of Chinese insurance regulation.

中国保险监督管理委员会成立大会
Inauguration of the CIRC

中国保险监督管理委员会第一任主席马永伟
Ma Yongwei, first chairman of the CIRC

时任国务院副总理温家宝与中国保险监督管理委员会全体人员合影
Wen Jiabao with Staff of the CIRC

二十、产寿险分业经营
Separately Operated Property & Life Insurance

1995年《保险法》颁布以前，保险公司可以同时经营财产险和人身险业务。进入90年代后，借鉴国际保险业实行产、寿险分业经营的通行做法，监管部门开始研究推动我国保险业产、寿险分业经营体制改革。《保险法》以法律的形式确立了产、寿险分业经营的原则。之后，各保险公司开始实施产、寿险分业经营体制改革。这一改革持续了6年时间。

除了1996年中国人民保险公司改制，2000年11月，新疆兵团完成分业经营体制改革，改为新疆兵团财产保险公司。2001年4月，太平洋保险公司改制为中国太平洋保险（集团）股份有限公司、中国太平洋财产保险股份有限公司、中国太平洋人寿保险股份有限公司。2002年4月，平安完成分业改革，成立了中国平安保险（集团）股份有限公司、中国平安财产保险股份有限公司、中国平安人寿保险股份有限公司和平安信托投资公司。

分业经营极大地促进了人身险业务的发展。1997年，人身险保费收入首次超过财产险。到2003年，人身险保费收入已占总保费收入的77.59%。

In 1990's, the *Insurance Law* set the principle of separate operation of property and life insurance, then, insurers started to implement the structural reform of separate operation of property and life insurance, which had lasted 6 years, greatly promoting the development of personal insurance.

关于中国平安保险股份有限公司名称变更为
中国平安保险（集团）股份有限公司
及设立中国平安财产保险股份有限公司
和中国平安人寿保险股份有限公司的
公告

根据国务院和中国保险监督管理委员会的批准，中国平安保险股份有限公司对人寿保险业务、资产以及相关的债权债务和财产保险业务、资产以及相关的债权债务进行了分业重组。

日前，中国平安保险股份有限公司正式完成分业改革，更名为中国平安保险（集团）股份有限公司，集团控股设立的中国平安人寿保险股份有限公司、中国平安财产保险股份有限公司也已正式成立。中国平安保险股份有限公司分业改革后，原由中国平安保险股份有限公司经营和拥有的人身保险业务和资产以及相关的债权债务将由中国平安人寿保险股份有限公司拥有或承担；原由中国平安保险股份有限公司经营和拥有的财产保险业务和资产以及相关债权债务将由中国平安财产保险股份有限公司拥有或承担；原中国平安保险股份有限公司人身保险业务、财产保险业务和资产及其相关债权债务以外的其他业务、债权债务和资产将由中国平安保险（集团）股份有限公司继续拥有或承担。

中国平安保险（集团）股份有限公司及其旗下各公司组成的平安保险集团将继续以“诚信”为基石，牢记自己对股东负责、对客户负责、对员工负责、对社会负责的企业使命，一如既往地致力于金融服务业的改革创新，努力把平安建设成为国际一流的专业化金融保险服务集团和金融业的百年老店。

中国平安保险（集团）股份有限公司
二〇〇三年二月十四日

中国平安保险股份公司更名为中国平安保险(集团)股份有限公司

Bulletin on China Ping An Insurance's renaming & establishment of Ping An Property and Ping An Life

中国太平洋保险公司产寿险分业经营机构体制改革暨思想政治工作会议(照片提供：刘力)

Conference by China Pacific Insurance Co. on Restructuring of institutions Separately Operating Property & Life Insurance & Ideology & Politics Work

二十一、国有保险公司的股份制改革和上市

Shareholding Reform and Listing of State-Owned Insurance Companies

中国保监会主席吴定富（右）与中国人保控股公司总经理唐运祥为公司揭牌。（照片提供：高星）

CIRC chairman Wu Dingfu (R) with PICC Holding president Tang Yunxiang at the unveiling ceremony

1999年9月，党的十五届四中全会《关于国有企业改革和发展若干重大问题的决定》指出："国有大中型企业，尤其是优势企业，宜于实行股份制的，要通过规范上市、中外合资和企业互相参股等形式，改为股份制企业，发展混合所有制经济，重要的企业由国家控股。"这为国有保险公司改革提供了难得的机遇。

2001年，保监会会同国家计委、财政部、人民银行、证监会和三家国有保险公司成立了保险业改革与发展调研小组，对国有保险公司股份制改革进行专题研究。根据2002年全国金融工作会议精神，中国人保、中国人寿和中国再保险公司分别制定了股份制改革方案，并得到国务院批准。

中国人保以审订评估后的净资产，联合其他发起股东，共同发起设立中国人民财产保险股份有限公司，对中国人保的全部资产进行全面重组，将主业经营性资产和业务全部纳入股份公司。中国人保改为中国人保控股公司，作为国家授权经营的股东代表，成为股份公司的股东之一，并经营管理非经营性资产。由控股公司发起设立中国人保资产管理有限公司。

2003年7月19日，中国人保控股公司、中国人民财产保险股份有限公司和中国人保资产管理有限公司正式挂牌成立。

The *Decision on Some Important Matters in the Reform and Development of State-Owned Enterprises* concluded at the 4th Session of the Fifteenth National Party Congress in September 1999 provided state-owned insurers god-given opportunity for reform. In 2001, Research Team of Reform & Development of Insurance was organized by the CIRC, National Development and Reform Commission, Ministry of Finance, PBOC, China Securities Regulatory Commission, and three state-owned insurers. Via reform, PICC Holding Co., Ltd., PICC Property & Casualty Co., Ltd., and PICC Assets Management Co., Ltd. were founded on July 19, 2003.

参加三家公司揭牌庆典的全体领导在纪念广告上签名

Signatures of all dignitaries on the ad celebrating the foundation of PICC Holding, Property, and AMC

2003年11月6日，中国人民财产保险股份有限公司在香港联交所主板市场以H股成功挂牌上市，这是内地第一家完成股份制改造的国有金融机构，也是内地第一家在境外上市的金融保险机构。中国人民财产保险股份有限公司共发行股票34.55亿股，募集资金62.2亿元港币。上市后股份总额为110亿股，其中国有股为80亿股。当日香港恒生指数下跌288点，但中国人民财产保险股份有限公司股票上市就以2.425元港币开盘，逆风飞扬，以2.7元港币收盘，涨幅达50%，成为市场追捧亮点。

On November 6, 2003, PICC Property & Casualty Co., Ltd., succeeded in listing at the main board of Hong Kong Stock Exchange with share H, hence the first domestic state-owned financial institution that completed shareholding reform and also the first inland financial insurance institution listing overseas.

在庆祝中国人民财产保险股份有限公司上市记者招待会上，中国人民财产保险股份有限公司董事长唐运祥(左一)与美国国际集团(AIG)主席格林柏格握手祝贺上市成功。(照片提供：高星)

Board Chairman of PICC Property & Casualty Tang Yunxiang (L1) shaking hands with president of AIG Maurce R. Greenberg to celebrate the successful overseas listing at the press conference of PICC P&C.

中国人民财产保险股份有限公司董事长唐运祥(左三)、总裁王毅(左四)、副总裁王银成(左五)与有关人员在香港交易市场上握手祝贺。(照片提供：高星)

Board Chairman Tang Yunxiang (L3), president Wang Yi (L4), vice president Wang Yincheng (L5) shaking hands to celebrate their company's listing in Hong Kong.

中国人寿重组改制为中国人寿保险（集团）公司，以1999版保单为界对业务、资产进行重组，1999年以前的老业务及相关资产负债进入集团公司。集团公司独家发起设立中国人寿保险股份有限公司，1999年及以后的业务及相关资产负债进入股份公司。集团公司和股份公司共同发起设立中国人寿保险资产管理公司。

2003年8月28日，中国人寿保险（集团）公司和中国人寿保险股份有限公司正式挂牌成立。2004年6月28日，中国人寿保险资产管理公司成立。

China Life Insurance Co., Ltd. has been restructured into China Life Insurance (Group) Company, which independently launched and established China Life Insurance Co., Ltd. The two companies were formally founded on August 28, 2003 and they jointly set up China Life Insurance Assets Management Company on June 28, 2004.

中国保监会主席吴定富为中国人寿保险(集团)公司揭牌(照片提供：许彬)
CIRC's chairman Wu Dingfu unveiling the plate for China Life Insurance (Group) Company

中国人寿大厦
(照片提供：王健)
Office building of China Life

中国人寿在香港联交所上市成功后，王宪章与董建华举杯同庆（照片提供：许彬）
Wang Xianzhang and Dong Jiahua drinking for China Life's successful listing in HKSE

中国人寿在香港联交所上市（照片提供：许彬）
China Life listing in HKSE

中国人寿保险股份有限公司分别于2003年12月17日、18日在美国纽约证交所和香港联交所成功挂牌上市，成为第一家在美国纽约和香港两地上市的国内金融机构。中国人寿此次公开发行融资34.75亿美元，创造了当年度全球资本市场融资额的最高记录。上市后国有股占总股本的72.2%。此次中国人寿在纽约和香港上市，全球机构配售部分的薄记总需求达554亿美元，相当于超额配售后发行规模的16倍。

China Life raised 3.475 billion US dollars via the IPO, hitting the top record of financing amount in the global capital market of the year. After the listing, state-owned share makes up 72.2 per cent of China Life's shareholding equity.

2003年12月17日上午9点30分，王宪章在纽约证交所交易大厅，为当天股市鸣响开业钟，这时，拥有210多年历史的纽约证交所外飘扬着五星红旗。随着中国经济的强劲发展，全球投资者看向中国。（照片提供：许彬）
Wang Xianzhang sounding the business—starting bell for the stock market of the day at the hall of New York Securities Exchange

中国再保险(集团)公司成立庆典
Inauguration of China Reinsurance (Group) Company, China P&C Reinsurance Co., and China Life Reinsurance Company

中国大地保险公司开业仪式(照片提供:阮凯丰)
Inauguration of China Continent P&C Insurance Co.

中国再保险公司经过重组，改制为中国再保险（集团）公司。集团公司主要经营存续期间的法定分保业务、资金运用及一些政策性业务和特殊风险业务等。集团公司作为主发起人，吸收境外资本，发起设立中国大地财产保险股份有限公司、中国财产再保险股份有限公司、中国人寿再保险股份有限公司。2003年12月22日，中国再保险（集团）公司、中国财产再保险股份有限公司和中国人寿再保险股份有限公司正式成立。

2003年10月20日，由中国再保险集团公司以控股60%作为主发起人发起设立的中国大地财产保险股份有限公司在上海挂牌成立，成为我国第一家由国有保险公司作为主发起人，吸收境内外多个投资人共同设立的保险公司。中再集团总经理戴凤举出任中国大地保险公司董事长，总裁由原中国再保险公司上海分公司总经理蒋明担任。中国大地保险在设立过程中，引进了9家境内外投资者。境外股东包括：亚洲联合企业公司、新鸿基地产保险公司、香港亚洲保险公司、泰国盘古大众保险公司、印度尼西亚保险公司，共占比10%。境内投资者中，太太药业以人民币1元/股的价格认购5000万股，占5%的股份，位列第四大股东。开业一年后，中国大地保险已经有22家分公司在全国开业，保费收入突破15亿元大关，市场占有率达到1.36%，在中资产险公司中排名第八位。

2004年，中再集团及下属再保、直保子公司共实现保费收入205.95亿元，同比增长5.71%。截至2004年底，中再集团的资产总额达到261.79亿元，同比增长6.7%，集团全系统资金运用余额达到了225亿元。

China Reinsurance Corporation, via reorganization, was transformed into China Reinsurance (Group) Corporation, which, by absorbing overseas capital, formally established China Contoinent Property & Casualty Co., Ltd., China Property Reinsurance Co., Ltd., and China Life Reinsurance Co., Ltd. On December 22, 2003. After one year's operation, China Contoinent Property & Casualty Insurance has had 22 branches operating business throughout China, with premium income exceeding 1.5 billion yuan and a market share of 1.36 per cent, ranking the 8th among Sino-funded property insurers.

二十二、政策性保险公司浮出水面

Policy-Support Insurer Emerged

政策性保险体制改革主要是在出口信用保险方面的突破。恢复国内保险业以后，中国人民保险公司和中国进出口银行同时经营出口信用保险业务。1997年全国金融工作会议决定，组建统一的政策性出口信用保险经营机构。1997年7月，《国务院批转整顿保险业工作小组保险业整顿与改革方案的通知》提出，改革出口信用保险体制，在中国人民保险公司和中国进出口银行出口信用保险部的基础上组建统一的政策性出口信用保险公司，其业务由保监会统一监管。2001年12月，中国出口信用保险公司正式成立，这是我国第一家政策性保险公司，标志着我国政策性保险体制改革取得重大进展。

Restructuring of policy-support insurance has gained breakthrough mainly in aspect of export credit insurance. After the recovery of China's domestic insurance, PICC and China Import & Export Bank simultaneously operated export credit insurance business. The whole country's Finance Work Conference in 1997 determined to organize a united policy-support export credit insurer. China Export and Credit Insurance Corporation (Sinosure) was formally founded on December 2001.

2003年，中国出口信用保险公司实现保险金额57.1亿美元，占我国一般贸易出口额的比重达到3.14%，累计保费收入9.96亿元人民币，支付赔款8.07亿元人民币。截至2003年底，公司总资产40亿元人民币，负债率42%，资产状况良好。图为中国出口信用保险公司领导班子合影，唐若昕总经理（中）、段景泉副总经理（右二）、曹圃副总经理（左二）、梁志东副总经理（右一）、刘康信纪委书记（左一）。

Leadership of Sinosure: president Tang Ruoxin (M); vice president Duan Jingquan (R2); vice president Cao Pu (L2); vice president Liang Zhidong (R1); secretary general of the Commission for Disciplinary Inspection Liu Kangxin (L1)

十六届三中全会明确提出要探索建立政策性农业保险制度，2003年以来，保监会进行了多次的深入调研，批准筹备设立专业性农业保险公司。

The 3rd Session of the 16th National Party Congress definitely brought forward to explore setting up policy-support agriculture insurance system and since 2003, the CIRC has carried out times of deep researches for approving preparation of specialized agriculture insurance company.

2004年9月17日，全国首家服务于"三农"的农业保险公司上海安信农业保险股份有限公司挂牌成立，这是全国首家专业农业保险公司，它以保险手段来转移和化解农业生产风险，增强抗御自然灾害的能力，为发展农村经济、保障农民生活撑起更有力的保护伞。在安信的成立大会上，安信的第一份保险单正式签下，上海市畜牧办公室代表全市22万户家禽专业养殖户，为8000多万只家禽上了第一份保险。图为公司董事长兼总经理李中宁（左二）、监事长苏仲（右二）、副董事长吴学锋（右一）、副总经理周伟国（左一）在公司开业典礼上。（照片提供：孙环民）。

On September 17, 2004, Chinese first agro insurer Shanghai Anxin Agriculture Insurance Co., Ltd. was founded to serve agriculture, farmers, and countryside.

Anxin's board chairman/general manager Li Zhongning (L2), supervisor general Su Zhong (R2), vice board chairman Wu Xuefeng (R1), deputy general manager Zhou Weiguo (L1) at the open ceremony of Anxin

全国首家相互农险公司——阳光农业相互保险公司，于2005年1月11日在黑龙江正式挂牌开业，标志着我国农业保险的发展迈出了重要一步。开业当日，阳光保险公司与中国再保险公司签署了再保合作框架协议，并分别与北大荒农业股份有限公司、黑龙江农垦九三奶牛协会签署938万亩粮食作物和5000头奶牛保险协议。（照片提供：孙振军）

Inauguration of Sun Agriculture Insurance in 2005.

二十三、保险资金入市

Insurance Capital Directly Enters Stock Market

自1980年国内保险业务恢复以来，我国保险资金运用可划分为三个阶段。第一阶段（1980－1987），资金运用还没有成为保险经营工作的主要方面，保险公司的资金基本上进入银行，形成银行存款。第二阶段（1987－1995），保险资金运用渠道全面放开，在投资权限分散、经验缺乏、管理滞后等情况下，保险资金广泛进入房地产、有价证券、信托业，形成了大量的不良资产。据不完全统计，仅1992年、1993年经济过热时期因保险业资金运用形成的不良资产就达100多亿元。第三阶段（1995年至今），表现为资金运用的力度和资金运用工作管理力度都不断加大。1998年10月，人民银行允许保险公司参与银行间债券市场从事现券交易，这使得国债市场现券空间打开。1999年5月，经国务院批准，保险公司可以在中国保监会的批复的额度内购买信用评级在AA+以上的中央企业债券，这使得高等级企业债券市场放开。1999年5月，《保险公司购买中央企业债券管理办法》颁布，规定保险公司购买的企业债券余额按成本价格计算不得超过公司上月末总资产的10%。1999年8月，保险公司获准进行银行间同业市场的回购交易，标志着银行国债回购市场对保险公司开放。1999年10月，中国人民银行批复同意商业银行可同保险公司办理协议存款，最低起存额3000万元，最低期限5年，利率由双方商定，这使得保险公司获准突破利率管制规定。1999年10月，《保险公司投资证券投资基金管理执行办法》颁布，标志着证券投资基金市场对保险公司开放，保险资金“间接入市”。2001年3月，保监会批准平安等三家寿险公司投资连结型保险帐户资金在投资基金上的投资比例从30%放宽到100%，是对保险投资的进一步开放与鼓励。2001年3月，保监会批复同意保险公司购买电信通迅类企业债。

至此，保险公司已成为资本市场主要的机构投资者，为资本市场的发展和稳定发挥了积极作用。2003年，我国保险资金运用实现收益235.03亿元，资金收益率为2.68%。

2004年10月24日，经国务院批准，中国保险监督管理委员会、中国证券监督管理委员会联合发布并实施《保险机构投资者股票投资管理暂行办法》。这标志着我国保险资金首次获准直接投资股票市场。

Since China's domestic insurance has been recovered, Chinese insurance capital applying can be divided into three phases: in the earliest (1980 – 1987), capital using hadn't been a major part in insurance operation and insurers' capital was basically put into banks, forming bank deposits; in the second period (1987 – 1995), the channels for insurance capital applying had been roundly loosened and widely flowed into real estate, securities, and entrusting, resulting in a large amount of non-performing assets; in the third stage (1995 so far), the development is mainly reflected in the constant strengthening in the applying ways and management of the capital, while insurers have been the main institutional investors in capital market.

2003年底我国保险资金投资渠道一览(资金总余额8739亿元人民币)

Investment Channels of Chinese Insurance Capital in Late 2003
(balance totaled 873.9 billion yuan RMB)

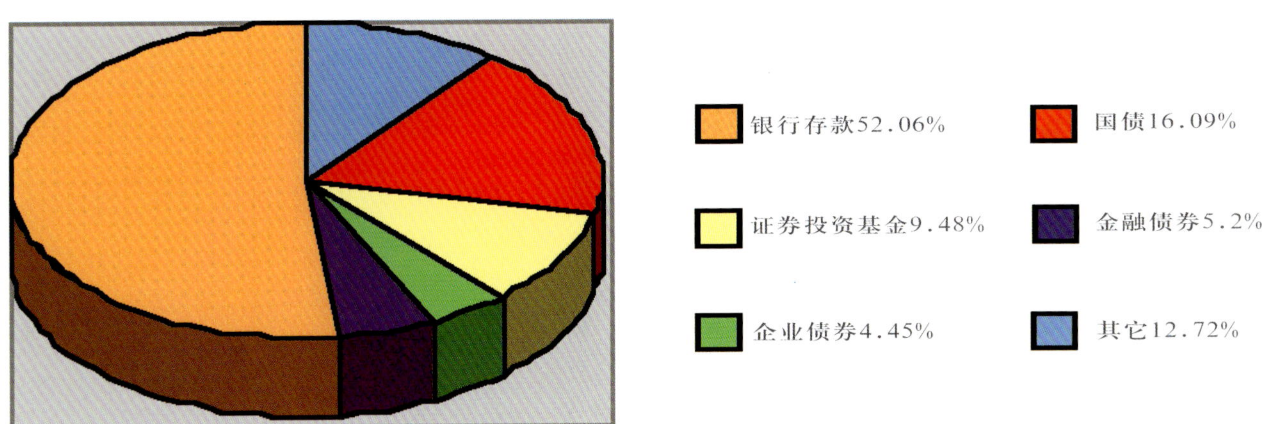

专业化保险资产管理公司现身

Beginning of Specialized Insurance Assets Management Company

保险资金的运用需要有质的提高，以现在国内保险公司内设投资部门的组织架构，显然很难满足保险资金专业化投资的需要。而保险资产管理公司的成立，提供了保险资金运用的有效平台，使保险自身业务和资金运用业务成为保险业发展的两个重要支柱。

2004年4、5月，《保险资产管理公司管理暂行规定》和《保险资金运用风险控制指引》发布，自2004年6月1日起正式实施。《规定》明确了保险资产管理公司的设立、变更和终止，经营范围和经营规则，风险控制和监督管理。《指引》对保险公司和保险资产管理公司建立运营规范、管理高效的保险资金运用风险控制体系，制定完善的保险资金运用风险控制制度提出了具体要求，被业内视为出台有关保险资金直接投资股票、投资境外资本市场、参与重大基础建设项目等投资管理细则的前奏。

中国保监会副主席吴小平曾在保险资金运用国际研讨会上指出，预计到2005年年底，中国保险市场上将一共成立6–9家保险资产管理公司，它们将逐步成为保险资产管理的主导力量。据中国保监会统计数据，截至2004年底，我国保险资产总额达到1.18万亿，保险资金运用余额达到1.03万亿元，保险资产管理已成为影响保险市场发展的重要因素。

2003年至2005年，中国人保、中国人寿、中国再保险和华泰保险的资金管理公司相继成立和获批。

Along with the gradual expansion of group members of new institutions like insurance assets management companies, the specialized organizing mode of insurance capital applying entity in China has started to appear.

Provisional Rules on Insurance Assets Management Company and *Instruction for Risk Control of Insurance Capital Applying* have been issued in April and May 2004 respectively and officially put into effect since June 1, 2004.

From 2003 to 2005, PICC, China Life, China Re, and Huatai Insurance, with the approval, set up their assets management companies in succession.

中国人保资产管理有限公司是国内首家保险资产管理有限公司，2003年7月在北京成立，注册资本金一亿元。人保资产管理公司、人保股份公司与中国银行曾进行过多次沟通，确定由中国银行作为托管银行，并分别签订了托管协议，确立了三方资产委托管理关系，及时办理了投资账户变更和资产移交等工作，使保险资金运用的安全性有了制度保障。经过一年多的运作，人保资产已经成为人保控股集中统一的资金运用平台，探索出一种适合保险资金专业化运作的新机制。2003年，按照香港会计准则核算，人保资产实现投资收益10.16亿元，综合收益率达到5.67%。2004年6月18日，中国人保资产管理有限公司迁至上海。

As the first insurance assets management company, PICC Assets Management Co., Ltd. was founded in July 2003 in Beijing, with registered capital of 100 million yuan. China Life Assets Management Co., Ltd., which is jointly funded by China Life Insurance (Group) Company and China Life Insurance Co., Ltd., was founded on June 28, 2004 in Beijing.

2004年6月28日，由中国人寿保险(集团)公司和中国人寿保险股份有限公司共同出资设立的中国人寿资产管理有限公司在北京揭牌成立。中国人寿资产管理有限公司注册资金为8亿元，管理的资产超过4000亿元，是中国内地最大的保险资产管理公司，也是中国内地资本市场最大的机构投资者。按这家公司高达8亿元的注册资本金来算，它未来受托管理的资产将不受额度限制。

With a registered capital of over 800 million yuan, China Life Insurance Assets Management manages assets valuing over 400 billion yuan, hence it the biggest insurance assets custodian in inland China, plus it's also the biggest institutional investor in the Chinese domestic capital market.

中再资产管理公司是由中国再保险(集团)公司发起设立，6家公司共同出资组建的，注册资金2亿元。中国再保险(集团)公司占该公司50.1%股份，瑞士再保险资产管理(亚洲)有限公司占该公司股比是10%，而中再集团下属三家成员公司，即中国财产再保险股份有限公司、中国人寿再保险股份有限公司、中国大地财产保险股份有限公司则分别拥有该公司10%股份，其余9.9%的股份则被来自上海的民营企业福禧投资控股有限公司持有。图为2005年2月28日，国内首家外资参股的保险资产管理公司——中再资产管理股份有限公司挂牌，中国再保险(集团)公司总经理戴凤举担任该公司董事长。(照片提供：仝春健)

On February 28, 2005, Chinese first inland insurance assets management company with foreign share China Reinsurance Assets Management Co., Ltd. opened.

二十四、海外保险机构的发展

Development of Chinese Insurers Abroad

我国海外保险事业的发展，划分为两个阶段，即解放前旧中国半封建半殖民地性质的阶段和解放后新中国社会主义性质的阶段。

早在20世纪30年代，中国银行投资创建的中国保险有限公司，由金城银行创办的太平保险有限公司开始向香港地区及东南亚地区开设机构。接着上海民安产物保险有限公司也在香港开设分公司。这些公司即构成了现在我国海外保险机构的主体。

建国以后，这些海外的保险公司都回到了祖国的怀抱，日益发挥着为祖国的经济繁荣提供保险服务和积累外汇资金的巨大作用，特别是在港澳地区，中资保险集团已成为一支不可忽视的力量。

中国保险（控股）有限公司（简称中国保险）前身为中国保险股份有限公司，1931年成立于上海。1949年中国人民保险公司成立后，中国保险成为中国人民保险公司的全资附属公司，并停办了境内保险业务，专营境外业务。1992年，中国人民保险公司成立了香港中国保险（集团）有限公司（简称香港中保集团），包括香港民安保险有限公司、太平保险香港分公司在内的港澳地区附属机构统一划归香港中保集团管理。1996年，中国人民保险公司改组为中国人民保险（集团）公司。1998年，根据国务院决定，中国人民保险（集团）公司撤销，其海外经营性机构划归中国保险；中国保险与香港中保集团实行"两块牌子、一套班子"的管理模式。

2002年8月20日，中国保险更名为中国保险（控股）有限公司，成为中国保险业第一家控股集团公司。为适应控股集团职能要求，在组建之初，中国保险采用重组合并、资本运作等措施，优化资源配置，集保险、证券、资产管理、信托投资于一体，完善了控股公司的框架结构。完成了保险主业的机构重组。重组了香港地区的产险资源，将中国保险香港分公司和太平保险香港分公司并入香港民安保险有限公司，合并后的香港民安保险成为香港地区最大的财产险公司之一；对新加坡的两家分支机构进行重组，将太平保险新加坡分公司并入中国保险新加坡分公司，并随后将后者子公司化。2000年2月，中国保险以中国国际再保险有限公司和华夏再保险顾问有限公司为主体，成立了中保国际控股有限公司，并于同年6月在香港联合交易所挂牌上市，成为中国保险业的第一家上市公司，构筑了中国保险资本运作的平台，扩大了中国保险对外的影响。通过一系列成功的资本运作，中国保险共筹集资金30亿港元，并进一步抓住利率处于低位的机遇，于2003年成功发行了1.75亿美元的10年期固定利率债券，开创了中资保险公司在国际市场融资发债的先河。

1964年6月28日周恩来总理接见中国保险股份有限公司代表
Premier Zhou Enlai with delegates of China Insurance Co. in 1964

中国保险董事长兼总经理杨超(左五)在香港联合交易所中保国际控股上市仪式上与嘉宾合影。(2000年6月29日)

China Insurance's board chairman/manager director Yang Chao (L5) with honorable guests at the listing ceremony of CIIH at Hong Kong Stock Exchange

2001年，经国务院同意，保监会批准，太平人寿和太平保险在国内成功复业。2004年，太平保险6家仅仅成立两三年的分公司实现了盈利；太平人寿更是被惠誉国际评级为BBB+，是国内保险企业中第一家由国际知名评级机构进行评级的公司，被中国保监会誉为中国保险业的一颗新星。截至2004年底，太平人寿在全国主要省市共建立二级机构22家，三级和四级机构110多家；太平保险共建立二级机构19家，三级和四级机构87家。

2004年，太平养老保险股份有限公司成立，成为第一批获保监会批准的企业年金试点单位，标志着中国保险在企业年金领域的探索和经营取得了实质性的突破。

香港民安保险有限公司成立五十五周年晚宴

Banquet for the 55th anniversary of Hong Kong Min An Insurance Co.

香港特别行政区行政长官董建华先生与中国保险董事长兼总经理杨超在庆祝特区成立五周年升旗仪式后合影

Hong Kong Special Administrative Region Chief Dong Jiahua with Yang Chao after the flag-raising ceremony for the 5th anniversary of the special zone

China's overseas insurance has experienced two periods in its development, i.e., the former period with the character of semi-feudal & semi-colony in old China and the later featuring socialism in new China.

In early 1930's, China Insurance Co., Ltd. founded by Bank of China, Taiping Insurance Co., Ltd. founded by Jincheng Bank, and Shanghai Min An Property Insurance Co., Ltd. made up of principal part of China's overseas insurance. China Insurance (Holding) Co., Ltd. (abbreviated as China Insurance) who, after the founding the PICC in 1949, became the whole-funded affiliated company to PICC via socialistic reform and, its inland insurance business was stopped but was specialized in overseas operation. On August 20, 2002, China Insurance was renamed as China Insurance (Holding) Co., Ltd., forming the first shareholding group company in China. In 2001, Taiping Life and Taiping Insurance succeeded in recovering domestic business with the approval from the State Council and the CIRC. In 2004, Taiping Endowment Insurance Co., Ltd was founded, which is among the first pilot units approved by the CIRC to run corporate annuity, making the substantial breakthrough in the exploration and operation of Chinese insurance annuity.

中国保监会主席吴定富和中国保险董事长兼总经理杨超在太平75周年图片展开幕仪式上

CIRC's chairman Wu Dingfu with China Insurance Co.'s board chairman/managing director Yang Chao at the inauguration of Min An

太平人寿保险有限公司在上海召开复业新闻发布会

News release conference on business recovery by Taiping Life in Shanghai

香港中环，中保集团大厦

Building of People's Insurance (Group) Company of China, Central Ring, Hong Kong

二十五、保险中介市场的发展

Development of Chinese Insurance Intermediary Market

1988年以前我国保险市场由人保公司独家经营，国内还没有专门的保险经纪机构。随着外商投资企业的增多和外国保险公司进入我国保险市场，运用保险经纪人进行展业成为保险业一种新的尝试。1993年6月，中国人民银行深圳分行和深圳市工商局分别批准了16家保险经纪公司开业。同时，国际上一些著名的保险经纪人看好中国保险市场，纷纷在华开设代表处，如威达信、怡安等。1993年5月，英国最大的保险经纪公司塞奇维克集团被批准设立“塞奇维克保险与风险咨询有限公司”，为外商投资企业提供服务。

1995年《保险法》颁布，第一次以法律形式承认了保险经纪人在我国保险市场的合法地位。1999年，保监会对保险中介市场进行了全面清理整顿工作，重点查处非法“地下保险经纪人”。在这次清理中，违规经营的塞奇维克中国公司被停业整顿三个月。

1999年5月15日，中国保监会首次举行保险经纪人资格考试，设两门科目：《财政金融知识》和《保险理论与实务》。共有4800人参加考试，162人两门科目合格。这162人成为我国首批获得保险经纪资格的保险经纪人。

首次保险经纪资格考试举行

本报讯【记者 刘景鹏】1999年保险经纪资格考试于5月15日举行。

推进保险市场竞争机制的形成发挥积极的作用。

唐运祥着重指出，中国保

《保险经纪人管理规定(试行)》，保护合法保险经纪行为，打击非法保险经纪活动，进一

风险管理咨询服务（中国）有限公司停业整顿，这是一个明确的信息：中国加大了

1999年5月15日，我国首次举行保险经纪资格考试。

A news report on the first exam for the certificate of insurance brokers in 1999.

Before 1988, Chinese insurance market had the exclusive operator PICC, without specialized insurance brokerage organ yet. In June 1996, 16 insurance brokers had been approved to open by the PBOC Shenzhen Branch and Shenzhen's Administration for Industry and Commerce respectively; meanwhile, some international well-known insurance brokers set up representative offices in China one after another, such as Marsh & McLennan and Aon, etc.

The *Insurance Law* promulgated in 1995, for the first time, legally recognizes the legal position of insurance broker in China insurance market.

2001年3月23日，中国第一家全国性、综合性的保险公估机构——方中保险公估有限公司在广州正式开业。

Inauguration of Chinese first nationwide, comprehensive insurance loss assessor: Guangdong Fangzhong Insurance Surveyors & Loss Adjusters Co. in 2001

从1999年底开始，我国保险经纪人进入快速发展阶段。1999年12月16日，中国保监会批准北京江泰、上海东大、广州长城三家全国性保险经纪公司筹建。2000年6月至7月，三家公司相继成立。到2000年底，保监会在全国共批设保险经纪公司8家。

上世纪90年代初，各保险公司为了赢得市场主动，在面临复杂的理赔项目时常聘请相关技术专家参加定损工作。而一些保户也开始求助于理赔中介机构来获得公正、公平的保险赔付，在这种社会需求下，我国保险公估业开始起步。1990年在内蒙古自治区成立的"保险理赔公估技术服务中心"是我国第一家商业保险公估组织。

从1993年开始，我国保险公估业快速发展。1993年3月18日，上海成立了东方公估行，1994年天津成立了"北方公估行"，杭州成立了"浙江公估行"，广州成立了"平量行顾问有限公司"，深圳成立了"民太安保险公估有限公司"等。2000年和2001年，保监会先后发布《保险公估人管理规定（试行）》、《保险公估机构管理规定》，奠定了保险公估的法律基础。

截至2004年底，我国通过保险中介渠道的保费收入为2902.7亿元，占全国总保费的67.2%。2004年底，我国共有保险代理机构932家、经纪机构199家、公估机构181家。

From later 1999, Chinese insurance brokerage has entered a rapid developing stage. On December 16, 1999, the CIRC authorized the preparation of the three countrywide insurance brokers: Jiangtai in Beijing, Dongda in Shanghai, and Great Wall in Guangzhou, which had been established in succession from June to July 2000 and by late 2000, 8 insurance brokers had been approved by the commission to found. Since 1993, Chinese insurance surveying & loss adjusting has initiated to make a rapid progress. Shanghai Oriental Surveying & Adjusting Co. was founded in Shanghai on March 18, 1993, following which a batch of loss assessors was set up in the next year.

2000年6月16日，中国第一家保险经纪公司——江泰保险经纪有限公司在北京人民大会堂隆重举行开业典礼，全国人大副委员长王光英应邀出席，并亲自为江泰揭牌。公司目前拥有员工600人，在全国40多个城市建立了分公司及服务网点。截止2003年底，江泰的品牌客户已发展到1800多家。

Inauguration of Guangdong Fangzhong Insurance Surveyors & Loss Adjusters Co. in 2001

二十六、保险教育状况
Chinese Insurance Education Market

从严格意义上说，中国保险教育培训工作的真正起步还是在1949年新中国成立之后。当时随着国民经济的恢复和不断发展，对保险人才的需求量越来越大，中国人民大学、南开大学、中央财政金融学院等高校先后开设了金融保险专业。1958年停办保险业务后，保险教育培训工作停顿下来。1968年经国务院批准重新开办国际保险业务后，中国对外贸易学院开始招收保险专业学生。十一届三中全会后，国内保险业务开始逐步恢复，到1984年，中国人民保险公司在全国各省、市、自治区、直辖市的分支机构全面开办业务，对人才的需求量急速增加。中国人民保险公司出资在全国17所高校招收保险专业生、专科学生，并经教育部批准独家开办了中国保险管理干部学院、哈尔滨保险学校、南昌保险学校、成都保险学校和广州保险学校。中国的保险教育由此得到迅速发展，形成了保险专业人才的梯次培养格局。

1998年11月18日中国保险监督管理委员会成立，为中国保险教育培训事业的发展提供了更加广阔的发展空间，保险教育培训本身也得到进一步细化和裂变。到目前为止，全国已有近百所高校开设了保险专业，年招生500人左右，很多院校还开始培养硕士研究生以上学历的高级人才。社会力量也在保险岗位培训、险种培训、营销团队培训等方面发挥着积极作用。

“中国保险教育论坛”于2003年由南开大学、武汉大学和西南财经大学共同发起成立，其宗旨是加强保险交流，提高保险教学与科研水平，同时在保险学术界与实务界之间搭起一座桥梁，为中国保险业的发展提供理论支持。

Strictly speaking, Chinese insurance educational and training work has been really started since the foundation of the PRC in 1949, as China Renmin University, Nankai University, and Central University of Finance and Economy, etc. had opened specialties of finance and insurance. However in 1958, the work had been stopped as a result of the closed-down insurance business.

After the recovery of domestic insurance, PICC funded 17 colleges and universities to recruit students for specialized courses and with the Ministry of Education's approval, PICC exclusively opened China Insurance Managerial Cadre College and Insurance Schools in Harbin, Nanchang, Chengdu, and Guangzhou. On November 18, 1998, the CIRC was founded, bringing much broader space for the development of Chinese insurance education and training.

二十七、中国保险业发展新思路

New Ideology of Chinese Insurance

2002年10月，吴定富出任中国保监会主席。

从2003年起，中国保险业有了新的发展思路：把一切保险业的发展都坚定地融入国民经济的发展大局中。

吴定富认为，为适应经济社会发展和全面建设小康社会的需要，保险业必须加快发展。一是要把保险业做大，提高保险覆盖面。发达国家20%的灾害损失是由保险公司赔偿的，而在中国，财政救济还是弥补经济损失的主要方式，保险还远没有发挥其应有的作用。保险业如果不加快发展，为国民经济和社会发展全局服务就只能是一句空话。二是要把保险业做强。大是速度和规模，强是质量和效益。没有大，谈不上强；不能做强，大也没有意义。加快保险业的发展并不是不要风险控制，而是在加快发展的同时加强和改善监管，坚持科学发展观，实现规模、效益、速度的统一，保持持续快速健康协调的发展。特别是要加强全行业的诚信建设，诚信是保险业的生命线，越是加快发展，越要讲诚信。

吴定富首次提出保险的三项功能：社会管理、经济补偿、资金融通。从经济社会发展全局的高度将保险业从片面强调自身发展的窠臼中解放出来，赋予保险新的、更广阔的内涵。

吴定富还提出了保险业发展的初级阶段论：初级阶段的中国保险业，主要矛盾仍然是国民经济社会的快速发展、人民生活水平的迅速提高对保险业的需求与保险业发展滞后的矛盾。保险业必须发展得更快，才能与国民经济的发展水平相适应，而全面建设小康的目标正给保险业发展以难得的历史机遇。

中国保监会主席吴定富（照片提供：王健）
Wu Dingfu, chairman of the CIRC

	2002年	2004年	增长率
保费收入	3053.1亿元	4318.1亿元	41.4%
保险总资产	6494.1亿元	11853.6亿元	82.5%
资金运用余额	5799.3亿元	11249.8亿元	93.9%
市场主体	54家	90家	66.7%
专业中介机构	63家	1298家	1960.3%
专业保险公司	0家	5家	500%
国有公司股改	0家	3家	300%
保险深度	3%	3.4%	13.3%
保险密度	237.6元	332元	39.7%
保险资金投资渠道	存款、国债、金融债券、投资基金	可直接进入股市等渠道	
对外开放地域	上海、广州、深圳、大连、佛山	取消地域限制	

吴定富(左二)在上海安信农业保险公司调研(照片提供:孙环民)
Wu Dingfu (L2) investigating at Shanghai Anxin Agriculture Insurance Co., Ltd.

2003年起,中国保险业接连发生着具有历史意义的变革:困扰保险业多年的资金运用渠道狭窄问题取得重大进展,保险资金可以直接入市了;国有企业的股份制改革取得突破,中国人保、人寿、再保三家公司股份制改革圆满结束;中国人保和中国人寿的股份公司相继在香港和纽约成功上市,为国内保险业引来巨额境外资本;三家国有公司的资产管理公司相继建立,为进一步提高保险资金运用效率打下基础;市场主体增加,市场竞争加剧,将中介机构的审批纳入正常程序,专业保险公司的分支机构经营区域也进一步拓宽,为打破垄断创造了条件;偿付能力监管迈出实质性步伐,发布《保险公司偿付能力监管规定》。

同时,吴定富务实的工作作风正在影响着各级监管队伍,各地保监办大兴调研之风。在他的号召下,各地保监办的官员主动向当地政府汇报工作,为保险业创造了积极的社会氛围。

"用开放进取的精神,看待目前存在的问题,争取用20年的时间做大做强中国保险业,我们要做现代中国保险市场的奠基人。"吴定富的信念给中国保险业带来全新的局面。

Substantial changes have occurred in China insurance since 2003 so far. Not only the reform of state-owned enterprises, as a matter of fact, Wu Dingfu who took the post of chairman of the CIRC in October 2002 integrated entire development of insurance into the major situation of the development of the national economy, lifting the height and depth of insurance development to a new level, with the new ideology on the sector's evolution.

Wu considers insurance must be accelerated to develop to meet the needs from the development of economy and society and roundly construction of Xiaokang (ideal society). Firstly, insurance should be built big to enhance the insurance coverage; secondly, insurance should be powerful. The "big" refers to speed and scale and the "powerful" carries quality and efficiency. Without "big", without "powerful"; if not powerful, the "big" has no significance.

二十八、中国保险业和WTO承诺

China Insurance under the Commitments for WTO Accession

2001年底，我国正式加入国际世贸组织。我国加入世贸组织关于保险业的对外承诺主要内容有：

经营区域：加入时，保险业对外开放上海、广州、大连、深圳和佛山；加入后2年内，开放北京、成都、重庆、福州、苏州、厦门、宁波、沈阳、武汉和天津；加入后3年内，取消地域限制。

业务范围：加入时，允许合资寿险公司向外国公民和中国公民提供个人（非团体）寿险业务；允许外国非寿险公司跨境从事国际海运、航空和运输保险业务，允许外国非寿险公司设立的分公司或合资公司从事没有地域限制的“统括保单”和大型商业险保险业务，允许提供境外企业的非寿险业务，在华外商投资企业的财产险，与之相关的责任险和信用服务；允许外国保险公司以分公司、合资公司或独资子公司的形式提供寿险和非寿险的再保险业务，但不允许经营法定保险业务；允许外国保险经纪公司跨境从事大型商业险经纪，国际海运、航空和运输保险经纪及再保险经纪业务，允许外国保险经纪公司设立的合资公司从事大型商业险经纪、再保险经纪以及国际海运、航空和运输及其再保险经纪业务，同时，在国民待遇的基础上提供“统括保单”经纪业务。

加入后2年内，允许外国非寿险公司设立的分公司，合资公司和独资子公司向外国和中国客户提供全面的非寿险服务。

加入后3年内，允许合资寿险公司向中国公民和外国公民提供健康险、团体险和养老金、年金服务。

公司组织形式：加入时，允许外国寿险公司设立合资公司，外资比例不超过50%，外方可以自由选择合资伙伴；允许外国非寿险公司设立分公司或合资公司，外资比例可以达到51%；允许外国保险公司以分公司、合资公司或独资子公司的形式提供寿险和非寿险的再保险业务；允许外国保险经纪公司设立合资公司，外资比例可达50%。

加入后2年内，允许外国非寿险公司设立独资子公司。

加入后3年内，合资经纪公司外资比例不超过51%。

2000年5月19日，中欧双边入世谈判结束。（新华社发）
Sino—Europe WTO—Accession negotiation succeed in 2000

2001年11月11日中国加入世贸组织签字仪式在卡塔尔多哈举行
Signing Ceremony on China's Accession to the WTO in Doha 2001

2001年11月22日中国保监会召开高峰会议，介绍入世谈判中有关保险的内容。
China's WTO Insurance Summit in 2001 introducing related insurance matters concerned in WTO-accession negotiation

2001年11月22日入世谈判组成员孟昭亿在高峰会上介绍中国保险业的有关承诺情况
Meng Zhaoyi introducing relevant commitments fulfilled by China insurance at the China Annual Summit in 2001

加入后5年内，允许外国经纪公司设立外商独资子公司。

法定分保：加入时，外资保险公司必须就非寿险、个人事故和健康险的基本风险的所有业务向一家指定的中国再保险公司进行20%的分保；加入后1年内，分保比例为15%；加入后2年内，分保比例为10%；加入后3年内，分保比例为5%；加入后4年内，取消强制分保。

外资公司设立条件：对外国保险公司和外国经纪公司营业许可的发放不设经济需求测试或许可数量限制。对外国保险公司发放营业许可的设立条件为：(1)投资者应为在WTO成员境内有超过30年经营历史的外国保险公司；(2)必须在中国设立代表处连续2年；(3)在提出申请前一年的年末总资产不低于50亿美元。

加入时，对外国保险经纪公司发放营业许可的设立条件为最低年末总资产为5亿美元，其他条件与寿险公司相同。加入后1年内为4亿美元，加入后2年内为3亿美元，加入后4年内为2亿美元。

2004年12月11日，中国保监会发布公告：根据中国入世承诺，自即日起，允许外资寿险公司提供健康险、团体险、养老金/年金险业务，取消对设立外资保险机构的地域限制，设立合资经纪公司的外资股比可至51%。这标志着中国保险业已经进入深度开放期。中国保险业正在以更加积极的姿态，张开双臂，拥抱世界。

In late 2001, China officially entered WTO, with main contents of commitments relevant with insurance. In terms of insurance operating regions, when entering WTO, Shanghai, Guangzhou, Dalian, Shenzhen, and Foshanin will be opened to outside world; within two years after the accession, Beijing, Chengdu, Chongqing, Fuzhou, Suzhou, Xiamen, Ningbo, Shenyang, Wuhan, and Tianjin will follow to open; within three years of the entrance, the geographical restriction will be deregulated.

On November 11, 2004, the CIRC released the announcement: in accordance to China's commitments to the WTO accession, from the very day, foreign life insurers are approved to provide health, group, endowment/annuity insurance; regional restriction is cancelled for establishing foreign insurance institutions; the proportion of foreign share in a joint venture of brokerage company to be founded can be up to 51 per cent, signing China insurance has entered a deep opening period.

二十九、中国保险第一传媒：《中国保险报》

China Insurance News: the Top Media of Chinese Insurance

1993年初，为适应中国保险市场迅速发展的需要，在中国保险市场占有特殊地位的中国人民保险公司开始筹备创立中国保险报社。1994年1月5日，中国保险业惟一公开发行的报纸——《中国保险报》正式创刊。

中国保险监督管理委员会成立后，《中国保险报》成为该会指定披露保险信息的报纸。

十一年来，《中国保险报》追赶保险市场快速发展的脚步，全程记录了中国保险业巨大变化，在业内产生了广泛的影响力，奠定了其中国保险业第一传媒的地位。

2004年，为进一步做大做强中国保险第一传媒，中国保险报社开始实行股份制改造。中国再保险（集团）公司作为中国保险报社的主管单位，会同中国人寿保险（集团）公司、北京畅想传媒投资集团有限公司、福禧投资控股有限公司、中国人保控股公司共同发起设立了中国保险报业股份有限公司，注册资本1亿元。

2005年4月18日，中国保险报业股份有限公司正式开业，成为中国第一家整体实行股份制的新闻机构。

In early 1993, PICC who dominates Chinese property insurance market began to prepare China Insurance News Press Office (CINPO), to meet the need of the fast developing Chinese insurance market. Since January 5, 1994, *China Insurance News* (*CIN*), the unique publicly issued newspaper of Chinese insurance, has been formally published.

After the foundation of the CIRC, *CIN* has been appointed by the commission to publish insurance news.

For 11 years, keeping up with the fast pace of insurance market, *CIN* has roundly recorded the great changes in Chinese insurance, produced widely influence in the sector, which laid the foundation for the paper to be the top media in Chinese insurance.

To further build up the media, *CIN*, in 2004, started to go on a stock-system reform. As the governing body of CINPO, China Reinsurance (Group) Company jointly launched China Insurance Media Corporation (CIMC) (with a registered capital of 100 million yaun RMB) with China Life Insurance (Group) Company, Beijing Changxiang Media Investment Group Company, Fuxi Investment Holding Co., Ltd. and PICC Holding Company.

Starting business from April 18, 2005, CIMC has been the first news institution run under stock system in China.

中国保险报业股份有限公司董事会
Directorate of China Insurance Media Company Limited

2005年4月18日，国家新闻出版总署署长石宗源（右一）、中国保监会主席吴定富为中国保险报业股份有限公司揭牌。（照片提供：王健）

Chief of the General Administration of Press and Publication Shizongyuan (R) with CIRC chairman Wu Dingfu at the unveiling ceremony of the CIMC.

中国保险报业股份有限公司股东简介：

中国再保险（集团）公司：是经国务院同意和中国报监会批准，于2003年成立的国有再保险集团公司，注册地点北京，注册资本为39亿元人民币。公司履行国家再保险公司职能，在中国再保险市场发挥着主渠道作用。

中国人寿保险（集团）公司：是国家大型金融保险企业，总部设在北京。中国人寿保险（集团）公司及其子公司构成了我国最大的商业保险集团。在《财富》杂志评选的2002年世界500强中，中国人寿位居290位，在中国500强排名中，中国人寿位居第6位。

北京畅想传媒投资集团：由高等教育出版社将其经营性业务与资产重组整合，联合5家企业共同发起设立的投资性企业集团，2004年9月成立，注册资本2亿元。高等教育出版社创立于1954年，是国内规模最大、综合实力最强的出版社。

福禧投资控股有限公司：是一家经国家工商总局批准，注册在上海的大型民营投资公司，是目前上海市规模最大的民营投资公司之一。2002年7月，公司凭借实力及诚信获得中国工商银行100亿元综合授信额度，这是目前国内民营企业获得的单笔最大授信。

中国人保控股公司：是1949年成立的、中国内地经营历史最悠久的保险企业——中国人民保险公司变更而来的，注册资本155亿元人民币。中国人保控股公司采用国际通行的金融控股公司模式，充分享有金融控股公司优势，代表国家投资并持有上市公司和其他金融保险机构的股份，经营管理存续资产。

Based on its predecessor China Insurance News Press Office (CINPO), China Insurance Media Corporation (CIMC) is a media company founded in accordance with the demands by the spirit of official instruction to CINPO's recapitalization from the General Administration of Press and Publication of the P.R. China and *Corporation Law*.

With registered capital of 100 million yuan RMB, CIMC is jointly founded by China Reinsurance (Group) Company, the main organizer and the superintendent over CINPO, China Life Insurance (Group) Company, Beijing Changxiang Media Investment Group Company, Fuxi Investment Holding Co., Ltd. and PICC Holding Company.

Under the premise of adhering to right guidance of public opinion and better social benefit, the object of CIMC is set to make great efforts in developing newspapering and relevant media industries with underwriting, finance, and economics.

三十、中国保险学会

The Insurance Institute of China

中国保险学会成立于1979年11月，会址设在北京市。业务主管单位为中国保险监督管理委员会。2004年9月23日在北京召开"中国保险学会第六届全国会员代表大会暨第六届理事会第一次会议"，完成换届工作，产生第六届理事会。中国保监会主席吴定富任名誉会长，中国再保险（集团）公司总经理戴凤举任会长，理事会副会长由中国人保控股公司副总经理邓昭雨、中国人寿保险（集团）公司总经理王宪章、中国保险（控股）有限公司董事长兼总经理杨超、中国出口信用保险公司总经理唐若昕、中国太平洋保险（集团）股份有限公司董事长王国良、中国平安保险（集团）股份有限公司常务副总经理孙建一、新华人寿保险股份有限公司董事长关国亮、泰康人寿保险股份有限公司董事长兼首席执行官陈东升、中央财经大学学术委员会名誉主任、前任校长王柯敬担任。中国再保险（集团）公司黎宗剑博士任秘书长。

中国保险学会是从事保险理论和实务研究的全国性学术团体，是由保险公司和保险中介机构、省级地方保险学会、有关高等院校、科研教学单位以及保险界和相关领域的专业人士自愿结成的非营利性社会组织。目前，中国保险学会共有128个会员单位和200个理事席位，其中常务理事57名、名誉会长1名、会长1名、副会长9名、秘书长1名、副秘书长9名。

20多年来，中国保险学会在科研出版方面硕果累累，先后出版发行了《中国保险史》、《外资保险与中国市场》、《中国保险年鉴》等一系列保险领域权威著作。作为中国保险学会会刊，《保险研究》至今已出版200余期，并成为全国中文核心期刊和全国金融保险类核心期刊。

Founded in Beijing in November 1979, the Insurance institute of China (IIC) is governed by the CIRC. As a nationwide academic organization engaging in the study of insurance theory and practice, the IIC is a non-profit social organization voluntarily organized by insurers, insurance intermediaries, provincial local insurance academies, related universities and colleges, scientific researching & teaching units, as well as professionals of related spheres, etc.

For over 20 years, the IIC has achieved much in aspect of scientific research and publication, such as *China Insurance History, Foreign Insurance in Chinese Market, China Insurance Yearbook* and a series of other authoritative works on insurance. More than 200 issues of *Insurance Research*, the journal of the institute, have been published, which has become the countrywide core journal in Chinese on finance & insurance.

中国保险学会与众多保险机构合作，整合资源，为多所大学和研究机构的保险专业学生和研究人员提供奖学金和研究基金。（照片提供：王健）

IIC 2004's Fubon Scholarship Awarding Ceremony

三十一、港澳台保险市场概况
Insurance in Hong Kong, Macao, and Taiwan

香　港　Hong Kong Insurance

香港保险业已有140多年历史，最早是于仁洋面保安行于1841年兼营保险代理业务。以后，相继有怡和、太古、太平、旗昌等洋行到港开办保险业务，但也都属于代理性质。随着香港对内地转口贸易的发展，保险公司不断增加，1941年后在港出单承保本地业务的保险公司约有100家。战后，香港保险业逐步复苏并迅速发展，在70年代间已臻于全盛时期，到1979年该业机构共335家，后由于《保险公司条例》的一再修订，不少公司受条例限制，尤其是受股本(从20万元增至不少于500万元)的限制，使该行业机构不断减缩。截至2005年1月31日，香港共有180名获授权保险人(当中约64%为一般业务保险人、25%为长期业务或人寿保险人，其余11%为综合保险人)。这些保险人当中，有91名在香港注册成立，其余则来自22个不同的国家及地区，其中以美国排列榜首(共17名)，紧随其后的是百慕达(共14名)及英国(共12名)。

香港保险业机构，依法可分为以下三种类型：(1)保险公司：是港府保险业监理处批准可以出单承保，按规定办理各种保险业务的专业保险公司。此外，还有一家香港政府属下的香港出口信用保险局，该局是政府为了鼓励并加强香港厂商开拓海外市场，向本港出口厂商提供商业保险；(2)保险代理：是受保险公司委托的法定代理人，代表该保险公司接受业务或为其缮写保险单，但如有失误，则由该保险公司负责。目前保险代理暂不受政府保险业监管处监管；(3)保险经纪或顾问：是接受保户委托代为设计或选择合适的保险品种，并介绍给对该险种较为专长的保险公司承保，同时也可为保险公司代为安排分保。目前保险经纪或顾问也不受政府保险业监理处监管。

截至2005年1月31日，香港有478名获授权保险经纪及4241名已登记行政总裁业务代表。而保险代理人(包括其负责人及业务代表)，在香港约有30459名获委任保险代理人及21026名负责人业务代表。以人均保费计算，香港是亚州第二大发达的保险市，仅次于日本。由于香港是亚洲主要的保险中心，吸引了不少全球顶级的保险公司。

据香港保险业监理处2005年3月7日公布的数字显示，香港保险业2004年的承保利润较2003年大幅增加逾6成。在2004年，一般业务的毛保费与净保费，分别取得7.2%的跌幅及4.5%的跌幅。2004年整体承保业绩较2003年有所改善，承保利润由港币13.43亿元上升至21.54亿元。其中，汽车业务的承保利润，更由5200万元激增至5.32亿元，增幅高达10倍。船舶及货运业务均明显好转，船舶业务由1.29亿元的亏损转为1.1亿元的利润，而货运业务的利润增加了1倍多。

With 140-year-plus history starting from 1841, Hong Kong insurance, with a few global insurance giants, has been the second advanced insurance market of Asia, just behind Japan.

中国保监会副主席李克穆(前左)与香港特别行政区政府保险业监理处专员袁铭辉在北京签署了《保险监管合作协议》

CIRC's vice chairman Li Kemu (front left) and Yuan Minghui, commissioner of OCI of Hong Kong Special Administrative Region signed the *Cooperating Protocol on Insurance Governing* in Beijing

何厚铧与澳门保险公会、银行公会等金融界代表会晤听取意见。
Macao Special Administrative Region chief He Houhua interviewing delegates from finance circle for opinions

澳　门　Macao Insurance

澳门保险业起源于葡萄牙的殖民贸易活动。1810年澳门出现了第一家保险公司——澳门保险公司，主要经营海上保险业务。1830年该公司倒闭。

1912年澳门颁布了最初的保险法，但这一时期澳门的保险业处在低迷状态，只有十几家保险代理公司主要代理香港保险公司在澳门的业务。

上个世纪70年代，随着澳门居民生活水平的提高，澳门保险业逐渐活跃起来。1981年澳门颁布了《保险活动管制法例》，明确由澳门货币暨汇总监理署保险监察处负责监管保险业活动。

1990年初，澳门已有保险公司19家，其中寿险公司3家，非寿险公司16家，保险从业人员近200人，专职保险经纪人300多人。1997年澳门当局重新制定了保险法，加大了保险市场监管力度。到了2003年底澳门已有保险公司26家，其中寿险公司11家，非寿险公司15家，有600多人获得保险代理人资格认可。

澳门属于微型经济，在世界54个微型经济体系中处于中上水平，属中等发达地区。今年上半年，在博彩旅游业的拉动下，澳门经济增长高达36%。

上个世纪80年代，澳门面积只有16平方公里，近20年来，通过不断的填海，其面积增长了70%，达到了27.3平方公里。目前澳门有人口44.8万人，平均人口密度为每平方公里16428人，是香港人口密度的2.6倍，最高的区域圣安尼堂人口密度达到了每平方公里98776人，是世界人口密度最高的地区。

在澳门这块狭小的半岛上活跃着26家保险公司，其保险市场竞争的激烈可想而知。2003年澳门总保费收入为15.85亿澳门元，比上年增长10.36%。其保险密度约和人民币3663元，同期北京的保险密度为1792元。

澳门非寿险市场已相对饱和，新公司进入相当困难。20多年来，非寿险公司数目非但没有增加，还略有减少。近10多年，澳门非寿险业的平均发展速度大体维持在4%左右。1991年澳门非寿险保费为2.25亿澳门元，市场份额64.6%。2003年澳门非寿险保费收入为3.95亿澳门元，比上年增长4.27%，市场份额下降到24.9%。

目前市场上的15家非寿险公司喜忧四六开，6家公司正增长，9家公司负增长。澳门非寿险市场现已被几大家保险公司把持，2003年4大非寿险公司市场占有率达到83.9%，中国保险位居第一，市场占有率26.1%，澳门保险与其比肩，为25.9%，随后是联丰亨和（18.6%）和亚洲保险（13.3%）。

和非寿险相比，近20年来澳门寿险业高速发展，已占据保险市场的主导地位。1987和1988年，寿险业增幅曾高达98%和100%。1991年，澳门寿险保费收入达到1.255亿澳门元，市场份额上升到36%。1995年，澳门寿险市场份额首次突破了40%。2003年，澳门寿险保费收入已到11.9亿澳门元，比上年增长12.54%，市场份额高达75.1%，远高于同期世界保险业寿险占56.9%的市场份额水平。

澳门寿险市场外资当家，位居前3名的公司均为外资，市场份额占到78.9%。美国友邦一马当先，保费收入6.18亿澳门元，市场份额占到51.9%；澳大利亚国卫和美国万通位居第二和第三，分别占14.9%和12.1%。

澳门寿险与非寿险相比，有着更大的拓展空间，这主要反映在澳门背靠大陆，寿险可凭借强劲增长的旅游业（今年二季度旅客消费增长133.6%），以及澳门寿险在服务和价格上的优势，吸引大陆居民到澳门投保。

Deriving from Portuguese colonial trade in early 19 century, Macao insurance, after the early downturn until in 1970s, has gradually been up and doing and, during the recent two decades, life insurance in the peninsula develops fast compared with the relatively saturated non-life insurance.

富邦产险荣获台湾第一届人才培训卓越奖、商品创新卓越奖、保户服务卓越奖、电子商务入围奖。
Fubon Property Won the first—session awards of talent training, product innovation, policyholders service, and standard e—commerce in Taiwan.

台 湾 Taiwanese Insurance

19世纪初，台湾海上贸易逐渐活跃。1836年，英商利物浦保险公司来台设立了代理处，开始为海上贸易提供保险服务。1854年，英商怡和洋行也在台设立了代理处，经营水险和火险业务。由此，台湾保险业开始兴起。

甲午战争后，台湾割让给日本，英商在台经营保险受到日本的限制。到1918年，英商保险机构全部退出台湾。当时，台湾人李景盛和日本人柳生义一合伙经营的大成产物保险公司是台湾自己的惟一一家保险公司，其余的31家产险公司和34家寿险公司都是日本保险公司在台设立的分公司。二战爆发后，台湾保险业受到重创，只剩下12家产险公司和14家寿险公司。

二战胜利后，台湾光复。1945年10月，台湾成立了保险业监理委员会，接管了日本人经营的26家保险公司，并合并为台湾财产保险公司和台湾人寿保险公司。1948年，资源委员会事务所、中央信托局、太平财产保险公司等在台设立分公司。

1960年，台湾对内开放了保险市场。产险公司由5家增至15家，其中公营3家，民营12家；寿险公司由2家增至9家。同年，台湾还提出了再保险计划。1963年中央再保险公司开始筹备，1968年10月，中央再保险公司正式成立。

1981年，台湾保险市场开始对外开放，准许美国保险公司来台设立分公司。到1990年底，已有美国的8家产险公司和8家寿险公司在台经营，但大都经营困难，市场份额很小。其后，台湾保险市场对外全面开放。

近10年来，台湾保险公司数量变化不大。1995年，台湾共有保险公司56家，其中产险公司25家（其中外资9家），寿险公司30家（其中外资14家），再保险公司1家。到了2005年初，台湾共有保险公司57家，其中产险公司26家（其中外资9家），寿险公司29家（其中外资8家），再保险公司2家。但这段时间台湾保险公司的分公司数量大幅度上升，产险公司分公司数量由119家发展到174家，寿险公司分公司数量由48家发展到135家。这些年来，台湾保险从业人员增长也很快，1993年台湾保险从业人员160749人（其中业务员142137人，内勤18612人，内勤占11.6%），2003年达到338333人（其中业务员299986人，内勤38347人，内勤占11.3%）。2003年台湾寿险从业人员的比重为78%。

2003年，台湾保险密度达到54949元新台币（其中产险4843元，寿险50106元），保险深度达到12.62%（其中产险1.11%，寿险11.51%）。近10年来，台湾总保费收入保持14%左右的增长率。2004年，台湾总保费收入为14185.2亿元新台币，寿险占91.9%。

Rising from 1836, Taiwanese insurance, though suffered heavy losses when Taiwan was ceded to Japan after the Jiawu War, has returned to the right path and developed at a relatively fast pace.

三十二、走过200年的中国保险市场概况

Brief of China Insurance Market after 200-year Development

2004年，全国保费收入4318.1亿元，同比增长11.3%，其中，财产险保费收入达1089.9亿元，同比增长25.4%；人身险保费收入3228.2亿元，同比增长7.2%。保险资金运用余额11249.8亿元，比年初增加2871.3亿元。保险深度3.4%，保险密度332元。截至2004年底，保险公司总资产11853.6亿元，比年初增加2730.7亿元。

2004年，外资保险公司保费收入98亿元，同比增长45%，占总保费收入的2.3%，同比提高0.6个百分点。在对外开放较早的上海、广州两地，外资保险公司的市场份额分别达到15.3%和8.2%。

In 2004, the whole country's premium income came to 431.81 billion yuan, a year-on-year up of 11.3%, of which, 108.99 billion from property insurance, a year-on-year increase of 25.4%; 322.82 billion from life insurance, a year-on-year growth of 7.2%. Balance of insurance capital using stood at 1124.98 billion yuan, increasing 287.13 billion yuan from the beginning 2004, with insurance depth of 3.4% and density of 332 yuan. As of late 2004, the total assets of insurers had been 1185.36 billion yuan, a rise of 273.07 billion over early 2004.

In 2004, foreign insurers reaped 9.8 billion yuan in premium revenue, an increase of 45% and 0.6 percentage points from the last year, accounting for 2.3% of the office premium; they grabbed 15.3% and 8.2% in Shanghai and Guangzhou respectively, which opened relatively earlier.

中国保险市场保费示意图(1980–2004)

Histogram of Premium in China Insurance Market (1980-2004)

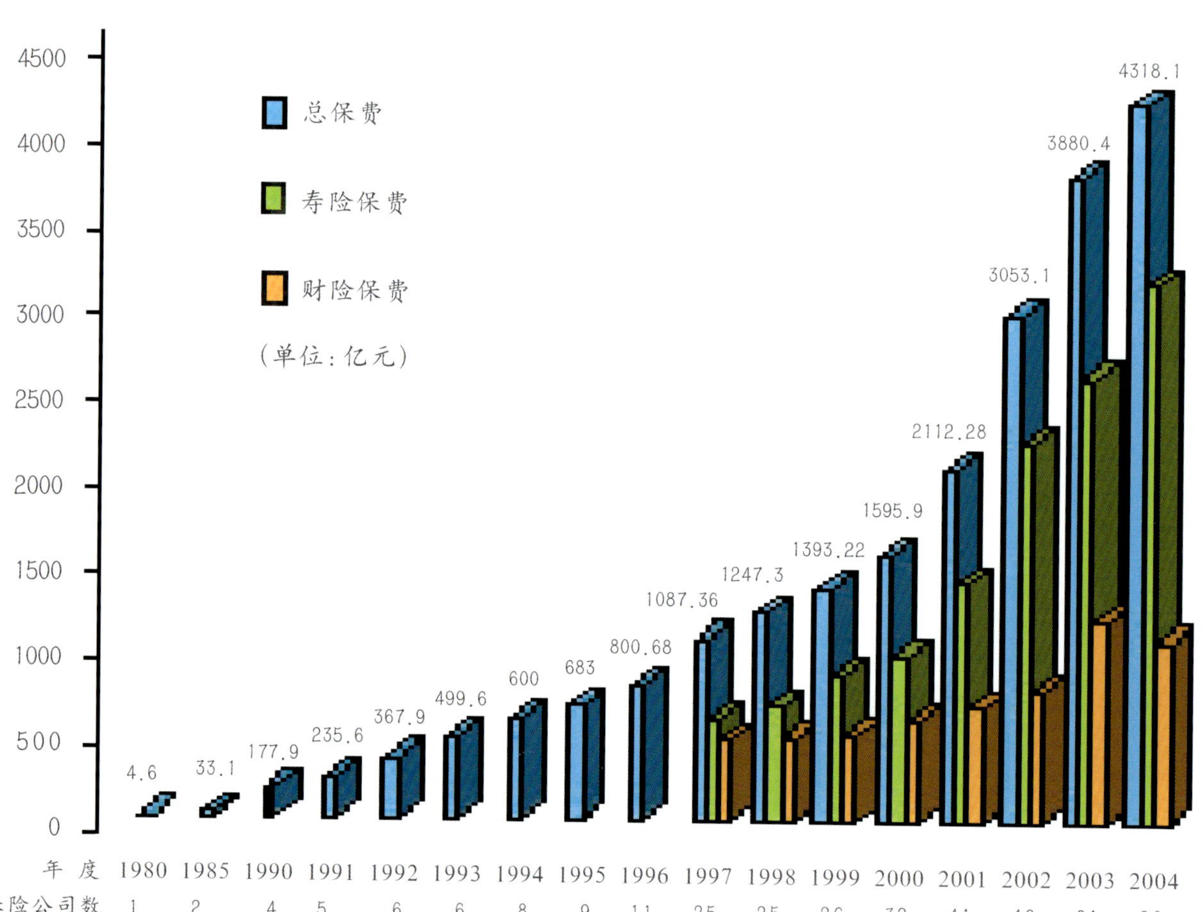

保险监管机构名录
Directory of CIRC & Its Local Bureaus

机构名称 Name of Organization	地 址 Address	邮编 Postcod	电话 Telephone
中国保险监督管理委员会	北京市西城区阜成门内大街410号	100034	010-66016688
北京保监局	北京市西城区宣武门西大街甲129号金隅大厦15层	100031	010-66416688
天津保监局	天津市南开区霞光道花园别墅34号	300381	022-23913020
河北保监局	河北省石家庄市维明北大街28号白楼宾馆迎宾楼4楼	050051	0311-7888888
山西保监局	山西省太原市并州北路31号	030001	0351-4193038
内蒙古保监局	内蒙古呼和浩特市东风路8号农业发展银行内蒙古分行大楼13层	010010	0471-4688832
辽宁保监局	辽宁省沈阳市沈河区北京街29号	110013	024-22596567
吉林保监局	吉林省长春市解放大路2677号光大大厦15楼	130021	0431-8400258
黑龙江保监局	黑龙江省哈尔滨市道里区通江街188号证券大厦13楼	150010	0451-84679941
上海保监局	上海市浦东南路360号33楼	200120	021-68862000
江苏保监局	江苏省南京市汉中路169号金丝利国际大厦12楼	210029	025-86795600
浙江保监局	浙江省杭州市中山北路366号中大广场A座27楼	310003	0571-85777751
安徽保监局	安徽省合肥市阜南西路166号润安大厦13楼	230061	0551-2820997
福建保监局	福建省福州市五四路111号宜发大厦21、22层	350004	0591-7829166
江西保监局	江西省南昌市永叔路15号(财政局八楼)	330009	0791-6692112
山东保监局	山东省济南市泺源大街150号中信广场五楼东	250011	0531-6038888
河南保监局	河南省郑州市农业路东段28号河南报业大厦15楼	450008	0371-5795993
湖北保监局	湖北省武汉市武昌区徐东路华电金融大厦10楼	430077	027-86611011
湖南保监局	湖南省长沙市芙蓉中路508号之3君逸康年大酒店10、11层	410007	0731-2327348
广东保监局	广东省广州市体育西路111号建和中心21楼	510620	020-38795001
广西保监局	广西南宁市滨湖路50号B座六楼	530028	0771-5536636
海南保监局	海南省海口市国贸大道45号银通国际中心18楼	570125	0898-68554322
重庆保监局	重庆市渝中区邹容路68号大都会商厦25楼	400010	023-89036695
四川保监局	四川省成都市八宝街88号国信广场9楼	610031	028-86252541
贵州保监局	贵州省贵阳市新华路9号乌江大厦18楼	550002	0851-5878262
云南保监局	云南省昆明市人民东路6号新华大厦9楼	650051	0871-3145599
陕西保监局	陕西省西安市高新一路2号国家开发银行大厦17层	710075	029-88377058
甘肃保监局	甘肃省兰州市城关区静宁路308号(信托大厦7-10层)	730030	0931-8833707
青海保监局	青海省西宁市昆仑路30号(96351部队招待所院内)	810001	0971-6108860
宁夏保监局	宁夏银川市文化东街123号信托大厦5层	750004	0951-6030867
新疆保监局	新疆乌鲁木齐市东风路2号中银大厦31楼	830002	0991-2313479
深圳保监局	广东省深圳市深南东路5008号农行大厦21楼	518001	0755-25939018
大连保监局	大连市中山区人民路23号虹源大厦38层	116001	0411-82823232
宁波保监局	宁波市江东区兴宁路47号宁波大学商务中心2楼	315041	0574-87848530
青岛保监局	青岛市东海西路39号世纪大厦28楼	266071	0532-5799129

国内中资保险公司名录

Directory of Chinese Insurers in China

公司名称 Name of Organization	联系电话 Telephone	地 址 Address	邮 编 Postcod
中国人保控股公司	010-62616611	北京市海淀区清华西路28号万春园	100084
中国人民财产保险股份有限公司	010-63156688	北京市宣武门东河沿街69号	100052
中国人保资产管理有限公司	021-38789922	上海市银城中路200号中银大厦10层	200120
中国人寿保险(集团)公司	010-66114433	北京市西城区冠英园西区5号	100035
中国人寿保险股份有限公司	010-85659999	北京市朝外大街16号中国人寿大厦23层	100020
中国人寿资产管理公司	010-88088866	北京市西城区金融街33号通泰A座9层	100032
中国再保险(集团)公司	010-66576666	北京西城区金融街11号中再大厦	100034
中国财产再保险股份有限公司	010-66576188	北京西城区金融街11号中再大厦	100034
中国人寿再保险股份有限公司	010-66576366	北京西城区金融街11号中再大厦	100034
中国大地财产保险股份有限公司	021-58369588	上海市浦东南路855号世界广场36楼	200120
中国保险(控股)有限公司北京办事处	010-63600605	北京宣武门西大街28号大成广场一门9层	100053
太平保险有限公司	0755-82960919	深圳市福田区江苏大厦17层	518026
太平人寿保险有限公司	021-50614888	上海市浦东新区民生路1399号	200135
中国出口信用保险公司	010-88382288	北京市西城区阜成门北大街5号	100037
民生人寿保险股份有限公司	010-65886669	北京市朝外大街20号联合大厦4楼	100020
中华联合财产保险公司	0991-4680869	乌鲁木齐南湖南路9号	830017
中国太平洋保险(集团)有限公司	021-58776688	上海市银城东路190号	200120
中国太平洋财产保险股份有限公司	021-58776688	上海市银城东路190号	200120
中国太平洋人寿保险股份有限公司	021-58776688	上海市银城东路190号	200120
中国平安保险(集团)股份有限公司	0755-82262888	深圳市福田区八卦岭八卦三路平安大厦	518029
中国平安财产保险股份有限公司	0755-82262888	深圳市福田区八卦岭八卦三路平安大厦	518029
中国平安人寿保险股份有限公司	0755-82262888	深圳市福田区八卦岭八卦三路平安大厦	518029
新华人寿保险股份有限公司	010-63903399	北京市丰台区莲花池西里8号新华保险大厦	100073
泰康人寿保险股份有限公司	010-66429988	北京市西城区复兴门内大街156号B座	100031
华泰财产保险股份有限公司	010-66218833	北京市西城区金融街35号国际企业大厦	100032
天安保险股份有限公司	021-50543255	上海市浦东大道1号18楼	200120
大众保险股份有限公司	021-63221111	上海市汉口路400号23楼	200001
华安财产保险股份有限公司	0755-82665888	深圳市宝安南路2001号华安大厦27楼	518001
永安财产保险股份有限公司	029-87233888	西安市北大街163号	710003
生命人寿保险股份有限公司	021-58773333	上海浦东新区浦东南路855号18楼	200120
东方人寿保险股份有限公司	021-62797268	上海市浦东新区丁香路716号	200135

国内外资保险公司名录

Directory of Foreign Insurers in China

公司名称 Name of Organization	联系电话 Telephone	地址 Address	邮编 Postcod
中宏人寿保险有限公司 Manulife—Sinochen Life Insurance CO.,Ltd	(021)50492288	上海市浦东新区世纪大道88号金茂大厦21楼	200121
太平洋安泰人寿保险有限公司 Pacific—Antna Life Insurance Company Ltd	(021)68863183	上海市浦东新区浦东南路360号35楼	200120
安联大众人寿保险有限公司 Allianz—Dazhong Life Insurance co., Ltd	(021)58798828	上海市陆家嘴东路161号招商局大厦16楼	200120
金盛人寿保险有限公司 AXA—Minmetals Life Insurance co., Ltd	(021)58792288	上海市陆家嘴东路161号招商局大厦12层	200120
中保康联人寿保险有限公司 China CMG Life Insurance Company Ltd	(021)58882288	上海浦东陆家嘴东路166号中国保险大厦21楼	200120
信诚人寿保险有限公司 CITIC—Prudential Life Insurance Company Ltd.	(020)87521966	广州市天河北路233号中信广场60楼6002—6008室	510620
恒康天安人寿保险有限公司 ohn Hancock Tianan Life Insurance Company	(021)68816658	上海市浦东南路528号南楼2203室	200120
中意人寿保险有限公司 Generall China Life Insurance Company Ltd	(020)83278888	广州市中山五路219号中旅商业城12楼	510030
光大永明人寿保险有限公司 Manulife—Sinochen Life Insurance CO.,Ltd	(022)23391188	天津市和平区南京路75号天津国际大厦四层	300050
首创安泰人寿保险有限公司 ING Capital Life Insurance Company Ltd	(0411)82531688	大连市中山区同街25号世界贸易大厦42号	116001
海尔纽约人寿保险有限公司 Haier New York Life Insurance Company Ltd	(021)50472188	上海市浦东新世纪大道88号金茂大36层3601	200121
中英人寿保险有限公司 Aviva—COFCO Life Insurance Co.,Ltd	(020)84108080	广州市滨江中路308号海运大厦19楼	510220
海康人寿保险有限公司 AEGON—CNOOC Life Insurance Company Ltd	(021)38784868	上海市浦东南路588号浦发大厦15楼	200120
招商信诺人寿保险有限公司 CIGNA and CMC Life Insurance Company Ltd	(0755)83196209	深圳市深南大道7088号招商银行大厦31楼	518040
广电日生人寿保险有限公司 Nissay—SVA Life Insurance Company Ltd	(021)62476633	上海市南京西路1468号中欣大厦37F	200040
恒安标准人寿保险有限公司 Heng An Standard Life Insurance Company Ltd	(022)88227575	天津市河西区宾水道增9号环渤海发展中心A座23层	300061
瑞泰人寿保险有限公司 Skandia SM Life Insurance Company Ltd	(010)85275488	北京朝阳区麦子店37号盛福大厦21楼	100026
中美大都会人寿保险有限公司 Sino—US MetLife insurance Co.,Ltd	(010)85180966	北京市东长安街1号东方广场东方经贸城E2座12层	100738
香港民安保险有限公司深圳分公司 The Min An Insurance Company (Hong Kong) Limited Shenzhen Branch	(0755)82170793	深圳市人民南路天安国际大厦C座12楼	518001
香港民安保险有限公司海口分公司 The Min An Insurance Company (Hong Kong) Limited Haikou Branch	(0898)68518888	海口市滨海大厦南洋大厦708室	570105

公司名称 Name of Organization	联系电话 Telephone	地 址 Address	邮 编 Postcod
美国友邦保险有限公司上海分公司 AIA Shanghai Branch	(021)63216698	上海市中山东一路17号友邦大厦	200002
美国友邦保险有限公司广州分公司 AIA Guangzhou Branch	(020)81321888	广州市中山六路218-222号捷泰广场18楼	510180
美国友邦保险有限公司深圳分公司 AIA Shenzhen Branch	(0755)82463830	深圳市深南东路5002号 信兴广场地王商业中心商业大楼11楼	518008
美国友邦保险有限公司北京分公司 AIA Beijing Branch	(010)65683338	北京市朝阳区建国路乙118号京汇大厦三层	100022
美国友邦保险有限公司苏州分公司 AIA Suzhou Branch	(0512)65225558	江苏省苏州市干将西路120号友邦大厦4、5、7楼	215005
美亚保险公司上海分公司 AIU Shanghai Branch	(021)63508180	上海市南京西路128号永新广场7楼	200003
美亚保险公司广州分公司 AIU Guangzhou Branch	(020)87311888	广东省广州市农林下路83号广发银行大厦18楼	510080
美亚保险公司深圳分公司 AIU Shenzhen Branch	(0755)82463755	深圳市罗湖区深南东路5002号 信兴广场地王商业中心商业大楼11楼	518008
东京海上火灾保险株式会社上海分公司 The Tokyo Marine and Fire Insurance Company Limited Shanghai Branch	(021)68414455	上海市浦东新区银城东路10号汇丰大厦38F	200120
丰泰保险(亚洲)有限公司上海分公司 Winterthur Insurance(Asia) Limited. Shanghai Branch	(021)68823351	上海市浦东新区浦东南路528号 上海证券大厦24层2404－2409室	200120
皇家太阳联合保险公司上海分公司 Royal and Sun Alliance Insurance PLC Shanghai Branch	(021)68411999	上海市浦东新区银城东路101号汇丰大厦9楼	200120
美国联邦保险股份有限公司上海分公司 Federal Insurance Company Shanghai Branch	(021)53067799	上海市浦东新区银城东路101号汇丰大厦32楼 上海卢湾区湖滨路222号企业天地1号楼1901	200021
三井住友海上火灾保险公司上海分公司 Mitsui Sumitomo Insurance Co. Ltd. Shanghai Branch	(021)68411034	上海市浦东新区银城东路101号汇丰大厦41楼	200120
韩国三星火灾海上保险有限公司上海分公司 Samsung Fire And Marine Insurance Co. Ltd. Shanghai Branch	(021)62080080	上海延安西路2200号上海国际贸易中心8楼812室	200336
中银集团保险有限公司深圳分公司 Bank of China Group Insurance Co. Ltd. Shenzhen Branch	(0755)25155678	深圳市罗湖区建设路2022号 深圳国际金融大厦31楼	518001
安联保险公司广州分公司 Allianz Guangzhou Branch	(020)38911889	广州市天河北路233号中信广场5107室	510613
日本财产保险公司大连分公司 Sompo Japan Insurance Inc Dalian Branch	(0411)83603092	大连市西岗中山路147号	116011
慕尼黑再保险公司北京分公司 Munich Reinsurance Company Beijing Branch	(010)64651901	北京市朝阳区亮马桥路50号燕莎中心写字楼C413室	100016
瑞士再保险公司北京分公司 Swiss Re Beijing Branch	(010)85188966	北京市东城区东长安街1号东方广场写字楼东二座1701	100738
利宝互助重庆分公司 Liberty Mutual Insurance Company Chongqing Branch	(023)89038737	重庆市渝中区中山三路131号庆隆希尔顿商务中心35楼	400015

保险学会、行业协会名录

Directory of Insurance Academies and Associations

机构名称 Name of Organization	地　址 Address	邮编 Postcod	电话 Telephone
中国保险学会	北京市西城区金融大街11号中再大厦7层	100034	010-66553701
中国保险行业协会	北京市西城区西交民巷22号	100031	010-66071116
北京市保险学会	北京市朝外市场20号中保大厦5层	100020	010-65035122
北京市保险行业协会	北京市朝阳区安贞西里四区23号楼4D室	100029	010-64410345
天津市保险学会	天津市和平区岳阳道88号福泰公寓C205室	300051	010-23328878
天津市保险行业协会	天津市和平区岳阳道88号福泰公寓C204室	300051	010-23328878
河北省保险行业协会	河北省石家庄市自强路134号1号楼二层	050051	0311-7887093
山西省保险行业协会	山西省太原市并州北路69号	030001	0351-4193075
内蒙古保险行业协会	内蒙古呼和浩特市东风路8号农发行大楼13层	010010	0471-4688831
辽宁省保险学会	辽宁省沈阳市皇姑区长江街17号沈阳中国石化大厦	110013	024-86280192
辽宁省保险行业协会	辽宁省沈阳市和平区市府大路157号泰利阳光饭店七楼	110002	024-22808710
大连市保险学会	大连市西岗区黄河路2号	116011	0411-83626388
大连市保险行业协会	大连市中山区世纪街39号	116001	0411-82827060
吉林省保险行业协会	吉林省长春市民康路11号四层	130041	0431-8973843
黑龙江省保险行业协会	黑龙江省哈尔滨市霁虹街99号B栋12层	150010	0451-84643316
上海市保险学会	上海市四川中路126弄18号308室	200002	021-63510762
上海市保险同业公会	上海市中山南路1228号8楼	200011	021-63155989
江苏省保险学会	江苏省南京市长江路69号保险大厦1608室	210005	025-84709743
江苏省保险行业协会	江苏省南京市中山东路18号国际中心2111室	210005	025-84791449
浙江省保险学会	浙江省杭州市天目山路148号浙江大学西溪校区	310028	0571-88273076
浙江省保险行业协会	浙江省杭州市中山北路46号	310003	0571-87065500
宁波市保险行业协会	浙江省宁波市国医街12号3楼	315000	0574-87345378
安徽省保险学会	安徽省合肥市淮河路180号1幢402	230001	0551-2623863
安徽省保险行业协会	安徽省合肥市阜阳北路1号太平洋大厦	230041	0551-5612175
福建省保险学会	福建省福州市五四路233号保险大厦	350003	0591-7092176
福建省保险行业协会	福建省福州市五四路233号	350003	0591-7092139
厦门市保险行业协会	厦门市湖滨北路68号税保大厦6楼	361012	0592-5316168
江西省保险行业协会	江西省南昌市中山路470号五楼	330009	0791-6692036
江西省保险学会	江西省南昌市永步路18号(吉安大厦二楼)	330003	0791-6383286
山东省保险学会	山东省济南市泺源大街88号	250011	0531-6108700
山东省保险行业协会	山东省济南市马鞍山路9号	250002	0531-2066346
青岛市保险学会	青岛市香港东路126号2-3-102	266071	0532-5921123
青岛市保险行业协会	青岛市香港中路100号中商大厦506室	266071	0532-5929703
河南省保险学会	河南省郑州市黄河路116号付26号	450003	0371-5990484

机构名称 Name of Organization	地 址 Address	邮编 Postcod	电话 Telephone
河南省保险行业协会	河南省郑州市红专路63—1荣华商务	450008	0371—5950229
湖北省保险学会	湖北省武汉市汉口黄浦大街27号三九国际大酒店17楼	430010	027—51245379
湖北省保险行业协会	湖北省武汉市汉口黄浦大街27号三九国际大酒店17楼	430010	027—51245379
湖南省保险学会	湖南省长沙市韶山路178号人寿保险大楼	410011	0731—4302257
湖南省保险行业协会	湖南省长沙市韶山路328—A号长岭宾馆900房	410007	0731—5796130
广东保险学会	广东省广州市天河广利路73号503室	510620	020—85593410
广东保险行业协会	广州市天河体育西路111号建和中心21楼F座	510620	020—38795503
深圳市保险学会	深圳市罗湖区松园路9号茂源大厦603室	518008	0755—82475017
深圳市同业公会	深圳市福田区新洲北路长景阁17楼B座	518034	0755—83529983
广西保险学会	广西南宁市滨湖路50号B座	530028	0771—5536812
广西保险行业协会	广西南宁市滨湖路50号B座	530028	0771—5536812
海南省保险行业协会	海南省海口市金龙路22号深发展大厦9层	570125	0898—68550860
海南省保险同业公会	海南省海口市金贸区金龙路22号深发展大厦六层	570125	0898—66225503
重庆市保险行业协会	重庆市渝中区民族路94号时新宾馆6楼	400010	023—63716092
四川省保险行业协会	四川省成都市梓潼桥西街39号	610017	028—86752029
成都市保险学会	四川省绵阳市南河路3号	610017	028—86761228
贵州省保险行业协会	贵州省贵阳市遵义路56号迎宾商务大楼401室	550002	0851—5573617
云南省保险学会	云南省昆明市拓东路80号绿洲大酒店A座27楼	650011	0871—3157190
云南省保险行业协会	云南省昆明市环城东路董家湾大厦13楼	650041	0871—3390958
陕西省保险学会	陕西省西安市南关正街1号泛美大厦7层	710054	029—87817417
陕西省保险行业协会	陕西省西安市南二环西段21号华融大厦A座10层	710061	029—82309828
甘肃省保险学会	甘肃省兰州市滨河东路719号	730030	0931—8484911
甘肃省保险行业协会	甘肃省兰州市静宁路337—345号	730030	0931—2166608
青海省保险学会	青海省西宁市新宁路20号	810008	0971—6301646
青海省保险行业协会	青海省西宁市五四西路2号	810008	0971—6381552
宁夏保险行业协会	宁夏银川市解放东街永康北巷1号工行3楼	750004	0951—6017497
新疆维吾尔自治区保险学会	新疆乌鲁木齐市西后街55号平安大厦	830002	0991—8835826
新疆维吾尔自治区保险行业协会	新疆乌鲁木齐市人民路21号	830002	0991—2819687

中国开设保险专业大专院校名录

Directory of Universities & Colleges with Insurance Specialty

院校名称 Name of Organization	电话 Telephone	地址 Address	邮编 Postcod
安徽财经大学金融系	0552—3112147	安徽省蚌埠市宏业路255号	233040
北京城市学院	010—62322616	北京市海淀区北四环中路269号	100083
北京大学中国保险与社会保障研究中心	010—82529127	北京市海淀区成府路方正大厦	100871
北京工商大学	010—68905929	北京市海淀阜成路11号	100037
北京联合大学管理学院	010—64900704	北京市朝阳区北四环东路97号	100101
保险职业学院	0731—5636308	湖南省长沙市天心区	410114
长春税务学院	0431—8919931	长春市人民大街3646号	130021
成都保险学校	028—3972612	成都市新都区桂湖东路三巷七号	610500
东北财经大学	0411—84711902	大连市沙河口区黑石礁	116025
东南大学金融系	025—83792452	江苏省南京市四牌楼2号	210096
对外经济贸易大学保险系	010—64495040	北京市朝阳区惠新东街	100029
复旦大学经济学院保险系	021—65643750	上海市邯郸路220号	200433
复旦大学太平洋金融学院	021—68257000—10252	上海市南汇区惠南镇拱北路168号	201300
广东金融学院	020—87033145	广州市沙河龙眼洞	510520
河北经贸大学	0311—7657068	河北省石家庄市学府路47号	071009
华东师范大学统计系	021—62232462	上海市中山北路3663号	200062
哈尔滨保险学校	0451—82116378	哈尔滨市动力区文启街18号	150040
湖南大学金融学院	0731—8684772	湖南省长沙市石佳冲6号	410079
吉林大学经济学院	0431—5168829	长春市前卫路10号东荣大厦8楼	130012
南昌保险学院	0791—5213039	南昌市南莲路176号	330001
南开大学风险管理与保险学系	022—23505936	天津市卫津路94号	300071
清华大学经济管理学院	010—62785001	北京市海淀区	100084
山东财政学院金融学院	0531—2911112	济南市舜耕路40号	250014
山东大学经济学院	0531—8364601	济南市	250100
首都经贸大学	010—83952256	北京市丰台区张家路口121号	100070
上海财经大学金融学院保险系	021—65640818	上海市国定路777号	200433
上海金融学院	021—58636545	上海市上川路995号(浦东校区)	201209
同济大学中德学院	021—65980327	上海市四平路1239号	200092
武汉大学商学院	027—87682134	湖北省武汉市武昌区珞珈山	430072
西安交通大学经济与管理学院	029—82668382	西安市咸宁西路28号	710049
厦门大学经济学院金融系	0592—2182395	福建省厦门市思明南路422号	350002
西南财经大学保险学院	028—87352302	成都市光华村街55号	610074
中国人民大学社会保障研究中心	010—62513013	北京市中关村大街59号	100872
中国人民大学财政金融学院	010—62511128	北京市海淀区海淀路175号	100872
浙江财经学院金融学院	0571—88922794	浙江省杭州市文华路269号	310012
浙江大学经济学院(保险研究所)	0571—88273076	浙江省杭州市天目山路148号	310028
中南财经政法大学	027—88044330	湖北省武汉市武昌区武珞路114号	430064
新华金融保险学院	027—88058159	武汉市武昌区武珞路114号	430060
中山大学岭南学院	020—84112820	广州市新港西路135号	510275
中央财经大学	010—62251188	北京市海淀区学院南路39号	100081
中央广播电视大学财经部	010—66490604	北京市复兴门内大街160号	100031

中国保险业大事记

Chronicle of Chinese Insurance

1805年　中国第一家保险公司英商谏当保安行(广州保险会社)在广州设立。
1824年　宝顺行在广州开设，兼营货物保险业务。
1832年　查顿·马地臣在广州设立英商怡和洋行。
1835年　英商宝顺行在香港开设于仁洋面保安行，也称友宁保险行。
1836年　怡和洋行接管并改组谏当保险行，改名谏当保险公司，1882年改称广东保险公司。
1841年　于仁洋面保险公司在香港注册。
1943年　魏源《海国图志》开始刊行。
　　　　怡和洋行抵达上海。
1846年　英商在上海开设“永福”和“大东方”两家人寿保险公司，这是中国最早的人寿保险公司。
1859年　洪仁玕自香港赴天京，其著述《资政新篇》在“法法类”中阐述了兴办保险的思想。
1861年　美商琼记洋行成为第一家在华充当美国保险公司代理人的美国洋行。
1863年　保家行(North China Insurance Company)在上海成立。
　　　　美商旗昌轮船公司设立扬子保险公司。
1864年　泰安保险公司(中国火烛保险行)在香港成立。
1865年　琼记洋行在香港设立保宁保险公司。
　　　　上海华商义和公司保险行成立，这是目前已知的第一家民族保险企业。
1866年　怡和洋行在香港成立香港火烛保险公司，这是中国最早的专营火险公司。
1871年　中外合股的华商保安公司在香港开业。
1873年　太古洋行成为英国暨海外保险公司和皇家交易保险公司的代理人。
1875年　第一家大型民族保险业——保险招商局诞生。
1876年　徐润、唐廷枢组建仁和水险公司。
1877年　香港成立华商安泰保险公司。
1878年　徐润、唐廷枢发起扩建济和船栈保险局。
1882年　第一家华商专营火灾保险公司——上海火烛保险有限公司开业。
1886年　仁和、济和合并，更名为仁济和保险有限公司。
1891年　重庆开埠，英商立德开设专保客货的利川保险公司。
1893年　台湾商人开始经营保险代理业。
1896年　日本海上保险株式会社在上海设立分支机构。
1897年　加拿大宏利人寿保险公司在上海设立分公司。
1898年　英商永年人寿公司在上海成立。
1899年　外商在上海设立海上保险协会。
　　　　日本明治火灾保险株式会社在台湾设立分公司。
1902年　莫斯科火灾保险公司在哈尔滨设立。
1903年　英商在重庆设立保家水险公司。
1905年　英商上海华洋人寿保险公司成立。
　　　　华商华兴保险公司在上海开业。
1906年　英商英京火险公司、永年人寿保险公司、永明人寿保险公司在重庆设立分公司。
　　　　华商华安水火保险公司在上海开业。
　　　　华商华成经保火险公司在上海开业。
1907年　上海华商保险公司发起组织华商火险公会，这是中国第一个保险团体。
　　　　徐锐去小吕宋、新加坡、槟榔屿集资办银行、航业、保险三大公司，并草拟
　　　　中国第一部保险专门法规——《保险业章程草案》。
　　　　华商华安人寿保险公司在上海开业。
1908年　华商长安保险公司、和乐联保火险公司、远乐火险公司在广州成立，后合并为冠球联保火险公司。
1909年　英商旗昌保险公司在香港成立。
　　　　华商延年人寿保险公司在上海开业。
1910年　荷兰望赉保险公司在上海设分公司。
1912年　华商上海康年保寿有限公司成立。
　　　　华商华安合群保寿公司在上海成立。
1913年　邮政部门创办保险邮件业务。
　　　　华商羊城保险置业公司在广州成立。

1914年　英商保禄斯在天津设立保禄洋行，下设保险部，该行于1953年结束。
张謇主编的《第一次农商统计表》出版，1912年保险公司为42家。
华商上海康年保寿有限公司成立。
1915年　华商上海联保水火保险公司成立，总公司设香港，1927年迁上海。
中国实业银行拨资成立永宁保险行。
日本保险商在“关东州”开设51家会社。
1916年　华商华年人寿水火保险有限公司在汉口成立。
华商永安水火保险公司在香港成立。
英商远东保险公司在香港成立。
1917年　华商福星小保险公司在福州成立。
上海华商火险公会更名为华商水火保险公会。
1919年　美国保险公会组织21家保险公司来华经营保险。
华商福建福星人寿小保险股份有限公司注册成立。
美国美亚保险公司在上海成立。
1920年　中日合股东方人寿保险公司在北平成立，1924年改为纯粹华股。
1921年　美商友邦人寿保险公司注册成立。
华商华侨银行设立华侨保险公司，总公司设在新加坡。
中央信托公司成立，1935年改名为中一信托公司。
1923年　华商大中华保险公司在杭州成立。
华商先施人寿保险公司成立，总部设在香港，广州、上海设分公司。
1924年　成立于1914年的华商香安保险公司在香港注册，在广州设分公司。
华商福田保寿公司在福州开业。
香港永安公司、永安纺织公司、上海永安公司、雪梨永安公司、永安水火保险公司等1927年在上海成立永安人寿公司，翌年总公司迁香港。
1925年　中国第一部保险学著作——王效文编写的《保险学》由商务印书馆出版。
宁绍商轮公司保险部成立，该部1935年脱离商轮公司，扩组为宁绍水火保险公司。
1926年　华商珠江保险公司在广州成立。
华商大中保寿储蓄公司和福康保寿公司在福州成立。
东莱银行在上海创办安平水火保险公司。
1927年　由陈光甫、刘鸿生等发起组织的华商大华保险公司在上海成立。
1928年　华商联泰水火保险公司在香港成立，广州设分公司，发起人为华侨李煜堂等。
华商肇泰轮船公司在上海设立肇泰保险公司。
1929年　上海华商水炎保险公会改名为上海保险公会。
华商滨江保商公司在哈尔滨成立。
金城银行在上海独资创办太平水火保险公司。
中国垦业银行创办天一保险公司。
国民党政府颁布《保险法》及《海商法》、《工厂法》。
1930年　英商四海保险公司在上海成立。
华商慎平火险公司在福州成立。
华商中国第一信用保险公司成立，这是中国第一家专营信用保险的公司。
1931年　法商法美保险公司在上海成立。
上海保险公会易名为上海保险业同业公会。
华商丰盛实业公司开办的丰盛保险公司在上海成立。
华洋合资的宝丰保险公司在上海成立。
华商中国保险股份有限公司在上海成立，1944年易名为中国产物保险公司。
华商宁绍人寿保险公司在上海成立。
1932年　总公司在加拿大的合众人寿保险公司在上海设分公司，该公司创立于1873年。
泰山保险公司成立，徐新六任董事长，史带任董事。
1933年　华商中国海上意外保险公司成立，主要发起人为丁雪农。
华商四明保险公司成立，发起人为孙衡甫、俞佐廷。
华商联合保险公司成立，发起单位为肇泰、华安、永宁、永安、先施、中国海上、通易信托公司保险部、宁绍商轮公司水火保险部8家。
金城银行将太平水火保险公司改组为太平保险公司。
华商四川聚兴诚银行在重庆设立兴华保险公司。

1935年 沈雷春主编的中国第一部保险年鉴——《中国保险年鉴》出版。
国民政府颁布《简易人寿保险法》、《简易人寿保险章程》和《保险业法》。
中国第一家保险学术机构——中国保险学会成立。
太平、安平、丰盛保险公司主办的《太安丰保险界》创刊，后易名为《保险界》。
中央信托局保险部成立。

1937年 修改后的《保险法》、《保险业法》以及《保险业法施行法》公布。
中国保险公司将寿险部划出而另组成中国人寿保险公司，并在香港设立"驻港总处"。

1938年 上海市保险业业余联谊会成立。
上海市保险业业余联谊会主办的《保联月刊》创刊，1940年改为《保险月刊》。

1941年 中共地下党支持的大安物产保险公司成立。

1942年 中国、太平、宝丰、兴华在重庆组成"四联分保办事处"。
以保井内盐险为主的中兴保险公司在重庆成立。
中国保险公司同其它10家华商保险公司成立久联保险集团。

1943年 国民政府财政部及行政院通过《强制保险草案》。
交通银行设立太平洋保险公司。
中共地下党办企业广大华行与民生实业公司合办的民安产物保险公司在重庆成立。

1944年 重庆永兴、亚兴、中兴、永大等保险公司组成再保险集团——新联保险公司。
中国农业银行独资开办中国农业保险公司。

1945年 中国人事保险公司开业。
中共上海保险业地下党建立上海市保险界民主促进会。
国民政府财产部公布《收复区商营保险公司复员办法》8条。

1946年 中华民国保险商业同业公会(简称中国保险业联合会)成立，罗北辰任理事长。
上海市保险业业余联谊会改称上海市保险界同仁进修会。

1947年 国民政府社会部成立中央社会保险局。
解放区哈尔滨人民政府批准成立亚洲、阜成、中兴三家私营保险公司。
中国人身保险合作社在南京成立。
中国在美第一家获准特许设立的水火保险公司——中央信托局保险分理处在纽约开业，
项馨吾任经理。

1948年 全国解放区第一家公私合营性质保险机构——哈尔滨联合保险公司成立。
东北人民政府公布《东北公营企业战时暂行劳动保险条例》。

1949年 共产党和人民政府领导的全国第一家人民保险机构——新华保险公司在哈尔滨成立。
人民政府东北保险总公司在沈阳成立。
上海市军事管制委员会财经接管委员会下属金融处设立保险组，开始接管清理金融保险业。
中国人民银行总行召开第一次全国保险会议。
中国人民保险公司在北京成立。

1951年 上海15家私营保险公司合并，由国营保险公司参股组成公私合营太平保险公司。
中国产物保险公司和中国人寿保险公司总管理处由上海迁往北京，专营海外保险业务。

1952年 中国人民保险公司机构发展到1300个左右，除西藏、台湾外，各省、直辖市、专区及全国
1／3的市、县都设置了分支机构。
上海13家私营保险公司由国营保险公司参股组成公私合营新丰保险公司。

1953年 国内停办农村保险。

1954年 1953年年初，全国行政大区撤销，保险公司各大区区公司在三月份陆续撤销。
为配合农业合作化复办农村保险。

1955年 公私合营新丰、太平保险公司合并为公私合营太平保险公司，与中国保险公司一起，
专门经营对外保险业务。

1958年 全国财政会议在武汉召开，正式决定停办国内保险业务。

1959年 中国人民保险公司复归银行管辖，同年停办国内保险业务，只在上海、哈尔滨两地，
继续办理保险，上海办企业财产保险、运输保险、公民财产保险和简易人身保险。
哈尔滨只办企业财产保险。

1963年 广州、天津等地恢复国内保险业务。
上海市政府批准《企业、机关、团体财产保险办法》和《国内船舶保险办法》。

1964年 中国人民保险公司再次独立建制，成为人民银行的局级机构。
广东省成立广东省保险公司，并草拟了"广东省地方国营、公私合营企业强制保险试行办法"。
经省人民政府批准自4月1日起在全省实行。

1965年 中国人民银行、财政部发出通知，明确国内业务统一由财政部管理；国际业务由中国人民银行管理。

1967年　上海、哈尔滨、广州、广东、天津等地国内保险业务被迫停办，自此，大陆范围内国内保险业务全部中止。
1969年　财政部在北京召开银行、保险国外工作座谈会。
1972年　中国人民保险公司制订船舶保险条款，恢复远洋船舶保险。
1979年　国务院批转《中国人民银行全国分行长会议纪要》。指出要逐步恢复国内保险业务，在各口岸和各省、市、自治区逐步设立保险分公司。
中国保险学会成立。
1980年　中国人民保险公司开始办理国内保险业务。中国人民保险公司除台湾、西藏外的28个省、市、自治区都恢复建立了分支机构。
中国保险学会和中国人民保险公司主办的《保险研究》创刊。
中央财政金融学院设立保险系国际保险专业。
1982年　国务院国发[1982]27号文件批转中国人民银行关于国内保险业务恢复情况和今后发展意见的报告的通知。
1984年　中国人民保险公司从中国人民银行分离出来，成为国务院直属经济实体。
中国人民保险公司主办的《中国保险》创刊。
1985年　国家教委批准在南开大学、武汉大学、辽宁大学和西南财大开设保险专业。
国务院颁布《保险企业管理暂行条例》。
1986年　经国务院引进智力办公室批准，在中国设立"英国特许保险学会(CII)北京考试中心。"
新疆建设兵团农牧业生产保险总公司在乌鲁木齐设立。
1988年　深圳平安保险公司成立。
1989年　国务院办公厅下发《关于加强保险事业管理的通知》。
1990年　农村灾害保险技术研究中心在北京成立。
1991年　中国太平洋保险公司暨上海分公司成立。
1992年　中国人民银行批准，平安保险公司更名为"中国平安保险公司"。
美国友邦获准在上海开业，这是改革开放后第一家获准进入中国的外资保险公司。
1993年　中国保险报社成立。
1994年　美国AIG获准在上海设立分公司。
《中国保险报》创刊。
天安保险股份有限公司在上海成立。
日本东京海上火灾保险株式会社获准在上海成立分公司。
1995年　大众保险股份有限公司在上海成立。
八届人大十四次常委会议通过《中华人民共和国保险法》。
1996年　中宏人寿保险有限公司在上海成立，这是中国首家中外合资人寿保险公司。
新华人寿保险股份有限公司在北京成立。
泰康人寿保险股份有限公司在北京成立。
华安财产保险股份有限公司在深圳成立。
永安财产保险股份有限公司在西安成立。
华泰财产保险股份有限公司在北京成立。
中国人民保险公司机构体制改革，组建中保集团，下设中保财产、中保人寿、中保再保险三家子公司。
中国人民银行公布《保险代理人管理暂行规定》。
1997年　德国安联保险公司和瑞士丰泰保险公司获准在上海营业。
1998年　《保险经纪人管理规定(试行)》颁布。
法国安盛、英国皇家太阳、美国安泰、澳大利亚康联保险获准在上海营业。
中国保险监督管理委员会成立。
1999年　中保财产保险有限公司更名为中国人民保险公司，中保人寿保险有限公司更名为中国人寿保险公司，中保再保险有限公司更为中国再保险公司。
1999年　我国首家中德合资保险公司——安联大众人寿保险有限公司在上海成立。
中国再保险公司在北京成立。
中国人寿保险公司在北京成立。
中保财产保险有限公司复名为中国人民保险公司。
全国(深圳市除外)统一的车险新条款及费率正式实施。
中国保监会勒令塞奇维克保险与风险管理咨询服务(中国)有限公司停业整顿。
中国首次保险经纪资格考试在京举行。
第一家中法合资人寿保险公司——金盛人寿保险公司在上海成立。
国家教育保险制度发布。
基金同盛向保险公司配售，保险资金通过证券投资基金间接进入证券市场。

2000年 《保险公司管理规定》开始施行。
中国保监会对三家严重违规的外资保险机构驻华代表处予以撤销。
中国保险市场首家保险经纪人——江泰保险经纪有限公司在京成立。
中澳合资的中保康联人寿保险有限公司开业。
新华人寿保险有限公司成为国内首家完成向外资招股的保险公司。
《保险公估人管理规定(试行)》颁布。
美国丘博保险集团的成员公司——美国联邦保险公司成立其上海分公司。
第一家中英合资人寿保险公司——信诚人寿保险公司在广州成立。
中国保险行业协会在北京成立。
我国首次精算师资格考试在北京、天津、上海、武汉同时举行。
新疆兵团保险公司更名为新疆兵团财产保险公司。

2001年 《保险公司最低偿付能力及监管指标管理规定》试行。
中美合资的恒康天安人寿保险有限公司在上海成立。
中银集团保险有限公司深圳分公司开业。
中国出口信用保险公司正式成立。
国务院公布《中华人民共和国外资保险公司管理条例》。
中国太平洋保险公司易名中国太平洋保险(集团)股份有限公司,下设中国太平洋财产保险股份有限公司和中国太平洋人寿保险股份有限公司。
中国第一家全国性综合性公估机构——方中保险公估公司在广州成立

2002年 《保险公估机构管理规定》、《保险代理机构管理规定》、《保险经纪公司管理规定》开始施行。
上海推出保险市场景气指数。
生命人寿保险股份有限公司成立。
美国ACE集团成为华泰财产保险公司第一大股东。
首家获准在北京经营的外资保险公司美国友邦保险有限公司北京分公司正式开业。
《保险法》完成修改。
光大永明人寿保险公司在天津开业。
首创安泰在大连开业。
国家税务总局下发《关于保险营销员取得收入征收个人所得税有关问题的通知》。
新疆兵团保险公司易名中华联合财产保险公司。
中国平安保险公司易名中国平安保险(集团)股份有限公司、中国平安财产保险股份有限公司、中国平安人寿保险股份有限公司。

2003年 中国保监会升格为正部级单位。
150多万从业人员绝大多数安全渡过疫期,"非典"赔付416.98万元。
中国人民保险公司更名为中国人保控股公司,并发起设立中国人民财产保险股份有限公司和中国人保资产管理有限公司。
中国人寿保险公司重组为中国人寿保险(集团)公司和中国人寿保险股份有限公司。
中国再保险公司重组为中国再保险(集团)公司,并设立中国财产再保险股份有限公司、中国人寿再保险股份有限公司、中国大地财产保险股份有限公司。
中国人民财产保险股份有限公司股票在香港联合证券交易所成功挂牌交易。
中国人寿保险股份有限公司股票在纽约和香港证券交易所上市。
中国人保股份董事长唐运祥当选2003CCTV中国经济年度人物。
中国人寿入选《财富》全球500强。
中国远洋运输集团公司之"富山海"轮在丹麦海域被撞沉没,中国人民保险公司赔付2920万美元,创我国船舶保险史之最。
泰康人寿保险公司支付820万元保险金给一病逝企业家张某之妻,创内地个人寿险赔付之最。

2004年 中国保监会原驻各地31个派出机构统一更名为"保监局",并新设立大连、青岛、宁波、厦门4个计划单列市及西藏自治区保监局。
《保险机构投资者股票投资管理暂行办法》,允许保险机构投资者在严格监管的前提下直接投资股票市场,参与一级市场和二级市场交易。
中国加入世贸组织三周年,中国保险业结束开放过渡期,迎来全面开放。
《保险公司管理规定》等系列规章制度出台。
全国第一家农业保险公司上海安信农业保险公司开业。
中国平安保险(集团)股份有限公司在香港联交所正式挂牌交易。

2005年 全国第一家相互制保险公司阳光农险在哈尔滨开业。
中国保险报社改制为中国保险报业股份有限公司,这是中国第一家整体实行股份制的新闻机构。